THE GRAND CONSPIRACY

0 50 100   200   300   400
MILES

A. JANCOVIC

CONFEDERATE AGENT

Captain Thomas Henry Hines. This photograph was taken in Toronto in 1864 for his sweetheart Nancy in Kentucky.

Confederate Agent

A DISCOVERY IN HISTORY

BY

JAMES D. HORAN

CROWN PUBLISHERS, INC.

NEW YORK, NEW YORK

For Patricia, Brian Boru, Gary Stephen and lovable little J. C., who have on occasion been known to rebel against constituted authority

CONTENTS

PART I

RAIDER AND GUERRILLA: *The Apprenticeship*

PART II

SECRET AGENT: *Underground Ambassador*

PART III

THE NORTHWEST CONSPIRACY: *The Preparation*

PART IV

THE NORTHWEST CONSPIRACY: *The Attacks*

PART V

THE AFTERMATH: *Dispersion and Reunion*

ILLUSTRATIONS

REPORT OF AN AUTHOR'S SEARCH FOR SECRET HISTORY

I FIRST became acquainted with Captain Thomas H. Hines, Confederate States of America, and the Northwest Conspiracy in 1951 while examining the loveletters and dispatches of Rose O'Neal Greenhow, the "Wild Rose of the Confederacy," among the captured Confederate correspondence, State Department Records, National Archives, in Washington, D. C.

I wanted to determine whether there was enough material for a full biography of the pretty Rebel spy. Unfortunately, her flamboyant life had to be confined to a chapter in a book about fascinating—and desperate—women. But among these papers was the story of her death in a howling storm off the coast of Wilmington, North Carolina, while trying to run the blockade. James Holcomb, who, with Horace Greeley, had attended the "peace conference" at Niagara Falls, was in the small lifeboat with Rose when it overturned. As the Richmond correspondent of the London *Times* reported, Holcomb barely escaped with his life but saved the "confidential documents" he was taking to the Confederate ministers Mason and Slidell in London.

Holcomb, the Wild Rose and secret dispatches from Niagara Falls . . . they all added up to a mystery that needed looking into. I knew something of the peace meeting at Niagara at which Greeley was hoodwinked by the smooth-talking Confederate agents. But why was Holcomb running the blockade to Richmond instead of London?

Greeley's Papers in the Manuscript Division of the New York Public Library and his published memoirs mentioned the conference. A man named George N. Sanders seemed to have been pulling wires, behind the scenes, to manipulate the actions of the Confederate agents. Who was this Sanders? Who were Captains Thomas H. Hines and John Breckinridge Castleman, C. S. A.?

A reading of Castleman's memoirs, *Active Service*, published half a century ago in Louisville, Kentucky, and the abridged version of their adventures in the *Southern Bivouac* gave me my first hint of the scope of the Northwest Conspiracy. Castleman's reminiscences of his boyhood on the family plantation are vivid, but the exciting adventures he shared with Hines are curiously blurred and disjointed, as though purposely abridged. However, they did reveal that Hines was the military commander of some secret project, with the Copperheads as its core. Two definitive books on that subject, George Fort Milton's *Abraham Lincoln and the Fifth Column* and Wood Gray's *The Hidden Civil War*, told me about the Copperhead movement. Gray, too, seemed intrigued with Captain Hines, "whose wartime exploits would merit the pen of an E. Phillips Oppenheim."

An evening with my friend Howard Swiggett who, in 1934, wrote *The Rebel Raider*, the biography of General John Hunt Morgan, confirmed my suspicions that the adventures of Tom Hines had the makings of a good book—if he had left any papers behind. At first, this seemed doubtful—what good espionage agent would? "The most competently dangerous man in the Confederacy," Swiggett called him that night.

What clues were there? A sketch in the *Biographical Encyclopedia of Kentucky* stated that Hines had died in 1898 in Kentucky. He had served two terms as Chief Justice of Kentucky's Court of Appeals. Were any of his descendants living?

Numerous letters were sent out to historians, regional and state historical societies, etc. Replies drifted back. One contained sad news: Clayton Torrence, of the Virginia Historical Society, whose advice was so eagerly awaited, had recently died. A friend said he thought the Hines family had moved to Mississippi; another suggested I write to the Tennessee Historical Society.

But one answer contained the first concrete clue. Miss Mabel Weaks, archivist of the celebrated Filson Club, Louisville, Kentucky, known to every historian and historical novelist for her prompt replies, unlimited patience and courtesy, had located the granddaughter of Captain Hines. She was Mrs. John J. Winn, wife of Chief Justice Winn, of Mt. Sterling, Kentucky.

Off went a note to her and in the return mail was a cordial invitation to come down to Mt. Sterling to look over Captain Hines' letters, reports and personal papers! What an exciting discovery! A check of sources in the Gray and Milton books showed neither author had had the benefit of the Hines Papers. Howard Swiggett was most enthusiastic. He had not seen the papers when he had written his book on Morgan.

The holiday spent with the Winns in the Blue Grass will not soon be forgotten, nor the touching letter from Nancy Sproule to her father describing the ride across Ohio to Kentucky where she married Tom Hines, at the hour when he was the most wanted man in America. It seemed fitting that Nancy's letters and Tom Hines' personal papers were stored in a hutch cupboard brought through the Cumberland Gap by one of Daniel Boone's wagons. As I took notes I was conscious of Hines, cold and handsome, staring down at me from his portrait on the wall.

The Hines Papers, now in the Margaret I. King Library, University of Kentucky, Lexington, were a rare find of decoded letters, unpublished memoirs, his diary, notebooks, expense accounts for revolution, etc. The library and its curator, Miss Jacqueline Bull, were most cooperative. I had only so many days, and Miss Bull and her staff helped me to hurdle the obstacles every author finds in his path while doing research: typists, telephones, help in making photostats, etc.

A period of sober analysis followed the initial sense of triumphant discovery. The scope of the Northwest Conspiracy was enormous; it was an eighty-seven-year-old jig-saw puzzle with pieces still missing that even the Hines Papers could not supply. Where could one find more about Colonel Grenfel, that fabulous soldier of fortune? Was Captain Ben M. Anderson the brother of the notorious guerrilla Bloody Bill Anderson? What effect did the Conspiracy have on the Union? Where did the money come from? Who was Bennett H. Young, the cavalier bank robber? And John Yates Beall?

Miss Weaks, Miss Bull and several other curators began working on leads. As letters poured in, I had the curious feeling that I was operating a widespread detective agency. Operatives would report that they had run into a blank wall or inform me by special delivery airmail that they had found the diary of someone who was in Fort Lafayette Prison with Acting Master John Yates Beall before he was hanged and did I want photostats?

The hunt became international when Miss Weaks gave me the address of Colonel George St. Leger Grenfel's grandson in Bucks, England, who sent on from his family archives the only existing picture of Grenfel. The Earl of Buckinghamshire also contributed background on his ancestor, Admiral Hampden, a favorite of Queen Victoria, who was the mysterious skipper of the ship which had sunk off Wilmington, sending Rose O'Neal Greenhow to her death and Holcomb and his mysterious documents into oblivion.

Still there were missing pieces. Dr. Oliver Wendell Holmes of the

National Archives made a cursory check and advised me to come to Washington. Hines and his men had used so many aliases it was impossible for one not familiar with his intrigues to trace him.

The Archives cannot be hurried through. Gems lie there under the dust of history, and one must read carefully lest he miss them. It was a lucky trip. A few days before I arrived, the government had released, on September 29, 1953, the controversial Baker-Turner Papers which had been sealed since 1866, by order of the Adjutant General's Office. *The Preliminary Inventory (No. 17) of the Records of the Adjutant General's Office,* compiled by Lucille H. Pendell and Elizabeth Bethel, Washington, 1949, gives the following description of these secret papers: "These records constitute the files of Brigadier-General Lafayette C. Baker, special agent or Provost Marshal of the War Department, appointed September 9, 1862, and Assistant Judge Advocate Levi Turner. The records relate to the investigations of fraud, examinations of civilians and military prisoners, and other matters pertaining generally to subversive activities in connection with the Civil War. The records were on file in the Office of the Judge Advocate General until 1895, when they were turned over to the Record and Pension Bureau, under orders of the Secretary of War dated May 15, 1894. Such portions of the Baker-Turner Records as the War Department deemed proper to make public have been printed in the *Official Records of the Union and Confederate Armies. The papers that were not published in this work have been held as strictly confidential in nature and have not been consulted except for official purposes.* . . ." In 1951 I had made an attempt to examine the papers, but my request had been refused.

To the ordinary reader it might seem somewhat ridiculous to keep under seal papers which have to do with a war and men long dead. But as the great entry book was opened and I selected the first documents, I could see some sense to the order. I found that the founder of a still active New York business, noted for his sobriety and a pillar of the church, stood charged therein with drunkenness on the battlefield. "He was so drunk he couldn't stand up," his accuser told Secretary of War Edwin Stanton. These were accusations only; there are no records of a hearing, no final disposition. He was an incompetent intelligence officer, but judging the man's personal character as he is known in history, that particular charge seems absurd. How his enemies would have loved it, half a century ago, when many of the Civil War figures were still alive.

The Baker-Turner Papers present, for the most part, a grim and deadly phase of the Civil War not fought on the battlefields. There are reports of spies, counterspies, mysterious women with descriptions worthy of Defoe ("She was one of those deep and dark women who can be so confidential without leading you into her profound secrets") and men hanged at dawn or sentenced to spend the "rest of their natural lives" in the hell of the Dry Tortugas.

The most startling discovery was evidence that the Conspiracy encompassed not only the Northwest, but also the Northeast, as shown in the confession of young Francis Jones, captured in the abortive Calais, Maine, bank robbery. Reading the dusty pages, one can imagine the excitement Secretaries Seward and Stanton must have felt when they read Jones' disclosures. From the reports of their own counterespionage agents they knew something was brewing; Jones was their first break. It is significant that Stanton sent Assistant Judge Advocate Turner hurrying to Maine to confirm Jones' confession.

Turner's report includes lists of secret agents all over the United States, Canada and in Bermuda. Many were respectable businessmen secretly in sympathy with the Confederate cause. One cannot help but experience an eerie feeling that he is really far in the future and reading secret reports, not of the Civil War, but of his own day. Surely the modern counterpart of secret agent Felix Stidger, who infiltrated the ranks of the Sons of Liberty, could be any F.B.I. counter-espionage agent of today. Even the explosive courtroom appearances seem familiar.

My research went on, but still the intricate puzzle had not been completed. Hines was assuredly the mysterious Doctor Hunter who wrote letters to the Chicago Copperheads, but there seemed to be almost nothing available on Colonel Grenfel. What was the inside story of the escape of H. H. Dodd, the Indiana Copperhead leader? Where were Hines' original orders? Where did he go after leaving Richmond in the spring of 1864? Where were the trial papers of John Yates Beall? Who was Colonel Ben M. Anderson? Was there any direct evidence Hines was in Indiana to pave the way for Morgan's raid of '63?

It was a laborious search. But finally the questions *were* answered. The story meshed, knitted together. Ben Anderson was identified. Secretary Seddon's orders were found. Hines was traced to Memphis and linked definitely to Doctor Bowles and his Copperheads. The pieces were falling into place.

Still the letters continued to come in. Miss Weaks sent a memoir of

Bennett Young, written by himself in the third person, and letters of Colonel Grenfel to his daughter in England while he was confined in the Dry Tortugas prison. Mrs. Winn patiently answered my lists of questions about the Hines family. Friends in the rare book business continued to dig up for me crumbling old pamphlets. The Ohio State Historical Society found a wonderful sketch of the escape of Morgan and Hines from the Columbus, Ohio, Penitentiary.

Still there was one thing lacking: an insight into the main character of the Conspiracy, Captain Thomas Henry Hines. There were narrow escapes, intrigue, brilliant failures, fantastic adventures and even a love story, but little illumination of the man himself, his philosophy of life, his hopes and dreams. The only warm and personal documents are Nancy's loveletters, but though their courtship was a highly romantic one, Hines never spoke of it. Another man might have sat by the fire in the twilight of his life thrilling his grandchildren with the grand tales of his life but not Hines. In war and in peace he was a cool, aloof man. He gave his friendship only to a few. Perhaps only Nancy really knew him. Her granddaughter recalls her mother held him in awe. He was in her words, "a scholar and a dreamer of violent dreams."

I had just completed a long novel when I began my research into Hines' life, and my lack of insight into his character resulted in a battle. It was the novelist versus the historian. The creative urge ached to supply the deep motivation, the final brush strokes, but at every step the historian would silently point to the facts. I had not created Captain Hines; he had to appear in this book as he had in life—a singularly passive young man who exaggerated nothing, sentimentalized nothing, feared nothing. The search for his secret history went on long after the manuscript had been finished. New material was constantly being inserted. At last a halt had to be called.

My private literary detective agency now stretched across the country, north to Canada and across the sea. Reviewing the "reports" of my operatives, I can only recommend them to the F.B.I., Scotland Yard and the Sûreté. I salute them, *con amore*.

✿   ✿   ✿   ✿   ✿

Many persons in the United States, Canada and England have helped to make this book possible. First, as always, there must be Gertrude, who should share in the bylines.

I would also like to thank John B. Heffernan, Rear Admiral USN (retired), Director of Naval History, Department of the Navy, Washington, D. C.; the staff of the Chicago Historical Society, Miss Margaret Scriven, librarian; Miss Elizabeth Baughman, reference librarian; Mary Frances Rhymer, Print Room; Miss Mabel C. Weaks, archivist, The Filson Club; Miss Jacqueline Bull, archivist, Margaret I. King Library, University of Kentucky; Mrs. Pope McAdams of Louisville, Kentucky, who graciously gave me permission to use Captain Allison's diary; Mr. John Melville Jennings, Director, Virginia Historical Society, Richmond, Virginia; Joe and Alvina Estrada and Anne O'Shea, who again helped to type a long manuscript; Mr. Howard Swiggett, whose friendship, as I have said in other books, can never be measured in words (no book on Morgan could be written without consulting *The Rebel Raider*); Bethania Meredith Smith of Lexington, Kentucky, whose excellent article, "Civil War Subversives," and advice were so helpful; Mr. Arthur A. Mayer, Jr., reference librarian, Ohio State Historical Society, who found and selected the illustrations for the 1863 escape; Mr. Melvin Nichols, who graciously allowed me to photostat the manifest of the ship on which the Rebels attempted to escape; Florence and Maureen, who watched the heirs and the hearth; Mr. William Kelleher, who sold me good books; and Mr. Samuel Stager of the Cadmus Book Shop, who went to so much trouble to find Headley's almost non-existent *Confederate Operations in Canada and New York*.

I shall always be grateful for the blue pencil and editorial skill of Helen Staeuble. And I certainly would be derelict toward old and dear friends if I forgot the hospitality of the colonel and his lady—Lieutenant Colonel Herbert Michau and his wife, Ann.

I must extend special thanks to Mr. A. H. Packe of Tile House, Dropmore Road, Burnham, Bucks, England, who searched for and found the picture of his grandfather, Colonel George St. Leger Grenfel.

As always, the staff of the American History Room, New York Public Library, were most helpful: Mr. Ivor Avellino, Mrs. Maud Cole and Mr. James Heslin; also Mr. Edward B. Morrison of the Manuscript Division. I would also like to thank Colonel Louis Sigaud and Mr. Sylvester Vigilante, now of the New York Historical Society, who interrupted his bear-hunt in Vermont to get me material on the St. Albans raid. Mr. Edmund Royce, photographer of St. Albans, Vermont, kindly supplied Lieutenant Young's picture, taken shortly after the raid in 1864. Mr. Edward C. Williamson, Librarian, Florida Historical Society, found much for me on the Dry Tortugas.

Despite the rush of the holidays, Miss Mary Crane Hone, of Morris-

CONFEDERATE AGENT

town, New Jersey, granddaughter of Captain Castleman, searched among her family archives for the original Lincoln letter which saved Castleman from the gallows. Unfortunately, it has not yet been located.

I desire also to express my sincere thanks to that distinguished couple of the Blue Grass country, Judge and Mrs. John J. Winn, of Mt. Sterling, Kentucky. As Mrs. Winn said of her grandfather, "He was a remarkable old gentleman," and with that statement I must agree.

I must also make a special tribute to the research efforts of Mr. Ray Flynn and Mr. Richard G. Wood, War Records branch, National Archives, who helped me trace Hines & Company in their North-western intrigues. I always leave their offices with this thought: wonderful people in a wonderful institution. And, again, it was Dr. Oliver Wendell Holmes who so kindly reconnoitered the way.

Horan's Boondocks, March 1, 1954.

Note. To keep abreast of Captain Hines and his raiders in the Northwest Conspiracy, both geographically and chronologically, is not too easy. As an aid in tracing their adventures see the supplemental material preceding and following the narrative.

DRAMATIS PERSONAE OF THE NORTHWEST CONSPIRACY

ANDERSON, Colonel Ben M., C. S. A., who turned traitor.

BAKER, Brigadier-General Lafayette, special agent or Provost Marshal of the War Department.

BARRETT, James, Commander of the Missouri Sons of Liberty.

BEALL, Acting Master John Yates, Confederate naval hero who was hanged in New York City.

BETTERSWORTH, Lieutenant J. J., C. S. A., who betrayed Hines in Chicago.

BICKLEY, Doctor George, founder of the Knights of the Golden Circle.

BOWLES, Doctor William A., Grand Commander of the Indiana Sons of Liberty.

BRECKINRIDGE, Judge Samuel, pro-Union uncle of Captain Castleman, who saw President Lincoln to save his nephew from the gallows.

BULLITT, Chief Justice Joshua, Commander of the Kentucky Sons of Liberty.

BURLEY, Acting Master Bennett R., C. N., second in command of the Lake Erie expedition.

CASTLEMAN, Captain John Breckinridge, C. S. A., second in command to Captain Hines.

CARRINGTON, Colonel Henry B., U. S. A., who broke the power of the Sons of Liberty in Indiana.

CLAY, Clement C., a member of the Confederate Mission in Canada.

COLE, Captain Charles, C. S. A., arrested as one of John Yates Beall's command in the expedition to capture the U. S. S. *Michigan*.

COLLINS, Captain William, C. S. A., leader of the Calais, Maine, expedition.

CONGER, Captain George, U. S. A., who rallied the citizens of St. Albans, Vermont, against the Confederates.

DODD, Harrison H., leader of the Indiana Sons of Liberty.

DUKE, Colonel Basil, C. S. A., second in command of Morgan's cavalry.

EASTIN, Lieutenant George, C. S. A., one of Hines' raiders.

EDWARDS, Doctor Edward W., leader of the Sons of Liberty in Chicago.

GREENHOW, Rose O'Neal ("the Wild Rose"), beautiful Confederate spy who died at sea.

GRENFEL, Colonel George St. Leger, C. S. A., the English soldier of fortune, sentenced to life for his part in the Chicago uprising.

HEADLEY, Lieutenant John W., C. S. A., second in command of the expedition to burn New York City.

HINES, Captain Thomas Henry, C. S. A., military commander of the Northwest Conspiracy who tried to set off a revolution in the northwestern part of the United States.

TIMETABLE

		The Radius of the Confederate Raiders
Civil War Operations in Broad Perspective	1861	
April — Bombardment of Fort Sumter. Lincoln calls for troops, declares blockade of Confederate ports. Battle of Bull Run.	April	Buckner's Guides, with Hines as their leader, are attached to General Albert Sidney Johnston's command.
July — Battle of Bull Run.	July	
November — Kentucky votes to secede and join the Confederacy.	November	Hines is commissioned a lieutenant, takes part in raid at Borah's Ferry, Kentucky.
	1862	
	January	The Guides are disbanded, leaving Hines without a command. Hines journeys to Richmond, war-time capital of the Confederacy.
February — Fort Henry and Fort Donelson in Tennessee are captured by the Union. Nashville is occupied by the Union. Southern Kentucky and Middle Tennessee are lost to Confederacy.	February	
March — Battle between ironclads *Monitor* and *Merrimac*.	March	
April — Battle of Shiloh. Surrender of forts at New Orleans.	April	Hines in Richmond hears of Morgan's exploits in Tennessee and Southern Kentucky.
May — Morgan's cavalry raids near Nashville. Morgan's cavalry defeated at Lebanon, Tennessee.	May	Hines enlists in the Ninth Kentucky as a private, is later commissioned a captain by General Morgan.
June — Cumberland Gap is occupied by the Union. McClellan is within sight of Richmond but is turned back in the Seven Days' Battle.	June	Hines meets the corps of officers who will serve with him in the Northwest Conspiracy. He is bushwhacked on his way to confer with the Kentucky Copperheads.
July — Morgan's first Kentucky raid.	July	
August — Second battle of Bull Run.	August	
September — Harper's Ferry. Antietam. Lincoln issues his Emancipation Proclamation.	September	Hines makes contacts and establishes his underground in Kentucky, joining his command at Lexington. Morgan gives him a three-week leave and Hines rides to Brown's Lock, near Bowling Green to see his sweetheart.
October — Battle of Perryville.	October	
November — Grant, whose section of the Union Army held northern Mississippi and west Tennessee, begins his campaign against Vicksburg, his mission: the opening of the Mississippi from the North.	November	
	December	Hines sees his sweetheart Nancy Sproule, is called back by Richmond, joins Morgan's retreat.

TIMETABLE—(Continued)

	Civil War Operations in Broad Perspective		The Radius of the Confederate Raiders
December	Morgan's "Christmas raid" to Kentucky. Battle of Stone's River, Tennessee, in which Braxton Bragg's courier failed to reach Morgan.		
	1863		
January	In 1863 the Union's primary objectives were: the opening of the Mississippi; the break-up of rail communication in the central South; the drive to Richmond; the continuing blockade.	January	Morgan steps up his raids. Hines takes part in many skirmishes. He prepares to raid and burn South Union Depot, Kentucky.
		February	Hines and his men are officially commended by Morgan for their expeditions into Kentucky.
May	Battle of Chancellorsville. Stonewall Jackson killed.	May	Copperhead leader Vallandigham is exiled to the South. Hines and Morgan (and possibly Vallandigham) confer on the great Ohio raid.
		June	Hines disappears from Morgan's headquarters, ostensibly to "recondition sick horses" in the Blue Grass country but actually to confer with the Copperheads about the projected raid.
July	Vicksburg surrendered to Grant. Morgan's raid into Kentucky, Indiana and Ohio. Battle of Gettysburg. The Army of Northern Virginia was never to cross the Potomac again. Draft riots spreading in the North. After Gettysburg and Vicksburg the South's hopes for foreign aid vanished. As Wood Gray noted in *The Hidden Civil War*, "the Confederacy was reduced to fighting a stubborn, slowly yielding defensive action that could have but one result—if the North were sufficiently determined to pay the cost."	July	Hines confers with Doctor Bowles at French Lick. The Indiana Copperheads fail to rise. Morgan and most of his command are captured. The Northeast facet of the Northwest Conspiracy collapses when one of the Calais, Maine, raiders confesses the plot for the Maine Coast raid.

Civil War Operations in Broad Perspective	*The Radius of the Confederate Raiders*
September Battle of Chickamauga. Rosecrans retreats to Chattanooga.	November Hines, Morgan and four captains escape from the Columbus, Ohio, penitentiary. Hines is captured twice but escapes.
November Battles of Chattanooga, Lookout Mountain.	

1864

March Grant made commander of all Union armies. Sherman put in command in the West.	March Hines is commissioned by Jefferson Davis as the military commander of the Northwest Conspiracy and is ordered north to make plans for the revolution in the Northwest and for the release of Confederate prisoners from Union camps.
April Battle of the Wilderness, Virginia. Morgan's last raid into Kentucky, is defeated in Cynthiana.	April Hines slips through the Union lines into Canada.
June Lincoln's draft call for 500,000 more men. Siege of Petersburg begun.	June Hines and the Confederate Commissioners confer with Vallandigham and the Copperhead leaders. In Kentucky the Union counterspy Felix Stidger infiltrates the Sons of Liberty. The Morgan raid into Kentucky fails.
	August The "peace conferences" at Niagara Falls fail. Confederate agents try to shake the inflated Union dollar by buying and exporting gold. The great Northwest uprising scheduled to coincide with the Democratic Convention in Chicago fails. Hines' plans for a revolution in Illinois, Ohio and Indiana are betrayed.
September Atlanta surrendered to Sherman. The capture of Atlanta cut off the South's remaining railroad artery.	September John Yates Beall commandeers the *Philo Parsons*, but the plan to capture the U.S.S. *Michigan* and sack the unprotected Northern lake

Civil War Operations in Broad Perspective

The Radius of the Confederate Raiders

	Civil War Operations in Broad Perspective	The Radius of the Confederate Raiders
		cities fails. Military transports at St. Louis are burned. Captain John Breckinridge Castleman is captured.
October		Bennett H. Young and his raiders rob the St. Albans banks.
November	Sherman leaves Atlanta for his "March to the Sea."	The revolution scheduled for Election Day fails to come off. The Chicago leaders of the Sons of Liberty are arrested in raids. Hines is hidden by friends from the Union patrols in Cincinnati, spirits his sweetheart from a convent school in Ohio, marries her in Covington, Kentucky. A party of raiders sets fire to hotels, ships and public buildings in New York City. General Ben Butler marches into New York City with 10,000 troops.
December	Sherman marches to Savannah.	Hines reports to Secretary of War Seddon and is ordered to return to Canada.

1865

	Civil War Operations in Broad Perspective	The Radius of the Confederate Raiders
February	Robert E. Lee made commander-in-chief. Petersburg and Richmond evacuated. Sherman starts north from Savannah.	During the early months of the year many of the raiders and Copperhead leaders are tried and sentenced to death or imprisonment for attempting to overthrow the United States government.
April	Army of Northern Virginia surrendered at Appomattox Court House. Army of Northern Tennessee surrendered at Greensboro, N. C. President Lincoln assassinated by John Wilkes Booth.	Hines disbands his command in the backwoods of Kentucky. Escapes from a mob in Detroit where he is mistaken for John Wilkes Booth. Commandeers a ferryboat to take him across to Canada, where Nancy later joins him in exile until they can safely return to the Blue Grass.
May	President Jefferson Davis captured in Georgia. Galveston surrendered. Last shot of the war	
June	fired by the Confederate cruiser *Shenandoah* in the North Pacific.	

PART I

RAIDER AND GUERRILLA
The Apprenticeship

I. THE MOST DANGEROUS MAN IN THE CONFEDERACY

THIS is the story of a grand conspiracy, a lost cause and the men and women who believed in it. At times it seems so incredible that one wonders if it ever happened. The existing records, some of them sealed by government orders for almost ninety years, tell us it did.

The full range of human emotions—love, hate, cowardice, courage and frivolity—runs through it, and, like a bright pattern in a crazy-quilt, is the love story of its young leader.

Let us first examine this Northwest Conspiracy in all its far-flung ramifications. Relatively little about it has appeared in print. The reason is simple: it was a secret plan and the men who took part in it kept their lips sealed, many until their deaths. In 1864 the *New York Times* hinted that it had been a vast Confederate plan to spread "a siege of terror from Maine to Minnesota." This was only partially true; the objective was not just to make raids on northern cities. The overthrow of the United States government by revolution was the principal goal of the Conspiracy.

Next, the cause. Of course it was the Confederacy—in the agonizing months when her gray columns began their slow but inevitable retreat. Most of her leaders knew she was doomed. Exchange Commissioner Colonel Robert Ould said to Mrs. Mary Boykin Chesnut, famous for her *Diary from Dixie,* in a memorable whisper, "We are rattling downhill."

And now, the men. They were young and handsome, mostly hard-bitten veterans of General John Hunt Morgan's command. The Rebel raider, as the North knew him. They were scholarly and men of good breeding. Those whom the court-martial boards convicted died in high Roman fashion. One of them, John Yates Beall, told the hangman, "As someone has said, we may be as near God on the scaffold as elsewhere."

This is their story. It begins on an April morning in 1861, with fifteen young men trotting south on the Newtown Turnpike. The riders were all neatly dressed in broadcloth, linen shirts, cocked hats and shining jackboots. They were armed with a strange assortment of weapons;

3

long squirrel guns, old muzzle loaders that had seen service in the Indian raids along the Kentucky frontier, horse pistols that had been fired at Buena Vista, double-barreled shotguns and a few old swords.

They all rode with the easy grace of men accustomed to the saddle since childhood. As they passed McCracken's farm on the pike they could see the orderly rows of daffodils, a bright yellow chalkline outlining against the fresh green lawns the winding driveway which led from the pike to the big white house.

They passed under the giant oaks and elms, shafts of sunlight flashing on the silver of their bridles. Overhead the mocking birds and the blue jays shattered the morning quiet with their eternal raucous feuds.

The fifteen riders had formed themselves into a troop of cavalry only two weeks before, the day after Fort Sumter had been fired upon, and since then they all had been whistling for action against the damn Yankees. It had been difficult to decide on a name for the troop. "Kentucky Raiders" and "Lexington Rifles" had been advanced and rejected. They liked the latter, but John Hunt Morgan's troop already had selected that name. "Buckner's Guides," honoring that great Kentucky military leader, General Simon Bolivar Buckner, finally had been accepted.

The officers, elected by the members, had been chosen for their personality and leadership. The Guides had cast only one vote to elect Tom Hines their captain. Hines, who had resigned from the faculty of the Masonic University, at La Grange, in Oldham County, the day after the troop had been formed, was well known to all of them for his coolness and leadership. Men always seemed ready to follow Hines in the classroom or elsewhere.

There was no snobbery in the Guides. The riders were sons of plantation owners, farmers, tobacco growers, storekeepers and members of the senior class and faculty of the university. One was a Latin instructor, another a fencing master. They had met twice a week in a pasture outside Lexington, performing there what an old Mexican war veteran said were cavalry maneuvers. Now at last, they voted they were ready for war. They had met early in the morning to avoid the Federal patrols on the roads leading out of Lexington, then had set out for General Albert Sidney Johnston's camp.

At the head of the column, Hines rode with the ease of a man who had spent eighteen of his twenty years in the saddle. He was a slender man, his weight no more than a hundred and thirty pounds, but he rode with such quiet grace that his slenderness, almost frailty, at-

A rare photograph of Captain Hines, Colonel Eastin and
General Morgan, taken about 1863 before the Ohio raid.

The only known photograph of Colonel George St. Leger Grenfel, a "soldier of fortune."

Courtesy, A. H. Packe, Bucks, England

Captain John Breckinridge Castleman, who served as second in command to Hines.

tracted no attention. From his grandfather, a surgeon in the English Army who had come to America before the French and Indian wars, had come the blue eyes that could be as cold as frozen seas, and the square-cut jaw; from the Dinwiddies of Virginia, on his grandmother's side, he had the slender, graceful body, hard as whipcord, the thick, black curly hair, slanting eyebrows and an instinctive appreciation for beautiful women, good music and fine horses.

He had a familiar look. A man might have looked twice at Hines, wondering where he had seen that face before. Suddenly it would have come to him: Hines bore a striking physical resemblance to another handsome young man of his day, John Wilkes Booth.

On that April morning Hines led his troops through the Blue Grass. At one toll gate they said they were Union cavalry and crossed the small stream without paying a toll.

It was about noon when they left the pike to turn into a side road. They splashed across a creek and rode up a small hill. Even before they were in sight of the camp they could smell the savory odor of frying bacon and pork roasting over a spit. They reached the top of the hill and General Johnston's camp spread out before them.

It had an almost medieval look: pavilions and tents decorated with streamers of colored cloth, pits of glowing coals and slowly revolving chunks of sizzling beef and mutton. Under the enormous shade trees were picnic tables covered with snowy cloths, cushions, chairs and benches. Ladies in hoop skirts holding colored parasols, like a flock of beautiful butterflies stopped in flight, and their escorts watched the riders in plumed hats above them wheel and turn. Their gentle clapping floated up to the men on the hill. Off on another side of the meadow the riders could see body servants, coachmen and maids dancing to the plunking of a banjo.

Hines raised his hand, then let it fall as his horse lunged forward. They rode down the winding road, leaving in their wake a towering wall of dust. They skimmed a pasture fence with the grace of fox hunters, then rode up the lane and into the meadow in perfect fours.

"Please tell General Johnston Buckner's Guides are reporting for duty," Hines told the orderly who greeted them.

Tom Hines had joined the war. Before its end he would become one of the most dangerous men in the Confederacy, plotting, and almost successful in touching off, a revolution in the Northwest.

From the very first, General Johnston used the Guides for raiding, burning military installations and capturing prisoners. They gained a reputation for boldness and daring. In those first months of the war the name of Tom Hines the guerrilla began to be known in Confederate headquarters and about the Federal campfires.

In November, 1861, Hines was commissioned a lieutenant by Major-General Hardee. On December 31 he, with ten men, executed a successful raid on the Federal garrison at Borah's Ferry, below Bowling Green, in Kentucky. But soon thereafter the Confederate fortunes took a turn for the worse. Forts Henry and Donelson were lost to Grant, and Hines and his Guides joined the Confederate retreat from Kentucky.

At Nashville, Tennessee, he and his men were detailed to another band of hard-riding bravos, Morgan's Lexington Rifles.

Hines and Morgan. They would have a strange bearing on each other's destinies.

II. MORGAN'S RAIDERS

J OHN HUNT MORGAN—the name had a magic ring to it. The man
himself had a strange, magnetic force that drew men to him. His
men and officers would never forget him; years after his death they
would unashamedly weep for him in their memoirs, forgetting his faults.
Tall, handsome, picturesque, he was a man of curious contradictions.

As a cavalryman he was superb. A technical military handbook as-
serts that he permanently altered cavalry tactics and operations by
using his command as riflemen. Another says he was the greatest partisan fighter since Francis Marion, the Swamp Fox of the Revolution.
But he excelled not in cavalry tactics alone. The love of conspiracy
was strong in his make-up, and might have attracted young Hines. The
two made a fine conspiratorial team. Both were close-mouthed,
shrewd and wily. Years after the Civil War, when he wrote his memoirs, Basil Duke, second in command of Morgan's cavalry, wondered
what lay between Hines and Morgan. Even in 1866, when he wrote
Morgan's Cavalry—the *Official Records of the Union and Confederate
Armies* (1880–1901) had not yet been published—Duke, who had
married Morgan's sister Henrietta in 1861, was unaware that his general and the young captain had secrets between them about which
only the high command in Richmond knew.

But neither Hines nor Morgan had any thoughts of conspiracy the
day they joined forces in Nashville, Tennessee, to keep order in that
terrified city. Rumors had spread with prairie-fire rapidity . . . the
Federals were at the gates . . . the Union steamboats could be seen . . .
the cannonading would soon start. . . .

On January 15, the city was evacuated. The gray columns marched
to Murfreesboro. There, according to Doctor James Blanton's unpublished account of Hines' career, now found among the Hines Papers,
the Guides were disbanded for the reason that "they were in a strange
region." Was war always to be fought in one's back yard?

Two weeks later Hines reorganized his small command, offering its
services to General John Cabell Breckinridge at Burnsville, Tennessee,

7

but was refused by that commander "because Congress had not given him authorization." Hines then traveled to Richmond, missing the battle of Shiloh and the great might-have-been victory for the Confederacy.

In Richmond he heard that his first general, Albert Sidney Johnston, had died, leading his men, at two o'clock that afternoon.

Hines stayed out of the war, in Richmond, for a month. This wartime capital, with the decay which attaches itself to all lost causes already too apparent, was to be no stranger to him in the months to come.

It was the magic of Morgan's name that brought Hines back into the Army. The name was already one to conjure with. In April they were telling stories in Richmond of how Morgan and his men had ridden into Murfreesboro and passed themselves off as Federal cavalrymen, to be cheered by the Union sympathizers who lined the sidewalks; of how in the college town of Lebanon they had suffered their first defeat, with the wounded Basil Duke watching Morgan in tears as the wounded streamed past him. They told of Morgan's gallant effort to capture the train which was taking his men as prisoners to Cave City in southern Kentucky, capturing instead a Federal payroll of eight thousand dollars, which helped ease the hurt of defeat.

In May, 1862, Hines enlisted as a private in Morgan's Ninth Kentucky, Company A, Captain John Breckinridge Castleman commanding. In the months ahead, Castleman and Hines would share incredible hardships. From their first meeting they struck up a friendship which was to last a lifetime.

Hines' qualities as an officer were not lost on Morgan. On June 10, 1862, he commissioned Hines a captain, assigning him to Company E, Ninth Kentucky.

Hines was now among the corps of officers who would later serve under him as his Northwest Conspiracy raiders. The story of his life and adventures cannot, of course, be separated from theirs. There was his close friend, Captain "Breck" Castleman, "born in the season of wild rose and elder blossom on June 30, 1841, at Castleton, Fayette County . . ." as he wrote of those early days; the handsome Colonel George B. Eastin, who was to fight a famous duel with a Yankee officer over a lady's hand; Lieutenant John W. Headley, who would think nothing of kidnapping a Vice President of the United States and holding him as a hostage; Captain Robert Cobb Kennedy and Colonel Robert Martin, who would put New York City to the torch; Lieutenant

Bennett H. Young, the cavalier bank robber whom St. Albans, Vermont, would never forget, and others.

In late June, a man who was neither a Kentuckian nor an American joined Morgan: Colonel George St. Leger Grenfel, one of the most fascinating but little known figures of the Civil War. It is hard to believe that he was flesh and blood and not from the pages of a G. A. Henty book. Soldier of fortune, white chieftain of a Moroccan desert tribe, veteran of four wars and revolutions, he was commissioned Inspector General under Braxton Bragg at the age of sixty-two.

When John Hunt Morgan formed his cavalry, Grenfel joined him, bringing with him the iron discipline and the tactics of the desert riders of Africa against whom he had fought and under whom he had served.

It was about this time, in the spring of 1862, that the first fires of the Copperheads in the North began to flicker. Isolated arrests were made by the Federal detectives who were ignorant of the vast scope of this American "fifth column."

Hines, Morgan and the high command in Richmond were all to be closely linked with the Copperhead movement. There is ample evidence that Hines served as a liaison between Morgan, the Richmond headquarters and the Copperhead leaders.

In the spring of 1862, Hines perfected his guerrilla tactics. He led several raids into Kentucky, destroying Federal rolling stock, burning bridges, tearing up railroad tracks and stealing horses. Union headquarters in Louisville or Lexington became familiar with the frantic messages from commanders of outposts in the Blue Grass, which usually read, in effect: "At ten o'clock this morning a Rebel force under the notorious Captain Hines crossed into this state, halting a train near Christiansburg, burning two cars and stealing one hundred horses. Lieutenant Jones and a patrol gave immediate pursuit, but the enemy had vanished. . . ."

The scene was always the same: Hines and his troopers sweeping out of the winter twilight or the gray dawn, the chilling Rebel cry quivering in the air; the ragged volleys, the surprised guards scattering for cover or dying at their posts; the arch of flame as the torches were flung into the warehouses or blockhouses; the grinding noise as crowbars ripped up the rails; the squeal of frightened horses herded through the forest; then gradually the shouts; the pounding hoofbeats dying out, leaving behind the crackling flames, the smoke and the dead men in the trampled snow.

That winter Hines tried his hand at conspiracy. He slipped in and out of Kentucky, organizing his underground and contacting that state's Copperhead leaders. From them Hines learned of the growing dissatisfaction in the North against the Lincoln administration and the gathering strength of the treasonable society, Knights of the Golden Circle, later to become the infamous Sons of Liberty. By the spring he was ready to deal with northern traitors and add their treason to the support of the Confederate cause.

Hines' raids and expeditions during that spring show how well he had learned the conspirator's role. He was now skilled in the use of disguises and had learned to cultivate Confederate sympathizers and recruit them as listening posts for his underground.

On June 27, Hines rode out of camp at Knoxville for Kentucky to make contact with Chief Justice Joshua Bullitt, of that state's Court of Appeals. Bullitt was Grand Commander of the Knights of the Golden Circle and a fervent Copperhead. On the way Hines was bushwhacked by Union guerrillas who shot his horse from under him, but escaped in a hail of bullets. For two nights he hid out in the brush. At twilight of the third evening, he came on a farmhouse owned by a "good Union man."

Throughout his adventures women, old and young, were captivated by the handsome young Kentuckian and would go to great lengths to warn him of Union ambushes or to conceal him. The daughter of this "good Union" farmer persuaded her father to hide Hines in an upstairs bedroom while she lied to the officer leading the Union patrol which had been set on Hines' trail by the guerrillas. Later, the farmer guided Hines over mountain passes and backroads to Columbia, Kentucky. From there he took a stage to Lebanon, south of Louisville, where the Federals had their headquarters. He posed as a horse trader and managed to slip out of the city on a stage to Bristown Station near Bowling Green.

He traveled through the woods to his home in Lexington to find his father had been arrested and his mother ill and being cared for by Hines' uncle. But Union informers told the provost marshal that Hines was back. They came up at a gallop, only to find Hines gone. Hines had more friends than enemies in the community; he had been warned before the patrol started out, and escaped through a back window of the house. Unwilling to remain at the homes of friends more than a few hours, he skipped across the county, avoiding the patrols with the skill of a checker player crowning his kings.

In the meantime, Morgan had moved out of Knoxville toward Sparta, Tennessee, one hundred and four miles away, to launch his first Kentucky raid. This was planned and intended as only that—a raid. It was not a part of what was to come—raids which would accompany revolution.

The Copperhead underground kept Hines advised of Morgan's progress across the state—Tompkinsville and Glasgow on July 7, Lebanon on the 11th, Harrodsburg (twenty-eight miles from Lexington) on the 13th, Versailles on the 15th. It was at Georgetown on the 17th that Hines emerged from the woods to join Morgan. What he reported to Morgan no one knows.

The next morning, the 18th, Hines returned to command Company E, Ninth Kentucky. He joined the column moving northeast for Cynthiana, while the company of his friend, Captain Castleman, pushed in the pickets posted on the outskirts of Lexington to mask the movements of Morgan's main force.

At Cynthiana, thirty miles from the Ohio River, they encountered four hundred Regulars and as many Home Guards. In the face of terrible fire, Morgan's men forded the Licking River, rifles and ammunition held over their heads. Men sank silently or thrashed wildly in the swift-moving stream when they were hit. But the line never wavered. They went on, stumbling on the mucky bottom or slipping on the moss-covered stones. The two companies under Castleman and Hines established a bridgehead after heavy losses. This was one of the amazing strains in Hines's makeup; he could make the transition from spy to a hard-riding cavalry leader without any difficulty.

The battle raged until that afternoon when the wild charges of Morgan's Texans and Georgians shattered the town's defenses. Four hundred Federals were taken prisoner. A hundred dead were counted.

The same day they headed south for Paris, the dust-covered wounded in the carriages groaning in the heat. On the 20th the whole command was safely across the Cumberland at Monticello.

Basil Duke's men blocked the twin tunnels of the Louisville & Nashville Railroad north of Gallatin by opening the throttles of two locomotives and sending them in a head-on collision at a hundred-mile-an-hour speed.

In September, the command made its triumphant entrance into Lexington. Hines had no eyes for the belles who waved the Stars and Bars and called out their greetings; he had thoughts only for pretty Nancy

Sproule, his boyhood sweetheart. Their love story is a clear, bright contrast to the dark, conspiratorial side of Hines' character.

Nancy's loveletters to Hines, now yellowing and crumbling, are beautifully written. They hint of the intense loneliness she experienced during the uncertain days when the armies were rolling back and forth across the dark and bloody ground of Kentucky. As she wrote, "You don't know how this word *alone* strikes upon my heart . . . oh, my darling, when I think of all the dangers which surround you, my heart grows sick with the intense longing to be with you and to share whatever fate may be intended for you. . . ."

Morgan gave Hines three weeks' leave and he set out for Nancy's home in Brown's Lock, near Bowling Green. This was no ordinary courtship; the town was occupied by the Federals who wanted him very badly. There were spies and informers to consider. But Tom's friends hid in the shadows near the Sproule house, to make sure the Union patrols didn't surprise "the fox," as they called Hines. Behind the drawn curtains Tom and Nancy forgot the war—even though they both knew there was a saddled horse in the back yard just in case the Yankees managed to sneak up suddenly.

They were to be together only a few days. Hardee of Braxton Bragg's army and Thomas of Don Carlos Buell's Union forces made contact at Perryville. Morgan sent an urgent message to Hines to rejoin his company. There was time only for a brief kiss before he was gone. He joined his men at Harrodsburg where the Confederates were concentrated. Under Federal pressure the Confederate Army retreated from Kentucky. Morgan's cavalry screened the movement.

September slipped into October. Hines took part in numerous skirmishes with the blue patrols. In November Hines' men entered Springfield, Tennessee, burning the bridges and trestles behind them. There was an ambush at Tyree Springs, where Morgan and Hines were almost captured. But they got away, soaring over the pasture fences like fox hunters on the chase.

November rains lashed the gray columns retreating deeper into Tennessee. The great guns dueled over the mountains. Morgan and Hines had no way of knowing the booming came from Murfreesboro where the Confederates, under Braxton Bragg, were fighting to the death at Stone's River. It was to be a blot on Morgan's reputation that the frantic courier sent out by Bragg could never find him.

Days and nights of hard riding passed. In the glare of campfires, shielding the precious paper from the rain, or swaying in the saddle from fatigue, Tom Hines reread Nancy's letters.

The retreat was bitter for all of them but perhaps bitterest for Hines when he tucked the precious letters inside his worn gray jacket. As he wrote her, "I thought we would meet next in heaven. . . ."

In the winter of 1863, with the high tide of the Confederacy running out, Morgan stepped up his raids. They created diversions, helped to diffuse the Union forces, gave sorely needed lifts to Confederate morale. On February 5, Hines led a company of men deep into Federal-held territory in Kentucky to burn South Union Depot, across the Green River just north of Bowling Green, and to burn a steamboat after dumping its valuable cargo of food into the river.

They were almost ambushed by the Federals on their way back to Morgan's headquarters at McMinnville, Tennessee, but escaped. The only casualty was a trooper who had been swept out of his saddle when they swam their horses across a swollen stream.

In thirty-six hours they covered one hundred and ten miles in a raging storm. His men would recall later how their clothes froze to their bodies, how the insides of their legs were worn raw from crotch to knee. Hines was an inexhaustible demon, riding up and down the single file, pleading, taunting, urging his men to keep riding. More than once a man slipped out of his saddle to sleep in the snow. While the column halted, a giant sergeant who had stayed with Hines from the days of Buckner's Guides, would rub the fallen trooper's hands and feet until blood again warmed numbed flesh.

Five days after they had left camp, Hines led his men, some sleeping as they rode, into McMinnville. Morgan was delighted with Hines' report. In General Orders 12, issued at McMinnville, he wrote:

> The General commanding this Brigade desires to call the attention of the troops to the gallantry and skill displayed by Captain Hines and Lieutenant Porter and the men under their command during the late successful expedition into Kentucky, in which they succeeded in destroying over half a million dollars' worth of U. S. Government property, capturing a train of twenty-one cars, burning a depot and steamboat full of valuable army stores, and successfully making

their escape, without the loss of a man killed or captured by the enemy. Such examples are worth emulation, and add new lustre to the already proud reputation of the Command. . . .

(Signed)

John H. Morgan,
Brig.-General

In 1863 Tom Hines had successfully completed his apprenticeship as a guerrilla and a conspirator. He had learned how to operate behind the enemy lines, he had found many vulnerabilities in the Union. There were weakly garrisoned supply depots, unprotected railroads, unguarded Federal payrolls and a powerful unexploited "fifth column." Here was a great opportunity for the Confederacy.

III. FIRES OF THE COPPERHEADS

WHILE Hines was burning Federal depots and supply trains in Kentucky, events were occurring in the North which were to bear closely on his life and adventures.

The brush fires of the Copperheads were now beginning to crackle along the borders of Ohio, Indiana and Illinois. Men were meeting in abandoned farmhouses, old quarries, in the woods, to raise their hands and swear treasonable oaths.

Federal warehouses mysteriously burned to the ground. Sentries were found with their throats cut. Men exchanged and acknowledged secret signs and symbols on the street, and walked off together to commit treason. There was talk of peace, whispers that only the industrialists wanted a war. Pictures of Jefferson Davis and Morgan began to appear in many Ohio homes.

Spies passed back and forth across the borders of the northwestern states. At General Rosecrans' headquarters in Tennessee an order was signed: "Dr. Cheatham and wife entertained a spy from Morgan. Execute sentence on them."

In Washington, a Senator electrified the Senate Chamber when he rose to ask point-blank if there was not an organization in the Democratic Party whose objectives were to demoralize the Army and to encourage desertion.

To understand the role Hines played in the Copperhead uprising, it is important to know something of the movement itself and the extent of its power during those uncertain days of 1863–64. To the ordinary reader, the term "Copperhead" is connected vaguely with the Civil War.

Copperhead was a catch-all phrase describing several secret societies, mostly composed of members of the radical wing of the Democratic Party. These included the Knights of the Golden Circle, the Sons of Liberty, Order of the American Knights, Corps de Belgique and several others. Their names were different, but they claimed a common aim: to seize political power and overthrow the Lincoln government.

15

During 1863–64, their followers destroyed government warehouses and military installations, cut communications, acted as arsonists, murderers, spies and couriers for Confederate leaders, and, in short, attempted to create a Trojan horse within the loyal northern states.

The story of the Copperheads, gaudy with secret symbols, passwords and other conspiratorial paraphernalia, is bloody and full of nightly terror. Beneath the theatrical props were real violence and fanaticism. The true scope of the Copperheads will probably never be known. When Richmond was burning, Secretary of State Judah Benjamin burned the records of his and of Hines' secret dealings with the Copperhead leaders. However, Hines kept copies of many of his reports and letters, which he sent to his wife with instructions to hide them.

The Knights of the Golden Circle may or may not have been the outgrowth of the Southern Rights clubs of the 1830's. Six ships, all equipped for piracy, were sent out on the high seas by the clubs, but they were captured and burned by the British.

In 1854 a wonderful old humbug, George W. L. Bickley, took over the clubs and organized the Knights of the Golden Circle, with headquarters in Cincinnati. Bickley had an impressive list of medical degrees—all forged, of course—and a suitcase of secret signs, symbols and a "book of rites." Under his management the Knights spread like wildfire through the cotton South. From hocus-pocus rituals they turned to violence and conquest when they tried to promote the extension of slavery by the conquest of Mexico.

Secession was their goal in 1860. "Castles," as the Knights called their lodges, sprang up in non-seceding states. Bickley, active in this work in Kentucky, was threatened with arrest and fled to Virginia. But the movement flourished in Kentucky, and became a real danger to the Union Army after war broke out.

Not all the Knights knew the secret aims of their leaders. Many solemnly went through the fantastic rituals, swore their oaths, believing themselves to be only Democrats preserving the freedom of the ballot against tyrannical Republicans. Only those who took the last two advanced degrees of the ritual were told—then only orally—of the violent goals their leaders had set. Armed sentries, sometimes the strength of a full company, guarded the meeting places.

In Illinois the Knights were openly gathering recruits for the Confederate Army in 1861. In Iowa they burned the homes of men who joined the Federals. In Des Moines the U. S. marshal found evidence that the Knights were gun-running into Missouri for Quantrill's guer-

G'rt &x "C"

V.

W. O. C. Gives * * *

K. L. Who cometh? Who cometh? Who cometh?

W. O. C. A man! We found him in the dark ways of the Sons of Folly, bound in chains, and well nigh crushed to death beneath the iron heel of the oppressor. We have brought him hither, and would fain clothe him in the white robes of Virtue, and place his feet in the straight and narrow path which leads to Truth and Wisdom.

K. L. Brothers! The purpose ye have declared touching this stranger is most worthy; let him advance to our Altar by the regular steps; instruct him in our chosen, solemn attitude, and let him give testimony of that which is in him.

K. L. DIVINE ESSENCE! GOD OF OUR FATHERS, whose inspiration moved them to mighty deeds of valor in the cause of Eternal Truth, Justice, and Human Rights. We, their sons, would fain recognize the same presence and inspiration in this V. of the T., consecrated to the principles which they inculcated by precept and by example, and defended with their lives, and their sacred honor. With the DIVINE PRESENCE let holiest memories come, like incense to our souls, and exalt them with emotions worthy of the ceremonies of the Supreme occasion. *Amen!*

Man! Thou art now in the V., and, if found worthy, will hence be ushered into the consecrated T., where Truth dwells amid her votaries; let thy soul be duly conscious of her presence, and go forth in exalted desire for her divine influence. Within those sacred precincts, reverence toward the SUPREME BEING, Patriotism, Love, Charity, and good fellowship, are inculcated and cherished. Infidelity to GOD, or our country, nor hatred, nor malice, nor uncharitableness, nor their kindred vices, must enter there. "Love one another," is the *hail* of the Order into whose inner circle thou wouldst fain be inducted. Direct thy thoughts within at this supreme moment, and declare, as thou wouldst answer to a good conscience, is thy soul pure and fitted for the indwelling of Truth?

Answer, "Yes," or "No."

Is thy heart quickened with genial emotions toward thy fellow man?

Answer, "Yes," or "No."

It is well. If thou hast not answered truly, in obedience to the promptings of thy holier nature, so shalt thou be judged in the last day when the secrets of thy heart shall be revealed, and the actions and purposes of thy life on earth shall return to thy soul their fruits

The Sons of Liberty ritual book, exhibited in the Indiana Conspiracy trial.

rillas. In August, 1862, the Chicago *Tribune* declared the movement had 20,000 members. Missouri membership was reported as from 10,-000 to 60,000, with Castles springing up in every section of the state.

There is no way of knowing exactly how many members the Knights really had. With death by torture the penalty for any Knight who revealed the secrets of his society, it is surprising that a few did find the courage to make public some details. But in May, 1862, a Federal grand jury in Indiana handed down a report on the activities of the Knights, in which they estimated their strength in the state at 15,000, all of whom were plotting to resist paying taxes and to prevent enlistments in the Union Army. The report pointed out that recruiting was almost at a standstill in the areas where they were strongest. The jurors also reported that delegates at the Indiana State Democratic Convention "openly exchanged the signs and symbols of the Knights of the Golden Circle."

In June and August, 1862, mobs spurred on by the Knights rode through towns of southern Illinois, cheering Jefferson Davis and John Hunt Morgan.

The Chicago *Tribune*, a bitter foe of the Knights, reported that Grant had had to disband the 109th Illinois Volunteers because it was virtually a branch of the Knights. In Indiana, Governor Oliver Morton began to govern his state like a dictator after the legislature had refused to grant him war appropriations and had begun to hamstring his war powers.

Undoubtedly the most prominent Copperhead of all was Clement Vallandigham, with whom Hines tried to carry out what he called "a revolution in the northern part of the United States."

Vallandigham is one of the strangest and most tragic figures of the Civil War. There is little known about him except the few facts in a "memorial" published by his brother almost seventy-five years ago. He was born in Lisbon, Ohio, in 1820, the son of a Huguenot minister who liked to boast that his family's traits were always "decision, moral courage and religious convictions." At two he knew the alphabet and at twelve spoke Greek and Latin fluently and was ready to enter college, but college authorities refused to accept him.

At seventeen he entered Jefferson College in Philadelphia. At nineteen he was principal of Union Academy in Maryland. A year later he was editor of the *Western Empire*, a powerful Democratic newspaper. He became interested in politics and at twenty was making major speeches for the Democratic Party. He resigned from his post as college principal to practice law in his home town of Lisbon. Ambition and love of power burned in Vallandigham's breast. He desperately wanted to be a leader of men, a champion of lost causes. In Lisbon he specialized in criminal cases which other lawyers refused because of the obvious weight of state's evidence against them. Vallandigham delighted in defeating the state's attorney. He seldom lost; juries were hypnotized by his clear, ringing voice and dark gray eyes, cold and flat as slate, under jutting brows. But politics continued to be his first love and from a Common Pleas judgeship he advanced to the office of Lieutenant Governor and finally Congressman.

The tall, hawk-nosed, moody man was soon a familiar sight in the halls of Congress. He had few warm friends. As one man recalled years later, "he was not what you would call a mixer." Hines found him a fanatical dreamer "who believed all that was told to him."

One hour of every day of his life was set aside for reading the Bible. Nearly all of his major speeches are sprinkled with Biblical quotations. As a youth Vallandigham had lived a monastic life, shunning liquor, women and dancing. The oil lamp in his room burned late as he devoured books on law, religion and philosophy. His favorite was a dog-eared collection of Calhoun's speeches. Like Calhoun, Vallandigham supported a political philosophy of states' rights. In Congress he was the leader of the radical, or anti-abolitionist, movement of the Democratic Party. In the elections of 1862 he was defeated—a stunning blow to his pride. He was a bitter man when he returned to Washington to deliver his last speech in the House, a ringing denunciation of Lincoln and his war administration. The speech was frankly defeatist. The North would never succeed in subduing the South, he cried. "Why carry on this terrible war? It is folly."

His protest was a trumpet call to the Copperheads and to that section of his party which advocated peace at any cost. Vallandigham's rise as the spokesman for the Peace Democrats in the North had begun. These were the crucial days of the middle period of the war. Grant was besieging Vicksburg without success. Rosecrans was still inactive and apparently helpless after the bloody battle of Stone's River against Bragg. Lee had invaded Maryland and there were rumors of a second invasion of the North. Lincoln's Proclamation of Emancipation was being assailed on all sides. Draft riots flared up in New York City, while the terrible casualty list from Fredericksburg mounted. In the North ardor for the war was indeed lessening.

On February 20, 1863, the Cincinnati *Gazette* predicted that, through the "United States Grand Jury at Indianapolis, important revelations are being made upon the persistent denials of rebel sympathizers of the existence of a treasonable society known as the Knights of the Golden Circle."

Governor Morton of Indiana, alarmed at the mushrooming growth of the Copperheads in his state, asked Secretary of War Stanton for assistance. Would he relieve Colonel Henry B. Carrington, a Yale man and close friend of Secretary of State Salmon Chase, of his duties in the Adjutant General's Office?

Morton's request was granted. Carrington arrived at Indianapolis and was told by the Governor "to organize a staff and break up the Copperheads." It was a difficult assignment, but Carrington accepted it with enthusiasm. He selected five investigators, all amateur detectives. In 1863, on the evidence they obtained, a number of Federal indictments were issued. But Carrington knew he had only scratched the surface. He sent out his investigators again. Among them was a young clerk named Felix Stidger. If Hines was the Confederacy's most dangerous agent, Stidger was his northern counterpart.

When Stidger's reports arrived, Carrington, a judicious man of sober judgment, thought his investigator's imagination had run away with him. But when Stidger predicted that certain Federal supply warehouses would be burned, and they were burned, Carrington acted.

On March 19, 1863, Carrington, in a direct wire to Lincoln, reported of Morgan's next raid that "he [Morgan] will leave the command and quietly reappear to raise the standard of revolt in Indiana. Thousands believe this and his photograph is hung in many homes. In some counties his name is daily praised."

It would appear, then, that by this time the purpose of Morgan's raids had expanded. Now according to Carrington's information, the Confederates—or at least Morgan—had made some sort of alliance with the Copperheads for a revolt in the Northwest.

In April, Burnside, who had been given the command of the Department of Ohio after the Fredericksburg debacle, issued his famous Order No. 38, which authorized the death penalty for Confederate couriers carrying secret mails, recruiting officers of secret societies and "persons found concealed in lines belonging to service of the enemy."

The following day three thousand wildly cheering Copperheads greeted Vallandigham at an open-air meeting in Dayton, to watch the former Congressman spit on a copy of the order and hear him denounce Burnside as a "usurper of American freedom." That afternoon Burnside heard of the speech. He immediately ordered the provost marshal of Ohio to arrest Vallandigham. The hour of midnight was melodramatic enough, but Vallandigham added a few tricks. Grabbing a pistol and barricading himself and his wife in a bedroom, he fired several shots from a window, shouting "Asa, Asa, Asa," into the darkness. What the words meant no one knows. It is said they were signals to secret agents who were watching his house night and day in case Burnside were to attempt to arrest him.

The soldiers smashed in the door, arrested Vallandigham and took him to the Dayton military prison. Word swept across the countryside. In towns and villages men fastened the copper Indian head of a penny in their lapels, armed themselves with rifles and pistols and marched on Dayton.

Thousands streamed into the city all day. Soldiers with bayonets ringed the jail three deep to stand off the shouting, jeering mob. When they were unable to break through the ring of steel, the mob, led by Copperhead leaders, took its revenge on the city. Public buildings were burned to the ground, stores looted, houses broken into and hundreds wounded by stray bullets.

In the morning the mob was gone, leaving behind streets littered with rocks, splintered glass and overturned wagons. A pall of smoke hung over the city. Across the sides of many buildings was painted: "Release Vallandigham!"

Vallandigham was whisked to Cincinnati, where several lawyers of distinction defended him. His defense was that no military court could try him as there was no rebellion in his state.

During the high excitement in the city, newly elected Commissioner of Schools Cathcart was badly beaten by a Union soldier when he loudly defended Vallandigham and the Copperheads' peace aims. Cathcart, at the most only a shadowy figure, moves in and out of Tom Hines' life in 1863. He will appear a few more times, then will vanish into history.

Meanwhile, demonstrations took place all over the state. In the newspapers were frequent accounts of bands of armed men galloping about the squares of small towns, firing pistols and shouting and cheering for Jeff Davis, John Hunt Morgan and Vallandigham.

On May 10 Vallandigham was arrested, found guilty of treason, and sent to Fort Warren in Boston. Lincoln reviewed his case and decided he could do less harm in exile than at home. He sent him to Rosecrans' headquarters to be sent through the lines. On the 25th he was taken to Murfreesboro and held there under guard. The next day he was placed on the Shelbyville Pike and before nine was riding into the Confederate lines to be escorted to Braxton Bragg's headquarters at Shelbyville.

Vallandigham stayed at Bragg's headquarters until June. Morgan, even though he detested Bragg, and Captain Hines, were in and out of Shelbyville that spring. Consider the cast: Morgan, Hines and Val- landigham. A year later, Morgan's secret agent and the exiled traitor would confer on how to touch off a revolution in the Northwest. If this strange triumvirate had met at Shelbyville—and Hines makes no mention of such a meeting anywhere among his letters or in his diary —what had been discussed? Unfortunately, there is no way of knowing. But we do know that Tom Hines vanished in the last week of May. It was said officially that he was going into the Blue Grass to "fatten his horses." Actually, his purpose was to lay plans with the Copperheads for Morgan's great Ohio raid.

His real objective was carefully shielded from the other officers of Morgan's command. Even Basil Duke would write of what appeared to be absolute disobedience by Hines in raiding as far as Indiana in- stead of reconditioning sick horses in Kentucky.

"I do not know," says Duke, "what explanation he made to General Morgan, but it seemed perfectly satisfactory." Although there is no di- rect evidence such as written orders, the probability is that Morgan had received orders for the raid from Jefferson Davis, Judah Benjamin or Secretary of War Seddon after receiving assurances from Vallandig- ham that the Copperheads in the Northwest would rise when Morgan invaded their states.

On June 2 Vallandigham left Bragg's headquarters for Chattanooga. He would next appear in Canada, a man without a country.

The opening act of one of the most fantastic melodramas in our his- tory had begun. Rogues, villains, cavaliers and cowards crowd its cast. Acts would be played in the burning cities of New York, Chicago, Cincinnati and Boston; aboard captured schooners on the Great Lakes and in the messroom of a Federal gunboat; in a darkened Pullman sleeper in which ten Rebel raiders waited with cocked pistols "to start the ball"; in the offices of three Vermont banks, in Federal dungeons and prisons and on the steps of gallows; in newspaper offices and in a freak show with a howling giantess. There would be daring prison es- capes, hand-to-hand battles on the platforms of trains, murder and arson.

There would be many players but one outstanding star: Captain Thomas Henry Hines, C.S.A.

PART II

SECRET AGENT:
Underground Ambassador

———•••———

IV. ON TO THE OHIO

O N JUNE 10, 1863, seven days after Captain Hines had disappeared, Morgan joined his command at Alexandria to inform his startled staff he was going on the Ohio raid, although Braxton Bragg had specifically ordered him not to go.

To his officers, including Basil Duke, his decision appeared to be foolhardy. Aside from Rosecrans' force, in Tennessee, there were twelve thousand Federal troops, including five thousand of General Judah's excellent cavalry, in front of him. Bragg's army was threatened, yet Morgan decided to remove his strong cavalry arm and move north into Ohio. Of course it seemed wrong, but Duke, Morgan's own brothers and the other officers knew nothing of Morgan's dealings, through Hines, with the treasonable Copperheads in Ohio and Indiana.

Hines came and went as he pleased, yet the other officers never suspected his secret service work. After the war Basil Duke said there was no talk of aid from the Copperheads before the move north to Ohio. Of course there wasn't; that subject was a secret shared only by Morgan and his favorite captain.

When Jefferson Davis wrote in 1886 to Basil Duke, then editor of the *Southern Bivouac* magazine, asking him not to reveal the names of the northern leaders of the Conspiracy in an article Hines was writing, Duke replied that he had "no connections" with the transactions of Hines and no personal knowledge of them. Not only was Duke in the dark, but many of the high command in Richmond had no idea of what Davis, Judah Benjamin and Secretary of War Seddon were plotting in the days of 1863–64.

They were no ordinary men who went out to deal with the Copperheads and plan the Northwest Conspiracy, Duke recalled in 1906. "The kind of men who could plan and execute it are the very men to keep a secret themselves, and to teach and coerce silence and discretion to others. In the very heat and strain of war the people of the North were startled by learning that while their armies were waging battle in the distant region of rebellion, revolt and danger were at their very doors and strife might at any moment break out in northern communities direr than that which had desolated Virginia and Tennessee."

When Basil Duke questioned Morgan about the proposed Ohio raid, he replied they would join Lee in Pennsylvania if they could not get back across the Ohio. This was on June 10, the very day Lee's First Corps moved north. Lee's objective was not generally known. Vallandigham by this time had run the blockade and was now living in Windsor, Canada, where Hines would meet him the following spring.

While Duke and the rest of Morgan's staff were wondering what was in their general's mind to go off on what appeared to be a foolhardy raid, Captain Hines and his raiders had crossed the Cumberland and entered Kentucky.

Hines had set out from a picket camp at Woodbury, Tennessee, with eighty picked men. Before they left he had made a short speech to his men telling them simply that they were going on a long and dangerous mission. As one trooper recalled the scene, Hines sat on his horse facing his men, telling them in his soft, almost inaudible voice, "We are going where there will be a great deal of fighting, and a great deal of hard riding. If there are any of you who do not wish to go, who feel they will dread the long and tiresome march, the weary and sleepless watches —now is the time for them to ride out. . . ."

There was a long taut pause. Not a man kicked his horse forward. The following year the trooper paid him simple tribute. "Not a man stepped out. We were all anxious to serve with our captain."

After crossing the Cumberland, they rode all that night, reaching Jimtown, a small crossroads village, at dawn. Later that day they captured a stagecoach with a Federal officer carrying mail and Louisville newspapers. The papers contained the railroad schedules of mail trains which carried gold shipments and Hines could not resist delaying the march for the chance to steal some Yankee gold.

They piled logs across the tracks of the Louisville & Nashville Railroad and waited in the brush. But no train appeared. Later they learned that the train schedules had been changed when word was received at Union headquarters that Hines and his men were moving across the state.

Brownsville was their next stop. The citizens believed they were Union troops and cheered them from the sidewalks. They stayed only long enough to clean out a Union sutler's store of fresh army shirts, boots and trousers before galloping off.

At Elizabethtown the local Copperheads told Hines a mail train was soon to pass through. A halt was ordered and again logs were placed across the tracks. This time the train did appear. As the engine chugged to a halt Hines and his men rode out of the brush, the high, keening Rebel cry on their lips.

The Federal paymaster turned over his box of greenbacks. How much it contained is a mystery. In the Hines Papers it is simply described as "a large sum of money, in greenbacks." It is believed that the money was sent to Justice Bullitt in Louisville to arm his Sons of Liberty.

From Elizabethtown they rode northeast, passing within a few hundred yards of a Federal garrison. Through the trees they could see the Union campfires and hear the voices of the sentries.

The next day, while the men were taking a swim, the flankers Hines never failed to post rode in with the news that a large Union force was attacking. Hines led his half-dressed command deep into the forest to play hounds and hare with the Union cavalry all that day and part of the night.

They kept moving north. A crossroads village supplied trousers and coats for the troopers who had to leave their clothes behind. On the banks of the Ohio, looking across to the Indiana shore, Hines told his men they were now to be known as "Indiana Grays," a unit of the state's Home Guard.

He also informed them their destination was French Lick, the home of a man named Doctor William Bowles. The name meant nothing to his men but to Hines it meant a great deal. Bowles was the leader of the Copperheads in Indiana. His home at French Lick was a well known Democratic Party gathering place. Bowles was a power in the state party and Richmond had heard he was eager to help start an uprising in the Northwest. As the Madison [Indiana] *Courier* noted: "Hines and his raiders have inquired repeatedly for William A. Bowles. . . ."

Near Paoli Hines met a strong force of Home Guards. With that marvelous aplomb which he was to employ in many future dangerous hours in the Northwest, he passed himself off as a Federal officer, and his command as Indiana Grays, "hunting deserters and absentees from the Army."

The Guards escorted them to Paoli, where the townspeople set a long table in the square to feed the weary "Union" troopers. In the middle of the meal there was a disturbance when troopers rode up to inform the town's mayor that he had been hoodwinked.

Hines managed to get his men out of town and, by a ruse, surrounded a meadow where another body of Guards was camped, and calmly demanded their surrender. To create the impression he had a superior force Hines had divided the men into two groups. As he and a lieutenant rode into the meadow to confer "on terms" with the Federal officers who were holding up hissing torches, the Confederates yelled, fired their rifles and raced their horses back and forth through the trees. The impressed Guards quickly surrendered. Hines took their best horses and rode off after he had "placed the Guards on parole," as one of his troopers recalled the following year.

But they paid dearly for their braggadocio. Federal and Home Guard patrols buzzed about them like angry hornets. It was run-and-fight all night long. At last, just before dawn, they managed to outride their pursuers.

Three days later Hines found Doctor William A. Bowles at French Lick, south of Paoli. He ordered his men to make camp in the woods just outside French Lick, and went on alone to the Bowles house.

Bowles, then about fifty-five, was a slight man with a prominent nose, glaring eyes and tufts of white hair which gave him the appearance of an outraged old eagle. Bowles had served as a colonel in the Second Indiana Volunteers during the Mexican War. To him was attributed the disgraceful retreat at Buena Vista.

His large white house at French Lick was a Rebels' roost of deserters and escaped prisoners of war. Hines found "Bowles' army" to be equipped with the fine Henry rifles and Navy Colt revolvers. An account of this Bowles-Hines meeting in the early summer of 1863 is contained in a confidential report dated August 23, 1864, made to the assistant chief of staff of the Department of Ohio by Carrington, then a Brigadier-General. He outlines the activities of Tom Hines in trying to pave the way for General Morgan's raid.

Hines, he said, had met and conferred with Bowles about raising an army of Copperheads who would take over the state, assassinating the state and local government officials, seizing the state arsenals and turning on the Home Guards.

Carrington said Doctor Bowles had promised Hines "he could command ten thousand men in twenty-four hours." But the discussion was ended abruptly when an informer rode up to tell Bowles a provost marshal's patrol was on the way to arrest "Hines, General Morgan's guerrilla."

Carrington sadly admitted, "Hines, however, eluded the patrol."

After Hines had left, Doctor Bowles openly defied Union headquarters at Indianapolis. When a patrol came up to arrest five deserters, Bowles led his ragamuffin army out of a barn, and told the officer in charge of the patrol to turn back or be shot down. As Carrington reported, "He is as defiant and threatening as if he commands a Rebel force of regular troops."

On June 19, Hines and his men reached the Ohio. The Federals had pressed them hard since they had left French Lick. It was day and night riding, cold meals and little sleep.

They captured a small tug near an island and started to cross the horses when a Union force, "regiment strength," arrived, accompanied by an armed steamboat. Hines retreated to the island and fought off the first wave of Federal troops that splashed ashore. But the *Izetta* lobbed shells all around them, forcing them to retreat back up the island.

Hines realized it was a hopeless situation. He gathered his men about him to give them the choice of surrendering or attempting to swim the river under fire to the Kentucky side. Twelve men followed him. Hines stripped to his drawers, put his money and revolver in his hat and struck out. The Federals tried to run them down with their tug, but the Confederates on the island kept up such a steady fire at the tug's bridge that its skipper was forced to pull back beyond the island. But before the tug had pulled away, Union infantrymen on the decks had killed three of Hines' troopers. One, directly in front of him, sank without a sound.

When they reached the Kentucky shore they turned and waved to their comrades, then vanished in the woods. The Confederates on the island raised a cheer, broke their rifles and marched down to the beach under a white flag to surrender.

Hines and his men clothed themselves by "pressing into service" clothing and horses along the way. On the 27th of June they passed through Elizabethtown. Bardstown and Shelbyville were next. On July 6, they reached the Louisville & Frankfort Railroad Junction. Hines said he had taken this route because of information he had

received that a train carrying a fortune in gold for Rosecrans was
scheduled to stop there. But there was more than gold aboard that
train. Among the passengers was a Colonel Harney, editor of the Louisville *Journal* and a prominent Kentucky Copperhead.

In Cincinnati the *Gazette* said the day after the train had been
stopped:

> Morgan is in the state [Kentucky]. . . . Colonel Harney,
> the Copperhead editor of the Louisville *Journal,* met Hines
> last night, saying "I'm delighted to meet you . . . Morgan is
> coming." This is enough. There is panic and it is increasing. . . .

There is no way of knowing exactly what took place between Harney
and Hines, but undoubtedly the editor gave Hines news of Morgan's
advance, and possibly a message from Morgan himself.

When Burnside received news of the train raid by Hines, he sent
an outraged note to the provost marshal at Lexington demanding that
Hines be captured at any cost. "Tell the captain [of the patrol sent out
after Hines] that I will give him a thousand dollars if he captures Hines
and his men," Burnside wired. Hines must have been a sensitive subject with Burnside to have him offer such a large sum to his own men
for the capture of a mere enemy captain.

Brandenburg, on the Ohio River, was one day's ride. On the morning
of the 8th, Hines and his men arrived there to join two other Morgan
captains who had been sent on ahead to capture a steamboat to transport the troops across the river.

Later that day Morgan and his command arrived at Brandenburg
wharf. As Basil Duke recalled in his memoirs, he found Hines at the
wharf, "with a sleepy, melancholy look—apparently the most listless,
inoffensive youth that was ever imposed upon."

Duke, as Hines' superior officer, was amazed and indignant when
he saw Hines. All that he knew was that Hines had been ordered to
recondition some horses in Kentucky but had disappeared. Reports
had him in Kentucky, Ohio and as far north as Seymour, Indiana.
Even on the banks of the Ohio, Duke did not know how important an
intermediary Hines was.

The Ohio was still curtained by the morning mists at Brandenburg
as Hines reported immediately to Morgan on the extent of support he

could expect from the Indiana Copperheads. Hines returned to his position on Morgan's staff, replacing a wounded captain in the second brigade.

When the sun came out, the column of fours could see the haystacks and farmhouses along the Indiana shore from which the Union militia was firing. The single battery of Morgan's Parrott guns opened up from the wharf to drive the Union troops back to a wooded ridge six hundred yards from the river bank. It was Morgan's Second Kentucky which had the honor of making the first crossing. There was laughing and yelling among the ranks as they crowded to the bow of the boats to watch the approaching Yankee shore. But to the weary Hines, in one of the first boats, the thrill of stepping ashore on Indiana soil was lacking. He had already been much farther north.

A bridgehead was established and an advance made to the ridge. This halted briefly while the troops watched a duel between the Morgan battery and a small snub-nosed boat firing bronze 12-pound howitzers through portholes cut in oak planking. The duel went on for an hour, with neither the battery nor the howitzers doing much damage. Finally, the gunboat backed up the river and the crossing continued.

The next day at Croydon, Indiana, Hines, in the advance guard, charged a band of militia firing from behind rail fences, and Morgan's acting adjutant was killed at his side. Passing through Croydon, the column took the Salem road, camping eighteen miles from the town. A short halt was made in Salem the next day to feed the troops and the horses. Hines burned several railroad bridges in and around the town. In Salem pillaging was so widespread the provost marshal reported to Duke he could not control it. "It was senseless and purposeless," Duke later recalled.

One man carried for two days a bird cage with three canaries. Another rode with a large chafing dish tied to the pommel of his saddle until an officer forced him to cut it loose. The weather was boiling hot, yet several troopers hung ice skates about their necks. The looting had its serious side. The homes of Copperheads, from which hung the lone-star flag of the Knights of the Golden Circle, as well as homes of Union men, were looted. In fact, the homes of Copperheads became special targets for Morgan's raiders. "Give for the cause you love so well," they told the protesting Knights.

Morgan himself was no exception. He took seven hundred and fifty dollars from a county treasury and accepted twenty hundred dollars in Federal greenbacks not to burn a flour mill. Perhaps Morgan thought the money was a greater benefit to the Confederacy than a pile of charred timbers could be.

Indiana was now aroused. Governor Morton sent couriers through the state to call all men to arms. Church bells rang continuously. An order was issued to all able-bodied men south of the National Road to arm themselves and form into companies of sixty persons each. Morton asked General Lew Wallace, who was fishing on the Kankakee River, to rush to the state capital and take control of the armed forces. Wallace accepted. He found Morton and the state officials wildly excited. Morton told him Morgan had but to march on Indianapolis and it would be his.

Outside the city was a Rebel prison with six thousand hard-bitten veterans. With these Confederates free to augment his own force, Morgan could simply sit back and allow the Knights of the Golden Circle to fulfill the promises they had made to Captain Hines, and Indiana would be in the Confederacy.

Wallace later said he realized this danger and that "such an organization not only existed but reached the danger line in Indiana, Illinois and Missouri. Its members held meetings in schoolhouses of my own county and drilled openly."

Morton met Colonel Carrington, the arch foe of the Copperheads, in a dramatic episode at the Bates House. Carrington never forgot that night. Years later he wrote Morton's son:

> Neither does any man living but myself know the extent of that disaffection. . . . Your father came to me at midnight and asked how to prevent the [Copperhead] legislature from getting control of the arms in the state arsenal. I took my pen and made a requisition upon him for return to the United States of all arms which the state had received from the Government and then wrote out a transfer which he signed so that he was able to notify the legislature that the state had no arms. That was never published. . . .

That was on July 10. That same night Conrad Baker, Acting Provost Marshal General of Indiana, wrote Colonel Fry, Acting Provost Marshal of Indianapolis:

> In consequence of Morgan's raid into this state and the fears I entertain that there is an understanding between him

and the Knights of the Golden Circle, I have instructed the several provost marshals that in the event of the militia being called away from the neighborhood of the headquarters, the rolls [of militia] shall be so secreted as to put it out of the power of domestic enemies to find them. I am apprehensive that domestic enemies may embrace the opportunity to destroy the rolls.

Only eleven hundred raw recruits answered Governor Morton's call to arms. General Wallace shrewdly asked Morton if he wanted to make a stand against Morgan or "have him pushed through [out of] the state as rapidly as possible." Morton wisely adopted the latter strategy.

Morgan's column continued to move across the state. Where the Knights were thickest "there was full information in Morgan's possession of all he wished to know." Both at Salem and at Croydon Morgan showed lists of every citizen who owned a Henry rifle and patrols brought the owners in. Excellent guides appeared at his headquarters voluntarily when he arrived. Hines had done his work well.

Indianapolis was Morgan's for the taking, but for some reason he turned east from Salem. Though they cooperated with information and assistance, the Copperheads did not rise up. Perhaps the looting and bank-robbing by Morgan's men disaffected enough of them, perhaps it was decided that the revolt in Indiana should wait until Ohio had overthrown its Union government.

In any case, Morgan turned away from Indianapolis and headed east for Vienna. There he put his telegrapher on the wires to intercept messages telling which roads ahead of them had been blocked. The next day the raiders turned north again for Paris. On July 12 they reached Vernon. Indianapolis was only fifty miles to the northwest. With pursuit hot on their trail, and no Copperhead underground army to aid them, the Confederate raiders were now averaging twenty-one hours a day in the saddle.

The Hoosier townsfolk of Dupont watched the weary fours pass from five until ten o'clock in the morning. South of the town the Confederates raided a packing plant. Hams now hung from the pommels of saddles, along with bird cages.

In Versailles five thousand dollars was taken from the public funds. At noon of the same day the raiders reached Harrison on the White

Water River, only twenty-five miles northwest of Cincinnati. The long column of weary men was now strung out for miles.

At four o'clock, after a two-hour halt, they pushed on to Cincinnati. Five hundred men and horses had been lost from exhaustion and straggling. That evening, from the outskirts of the city, Morgan sent in two officers to reconnoiter the city's defenses. One was Captain Taylor, who worked with Hines in rallying the Copperheads from May to November, 1863. A reporter for the *Gazette* saw him ride leisurely up Front Street to Sycamore, then run down the river bank and disappear.

The night of July 13 the command bypassed Cincinnati, riding around the city with torches made from bolts of stolen calico. Morgan didn't know it yet, but Gettysburg had been fought and that same night Lee's army was crossing the Potomac back into Virginia.

Those who were with Morgan that night never forgot it. The terrible fatigue unnerved them all. Companies, squadrons and even brigades bumped into one another and lost their way. After the war Basil Duke recalled how in the torchlight they looked for the lather from the horses' mouths to trace their own advance. Men fell out to crawl into fields and sleep. Others dropped like dead men from their saddles. Officers, themselves half asleep, kicked and dragged men awake whenever they found them.

Dawn, fresh and sparkling, came at last to restore their spirits. At Williamsburg, at four o'clock that afternoon, Hines and Taylor, who had ridden into town, reported back to Morgan that all was well. A halt was ordered. The weary column slept all day and night.

It was about this time that the draft riots were spreading. In Buffalo, Philadelphia and Easton the draft lottery was suspended. In Denver the draft could not be enforced. Iowa told Washington if New York couldn't enforce the draft, why should she?

But the revolt did not flame in Ohio or Indiana. There was no general uprising. The militia, expected to rise up and fight alongside Morgan's troopers, turned and fought against them, most of the time to defend their own homes. Why should the Copperheads of Indiana and Ohio rally to the standard of a man whose troops were burning their homes, looting their furnishings, stealing their tax money and robbing their banks? On July 17 the columns reached Chester.

That same day Colonel Carrington's special detectives made a strange arrest in Louisville—a well-dressed fat man with a pompous air. He said he was on his way to Cincinnati and he had a pass signed by Rosecrans himself. Yet something about him did not ring true. Carrington ordered his luggage searched. A secret code and the original brass plate seal of the Knights of the Golden Circle were found, along with a small package of red dust, a number of incriminating papers and two small stars from a general's uniform, which were being used as Copperhead symbols.

He was "Doctor" George W. L. Bickley, the old humbug who had founded the Knights before the war. He tried to bluff his way out, but Carrington threw him into the Federal Penitentiary at Columbus, Ohio.

Behind Morgan the blue forces were forming: Burnside, the Ohio militia, three Ohio regiments from Fayetteville, West Virginia, and the splendid Federal cavalry under General Judah.

Morgan's command had been in the saddle in enemy country for fifteen days. For Hines and his little company these fifteen days with Morgan were on top of thirty-four days of almost endless riding and fighting before they had joined Morgan at Brandenburg.

At Chester, Morgan stopped long enough to rest his horses and find a guide to show him the way to the fords of the Ohio at Buffington. He reached Buffington after dark; it was impossible to cross until morning. Besides, three hundred Federals in trenches were guarding the fords.

Morgan was faced with making the decision to take the trenches, which meant charging across unknown terrain at night or waiting until dawn. He waited. At dawn the Fifth and Second Kentucky made ready to attack. The east was no longer black when they moved out. But the trenches were empty! The Federals had vanished during the night.

Later that morning a rear guard covering the crossing at Pomeroy Road made contact with Federal General Judah's advance elements. The Kentuckians, bone-weary yet still full of fight, beat off Judah's riders. But the blue flood could not be stopped, and soon the rear guard was driven in. With Basil Duke and Colonel Johnson holding his flanks, Morgan began to draw off toward the river. Twenty-eight men died on the banks. Then with a wild howl the Seventh Michigan cavalry tore down the road and routed the Confederates. There, at Buffington Island, they captured Basil Duke, Morgan's younger brothers, Hines and a number of other officers.

But Morgan succeeded in drawing off, managed to rally a thousand troopers and cut his way through the Federals. He kept going east through Ohio. The night of July 20 Morgan and his men were almost surrounded, but the Union leaders, confident that surrender was only a few hours away, did not attack. Under cover of darkness, the Confederates slipped away. The towns Morgan's men now passed through had lights and flags in the windows celebrating the great Union victories at Gettysburg and Vicksburg.

While Morgan led the remnants of his command along the dusty roads, Justice Bullitt of Kentucky was meeting in Chicago with the leaders of the Knights of the Golden Circle. He had word of a two-million-dollar Federal payroll captured by the Knights at Red River, Arkansas, which would be used for the uprising. The leaders were so confident of Morgan's victory that they decided at the meeting that "only homes which fly the Confederate flag shall be spared from burning. . . ."

But in the still July heat, with the taste of defeat on his parched lips, there could have been no conspiratorial thoughts in the reeling brain of Captain Tom Hines as he stretched out on the bank of the Ohio, at last a prisoner of the Union.

By the 26th Morgan and his men could go no further. The help they had expected never materialized. The pursuit, growing in strength, was too vigorous to withstand. As they neared the sleepy little village of East Liverpool, Morgan surrendered to Major George W. Rue of the Ninth [Federal] Kentucky. It was a Sunday morning. The exhausted troopers fell out of their saddles, stretched out in the dust and slept as the soaring voices of the choir drifted through the open windows and door of the white clapboard church. As Basil Duke recalled, a housewife brought a glass of cool water to a wounded trooper who was carried to a porch and put in the shade. He was very young and so badly wounded he couldn't give his name. She held his head in her lap whispering and soothing him as a mother would do; then when he closed his eyes and died, she laid his head back gently and carefully folded his hands across his breast.

The great Ohio raid was ended.

V. PRISON

THE Confederate prisoners taken at Buffington Island were sent down to Cincinnati on boats. It was a three-day journey for Hines on a crowded hurricane deck. Several troopers escaped by slipping over the side and swimming to shore. But Hines was allowed no opportunity to escape. Of all the officers he was the most carefully guarded. Telegraph wires across the state were crackling with news of his capture.

General Judah sent a courier to Burnside with the news that the prisoners on their way to Cincinnati numbered seven hundred and four, with forty-eight commissioned officers. Hines was selected for special mention. "We are keeping close watch over him," Judah said.

Burnside, in turn, wired headquarters that the bag of prisoners amounted to six hundred, "among them Duke, Colonel Morgan and the notorious Captain Hines. . . ." The great Duke and Morgan's brothers are listed, but again it is Hines who is singled out.

At Cincinnati they were met by jeering mobs who spat at them and urged the guards to use their bayonets. Privates were sent to Camps Morton and Douglas, while the officers were kept at the city prison in the center of Cincinnati for three days. Here they received news of Morgan's capture and his removal with his officers to a prison in Columbus, Ohio.

On the morning of the fourth day Hines and the other officers were transferred from Cincinnati to Johnson's Island in Lake Erie not far from Sandusky, Ohio. At every station large crowds chanted, "Hang Morgan's horse-thieves!" over and over. At Sandusky they were taken under heavy guard to a small steam tug. In twenty minutes they had crossed the arm of the lake which separates Johnson's Island from the mainland and marched into the prison camp to the cries of "Fresh fish" by the other prisoners.

The first man Basil Duke saw was one of his young lieutenants who had been captured a month before. Before Duke had set out on the

35

Ohio raid he had seen the boy's father, who asked him to send his son his greetings if he ever saw him.

"Lieutenant," Duke said, "your father asked me to send you his best wishes."

"Why, thank you, sir," said the young officer. "May I show you around?"

That night Duke and Hines listened to several prisoners taken at Gettysburg describe that battle in all its terrible detail. They went to bed whispering a prayer for "Uncle Robert" and his gallant Virginians.

Johnson's Island held several thousand prisoners. As their memoirs testify, two things occupied most of their thoughts: escape and food, in that order. Canada lay across the lake and plans were made every day to cross the waters on makeshift rafts, start an army across the border and come down on the Yankees' back. It was a favorite thought of Hines. As they sat in the shade of the prison barracks, he would draw maps with a pointed stick in the dust and show his fellow-prisoners how it could be done.

Finally, an escape was planned. They were to take over the prison by force, bind and gag the keepers and steal boats to cross the lake. It was a wild plan but it might have worked. Hines says two hundred men were ready to overpower the guards when an informer told the prison commandant, a Federal colonel. The colonel stormed into Basil Duke's quarters to denounce Hines and the rest of them as horse-thieves who should be hanged. As punishment, they were to be shipped to the penitentiary at Columbus.

The colonel walked out, followed by his large black Newfoundland dog. Sitting outside in the shade, one of Hines' troopers thoughtfully eyed the dog. The next day the animal was missing. The commandant stormed about, "making a great deal of a racket about his hound." He demanded that the dog be brought back before nightfall or the camp would suffer. The dog was never returned.

The following day Basil Duke, Captain Hines and forty-two of Morgan's officers were transferred to Columbus. Left behind them, pinned to a bunk, was a verse written by the hungry trooper:

> Dear Col.
> For want of bread
> Your dog is dead
> For want of meat
> Your dog is eat.

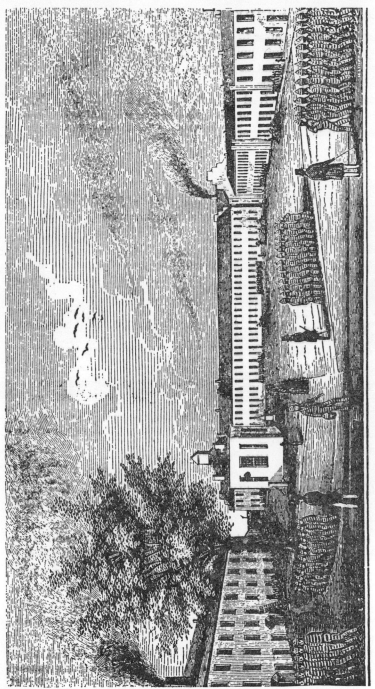

SCENE AT THE OHIO PENITENTIARY, COLUMBUS.

The view was taken within the inner enclosure of the Penitentiary, and shows the manner in which the prisoners march to and from their work. Their shops appear on three sides of the area, while the Prison building bounds it on the fourth.

Hines arrived at Columbus to find the penitentiary a miserable collection of stone houses surrounded by an inner and outer wall. The prison, he recalled, "was hot as an oven in the summer, and cold as the northern poles in winter."

The treatment they received on their arrival enraged them. Negro attendants with horse brushes and coarse soap scrubbed them in hogsheads filled with filthy water and a barber shaved them and clipped their hair short.

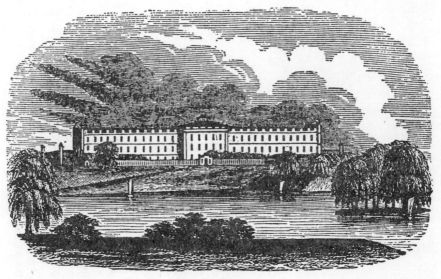

Ohio Penitentiary.

Courtesy, Ohio State University

Contemporary view of the Ohio State Penitentiary in Columbus from which Hines, Morgan and four of his captains escaped in November, 1863.

When Basil Duke walked into the cell block he said "hello" to a man he thought was a convict. The man laughed; Duke looked closer. It was General Morgan, unrecognizable without his beard and moustache. A Colonel Smith had his waist-long beard shaven off. His thin face and scrawny neck gave him the look of an angry turkey cock. Duke tried to turn a joke, but Smith, one of his oldest friends, snapped, "This is no jesting matter, sir."

Captain Hines had his corsair's moustache shaven off. With it went several years. The men who were with him in the prison always re-

membered how young he looked as he peered insolently at the guards
through the bars of his cell.

They raised such a fuss about their beards that it reached the ears
of Burnside, who sent a telegram to Warden Merion saying they
shouldn't be shaved if they didn't want to be. But the damage had
been done; their lovelocks were shorn.

Morgan and sixty-nine of his officers were imprisoned in the "East
Hall" of the penitentiary. Several large windows looked out over the
town, but the men were forbidden to go near them. The cells were
three and a half feet wide and seven feet long, arranged in five tiers
called Range One, Two, Three, Four and Five. In front of each tier
was an "alley," sixty paces long and twelve feet wide. Iron ladders
connected the tiers. Exercise was permitted in the alley during the day.

The first and second tiers were occupied by Morgan and his officers.
The other tiers were empty. General Morgan's cell was in the second
range. Captain Hines' was No. 20, in the dead center of the first floor
block. In each cell was an iron bed which could be hooked up to the wall,
and a straw bedtick. Usually they kept the beds lowered on their inch-
square wooden "bed props," to sit on to read or write letters.

As Hines writes:

> Sixteen out of the twenty-four [hours], we were confined
> in these cells and not permitted to recognize the presence of
> each other, even by a whisper. The remaining hours of the
> twenty four we were permitted by his highness, the warden,
> to promenade in the narrow hall in front of our cells, which
> was sixty paces in length and twelve feet in width. We were
> forbidden correspondence with our friends except of the
> most meagre nature and that subject to the censorship of both
> civil and military authorities. . . .

On the way to breakfast the guards allowed them to wash in the
trough. At two and at seven they were marched to the dining room
in the main building across the yard. Hines never forgot the steady, far-
off tramp of the convicts in the West Hall marching to their dinner.
The warden thought it was a huge joke that the regular felons were
forbidden to sit at the same table with "Morgan's horse-thieves."

The cells were locked for the night when a particularly obnoxious
turnkey named Scotty rapped on a stove lid with his ring of keys. The
cells were inspected at ten o'clock, midnight and at three by an evil-
faced ghoul in carpet slippers who tried to catch the prisoners with

lighted candles after lights out, and who liked to thrust his "coffee-pot" lamp into the cells to awaken those who had at last fallen asleep.

He was Hines' special bait. After the trusty inspected his cell and was beginning to climb up to Range Two, Hines would call, "Turnkey!"

The trusty would shuffle down the long alley to Hines' cell only to hear the Confederate whisper slyly, "Goodnight, sir."

The laughter traveled from range to range to echo about the domed ceiling when the old keeper angrily cursed Hines, who would protest indignantly that he was only being polite.

During the long day they paced endless miles up and down the alley, wrote hundreds of letters or played countless games of marbles with what Basil Duke called "restless lethargy." Merion permitted Hines to buy a chess set and his cell became a meeting place for the expert players. Chess books were bought and studied as carefully as any book on tactics. Captain Hines demanded and was allowed to buy some Waverley novels. Next he ordered two French romances and Gibbon's *Decline and Fall of the Roman Empire*.

Warden Merion insisted on strict discipline. Captain Hockersmith, whose memoirs are in the Hines papers, remembered that the principal rules were:

> No spitting tobacco juice on the floor.
> No dust or dirt allowed on the floor.
> No apple cores or peach pits permitted on the floor.
> No loud talking, joking or boisterous language.

The trusty Scotty was always inspecting the cells to make sure they were spotless. Infraction of the rules resulted in drastic punishment. Two of Morgan's captains were sent to the prison's dungeon, "Hell's Pit"—as they called it—for forty-eight hours. Both emerged pale and shaken from their experience.

The Copperheads of Ohio were finally on the march. Torchlight parades moved through the streets of Dayton. Homes of Union men were burned, and their cattle poisoned. It is curious that despite the failure of Morgan's Ohio raid, the Copperheads seemed to grow in strength. This may have been a result of the meeting of the Grand

Commanders during this same month in Chicago. Here plans were laid, and funds distributed, for insurrection.

On July 29 Mrs. Morgan arrived at Columbus to see her sons. General Burnside denied her request.

J. B. Jones in his *Rebel War Clerk's Diary* noted on the day that Mrs. Morgan was refused permission to visit her sons, Adam Johnson of the Tenth Kentucky and some three hundred of Morgan's men who had escaped reached Lynchburg. They had traveled down through the Kanawha Valley by back roads to find their first refuge in Wytheville, West Virginia.

Wytheville was a town of strong Rebel sympathies. When the Federal troops marched in, the townspeople cried out from windows and rooftops, "No quarter," and "Black flag" while sharpshooters picked off the officers. Learning that Morgan's men had hidden there, the Federals left the town in ashes.

In Richmond, Adam Johnson reorganized Morgan's command to join Bragg before Chattanooga. Bragg, Morgan's eternal enemy, was making the most of Morgan's disobeying his order not to go on the Ohio raid, telling all who would listen that had Morgan's cavalry been there to support him at Murfreesboro, when Rosecrans rolled out, things might have been different.

The bickering, petty feuds and quarrels at Richmond never reached Columbus, where the broiling hot days made life miserable for Morgan and his officers. But the mysterious and accurate grapevine which seems to exist in every prison told them of Lee's resignation in August and its refusal the next day.

In the theatre of war, Bragg evacuated Chattanooga, retreating twenty-five miles to Lafayette, Georgia. On September 9 Rosecrans was in Chattanooga. Longstreet's First Corps with the Hood and McLaws Division started down from Virginia to support Bragg. Buckner was recalled from Knoxville with his division and Breckinridge joined him with some troops from Mississippi.

Four days later, on September 22, Rosecrans limped back into Chattanooga after the terrible day of Chickamauga. Morgan's men under Adam Johnson had led the attack. Forrest took off his hat in their honor as they passed.

The great news filtered back into the cells at Columbus. Hines and the officers went wild with joy. There was other good news. The Copperheads had nominated Vallandigham for Governor and Ohio was at a fever pitch. There were more torchlight parades in Ohio and Indiana cities. It seemed almost every man on the street wore on his lapel a tiny copper Indian head carved from a penny.

Discipline was tightened at Columbus. Merion, the warden, threw one of Morgan's colonels into solitary confinement and later transferred him to Johnson's Island, where he died of diphtheria.

In October Morgan protested to the Army Commander in Columbus against the increasing rigor of their imprisonment. In his list of complaints he stated they were locked in their cells every Sunday all day, allowed but one hour for exercise, returned to their cells daily at five o'clock and let out at seven-thirty. From Saturday to Monday they were in their cells more than forty hours.

November, 1863, is the most mysterious month in Hines' life. The yellowing memoirs tell only a part. After ninety years the whole story is yet to be told. It probably never will be.

That month Hines planned and executed the escape from Columbus of Morgan and his captains, one of the most thrilling prison escapes of the war. Hines claims this achievement was the reason why Richmond officials chose him to command the Northwest Conspiracy and the uprising of the Copperheads the following year. However, that was only partly the reason why Secretary of State Judah Benjamin selected Hines. The fact that the Copperhead leaders knew him from previous dealings was also an important factor.

One fall day says Hines, he was "rudely treated" by Warden Merion. Later, as he was reading of Jean Valjean's escape in *Les Misérables* and brooding over the "insult," he decided to break out of Columbus. As he sat outside his cell, the book in his lap, he noticed for the first time that the floor of his cell, built on a level with the ground outside, was dry and free from mold. Hines' logical mind began to function. He soon came to the conclusion "that this dryness could not exist unless there was underneath an air chamber to prevent the dampness from rising."

Hines made some "casual inquiries" which confirmed his deductions.

He realized that if he cut through the floor of his cell he would have "an excellent base for future operations."

Hines took Captains Hockersmith, Bennett, Taylor, Sheldon and Magee into his confidence. They eagerly agreed to help. That afternoon Hines went to Morgan's cell to outline his plan. Morgan told him to go ahead.

With his wooden bed prop Hines tested the floor of his cell and the adjacent ones. Each thump gave off a hollow sound. He was sure now that some sort of an air chamber had been built below the floor of the jailhouse.

His plan was to cut through the concrete floor of his cell. But there was no way of knowing how thick the floor might be, and a council of war produced only one broken penknife. Hines knew that two of the officers in the second range were sick and that their meals were brought in. Hines detailed Taylor and Sheldon to visit those officers and persuade them to steal the cutlery. Later Taylor and Sheldon returned with the knives.

Hockersmith, who had been a bricklayer in civilian life, and Taylor, who had been a mechanic, were assigned by Hines to begin the digging. Hines, seated on the edge of his bed with Gibbon's *Decline and Fall*, was to act as lookout.

Two men were to work at a time while the others "promenaded" the alley. The digging detail was relieved every hour and worked from four to five hours a day. Hines made up a system of signals. One tap on the floor with the bed prop was to commence work; two taps: stop; three: danger and come out of the hole at once. Work was to begin as soon as the cells were opened and to stop just before they were ordered to fall into line at seven to be marched out for dinner.

All rubble was to be hidden in Hines' bed-tick. The danger was great that the trusty Scotty or Warden Merion might find telltale gobs of clay on the floor. Hines proposed he buy his own broom and make a great show of obeying Scotty's rule of spotless cell floors. The captains agreed and Hines bought a broom for twenty-five cents.

Before he used his broom for the first time Hines littered his cell with scraps of paper and peach pits. When he saw the trusty coming down the hall he carefully backed out of his cell, sweeping up the paper and peach pits. Scotty stopped and glowed.

"Ah, that's more like it, Hines," he said and went on.

"Yes, sir," Hines replied. The trusty could not see the contempt in his cold blue eyes.

But suppose the noise of the digging could be heard, or the tapping of the men in the hole on the floor of the cell? Captain Bennett had an answer.

"We'll just sing 'The Old Cow Crossed the Road,' 'Grasshopper Sittin' on a Tater Vine' or any one of the old songs," he said, "and dance around the guard who happens to be near."

"Suppose they don't like to be danced around?" Hines asked dryly.

"Captain Magee is always hammering on something to make a ring or breastpin," Taylor said. "We can signal him to begin hammering."

"We'll do them both," Hines said. "Whatever is handiest."

Hines himself puts November 2 as the day the actual digging began. Captain Hockersmith, he says, placed the blades of the stolen kitchen knives together, serrating the blades by striking the edges with a poker.

The date is important for other reasons. On that day, as Warden Merion later testified, he turned over to the military authorities the sole control of Morgan and his captains. This was disputed by the Federal Army Commander in Columbus, who said the Army did not take over control of the celebrated prisoners but had sent to Warden Merion a Sergeant J. W. Moon, as prison steward. Sergeant Moon's duties are still a mystery.

Also on that date, inspection of the cells was discontinued. Later it was established that Moon "received and disbursed" the funds of Morgan and his officers.

Back in Hines' cell the work had started. The two stolen knives were made of soft iron and their square clumsy handles made the chipping very difficult. The teams of two captains casually sauntered in and out of Cell No. 20 all day. Hines, as lookout, sat on the edge of the bunk, apparently deeply engrossed in the glories of ancient Rome.

"My recollection is that we worked all day but at night could scarcely tell what had been done," Hockersmith says in his diary. "The concrete proved to be harder than ordinary rock. Our knives of soft iron made but little impression on the floor. Consequently, Captain Sam Taylor had not much more than his vest pocket full of rubbish to dispose of. Captain Hines was at his post all the while, keeping a sharp lookout lest some intruder should step in unawares."

The next day Bennett and Magee took their turns at chipping at the cement floor. Taylor, Sheldon and Hockersmith stayed out in the hall, doing their best to keep the attention of the guards focused on a game of marbles. As Hockersmith says, "Hines insisted that each man take a turn of not more than an hour because the guards were familiar with their faces and if they didn't see a man about in the hall they made it a practice to walk down the row of cells and inquire after him."

On the third day they made good progress. A hole about fourteen inches in diameter was gouged out of the cement floor. When their pockets were stuffed with chips of cement Hines called a halt. The rubble was put into his bed-tick from which the straw had been removed. Hines was to recall his bed felt like a Hindu torture platform.

Meanwhile there was wild excitement in Cincinnati. About the same time that Hines and his men had begun chipping at the concrete cell floor, the Gazette was on the street with stirring news. Charles W. H. Cathcart, Ohio State School Commissioner, had been arrested in a large Copperhead plot to overpower the guards at Camps Morton and Chase, Indiana, and then to release Morgan and his men at Columbus. Cathcart, it should be remembered, was the same man who was struck down by a Federal trooper for praising Vallandigham, the day the Copperhead mobs burned and looted Dayton in protest against Vallandigham's arrest.

The Gazette said that "thousands were waiting the signal to rise." Two women, one a mail courier between the Copperheads and the Confederate agents, and a laundry worker "who had access to the prisoners" [Morgan and his officers] were also arrested.

The next day the digging continued. On November 4, Hockersmith came out of the cell, yawned and stared down at Hines, who closed his book and looked up.

Hockersmith's lips formed the words, "We're through the floor," and then went back to his "chess game."

A guard came up and Hines began humming, "The Old Cow Crossed the Road." When he looked in the cell the guard saw Taylor and Hockersmith bent over a chess board. They both seemed a thousand miles away.

The guard stared down at Hines' book and asked its title. Hines told him. The guard wanted to know what the "story" was about. Hines went into a long and detailed description of Gibbon's work. But the guard became bored, as the Confederate knew he would, and walked away. The digging went on.

That night Hockersmith told Hines they had gone through the floor to reach a red brick arch on which the floor had been built. Below the arch was the air chamber. The mortar in the arch was old, he said, and it would take only a few hours to break through.

There was breathless excitement that night as word was sent through the grapevine to General Morgan. He whispered back his congratulations to Hines and the others.

At two o'clock on the afternoon of November 5, Hockersmith's knife slipped through a joint of mortar between two of the arched bricks. Thirty years later Hockersmith could recall the tremendous excitement he felt at that moment. Carefully he worked his knife up and down the slit. The mortar crumbled. Two loose bricks were lifted out of the hole. The others he tapped gently and they fell into the darkness below. In a few minutes he had made a hole wide enough to allow the passage of a man.

Hockersmith notified Hines, who played sick, refusing his dinner. When the others had marched out, he scrambled down into the air chamber with a candle. He found it to be about five feet high and twenty feet long. The foundation of the building was squared granite stone. Hines chipped at the mortar of the foundation with a knife. It crumbled easily. He dug at the dirt floor. It was soft. As he squatted in the hole, the tiny flame casting dancing shadows on the old stone, he told himself they had one of two courses to take: remove the large stones from the foundation and dig a tunnel across the jailyard, or burrow under the foundation. He decided to let Hockersmith the bricklayer advise them. Then Hockersmith went down into the hole. He told Hines he recommended removing one or two large foundation stones and digging out into the prison yard. They all agreed to accept his recommendations.

When the others returned from dinner, Hines told Morgan, who scarcely believed the story. He asked to see the hole. Hines escorted him to his cell and dramatically pulled aside a strip of black carpeting.

"There it is, General," he whispered. Morgan stared down into the hole. Then he nodded, saying he was "satisfied with the result."

Before the cells were locked, the rubble from Hines' bed was dumped into the air chamber. For the first time since they had started digging, Hines was able to sleep.

On November 6, Hockersmith went back into the chamber. When he came up he said he had found a small, boarded-up grill at the far end of the chamber. But he was puzzled why he couldn't see daylight through slits in the boards. Work was called off until they could find out what was blocking the grill. Fortunately, it was the day they washed their clothes in the yard.

At the trough they scrubbed and wrung their shirts, drawers and pants with a great deal of noise and laughter. Hockersmith casually strolled across the yard. When he reached the spot where he judged the grill to be he stopped and stared in disgust. Forty bushels of coal had been dumped against the wall. If the grate were removed, the coal would pour into the chamber like an avalanche.

On the morning of November 7, as they were washing at the wooden trough in the jailyard, Hines saw a small rusted shovel with a broken handle. He hid the excitement he felt by plunging his face into the cold water. As he came up dripping, he hid his face in his towel. Taylor, who was next to him, was kicked in the shins. He caught on and leaned to Hines to receive the muffled instructions.

It was the custom for the guards to allow the captains who had finished washing first to engage in some horseplay while waiting for the others. Wrestling and leap frog were some of the games. Taylor whispered to Hockersmith, Bennett and Sheldon. Hines was already prancing about. The bricklayer, a big man, lunged at him playfully. Hines dodged. Hockersmith tried again; Hines whirled away. He was now halfway across the yard and near the shovel. The guards at the trough grinned and then turned away to exchange the gossip of the morning. Taylor, who had his army coat on, came running after Hines. Bennett joined Hines. The four men wrestled about the yard, laughing and shouting insults at one another. When they reached the shovel, Bennett seemed to trip. Hines fell on top of him, Hockersmith and Sheldon stood in front of them, blocking off the view of the guards at the troughs and the one in the sentry box on the wall. In a moment Bennett had the shovel under his coat and down the waist of his pants. Laughing, Hines gave him his hand and helped him to his feet.

"That's enough, fall in . . . fall in . . .," the guards shouted. They did not notice the ramrod stiffness of Captain Bennett's back as he marched into the dining room and sat at the table. The shovel had a pointed end, and "was used by us to good advantage," Captain Bennett wrote the following year as he recalled for a friend the thrilling escape.

The same day they stole the shovel, a United States grand jury had indicted School Commissioner Cathcart and his co-conspirators for "treason in endeavoring to release John Morgan and his officers from the Ohio Penitentiary, to release Rebel prisoners from Camp

Chase, and conspiring to capture the U. S. steamer *Michigan* on Lake Erie. . . ."

The 8th, 9th and 10th were used to cut through the foundation of the jail building. It was laborious work. Taylor's hands began to bleed where blisters were rubbed raw from the square handle of the iron knife. Hines ordered him to stop digging for a few days.

Patiently they scraped away the mortar around a large rock with a pointed end. Hockersmith, Sheldon, Bennett and Magee took an hour each. Hines never left the cell door. His eyes seemed glued to Gibbon. The guards never failed to stop and ask questions about Rome. Was it true about Nero and his fiddle? What kind of people were these Romans anyway? Hines, with elaborate patience, would go into a scholarly discussion of Gibbon. It was too scholarly for the guards. They always walked away.

It took three days to loosen the big rock. Finally, when the others were able to get the attention of the guards, Taylor and Bennett joined Hockersmith to pull the rock into the hole. But the walls were thick and there were more rocks to remove before they could reach the outside. The work went on.

On the 12th disaster struck. Hockersmith was alone in the hole. Hines, whose duty it was to tap for Hockersmith to come out for dinner, was called to Morgan's cell for a conference. Another captain took his place. The guards came into the hall shouting that dinner was ready.

Cell by cell the officers fell into line. The man at the entrance of Hines' cell, who had forgotten to tap the floor with the bed prop, joined the others. Below, Hockersmith went on chipping the mortar away from the big rocks.

It was Hines who observed that Hockersmith was not in line. General Morgan was behind him. As he was about to pass out into the hall, Hines whispered a warning to Morgan. General Morgan caught on at once. He stopped and turned to a guard.

"Guard, I feel ill tonight. I won't have dinner," he said.

"Very well, General, as you wish," the guard said.

Morgan walked to Hines' cell, "for the chess game," and managed to tap the floor gently with the bed prop. Hockersmith scrambled up out of the hole. Morgan told him quickly what had happened. Hockersmith dived into his own cell, brushed his clothing and threw himself on his bunk. As he did so, he heard the chief keeper, who had missed

Hockersmith at the table, ask Morgan, "Where is Captain Hocker-smith, General Morgan?"

"I saw him lying on his bunk as I came into Captain Hines' cell for the chess game," Morgan replied casually. "I believe he said he was ill."

The keeper, in a suspicious voice, said, "Let's go and see if he is there."

"Very well, sir," Morgan replied.

They found Hockersmith on his bunk groaning and holding his stomach. When the keeper asked him what was "his disease," Hocker-smith said he was ill to his stomach and needed "a sick diet." The keeper felt his forehead, agreed he felt hot and went back to the kitchen to order toasted bread and weak tea sent into the sick man's cell. The prison physician, a loud, coarse man, came in later to insist that Hockersmith swallow some evil-looking medicines. Hockersmith later emptied the rest of the bottle into the stove.

Hines decided Hockersmith would have to remain on the "sick list" for the next day, despite the bricklayer's insistence he would rather dig in a musty dark hole than swallow any more of the prison doc-tor's medicines. Bennett, Sheldon and Magee did that day's digging.

Late on the 13th they broke through the foundation of the prison building to reach solid earth.

A tunnel was now needed for the distance across the jailyard to the outer walls. But Hockersmith said he needed an idea of the lay of the land outside, to make sure they would not dig under the coal piled against the walls of their cell building.

General Morgan himself solved the problem. He engaged Scotty, the trusty, in a conversation about two prisoners who had escaped by climbing up the bars of the "balconies" in front of the cells to the ceiling where two large windows and a skylight were located. The prisoners had climbed out the skylight onto the roof and slid down a waterspout to the jailyard. It was Scotty's favorite story and he never tired of repeating it.

"There's no other man on earth who could do what those fellows did," Scotty said.

"Why, Captain Taylor, small as he is, can do it," replied Morgan.

Scotty shook his head. Morgan insisted Taylor could make the climb. The other Confederates gathered around. They began sneering at Scotty's story of the two convicts. The trusty blustered but finally agreed to let Taylor make the try. The captain, who knew what his general was up to, took off his coat and began climbing.

It was a dramatic scene: the nimble Confederate prisoner climbing up hand over hand while below, Morgan, Hines and the rest, their nerves on edge, silently watched him, a prayer in their hearts. Taylor reached the top, hung on the bars for a moment as he looked out, studying the yard below. A cheer rose. Scotty shouted for him to come down. After a long look, Taylor climbed back down.

That afternoon, after a conference with Taylor, Hockersmith began digging the tunnel. The first eighteen inches of loose dirt they pulled back into the main hole by using shirts as bags. They were all jubilant that night, with Hockersmith predicting they would be finished in a few days. But the next day was a different tale.

After the stratum of loose dirt they struck hard, tough clay which broke one of the knives. From an old convict, probably through a bribe, Hines secured a large old-fashioned razor which proved best for cutting through the clay. The work progressed by inches. On the 16th Hockersmith's hands were so cramped from holding the razor he could not dig. They all rested that day.

The tunnel was five feet deep when Captain Taylor found a small box which he managed to smuggle into his cell. With the razor they cut a hole in one end of the box to which was tied a cord made of twisted strands of bed-ticking. A bed prop was used to push the box into the tunnel where the digger filled it with earth and clay. At a single jerk of the cord, the man back in the hole would pull out the box and empty it.

Next Bennett came down with blistered hands and couldn't work. On the 18th it was Taylor. Once a guard nearly caught them, but Hines managed to tap twice on the floor. They were bending over the chess game when he looked in.

In seven days they dug a tunnel twelve feet long, three feet high and eighteen inches wide. Hockersmith said nine pounds of candles were used.

On the 19th, Hockersmith's absent-mindedness almost trapped them all. As Hines tells the story, Hockersmith had bought a small striped hat from one of the other convicts to protect him from the dirt and clay. In the afternoon he came up for additional candles. Unthinkingly, he still wore his convict's cap.

"I need some more candles," he began but stopped. Hines was staring at his clay-smeared hat. At the far end of the corridor a guard was starting to turn around. Hockersmith whipped off the hat and threw it into the cell. The guard sauntered up to them.

"Reading about those Romans again, Captain?" he asked.

Hines smiled and nodded. Hockersmith held his breath. On the floor behind them in plain view was the dirty cap. The guard didn't seem to be in a hurry. Rocking back and forth on his toes, he kept up a conversation. Hines did most of the talking. Hockersmith's tongue seemed glued to the roof of his mouth. At last the guard walked away. Both men stared at each other. Luck was still with them.

On the morning of the 21st, the tunnel was almost completed. The escape had to take place at night but the problem of how to get the cell doors open presented itself. A plan to cut holes in each cell, working from underneath so the crust could be tapped through, was agreed upon. But how would Hockersmith and the other diggers know at what point in each cell floor to dig the hole? Hines' steel-trap mind solved the problem.

A makeshift rope the length of the cell block was woven together. To avoid suspicion, a friendly argument as to the exact length of the block was begun when Warden Merion appeared. The warden was to judge the various estimates. Then to arrive at the correct length Hines produced the rope as a measuring tape. The "argument" was settled—and Hines had marked off the points in the cell where they were to dig the escape holes.

On the 24th, Commissioner Cathcart in Cincinnati claimed he was ill and asked the courts to reduce his bail. It was reduced to two thousand dollars. He posted it and returned to Columbus on Thanksgiving Eve.

On the 25th, Hockersmith told Hines the tunnel would be finished within two days. That night, according to his own version, he had a curious interview with General Morgan, in which the general offered him ten thousand dollars "if we made our escape and I went with him to Richmond." Hockersmith claims he replied that it was liberty and not gold he was after. "That makes no difference; you must have the money," he quotes Morgan as saying.

Hockersmith's version is in the Hines Papers. Attached to it is an affidavit by Bennett testifying to the truth of the story. Hockersmith also said that Morgan offered to give anyone fifty or a hundred dollars to exchange cells with him so he could be next to No. 20, Hines' cell, the night of the escape. His brother, Colonel Richard Morgan, offered to let him have cell No. 21 and Morgan accepted.

VI. THE ESCAPE

O N THE morning of the 20th, Thanksgiving Day, the tunnel was completed. Hockersmith told Hines he had driven a wire up through the remaining foot of earth and had seen daylight. The task of cutting up through the floors of the six cells also had been completed. There remained only a thin crust to stamp through. Also, a rope was needed to enable the fugitives to get over the outside walls of the prison.

Colonel Morgan provided the rope which he had braided from strips of bedticks. A poker was bent into the shape of a hook and tied to one end. Every three feet in the rope a "climbing loop" was made. Now all was set. Ten minutes past midnight, after the old keeper had finished his rounds, was selected as the hour of the escape.

The day was wet and dreary, with a low overhanging sky. At dusk Hines told his general that "falling weather was coming." The dull, monotonous hours passed, broken only by the visit of Mrs. Lucy Dorsey, of Carlisle, Kentucky, who told Warden Merion she had come to see "her sweetheart," later identified as one of the Morgan brothers. It is curious to note the visit was permitted.

Two things happened that afternoon. An informer wrote to Secretary Stanton in Washington, "It is rumored and generally believed [in Columbus] that the party of John Morgan's Rebels now in our penitentiary are feasted and toasted and waited upon by the Copperheads in the community."

General Morgan sent for Sergeant Moon, the "prison steward," to give him his watch to take to a jeweler's to be repaired. Without asking permission Moon left the prison.

The dull twilight slipped into blackness. The prison was still as a tomb. In their cells the men who were going to escape, and those who were not, lay in their hard bunks listening to the beat of the rain against the windows and the steady tramp of the convicts on their way to the dining hall.

At midnight the door opened. The old trusty in carpet slippers shuffled along the cells, holding his "coffee-pot lamp" high so the light fell across the bunks and silent figures. Hines counted the steps. In his mind's eye he could see the old man climbing the ladder to the second tier. While they had distracted the guard's attention just before the cells had been locked, General Morgan had changed cells with his brother. Would the old man notice this?

The shuffling steps went along the second balcony, then down the ladder. The door had at last clanked shut. Hines leaped from his bunk. Extra shirts and drawers were made into a dummy. In their cells Hockersmith, Sheldon, Bennett, Taylor, Magee and General Morgan did the same thing.

That afternoon Hines had written a note. Now he took it from Gibbon's *Decline and Fall* to pin it to the dummy in his bed. It read:

> Castle Merion, Cell No. 20.
> Commencement November second, 1863. Number of hours of labor per day; five. Tools, two small knives. *La patience est amère mais son fruit est doux.* By order of my six honorable Confederates.
>
> T. H. Hines,
> Captain, C.S.A.

Hines slid down into the air chamber. He found Taylor, who had lit a candle. Together they knocked on the floor of each cell. The other six stamped through the thin crust and let themselves down into the air chamber. Above them the other captains lay awake, hearts pounding and ears strained for any noise that could be heard above the gusts of wind moaning in a spirit's voice about the corners and caves of the old prison.

One by one they crawled into the tunnel. Hockersmith clawed at the remaining earth with the razor and with his hands. Flat on their stomachs the others waited. A century passed for them before the bricklayer broke through the final foot of earth into the prison yard. Hockersmith first felt the rain on his hand, then on his face as he squirmed out. Panting and dripping with sweat, he paused to catch his breath. Taylor was next. Then the others.

The wind was up, riding the back of a dismal, bone-chilling rain. Somewhere on the buildings a shutter slammed in the wind. They moved cautiously, but the yard was deserted. The guards and their dogs had sought cover.

Contemporary sketch showing Hines, Morgan and the four captains escaping from the Ohio Penitentiary, Columbus, Ohio, in the fall of 1863. The artist, however, was in error. There is no evidence that there were any guards outside the walls or inside the prison yard when the Confederates crawled out of the tunnel they had dug under the very floors of their cells.

There were two walls to scale; one was twenty feet high, and the other five feet higher. After the third cast Taylor managed to hook the bent poker over the top of the first wall. He climbed up, using the loops in the rope, and reached the top. The others followed quickly. Then the second wall was scaled.

With the wind buffeting them they crawled along the wall to the

Governor Oliver Morton of Indiana, who became the virtual dictator of his state during the Civil War.

Colonel Henry B. Carrington, who arrested the Copperhead leaders for their attempted insurrection.

Felix Stidger, the Union counter-spy who infiltrated the top ranks of the Copperhead Sons of Liberty.

Basil Duke, second in command of Morgan's cavalry. He was captured along with Hines on the Ohio raid.

A rare photograph of General John Hunt Morgan, believed to have been made after he escaped with Hines from the Ohio Penitentiary.

The cell block of the Ohio Penitentiary in Columbus where Morgan and his officers were imprisoned. They dug a tunnel from Hines' cell which was 20 (see arrow), eighth from right.

Courtesy, Mrs. John J. Winn

Courtesy, Department of Photography,
Ohio State University

Jacob Thompson, appointed
by Jefferson Davis as chief of
the Mission sent to Canada.

Courtesy, National Archives

Commissioner Clement C.
Clay, an ailing member of the
ill-fated Confederate Mission.

Courtesy, National Archives

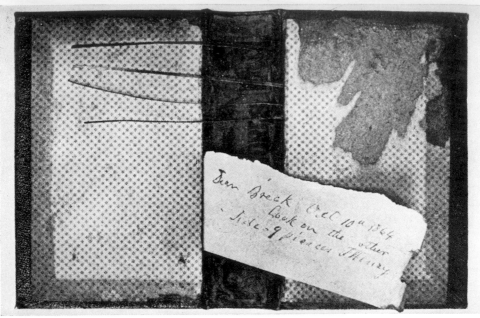

ABOVE: Cover of the New Testament in which Captain Hines hid thirteen saws made from a watch mainspring and sent to Castleman in prison.

BELOW: These particular verses were marked by Captain Hines to draw Castleman's attention to the bills and saws hidden in the Testament.

southeast corner near the railroad tracks where there was a sentry box used by a guard during the day. The rope was then fastened to an iron rod and they slid to the ground.

They were about to run off into the darkness when Morgan discovered he had left his carpetsack behind. What it contained that was so important we do not know, but Hockersmith and Taylor returned to the jailyard to recover it.

As had been prearranged, they split up into pairs, with the exception of Magee, who consented to go off by himself. These were Morgan and Hines, Taylor and Sheldon and Bennett and Hockersmith.

There was a final handshake before the six men split up, some of them never to see each other again.

Hockersmith and Bennett found their way to the railroad depot where they bought tickets on the night express for Cincinnati. They had just seated themselves in the crowded car when Hines strolled in. He gave them a wink and sat down at the far end of the car. Morgan came in a few minutes later, took a seat in the center to stare out the window.

Just as the train started a Federal colonel came in, stared around the car and then took a seat next to Morgan. The Confederate general nodded good evening. The colonel took off his coat, settled himself down and brought out a bottle of peach brandy.

He offered the flask to Morgan. "Will you join me, sir?"

"Certainly, sir," Morgan replied and tossed off a drink.

Just then the train passed the penitentiary. "This is the hotel at which Morgan stops, I believe," the Federal said with a laugh.

"And will stop, I hope," Morgan replied. "He has given us his fair share of trouble and will not now be released." He raised the flask. "I drink to him. May he ever be as closely kept as he is now."

"I'll drink to that," the Federal said and did.

From where they sat, Hines, Hockersmith and Sheldon could hear the conversation. Once Morgan looked over at Hines and, as if he had seen him for the first time, excused himself and walked down the aisle, greeting Hines with a strong handshake, questioning him about his family in Kentucky. Both men spoke animatedly for several minutes like two old friends who hadn't seen each other for years, instead of two prisoners of war who had just escaped together.

Morgan went back to his friend, the Federal colonel, to spend the night in an amiable discussion of the war and past campaigns. The Union man got off before Cincinnati and Morgan settled down for some sleep. Hines and the other two captains relaxed for the first time since they had boarded the train.

At dawn the train reached the outskirts of Cincinnati. All four men walked to the platform at the rear of the car. Hines proposed they swing off before entering the city. But Hockersmith and Sheldon said they had bought tickets to Covington and wanted to go on. With a wave, Hines jumped from the train. Morgan followed him.

Three soldiers sitting on a pile of lumber watched them. "What the hell are you jumping off the train for?" one asked suspiciously.

"What the hell is the use of a man going into town when he lives out here?" Morgan snapped. "And besides, what matter is it to you?"

Under his cold stare the soldier mumbled something and turned away. Morgan was still a general.

In Newport, Kentucky, Hines and Morgan found friends who hid

$1,000!
REWARD.

Head Quarters U. S. Forces,
Columbus, O., Nov. 28, 1863.

GEN. JOHN H. MORGAN
Captains J. C. Bennett, L. B. Taylor, L. D. Hockersmith, Sheldon T. H. Haines, and G. S. Magee,

Escaped from the Ohio Penitentiary on the night of the 27th instant.

A Reward of $1,000!

Will be paid for the apprehension and arrest of John Morgan, and a suitable reward for the apprehension and arrest of the others.

WM. WALLACE,
Colonel 15th O. V. I. Commanding.

This is the poster Federal authorities issued shortly after General John Hunt Morgan, Captain Hines and four other captains escaped from the Ohio Penitentiary in Columbus. Hines noted that his name had been incorrectly spelled "T. H. Haines."

them. Just before they left, they heard that news of their escape had electrified the South. In Boone County fresh horses, clothes, and guides were given to them. It was a happy, relaxed journey for both men through Boone, Harrison, Scott, Anderson and Nelson Counties to the Tennessee line. On the way they played various roles: government contractors, horse buyers, invalided army officers, cattle buyers and federal quartermasters.

After they had reached the Little Tennessee, their troubles began. Morgan was continually recognized and crowds gathered about him when he stopped in small towns. But the section was strongly pro-Union and Hines had to keep urging his general to ignore the adulation and move on.

Escaped prisoners of war from Camps Chase or Morton joined them until Hines and Morgan were leading a band of thirty ragged veterans. They had crossed the Little Tennessee when a company of Federal cavalry chased them. It was a running gunfight, but Hines led the way up a mountain trail and lost the blue patrol. Darkness fell and they stopped to breathe their horses. They agreed there would be no hiding places in the forest; it would be best to run the line of pickets guarding the other side of the mountain.

They led their horses down the mountainside in a misty rain to find the pickets asleep around a campfire. They flanked the camp, finding their way to a farmhouse where they hid in an attic.

Two nights later, Hines left Morgan in the road to inquire at a farmhouse for the correct road to Athens. He returned to see a Federal patrol galloping up. With quick presence of mind, Hines rode straight at them. The startled patrol pulled up short.

"This way, men," he shouted. "Morgan's gone down the road!" The magic name was enough to make the patrol of Home Guards follow Hines. After the first few miles, the Guard leader pulled up to Hines, shouting, "Who are you?"

"He's only a few miles further," Hines shouted back, adding fiercely, "He can't get away." Each time the patrol leader pulled up, Hines would shout something and pull away, leaving the Federals nothing to do except follow him. At last the Home Guard officer pulled his pistol and threatened to shoot Hines. Only then did the Confederate pull up.

"You're a damn Rebel," he shouted.

Hines said quietly, "That's true, sir. I'm your prisoner."

One of the enraged patrol riders threw a noose about Hines' neck, begging his captain to allow him to let the Confederate swing. Hines talked rapidly. He cited the Articles of War, his own treatment of Federal prisoners and everything else that came into his mind. As the minutes passed, tempers cooled. The noose was removed. He was taken back to the Home Guard camp and put in a small log hut for the night.

As Basil Duke says, Hines "made himself agreeable." His marvelous sense of mimicry soon had the sentry at the door chuckling. After supper Hines continued telling his funny stories. At one·point he deliberately lowered his voice.

"What's that?" the guard said.

Hines chuckled and slapped his leg as if the joke's ending were almost too hilarious to repeat. When he wiped his eyes, he mumbled something. As the guard leaned toward him to catch it, Hines leaped up, his knee catching the sentry in the pit of the stomach. In a flash he was out the door. As he ran through the darkness he could see the figures of the horses outlined against the leaping fire. Hines was galloping past the Home Guards as the guard came stumbling from the log hut. Rifles banged but the balls flew wide of their mark.

Before he reached the Confederate lines Hines was caught a second time. Again his glib tongue saved him, as a noose was flung in front of his face. It was another patrol of Home Guards led by another gullible leader. As the Federal officer listened, Hines dug his spurs into his horse. His mount reared and danced. The Federals scattered out of the way. Hines was gone in a flash, Lady Luck riding his coattails.

Morgan and Hines were safe behind their own lines and among friends when the man hunt took a bizarre twist. In Windsor, Canada, a man walked into the leading hotel, signed his name on the register and was assigned a room. The clerk gave a start when he read: "J. H. Morgan."

Who alerted the Federal authorities is not known, but that day the hunt for Morgan and Hines swung north to Windsor. Union detectives swarmed the city. "I credit the rumor Morgan is in Canada," Governor Tod telegraphed Warden Merion.

The Morgan registered at the hotel was an elusive fellow and it took the Federal detectives some time to establish that he was not the Confederate general but a respected citizen of Windsor who had the identical name.

When Hines wrote an abridged version of his escape after the war he passed the incident off as a humorous one. But evidently it was more than that. Letters in the Hines Papers show that the Windsor,

Canada, Morgan was a friend of Hines' who had tried to establish him in business after the war in Canada. Whether he had been a Rebel agent stationed in Windsor, later a headquarters for Hines when he was military commander of the Northwest Conspiracy, is not known. But certainly the incident of the Canadian Morgan signing his name to the hotel register did divert the hunt away from the two fugitives and was hardly as casual as Hines wanted people to believe, even twenty years after Appomattox.

This is the story of the escape from the Ohio Penitentiary according to the versions by Hines and others who took part in it. Obviously there are gaps. It is curious to note that Hines, when he was leading the Northwest Conspiracy the following year, put down a number of secrets on paper in letters to Nancy and to friends, any one of which could have sent him to the gallows. Yet, strangely enough, Hines never went into any details of his escape that involved accomplices. Nancy and his father were told about the air chamber, the tunnel and the close calls in Tennessee, but that was all. Items such as Commissioner Cathcart's arrest, Sergeant Moon, Morgan's watch, the pretty Kentucky girl who saw her sweetheart the day the tunnel was completed, were never mentioned.

Howard Swiggett, in his excellent biography of General John Hunt Morgan, *The Rebel Raider,* believes that no tunnel was dug but that bribery opened the doors for Morgan and his captains. Despite the fact he did not have the Hines Papers at his disposal, he makes an impressive case with circumstantial evidence. He includes the theory of J. Winslow Ayer, a medicine peddler who was used in a minor spying role by the Federals in Chicago, and a statement of the warden of the Ohio penitentiary in 1933. Ayer, in his memoirs, claimed the tunnel was never dug. However, he cites no authority for his statement but his own omniscience. He is true to character, for his own adventures are wildly exaggerated.

The warden of the prison in 1933 wrote to Swiggett that in 1913, while excavating, he found a tunnel made from the block from which he [Morgan] escaped, extending about six feet but ending there, with "virgin earth" from there on. As he wrote, "the tunnel was never made and never used." The warden neglected to explain one thing: how he was ever able to determine what was "virgin earth" forty-nine years after the tunnel had been dug and then filled in the morning after the escape?

The present author agrees with Swiggett that bribery paved the way for the escape but he disagrees that Hines and the other captains never dug their tunnel. Supporting this theory are the original reports of Governor Tod's investigators who appeared at the prison the morning the escape was discovered, and the subsequent investigation made by General Wright, and report submitted to Tod and Union Army headquarters at Cincinnati; also the narratives of Hines, Captain Hockersmith's diary and the account of Doctor Blanton among the Hines Papers and Basil Duke's memoirs. In 1864, in one of his orders sending Hines north to touch off the revolution in the Northwest, Secretary of War Seddon also recognized the authenticity of the escape tunnel by identifying Hines "as Captain Hines, who made possible General Morgan's escape."

First, let us examine the report of F. N. Dessellem, who was sent to the prison by Governor David Tod on the morning the escape was discovered. The later inquiry by the army was concerned with placing responsibility for the escape, but Dessellem confined his investigation to the *physical* layout of the tunnel and the holes in the floors of the six cells.

He wrote:

> To obtain access to the air chamber below cell No. 20, [Hines' cell] an opening was made in the left inside corner of the cell. The space between the cement floor and the top of the arch is about twenty-six inches.
>
> The lower stones of the foundation were loosened and removed by scraping the dirt beneath them, others in the same way until an irregular arched hole was dug through the wall at one point five feet wide. The passage was a right-angle hole, eighteen inches wide and thirty inches high, carried on like this for five feet, widening as it went. The stones and dirt were pushed back into the air chamber. The hole which led to the prison yard was not opened previous to the night of the escape.

Dessellem then went on to describe the holes in the floors of the six cells. His report confirms all that Hines wrote a few months later.

The opening for six of the cells into the air chamber had been formed from below and in the same manner; that is, from the center of the arch the brickwork and mortar above it had been taken down and scraped away without disturbing the cement floor of the cells, a sufficiency of which had been moved to permit the easy passage of a large body. The appearance of the rubble [below in the air chamber] indicates that a noiseless push of the foot broke through the cement flooring at the proper time, thus opening a free passage.

Dessellem described the air chamber, as "dry and absolutely dark. The stones and dirt removed from the passages had been pulled back into the [air] chamber east of the opening, forming an irregular heap about twenty-four feet long, and of average depth about sixteen inches." The work, he said, had been done with a stolen shovel, "common" table knives, three makeshift candlesticks, a small wooden box, numerous candles and two wooden dishes, "all of which had been left behind in the hole."

Dessellem overlooked one important question: where did the escaped prisoners get the shovel, the huge amount of candles, the box and wooden dishes? Obviously, gold had passed hands to buy the candles. We know where the shovel and the box came from; the two wooden dishes were probably smuggled out of the dining room. Hines said in his own account that he had bribed a prisoner who acted as a trusty to get a straight razor to hack at the hard clay. The prisoner undoubtedly also supplied the candles.

The six prisoners, Dessellem said, had let themselves down from the guardhouse at the southeast corner of the wall. The rope, which he examined, was still whipping in the wind when he arrived, Dessellem said. He reported that it was "constructed of bed ticking and old towels braided in loops to make a crude but efficient ladder."

After receiving Dessellem's report, Governor Tod, deluged with telegrams from the Army and from Washington—(Stanton telegraphed, "I hear Morgan escaped. Is that true?")—sent General Wright of the Quartermaster Corps, along with a private secretary, to determine which heads should roll.

The hearings were held in Warden Merion's office. Wright first questioned Colonel Morgan, who readily admitted that he had changed cells and clothing with his brother. He said that when Scotty, the trusty, had thrust his lamp against the bars the night of the escape, he had turned his back to the bars.

Morgan said Scotty had called out, "Are you all right, General?" and he had replied, "Yes, sir."

"At no time did the change [of clothing] enter the mind of the trusty," General Wright reported.

Among Merion's files was the original telegram from Governor Tod, which had arrived the day the prisoners entered the penitentiary. It was a vigorous message, counseling Merion to keep them under the closet surveillance, "not permitting any one to hold an interview with the prisoners in writing or in person unless by express permission of General Burnside."

The diary of Warden Merion was next introduced. The day-by-day items show that he had gradually relaxed the strict rules of the governor. On August 3 there was an item that Captain Hines had been allowed to buy some Waverley novels.

When Wright learned that Sergeant Moon had been brought into the prison as "the prisoner's steward," two days after Hines had started his digging, he began concentrating on Moon, his appointment and his duties. He discovered that Moon was a personal choice of Brigadier-General Mason, military commander of Columbus. Mason's actions prior to the escape are suspicious and questionable, as Wright's investigation shows.

On November 3, 1863, a meeting of the board of directors of the penitentiary had been held. Suddenly Mason appeared with the request that the task of guarding the prisoners be taken over by his department.

The board of directors agreed. When the subject of having a guard sweep out the cells of the Confederates was brought up, someone—he was never identified—said, "Oh, let those goddamned Rebels do their own sweeping."

When Mason was summoned by Wright it developed the Army had transferred him to San Francisco. Mason, it seemed, left hurriedly, "without waiting for a successor." Wright found that Mason had been in charge of the prisoners' funds, with Lieutenant Judkins the disbursing officer.

Wright immediately relieved Judkins of his duties. Wright tracked down Mason in Steubenville, Ohio, where he was on leave before going out to his new command. Mason, in a reply to Wright's letter, admitted that "no instructions were given to Moon with reference to the inspection of the cells." He promptly put the blame on Lieutenant Judkins' head.

Mason ended his report with: "The escape must have a full investigation. There must have been bribery and corruption."

Wright also questioned the propriety of allowing Mrs. Lucy Dorsey, of Carlisle, Kentucky, to be admitted to the prison to see one of the Morgan brothers.

Guards Watson and Scotty testified that the digging must have gone on in the day because of "an absolute stillness at night in the cells. The slightest jar could be heard by us."

Although Wright went through the motions of conducting a vigorous investigation, his summary was a whitewash for the Army. He explained the reason for the escape as "a misunderstanding" between Warden Merion, as the civilian control, and the Army over who should inspect the cells every night and morning.

Wright failed to make any recommendations, and although he had accumulated enough evidence to interest any grand jury, he did not suggest that the case be turned over to the United States District Attorney at Columbus.

I believe what happened was this: Hines began his tunnel two days after Moon had appeared and cell inspection was discontinued. It must have been the signal that all was clear, that gold had been paid. Outside help had come from Cathcart and the Ohio Copperheads who had brought the state to a white-heat of insurrection. Hines knew all the leaders. The following spring he would be working with them to bring about a revolution in the Northwest.

It also must be recalled that "Doctor" Bickley, who started the Knights of the Golden Circle, and was considered dangerous enough by the Union to be confined in the penitentiary, was still active in the Copperhead movement even behind bars. Bickley was known to Captain Hines. It is possible he had something to do with supplying the outside help.

Moreover, if the tunnel *was* the "Big Lie" of the Civil War, it is incredible how many different men of excellent reputation repeated it in minute detail through the years.

After the war jealousy flared up among some of the captains who had taken part in the escape. When Hockersmith was running against Hines for the seat of County Judge of Warren County, Kentucky, he tried to claim credit for originating the plan of escape. Evidently it didn't do him any good. It seems strange that if he were out to discredit Hines as the "hero" of the escape, he didn't simply deny the existence of a tunnel. Such a story, from an eyewitness, would have been sensational and might easily have ruined Hines' chances of election.

There is no doubt that Hines did not tell the whole story. Too many people had to be protected. Sergeant Moon was twenty-six years old at the time of his discharge from Camp Chase in July, 1865. We do not know when he died or what he knew. Also involved were people in the prison who had to be bribed and Copperheads outside. In all his secret dealings Hines never betrayed anyone. Nancy was the only one to whom he sometimes told guarded secrets. When he felt the secrets were too great even for Nancy, he commanded her not to open the letters or dispatches but only to hide them in a safe place, "and guard them as you would your husband's life."

When Hines died, in 1898, two weeks after Nancy, he carried to his grave the real story of what took place during the long days in the Ohio Penitentiary in 1863 and on that windy night in November when they all crawled out of the earth to feel rain on their faces and breathe the air of freedom.

PART III

THE NORTHWEST CONSPIRACY
The Preparation

"The plan for creating a Revolution in the West by the release of prisoners was first presented by me to the authorities at Richmond in the month of February, 1864. The following month I was commissioned for this purpose and furnished with everything deemed necessary for carrying the plan into execution. The military government and command were exclusively and entirely in my hands as my commission as Maj. General 'pro tempore' will fully prove."

August 27th, 1865. Toronto

(Hines' comments on the Northwest Conspiracy, inscribed in the margin of an *Atlantic Monthly* article, July, 1865. See next page.)

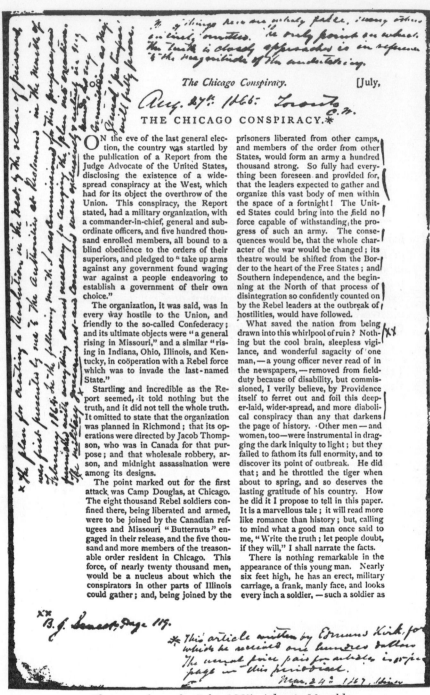

THE CHICAGO CONSPIRACY.*

ON the eve of the last general election, the country was startled by the publication of a Report from the Judge Advocate of the United States, disclosing the existence of a widespread conspiracy at the West, which had for its object the overthrow of the Union. This conspiracy, the Report stated, had a military organization, with a commander-in-chief, general and subordinate officers, and five hundred thousand enrolled members, all bound to a blind obedience to the orders of their superiors, and pledged to "take up arms against any government found waging war against a people endeavoring to establish a government of their own choice."

The organization, it was said, was in every way hostile to the Union, and friendly to the so-called Confederacy; and its ultimate objects were "a general rising in Missouri," and a similar "rising in Indiana, Ohio, Illinois, and Kentucky, in coöperation with a Rebel force which was to invade the last-named State."

Startling and incredible as the Report seemed, it told nothing but the truth, and it did not tell the whole truth. It omitted to state that the organization was planned in Richmond; that its operations were directed by Jacob Thompson, who was in Canada for that purpose; and that wholesale robbery, arson, and midnight assassination were among its designs.

The point marked out for the first attack was Camp Douglas, at Chicago. The eight thousand Rebel soldiers confined there, being liberated and armed, were to be joined by the Canadian refugees and Missouri "Butternuts" engaged in their release, and the five thousand and more members of the treasonable order resident in Chicago. This force, of nearly twenty thousand men, would be a nucleus about which the conspirators in other parts of Illinois could gather; and, being joined by the prisoners liberated from other camps, and members of the order from other States, would form an army a hundred thousand strong. So fully had everything been foreseen and provided for, that the leaders expected to gather and organize this vast body of men within the space of a fortnight! The United States could bring into the field no force capable of withstanding the progress of such an army. The consequences would be, that the whole character of the war would be changed; its theatre would be shifted from the Border to the heart of the Free States; and Southern independence, and the beginning at the North of that process of disintegration so confidently counted on by the Rebel leaders at the outbreak of hostilities, would have followed.

What saved the nation from being drawn into this whirlpool of ruin? Nothing but the cool brain, sleepless vigilance, and wonderful sagacity of one man,—a young officer never read of in the newspapers,—removed from field-duty because of disability, but commissioned, I verily believe, by Providence itself to ferret out and foil this deeper-laid, wider-spread, and more diabolical conspiracy than any that darkens the page of history. Other men—and women, too—were instrumental in dragging the dark iniquity to light; but they failed to fathom its full enormity, and to discover its point of outbreak. He did that; and he throttled the tiger when about to spring, and so deserves the lasting gratitude of his country. How he did it I propose to tell in this paper. It is a marvellous tale; it will read more like romance than history; but, calling to mind what a good man once said to me, "Write the truth; let people doubt, if they will," I shall narrate the facts.

There is nothing remarkable in the appearance of this young man. Nearly six feet high, he has an erect, military carriage, a frank, manly face, and looks every inch a soldier,—such a soldier as

The page from the July, 1865, *Atlantic Monthly*.

VII. THE MISSION IN CANADA

THE year of 1864 turned on a note of gloom for the Confederacy. Everywhere her arms had sustained reverses. Vicksburg had fallen and the guns of the Federal men-of-war controlled the Mississippi from St. Louis to the Gulf. Missouri, Arkansas and Louisiana were completely separated from their sister Confederate states east of the Mississippi. Military cooperation was almost impossible between the Trans-Mississippi Department and other Confederate territory.

The greater part of Mississippi and northern Alabama were either in Federal hands or were vulnerable targets for the slashing raids of the blue patrols. In March Grant took over the command of the Army of the Potomac, more formidable in numbers, matériel and morale than ever before. It was apparent to all that the last great struggle was near at hand. In the South iron and rolling stock were either worthless or wearing out. Ordnance stores were turned out only by a few manufacturers or brought through the blockade from Europe. The supply of food was limited. In some areas the civilian population was on the verge of starvation.

But if it was difficult to replace rolling stock, arms and ammunition, it was still more difficult to fill the gaps in the shattered regiments. Conscription had gained little. The only way to get the needed manpower seemed to be by recovering the veterans in the northern prison camps. The cartel of prison exchange had been broken in July, 1862, by the North. The Union had enough reserve manpower that it could afford to lose men in Libby Prison and other Confederate camps, but that was not the case in the South. Judah Benjamin knew this well.

There were reports of growing unrest in the North over the draft calls, Lincoln's long and vigorous prosecution of the war, and the suspension of the sacred writ of *habeas corpus*.

The Copperhead Societies were not only defiant but growing in strength. A Captain Longuemare of Missouri had outlined for President Jefferson Davis a plan for a general uprising of secret Copperhead societies in the North. State and municipal governments were to be

67

overthrown and their leaders murdered. All Confederate prisoners were to be freed from their camps. Chicago and New York City were to be burned. All this was to be accomplished in conjunction with a powerful thrust north by Morgan's entire command.

In the Maule Papers, Western Reserve Historical Society, is Captain Longuemare's account of his meeting with the President of the Confederacy. Captain Longuemare described Davis as "jumping to his feet with the quick nervous motion peculiar to him." He began pacing up and down.

" 'It is a great plan,' he said. 'In the West you have men, in the East only mannequins. You show me that this conspiracy is engineered and led by good men. I want military men: men that were connected with West Point. Give me some, even if only one or two, and I will have confidence in it.' "

"Davis then left," Longuemare says, promising to "communicate at once with Generals Forrest and Morgan," though neither was a West Pointer.

Those winter days in Richmond when he stared out the window to watch the carts and wagons making their way down the muddy streets, Secretary Benjamin weighed all these factors. The idea of freeing the prisoners while the Copperheads staged a revolution in the Northwest sounded excellent, but there was an important hitch. The Copperheads, for all their grand strategy, had no military leaders.

In February, Hines appeared in Richmond, as he says, to discuss his plan of creating a revolution in the Northwest with the aid of the Copperheads and of the Confederate prisoners to be released from Northern prison camps. Although Captain Longuemare, the Missouri captain, had previously sketched for Jefferson Davis a plan of terrorism against the North, Hines' prior contact and considerable experience with the Copperheads on his own and on the Morgan raids made him the logical man to head the military command of such a project.

Hines claimed for many years that he was commissioned a major-general "pro tempore" to head the Northwest Conspiracy's military activities. The commission is not among his papers today, but an explation for its disappearance may be this: in the late eighties Hines gave all his papers to Castleman to write an article on the Conspiracy for Basil Duke's *Southern Bivouac*. Evidently not all the papers, among them Hines' commission, were returned. Also missing is the *Official Journal* of the Confederate Mission in Canada. Castleman stated in his memoirs that Hines had been commissioned a major-general when he went north. Newspaper obituary accounts and regional histories also make the same claim.

Hines spent a busy winter in Richmond. Nancy wrote regularly, and once he was able to slip through the Federal lines and spend a few hours with her.

Hines never saw Morgan again after the day in the Tennessee hills when Hines had sacrificed himself for his general. The general, after hearing how Hines had been recaptured in Tennessee, sent off a note to Hines' father, praising his favorite captain. He added cheerfully that "He has been recaptured by them, but I am sure he has only been recaptured to escape again. They cannot hold your brave and gallant son."

Hines may have met in Richmond Colonel George St. Leger Grenfel, that fabulous soldier of fortune who was to join him in the Northwest with such tragic results.

In March, 1864, from Richmond, Grenfel wrote to his daughter, Marie Pearce Serocold, in England, that he had planned to return to Europe after he had resigned his commission, but Morgan after his escape, "had again put his claw on me." Grenfel wrote that although his passage for Nassau had been booked and his horses advertised for sale in the Richmond *Examiner,* he had agreed to become Morgan's Adjutant-General, "so look for a fresh raid on Kentucky."

Hines and Morgan were in and out of Richmond in December, January and February, yet their paths never crossed. In January, the Richmond City Council met to plan a reception they intended to give the general. Simultaneously, a group "of distinguished citizens" of Richmond invited Hines to a private dinner, honoring him for his part in the prison escape.

On the 4th of February "subscription books" were opened in Atlanta to remount Morgan's cavalry. Four thousand dollars was subscribed. His star was dimming, but his name could still stir the hearts of his countrymen.

On the 7th, they gave a great ball in Morgan's honor at the Ballard House. Before it ended, J. E. B. Stuart came in to meet Morgan for the first time. A. P. Hill joined them in a glass of peach brandy. Stuart, Morgan and Hill—the chariots were coming for them all.

Early in March, Hines and Nancy prepared to announce their engagement at a small party held at Nancy's house in Brown's Lock. Only their closest friends were invited. Federals still patrolled the town.

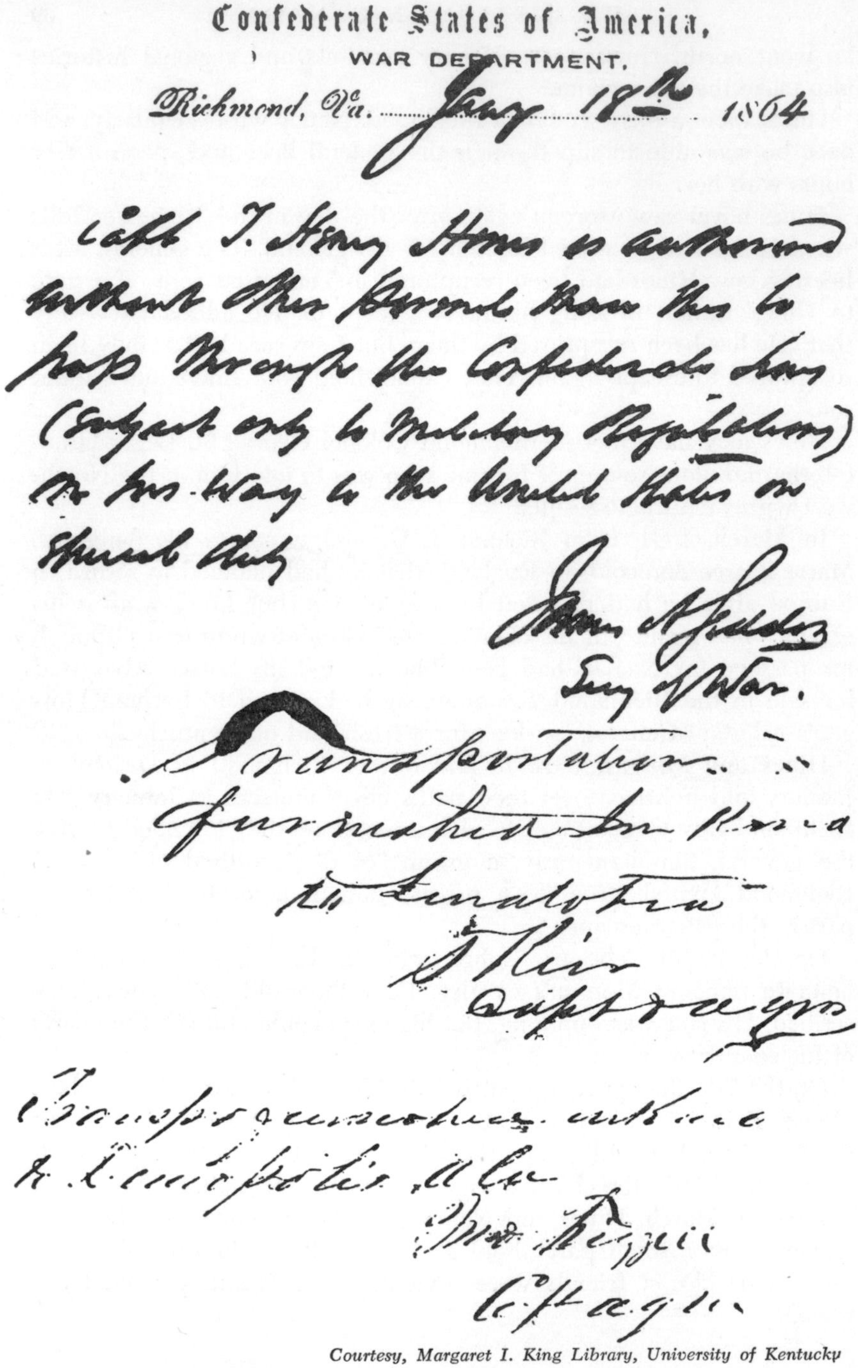
Confederate States of America,
WAR DEPARTMENT,
Richmond, Va. Jany 18th 1864

Capt. T. Henry Hines is authorized without other papers than this to pass through the Confederate lines (subject only to Military Regulations) on his way to the United States on special duty

James A. Seddon
Secy of War.

Transportation furnished [illegible]

Courtesy, Margaret I. King Library, University of Kentucky

Secretary of War Seddon's order detailing Captain Hines to "special duty."

It was a wonderful evening. The announcement would not come as a surprise. As Nancy said, "As all know, Tom had spoken for me, many years ago. . . ." Captain Sproule was about to make his announcement and call on his guests to toast Tom and Nancy when there was a knock on the kitchen door. When Hines went out, a man emerged from the shadows. He was a courier from Richmond with an urgent message for Hines from Secretary of State Benjamin to come at once to Richmond.

The engagement was announced quickly. Nancy kissed Tom goodbye on the back porch, whispering, "Please come back very quickly, my beloved . . . I love you so much. . . ."

He promised he would, then joined the messenger. A few minutes later they were on their way to a "friend's house" where horses were saddled and waiting.

This was Tom Hines' summons to Richmond in the first week of March, 1864. He was on his way, as he said himself, "to play a dangerous game."

In Richmond, Hines saw Davis, Benjamin and Secretary of War Seddon. In his interview with Davis he received certain "verbal orders," the nature of which he never disclosed. His formal orders of March 14, signed by Secretary of War Seddon, read: "You are to travel to Toronto to carry out the orders which we discussed last night, and to collect and organize, for the accomplishment of this mission, all of the Confederate soldiers in Canada, most of whom are escaped prisoners. . . ."

What were these verbal orders, so important and secret they could not be trusted to paper? The destruction of the northern cities by the torch? Instructions for the Copperheads? We do not know.

The week of his departure was a busy one for Hines. On the 16th, after his interview with Seddon, a signal officer in Richmond sent an order through channels ordering one of his command to instruct Hines in the use of their cipher.

"Agree with him on a convenient key word and make sure that key word is placed immediately in the files of the signal office," the order read.

On March 16, Seddon amended Hines' authority. Three Com-

War Department,

SIGNAL BUREAU.

*Richmond, Va. March 16ᵗ*_____ *1864.*

Capt. H. N. Barker

    Signal Officer &c :—

        Please instruct Capt Henry Hines in the use of cypher. Agree with him as to a convenient key word — His obligation with key word forward to this office & place on file.

        By Comd. Major W Norris—

            Alex: W Weddell

                Ch Signals &c

Order sent to a signal officer in Richmond requesting that he instruct Hines in the proper use of the cipher. A key word was to be placed on file.

missioners were to be appointed by Davis to head the Mission in Canada. Although he held the military command, Hines had to clear his plans through them. Seddon's order reads:

Confederate States of America
War Department
Richmond, Va., March 16, 1864

Captain T. Henry Hines:

Sir—You are detailed for special service to proceed to Canada, passing through the United States under such character and in such mode as you may deem most safe, for the purpose of collecting there the men of General Morgan's command who may have escaped, and others of the citizens of the Confederate States willing to return and enter the military service of the Confederacy, and arranging for their return either through the United States or by sea. You will place yourself, on arrival, in communication with Hon. J. P. Holcomb, who has been sent as special commissioner to the British Provinces, and in his instructions directed to facilitate the passage of such men to the Confederacy. In passing through the United States you will confer with the leading persons friendly or attached to the cause of the Confederacy, or who may be advocates of peace, and do all in your power to induce our friends to organize and prepare themselves to render such aid as circumstances may allow; and to encourage and animate those favorable to a peaceful adjustment to the employment of all agencies calculated to effect such consummation on terms consistent always with the independence of the Confederate States. You will likewise have in view the possibility, by such means as you can command, of effecting any fair and appropriate enterprises of war against our enemies, and will be at liberty to employ such of our soldiers as you may collect, in any hostile operation offering, that may be consistent with the strict observance of neutral obligations in the British Provinces.

Reliance is felt in your discretion and sagacity to understand and carry out, as contingencies may dictate, the details of the general design thus communicated. More specific instructions in anticipation of events that may occur under your observation cannot well be given. You will receive a letter to General Polk in which I request his aid in the transmission of cotton, so as to provide funds for the enterprise, and an order has been given to Colonel Bayne, with whom you will confer, to have two hundred bales of cotton purchased in North Mississippi and placed under your direction for this purpose.

Should the agencies you may employ for transmitting that be unsuccessful, the same means will be adopted of giving you larger credit, and you are advised to report to Colonel Bayne, before leaving the lines of the Confederacy, what success has attended your efforts for such transmission.

Respectfully,
(Signed) James A. Seddon,
Secretary of War

Instructions were also forwarded to Lieutenant-General Leonidas Polk, as follows:

Confederate States of America
War Department
Richmond, Va., March 16, 1864

Lt. Genl. L. Polk
Comd'g General—I shall have occasion to send Capt. T. Henry Hines, an enterprizing officer, late of Gen. Morgan's command, who was so efficient in aiding in the escape of that General and others from the Ohio penitentiary, on special service through the lines of the enemy. To provide him with

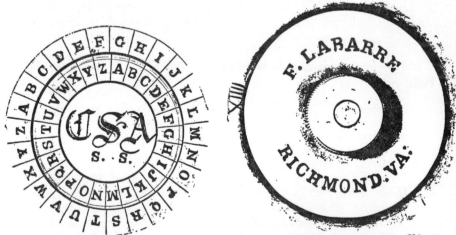

Courtesy, Margaret I. King Library, University of Kentucky

A message in cipher, believed to be in Hines' handwriting, found among his papers. This same dispatch, apparently decoded, appears on the opposite page.

Courtesy, Ralph Newman, Chicago

A Confederate decoding machine used by headquarters in Richmond to break down the secret messages sent by Captain Hines, the Confederate Commissioners in Toronto and other Confederate agents in the North. Only six of these specially made devices are known to be in existence today.

17ᵗʰ march /6⁵ *Translation–;*

Cir, Seventh St–

Send (the) boys (not–) more (than)
two together, to one hundred broad–;
(all (for) Cousin Dan; give (each)
party (a) letter such (as I) had
signed Present Anderson, Let–
first come Twenty– others follow
will get —— (12) Rifles;(4) teen
pistols – Some men;

Thomas.

Addressed to Wallace Pope
Amherstburg

A decoded dispatch, apparently the cipher message shown on page 74, probably referring to the New York raid. "Thomas" is Thomas Henry Hines.

funds for the accomplishment of the purpose designed, it will
be necessary that I shall have transferred to Memphis some
two hundred (200) bales of cotton, which I have ordered an
officer of the Bureau to have purchased at some convenient
point in North Mississippi.

Capt. Hines will himself arrange the agencies by which
the cotton can be transferred and disposed of, so as to place
funds at command in Memphis, and I have to request that
facilities, in the way of transportation and permission to pass
the lines, may, as far as needful, be granted him and the agent
he may select. You will please give appropriate instructions
to effect these ends to the officers in command on the border.

Very respectfully,

(Signed) James A. Seddon,

Secretary of War

On the 18th, Hines was arranging the sale of the cotton assigned
to him by Secretary of War Seddon. In a letter to Colonel T. L.
Bayne, Bureau of Ordnance, Richmond, he asked that a Major Wintersmith of Bayne's department be assigned as his agent in the "purchase,
sale and transportation of the cotton. He is directed to proceed immediately to the execution of this order." The money, Hines said, was to
be placed in his credit in the Montreal Bank, "and in the meanwhile I
shall use my private funds. . . ."

Colonel Bayne, who probably didn't like captains, even celebrated
ones in Morgan's command, sending him orders "by hand," didn't
reply. Hines promptly went to the top. Two days later Secretary of
War Seddon sent off a terse note to the colonel, asking that he "immediately" send Hines "ammunition, pistol and currency" and to appoint
Major Wintersmith as his agent for the sale of the cotton.

Seddon quoted parts of a letter Hines had sent to him after having
been ignored by the Ordnance Bureau. Underlined are the lines,
"Captain Hines wishes to depart on his mission as soon as possible."
The next day Hines received a Navy Colt revolver and an order permitting him to pass through Confederate lines.

Why Seddon placed the burden of a complicated financial transaction on the shoulders of a man who was to be engaged in such
dangerous activities, instead of giving him cash, is not known. The
answer may be that the Bureau of Ordnance informed the War Department that 200 bales of cotton, worth their weight in gold, were at
Memphis, and Seddon simply turned them over to Hines for conver-

C. S. A. War Department
Richmond, Va. March 14, 1864.

Lt. Genl. L. Polk

Com'd'g &c
General   I shall have occasion to
send Capt. T. Henry Hines, an enterprizing
officer late of Genl. Morgan's command who
was so efficient in aiding the escape of that
General and others from the Ohio penitentiary,
on special service through the lines of the
enemy. To provide him with funds for
the accomplishment of the purpose designed,
it will be necessary that I shall have transferred to Memphis some two hundred (200) bales
of cotton, which I have ordered an officer
of the Bureau to have purchased at some
convenient point in North Mississippi.   Capt.
Hines will himself arrange the agencies
by which this cotton can be transferred
and disposed of, so as to place funds at
command in Memphis; and I have to
request that facilities, in the way of transportation and permission to pass the
lines, may, as far as needful, be granted
to him and the agent he may select.
You will please give appropriate instructions
to effect these ends to the officers in command on the border.
                Very Respectfully
                    James A. Seddon
                        Secretary of War

C. S. A. War Department
Richmond, Va. March 15, 1864.

Courtesy, National Archives

Secretary of War Seddon's dispatch to General Polk advising him of Captain
Hines' secret mission to Canada. Funds were to be placed at Hines' command.

sion into cash. In the end it wasn't Hines but one of Bayne's officers who had to see the financial transaction through.

On March 28 Hines was writing his father from Columbia, South Carolina. In the morning, he said, he was going on to Augusta, Georgia, then to Demopolis, Alabama. The letter reveals that soldiers of the Civil War, like soldiers of World War II, never let an opportunity slip by to sell a magazine their memoirs.

Along with his letter Hines enclosed "some papers to file with the doctor (Doctor Blanton was a local historian of Lexington, Ky., whose long, unpublished story of Hines' raids and prison escape are among the Hines Papers). How soon will the doctor produce his book? I have written to *Atlantic* [magazine] for the sale of the escape [from the Ohio penitentiary at Columbus]. . . ." It was a strange war. Thousands could fall in the field, but a Confederate officer could write to a leading magazine in Boston to negotiate the sale of the story of his adventures!

In the first week of April, 1864, Hines reported to General Polk. From there he traveled to Grenada, on the Yalobusha River in Mississippi, to see how Major Wintersmith was getting on with the sale of the two hundred bales of cotton. In Grenada, Mississippi, he recruited two French engineers for his northern command.

On April 18, Aleide Gaschet de L'Isle and his brother wrote to Secretary Seddon from Camp Watts, complaining that the provost marshal of Mobile, Alabama, "not knowing by what authority Captain Hines had issued the enclosed orders for us to join him in a secret mission in Canada, sent us to Camp Watts. Captain Hines said he desired my brother and I because we are engineers and speak French fluently, and that we have a great many friends north and in Canada that might be of great service toward carrying out his plans. . . ."

Seddon sent an immediate reply to the provost marshal explaining that Hines was on "secret missions for this department with authorization to recruit men whom he might find useful."

The two Frenchmen were ordered released but by this time they had joined the Orleans Guard Battery. Hines went north alone.

There is a legend in the Hines family, vouched for by his son, that a banquet was tendered to Hines on the eve of his departure for Canada. Over the champagne he made a wager with another officer that he would pass through Washington and shake hands with Lincoln with bonds he was going to use to finance his Northwestern revolution sticking out of a coat pocket. It is claimed that after the war he met the other officer and collected the wager. Since Hines looked enough like John Wilkes Booth to be his twin, one wonders if he presented himself to the President as the actor.

The story may not be so fantastic as it sounds. Reconstructing his route from the passes and his letters home, Hines seems to have left Mississippi to return to Richmond, where he reported briefly at headquarters. The reason may have been to give an accounting of the sale of cotton, which had netted seventy thousand dollars. He crossed the Potomac River at night and slipped into Washington. There were plenty of Rebel agents in the capital to hide him. After shaking Lincoln's hand, as his son said he did, Hines left for Cincinnati, where he stayed at the home of his friend, Sam Thomas. From Cincinnati he traveled north by train to Detroit, to take the ferry to Windsor, Canada. Hines always ran the Union lines on land. He never took the favorite route of running the blockade from Wilmington, N. C., to Bermuda, then by mailboat to Halifax.

While Hines was moving north, reports from Confederate spies and agents in Illinois, Ohio and Indiana were arriving at the office of President Davis. One memorandum was marked "for the President alone." It told Davis what he already knew from Hines: that secret societies existed in the Northwest; that out of four hundred and ninety thousand members only two had been found disloyal to their oath and that these two had mysteriously disappeared; that plans were being formed to burn Grant's western transport service.

The message ended: "The matter is worthy of the closest cooperation."

How Davis must have smiled as he put the letter down.

Hines arrived in Toronto the week of April 20, 1864. He took quarters in a small boarding-house run by a Mr. Marsh, paying ten dollars a month. He soon discovered the center of Confederate activity was the Queen's Hotel and he established headquarters at once in the bar.

Toronto at the time must have been like Lisbon during World War II. Agents of the Confederacy, and detectives for the Union, walked in and out of the Queen's bar, buying, selling and trading information, much of it worthless, from the free-lance agents who had run the land route via the Detroit ferry to Windsor or the sea blockade from Wilmington to Bermuda, then to Canada.

There was no mistaking the escaped Rebel prisoners. They hung around the lobby and bar of the Queen's, trying to appear respectable in worn gray coats and cracked jackboots or in castoff clothes they had robbed from some clothesline after climbing the board fences of Camps Chase, Morton or Johnson's Island. They were gaunt, hollow-eyed men, with faces lined and tanned the color of old leather by the relentless sun which had scorched the treeless prison yards that rainless summer.

The first morning Hines walked into the bar he was recognized. A captain with whom Hines had served walked up and introduced himself, saying he had escaped from Johnson's Island. After watching the captain wolf down a welcome breakfast, Hines asked him if he could locate some of the other escaped prisoners. The Rebel officer nodded. He said he would get word to the others that Tom Hines had just arrived from Richmond and wanted to see them. Before the week was out, Hines found himself feeding and clothing more than fifty escaped prisoners.

Hines also made trips to Montreal to confer with informers and agents. But that city made him uneasy; strangers, obviously Federal detectives, appeared beside him in the depot, in restaurants and in the lobby of the Montreal Hotel. Toronto seemed much less dangerous and Hines was glad to return to the Queen's bar.

Meanwhile, back in Richmond, Jefferson Davis was searching about for three commissioners to send to Canada. He was finding it difficult.

On the 15th, Davis wrote to Hines, sending his dispatch by courier. The letter, addressed to Senator Hunter of Virginia, reads:

> I have your note of the 11th with enclosure. I have made attempts to engage for the service in Canada several gentlemen deemed competent. The subject is too delicate to permit entering into details until I have the pleasure of seeing you. I confine myself to saying that two persons specially qualified are now on their way here from the South, and I have reason to believe that they will depart for their duty in a few days. One of them is known to you.

Davis referred to Jacob Thompson, of Mississippi, former Secretary of the Interior under Buchanan, whom he appointed as Chief of the Mission. The other two Commissioners were Confederate Congressman and former U.S. Senator Clement Clay of Alabama and James P. Holcomb of Virginia.

On April 27, 1864, Davis wrote Thompson:

> Confiding special in your zeal, discretion and patriotism, I hereby direct you to proceed at once to Canada, and there to carry out the instructions you have received from me verbally, in such manner as shall seem most likely to conduce to the furtherance of the interests of the Confederate States of America which have been intrusted to you. . . .

Thompson and Clay, along with a mysterious, shrewd Irishman named William W. Cleary of Kentucky, a friend of Hines, who had been appointed secretary of the Mission, left Richmond on the 3rd of May for Wilmington. On the 6th they ran the blockade aboard the *Thistle*, a swift Clyde-built steamer. Holcomb was already in Montreal. Early in December, 1863, he had been sent there to look after an admiralty case in which Secretary of the Navy Mallory had been interested.

It was a close call for the Commission. Cleary later recalled how a Federal gunboat had nipped at the *Thistle*'s stern for most of the journey. Cleary told Hines (later included in the *Southern Bivouac* article):

> We left on the morning of the 6th of May, 1864, and slowly steamed down the Cape Fear River to Fort Fisher, reaching the fort about four P.M. We waited until it was quite dark, and then started to run out of the harbor. We could plainly discern out at sea the United States blockading squadron, thirteen ships in number. The *Thistle* was very fast. It was said she could make near fourteen knots an hour. She was a long, narrow side-wheel steamer, lying low in the water, painted gray or nearly white, so that she could scarcely be seen at night. White has been defined to be the absence of color, so that I may say she was colorless. All of the blockade runners were so painted. Her machinery was perfect and in exquisite order. It was a pleasure to visit her engine-room. Everything was clean and tidy, and the brass and steel burnished until they looked like gold and silver. All the parts of the machinery were kept well oiled, so that they worked noiselessly. When we began our run every light was extinguished. We burned anthracite coal and made little or no smoke, and a sort of hood was put over the furnace to prevent any reflection of its fires being seen.

The landlubbers aboard were smartly excited; we were un-used to that sort of thing, and when we crossed the bar, about eight P.M., and were creeping along and twisting our devious and perilous way through the huge blockaders, whose tower-ing hulls we could easily distinguish although they could not see us, we felt queerly. It seemed at times as if a stone could have been pitched from our vessel into one of these danger-ous neighbors. If we were detected we might expect a broad-side. Our Captain said, however, that the real danger would come with daylight—just at daylight—when we could be seen, and, not far away from the harbor, might find our ship close to some war vessel ready to give chase.

Then we would have to run for it. A blockade-runner was not built to fight, but intended to trust to her heels. A man always kept at the mast-head, scanning the horizon with a powerful glass. He paid no attention to sailing vessels, but as soon as he discovered a steamer notified the Captain, who changed his ship's course. These blockade-running steamers often ran away from each other. About seven A.M. on the 7th, the lookout gave notice that he had sighted a steamer. Our course was at once changed. The stranger immediately changed her course; and so on again and again, until it was plain that we were being pursued. We could see the black smoke pouring out from the chimneys of the pursuer, and our Captain said she was gaining on us—in a few hours she would be near enough to fire into us. This was pleasant intelligence to gentlemen going out on diplomatic business. I thought I might as well have remained and have been shot in the reg-ular way on land. The Captain thought this pertinacious steamer was the United States war steamer *Connecticut,* re-puted to be very fast. We made all arrangements to burn our mail and papers, and to distribute the money. Each passenger began to prepare his little story, that he might be able to properly entertain his captors.

All these dispositions finished, we thought it best to pledge our resolutions and fortify ourselves for the coming encounter with some excellent "Dutch courage" furnished from the Cap-tain's stores. We all agreed afterward that we were very cool and calm—that is, each man said he was—and that we would have tried with patriotic integrity to escape a fate not pro-vided for in our instructions. Fortunately, we never learned how we could have stood the racket. The chase lasted five hours. We were taking in more courage during all that time.

The Yankee seemed to gain on us rapidly. All at once our Captain got excited for the first time, and announced that we were running away from the enemy. He supposed that some part of her machinery had failed. At any rate, we got away, and in a short time were out of sight of that ominous black smoke.

Without further adventure, we ran safely into the Bermuda Islands and the port of St. George. The British flag flying on the fort in the harbor saluted the Confederate flag displayed from the *Thistle*.

At the Bermudas Messrs. Thompson, Clay and Cleary met Mr. Wellsman, of South Carolina, the Charleston partner of the firm of Frazer, Trenholm & Co. and Colonel Blanton Duncan, who were also en route for Canada. The whole party sailed from St. George on the 10th, on the British mail steamer *Alpha*. The commissioners arrived at Halifax, Nova Scotia, on the 19th. On May 21st, Messrs. Thompson and Cleary set out for Canada, crossing the Bay of Fundy to St. John's, New Brunswick, thence proceeding up the St. John's River to Tobeque, then overland to Rivier du Loup, there taking rail to Montreal, where they arrived May 29th.

Hines received a coded message by courier on May 10, telling of the commissioners' departure. But there was other news which stirred him more.

On May 9, Morgan and his troopers had defeated the Union columns marching on Saltville, in Western Virginia. The bluecoats were piled back up the Kanawha valley. The threat to the South had been a serious one; the Federals had been out to cut communications with Lee's army and destroy the salt works. That night in the bar at the Queen's in Toronto men in ragged gray lifted their glasses to toast the gallant Morgan and roar out the words of "The Raiders Ride Tonight."

VIII. THE FOX AND THE COPPERHEADS

I<small>T WAS</small> ten o'clock on the morning of May 29, 1864, that the Confederate Commissioners Clay and Thompson arrived in Montreal. Holcomb and Hines were on hand to greet them.

Instead of two competent leaders of men, wise in the ways of secret service, Hines saw a peevish invalid and a man with a brown spade beard whose main concern seemed to be his feverish, sore eyes at which he constantly dabbed with a handkerchief. Holcomb made the introductions. The invalid was Clement C. Clay; the man with the sore eyes was Jacob Thompson, Chief of the Mission.

"Have you made hotel reservations, Captain?" Clay asked in an irritable voice which Hines was to detest so much.

"Yes, sir," Hines said.

"We can't stand here, Captain," Thompson said. "There are too many Federal detectives. It is best we move on to Toronto."

This made sense to Hines, who remembered his uneasy visit to Montreal. He was about to agree with Thompson when Clay shook his head.

"I'm not going to do any more traveling, Jacob," he said to Thompson. "I'm tired. I want a hotel suite right here in Montreal."

Thompson shook his head doggedly. "We must move to Ontario."

Clay banged the street with his cane. "And I say I'm going to stay here!"

As Hines listened in horrified silence, the two Confederate Commissioners began bickering. Holcomb, his face troubled, tried to soothe them but without success.

Finally, his voice rasping like a saw cutting through ice, Thompson told Clay he could stay only overnight in Montreal and would leave the next day for Toronto. Clay seemed almost glad that he was to be alone. But before Thompson left, he demanded that the Mission Chief deposit ninety-five thousand dollars in the Bank of Montreal in a personal account in his name! Hines, speechless, stared at Thompson when he agreed to do so.

Clay's account was opened that afternoon in the Montreal bank by Thompson. Hines and Holcomb stayed one night at a Montreal hotel—where Clay had hired a suite—then set out the following morning for Toronto. Upon their arrival there, Hines found lodgings in a side-street boarding-house for himself and the Commissioners, while Holcomb and Thompson opened an account at the Bank of Ontario. (There is no record of the total amount that Thompson deposited, but from the receipts in the Hines Papers for guns, ammunition and chemicals for Greek fire, and Thompson's own reports, it must have been a fortune.)

Thompson made it clear he was head of the Mission, with superior authority over the other two members. Hines was military commander, but subject to final approval by Thompson. Because of the difficulty of communication with Richmond, the Mission Chief "was compelled to regulate his action very largely by circumstances," Hines said. This was disastrous power to be given to a man of Thompson's obstinacy and uncompromising opinions, lack of imagination and awe of persons who claimed "high connections" with those in high places in Richmond.

But for all his failings, Thompson, agreed Hines and Castleman, was the most competent of the three. In 1866 when he wrote of his work in Canada, Hines said Clay possessed an incredible naiveté. He was "willing to believe anybody and anything." He loved good food and wines. To the dismay of Hines he was always "confiding to parties whom he had known previously and under conditions altogether different from those he was required to meet."

Clay could never believe that the man who had been his genial dinner guest in Richmond or Washington before the war could possibly be an agent in the pay of the Union. His health also was a terrific drawback. He was a frail, sickly man, racked by a hacking cough which made him feverish, impatient and impulsive. He hated the biting cold of the Canadian winter and longed for his beloved Alabama.

As Hines said, "Commissioner Clay's health at the time of his appointment was of itself enough to disqualify him for the important service with which he had been charged."

Holcomb, junior member of the Commission, was a scholar and a polished gentleman, suited more for a diplomatic role than as a leader of what today might be called super-O.S.S. men. When he met with Hines and the Commission, he invariably wore a black suit and tie which made his thin, ascetic face seem deadly pale. Wherever he went he carried a slender, red leather-bound book of poems. He made an incongruous picture as he stood by the window, the slim volume in his hand, his lips moving as he followed the flowing phrases of the masters, while off to one side of the room Hines or Castleman outlined their bold plans to Thompson.

On their arrival in Toronto, Thompson impressed upon Hines and Holcomb Jefferson Davis's last-minute instructions. Above all they were to respect the neutrality of Canada. Secondly, they were to try all diplomatic means to gain a peace "and failing in that, to adopt measures to cripple and embarrass the military policy of the Federal Government by the destruction of military and naval stores, preventing the preparation and dispatch of expeditions against the Confederacy, retarding or hindering the forwarding of supplies, but to carefully avoid all transgressions of the laws of war as observed by open belligerents, and to neither command nor to permit the destruction of private property."

As Hines recalls, Thompson repeatedly warned his raiders they were restricted to that order in their guerrilla warfare. Of course, that was not possible. And if it were, the obstinate, unimaginative Thompson was not the man to make a band of hard-riding raiders who knew what the torches of Sherman's men were doing to their own homes, obey such a restriction.

In another letter, sent the week of May 29 to Thompson, Secretary of War Seddon gave Thompson *absolute* authority over Hines and his raiders. The decoded dispatch reads in part:

> He [Hines] is to report and confer with the Hon. Jacob Thompson, Special Commissioner of the Confederate States Government in Canada, and be guided by his counsel in his proceedings and actions in his present service. He may consider his instructions from this department [of War] subject to modification and change or revocation by the said Commissioner, and will take further instructions from him.

About this time appeared one of the strangest and most mysterious men in the history of the Civil War. His name is George N. Sanders, an *ex-officio* member of the Confederate Mission. An evil figure, he flits in and out of Hines' letters and reports. From a crumbling clipping of the New York *Herald* he was still meddling in state affairs in 1875 and had the ear of men in high place in Washington. He was a tall, debonair, smiling man who did much to ruin the work of the Mission. One wonders if he was perhaps a secret Union agent.

Fifty-five years after meeting him, Captain Castleman was still wondering about Sanders. "I never knew of another man like him," he wrote in wonderment. Hines spotted him immediately as a dangerous meddler. They evidently hated each other at sight.

Sanders was never without money or beautiful women. He was a friend of presidents and kings. When President-to-be Buchanan arrived at the Court of St. James's as American ambassador, it was Sanders who welcomed him with one of the most lavish parties that London had seen in many years. "Fantastic," the London *Times* called it.

Hines evidently was fascinated as well as repelled by his evil genius. Down through the years he jotted reminiscences of Sanders and saved anything written about him in the newspapers. Among his papers there is one clipping from the London *Times* that gives this picture of him:

> He [Sanders] sees everybody, talks to everybody, high and low. He has little reverence for great men. He would criticize George Washington to his face if he were alive. He is one of the most adept wire-pullers in the United States. . . .

Once, when a Congressional committee was investigating him, its investigators discovered that Sanders had called the first meeting held in the United States for the annexation of Texas, in a tiny tailor shop in Ghent, Kentucky. In the earlier fifties he was appointed American consul in London, although the Senate refused to confirm his appointment. It was only after the intercession of Seward, his bitter political foe, that he was approved!

Soon after his arrival in Montreal, Sanders had cultivated Clay. He gave large and lavish dinners at which Clay was the guest of honor, but, more importantly, he was a good listener while the ailing old man, lonely and homesick, aired his grievances against Thompson and Holcomb and that damn young firebrand, Tom Hines.

Sanders soon attained his objective. Clay at first turned to him for his opinion, then sought his approval. There is no reason to doubt Hines' opinion, taking into account his violent dislike of Sanders, that the wire-puller's hold on Clay did much to defeat their great plans.

From March to early June, 1864, Hines spent most of his time rounding up escaped prisoners of war, feeding and clothing them. He carefully investigated each man. Those officers he knew and trusted he asked to stay with him "on special service" in Canada. To others he gave sums of from fifty to a hundred dollars for their journey home.

To protect each man in case of arrest by Federal detectives, he had "certificates of citizenship" printed, on which the returning prisoner swore that he was a resident of a southern state and a member of the Confederate Army or Navy. Each form was notarized by a Toronto justice of the peace.

The money receipts and IOU's among the Hines Papers raise the question of exactly how much the Confederates did spend in Canada on the Northwest Conspiracy and the Copperhead uprisings. Although there are no exact totals, the factual and the possible figures are almost incredible.

Although it will never be known exactly how much the Confederates spent "to bring a siege of terror from Maine to Minnesota," as the *New York Times* described the Northwest Conspiracy, it appears that a million dollars might not be a fanciful figure.

In the winter of 1864, when he returned to Toronto, Hines was horrified to learn how easy it was to get gold out of Thompson. Every "scoundrel" who dreamed up a wild tale of how he was preparing to spread havoc among the Federals by burning army transports or military installations, would come to Thompson and demand anywhere from ten thousand dollars to fifty thousand dollars, "to equip my organization," as one said. Thompson usually turned over the money. Thompson himself tells how one man who had come from Richmond supposedly on the orders of Secretary Benjamin demanded ten thousand dollars for arms but couldn't produce his official orders. He promised to return to Richmond to get another copy—if Thompson gave him three thousand dollars. Thompson did. The supposed raider, of course, never appeared again.

For a more detailed analysis, see "A Financial Accounting of the Northwest Conspiracy," page 293.

While Hines rounded up the escaped prisoners of war to form his tiny "squadron," as he would call it in later years, Thompson set out for Niagara Falls to contact "potent men of the North" to learn how they felt about peace. Leading Copperheads like Fernando Wood, ex-mayor of New York City, and ex-governor Washington Hunt of New York, met with him at the Clifton House. New York and the East were

not ready for peace or an uprising, they told Thompson. War manufacturers there were too powerful and were on the alert to "neutralize"
any peace efforts.

Thompson next turned to Secretary Benjamin's favorite project: trying to create a financial panic in the North by buying up gold and
smuggling it out of the country in order to weaken the gold security
for the Union dollar. A Nashville banker named Porterfield, who was
living in exile in Montreal, was selected by Thompson as the proper
man to set this in motion.

Porterfield was furnished with fifty thousand dollars. He went to
New York, opened an office under a fictitious name and began to purchase gold, which he exported to England and sold for sterling bills
of exchange. Then he converted the sterling bills into dollars which
he used to buy more gold. The transaction was a costly one, showing
a loss due to the cost of operations, trans-shipment, etc. Porterfield
continued until his losses were twenty thousand dollars. By this time
he had exported five million dollars in gold, "and had induced others
to ship much more [gold]." His buying up gold and sending it out
of the country began "showing a marked effect," as Thompson said
in his official report to Richmond, when the Federals cracked down.

A former partner of Porterfield's was arrested by General Ben Butler
for exporting gold, and thrown in Lafayette Prison in New York Harbor. Porterfield fled back to Canada. However, he still retained the
twenty-five thousand dollars remaining to continue the exporting of
gold through "fronts" in New York.

By the first week in June, 1864, Hines was in touch with his Copperhead friends in Ohio, Indiana and Illinois and in communication with
Vallandigham, who was now living in Windsor. A meeting was set
for the 14th to plan the Copperhead uprising and the release of the
Rebel prisoners in Camps Douglas, Morton, Chase and Rock Island.

Hines and Thompson met with Vallandigham on the afternoon of
the 14th in a dim front parlor of a boarding-house in St. Catharine's,
Canada. Vallandigham, now a man without a country, detailed for
Hines the strength of the Copperheads. Membership totaled about
300,000. Illinois had furnished 80,000, Indiana, 50,000, Ohio, 40,000
and Kentucky and New York State, the rest. A "feeling of fatigue" was
sweeping through the North, Vallandigham told them, following Lincoln's draft call for 500,000 more men.

It was at this meeting, according to Hines, that he first learned that
not all the Copperheads favored the Northwest Conspiracy and a

separate Confederacy of the United States. Some of them wanted peace "based on the desires of the Lincoln administration."

Hines quotes Thompson as replying to Vallandigham: "We will be more free with our arms and money if they are used to promote and protect a Northwest Conspiracy."

Vallandigham at this first meeting refused to give clear-cut approval to the Conspiracy project. He cautiously referred Thompson and Hines to his Richmond speech in which he had expressed friendship for the South but said he could not be identified with their cause. The following day Vallandigham sneaked into Ohio, boldly inviting the authorities to arrest him. Burnside was wiser this time. To Vallandigham's disappointment, he and his soldiers ignored him. In his first speech after his return, at Hamilton, Canada, Vallandigham evidently had changed his mind about the Conspiracy, when he declared the existence and purpose of the secret societies.

"But I warn also the men in power," he thundered, "that there is a vast multitude, a host whom they cannot number, bound together by the strongest and holiest ties, to defend by whatever means the exigencies of the times shall demand, their natural and constitutional rights as free men, at all hazards and to the last extremity."

This was more to the liking of the Confederate raiders, waiting impatiently for direct word from the Copperheads. It finally came. Another meeting was held at St. Catharine's. This time the national leaders of the Copperheads were present. There were Charles Walsh, political boss of Chicago's Cook County; Amos Green, commanding Copperheads in Illinois; James J. Barrett, Adjutant-General and Grand Lecturer of the Sons of Liberty; H. H. Dodd, whom Tom Hines knew from Indiana; T. C. Massie of Ohio, and Hines' old friend, the powerful Justice J. Bullitt of Kentucky.

Vallandigham introduced them as his "efficient and determined leaders." He added: "If provocation and opportunity arise, gentlemen, there will be a general uprising."

Thompson offered Vallandigham twenty-five thousand dollars to arm his followers, but Vallandigham, with a great show of righteousness, held up his hand and refused. The high priest could not soil *his* hands with filthy gold. However, he turned to Barrett, "thoroughly endorsed his reliability and energy" and told Hines to turn over the money to him.

Thompson proved to be an enthusiastic supporter of Vallandigham and his Copperheads. He predicted a general uprising and bloodshed

Copy, from   To Hon James A Seddon
Cisher.   Secretary of War,
                              Richmond. Va

I have the honor to inform you that, in
compliance with instructions received from
the   of April 27th I have
placed myself in communication with Hon
J. Thompson and am requested by him to submit
to you. The proposed plan for a revolutionary
movement in the West and to request, if
compatable with the good of the public service
that a force may be sent

or to any other point you may deem necessary
in order to create a diversion in favor of the
movement. The Confederates in Canada together
with two regiments in process of formation at
Chicago will be placed under my command
to move upon that place for the release of the
prisoners confined at Camp Douglass.
Simultaneous with this movement the Democrats
in every county of Ill. and portions of Ind
and Ohio will rally to arms. A force of
Three Thousand democrats under a competent
leader will march upon Rock Island for the
release of the Seven Thousand prisoners at this
point. Five Thousand will move up of Indian
apolis where there are Six Thousand prisoners.

The remainder will concentrate upon
Chicago and Springfield. The State governments of
Ind. Ohio and Ill. will be seized and their
executive heads disposed of. By this means we
hope to have; in ten days after the movement
has begun, a force of fifty thousand men.
We hope to make a certainty of releasing the
prisoners at

Hines' first report from Toronto to Secretary of War Seddon, outlining
his plan to liberate Confederate prisoners in Camps Douglas and Rock Island.

unprecedented in the history of the United States. In later years Hines tried to appear as if he had been skeptical of the promises made by the Copperheads, but his own letters and reports written in 1864 show this was not true. For all his combat experience Hines was only twenty-three and engaged in a daring enterprise which stirred his young heart. There is no doubt that he, like Thompson, believed all that Vallandigham and his cohorts promised.

"I doubted whether men bound together by political affiliations and oaths behind which there was no real authority could be handled like an army," Hines was to write when he was Chief Justice T. H. Hines of Kentucky and thirty years removed from the handsome young cavalier of Morgan's raiders. But in the days of the sinister meetings in the front parlor of the boarding-house in St. Catharine's, he was writing Richmond that the revolution in the North was about to burst into flame.

Hines made his first report to Secretary of War Seddon in June, 1864, from Toronto. The dispatch was written in cipher and decoded by a departmental clerk.

Hines reported that he had met Thompson and had been requested by him to "submit to you [Seddon] the proposed plan for a revolutionary movement in the West."

> Two regiments now in the process of formation in Chicago will be placed under my command to move upon Camp Douglas and free the prisoners.
>
> Simultaneously with this movement, the Democrats in every county of Illinois, and portions of Indiana and Ohio will rally to arms. A force of 3,000 Democrats under a competent leader will march upon Rock Island for the release of the 7,000 prisoners at that place.
>
> The remainder will concentrate upon Chicago and Springfield. State Governments of Indiana, Ohio and Illinois will be seized and their executives disposed of. By this means we hope to have, within ten days after the movement has begun, a force of 50,000 men. We hope to make a certainty of releasing the prisoners.

Thompson and Hines met Vallandigham again a few weeks later. It was after this conference that Thompson sent a secret dispatch to Secretary of State Judah Benjamin, detailing the progress he had made and suggesting that a raid be made by Confederate cavalry into Kentucky or Missouri to coincide with the uprising. It is a bloodthirsty note and reads in part:

> Although intending this as a Western Confederacy and demanding peace, if peace be not granted, then it shall be war. There are some choice spirits in this enterprise [the uprising] and all that is needed for our success is unflinching nerve.
>
> For our part it is agreed that Captain Thomas H. Hines shall command at Chicago and Captain John B. Castleman at Rock Island. If a movement could be made by our troops in Kentucky and Missouri, it could greatly facilitate matters in the West. The organized forces of the Federal government would thus be employed elsewhere, and this would give courage and hope to the Northwestern people. The rank and file are weary of the war, but the violent abolitionists, preachers, contractors and political press are clamorous for its continuance. If Lee can hold his own in front of Richmond and Johnson's defeat [sic] in Georgia prior to the election, it seems probable that Lincoln will be defeated.
>
> Nothing less, however, can accomplish this end. It is not improbable that McClellan will be nominated by the war Democrats. His recent war speeches have broken him down with the war party but in my opinion no peace candidate will be offered, [sic] unless disaster attend the Federal armies in Virginia and Georgia.
>
> In short, nothing but violence can terminate the war. . . .

Perhaps this dispatch best illuminates the narrow-mindedness, the provincialism, found in many of the leaders of the Confederacy. They could never understand that Lincoln's high ideals of Union forever really inspired a large section of the North. It was this blind prejudice which made them believe that they could overthrow the Republic. Relying on the ignorance and credulity of men, in the end they deceived only themselves.

In this dispatch Thompson shows, as Hines suspected, that he was not the man to whom to entrust absolute authority over a secret espionage mission. Thompson had committed the unpardonable error of belittling his enemy.

With the Copperheads stirring, arms had to be bought and smuggled into the Northwest at once. Cleary, the handsome young Irish secretary of the Commission, was selected to visit New York and buy rifles, revolvers, and ammunition. Fernando Wood and the other Copperhead leaders, Hines later recalled, helped him to assemble these.

The meeting place for the New York City "subversives" was a tiny violin shop off Washington Square. There Cleary bought thirty thousand dollars' worth of rifles, pistols, chemicals for making Greek fire and powder and ball. The arms were smuggled aboard a ship at Canal Street and taken to Canada, where the Confederates smuggled them in wagons across the border into Ohio and Indiana. They were later found buried in graveyards, in haystacks and in barnyards. The boxes were stenciled "Prayer Books" or "School Books."

In the early summer of 1864, Clay, who hated and feared the "firebrand boys" and their violent methods, held one of his rare conferences with Thompson and Hines. He reminded them of President Davis's instructions to try to persuade the North to accept peace. He urged Thompson to begin a campaign for peace in the North. Thompson agreed. What they needed was to buy newspapers to trumpet peace, peace, peace. New York City had the largest newspapers and was the logical place to start shopping. Cleary, finishing his arms-buying spree, was ordered by Thompson to find a newspaper that could serve as the house organ for Confederate aims.

The New York *Daily News* was the logical selection. The paper was owned by Fernando Wood, ex-mayor of New York, and his brother, Benjamin, both prominent Copperheads. By "Faithful Schultz," the Hines courier, twenty-five thousand dollars was sent by Thompson to Cleary in New York, to turn over to Phineas Wright, the editor of the *News*. Wright was an expert propagandist and one of the more sinister figures in the Conspiracy. In the summer of 1863, he had moved his law practice from New Orleans to St. Louis. There he became associated with the Corps de Belgique, a society similar to the Knights of the Golden Circle. Its membership among the pro-Confederate Missourians was considerable.

Wright changed the name of the society to the Order of the American Knights. It spread rapidly and absorbed many of the former Knights of the Golden Circle. In February, 1864, the Order of the American Knights was again changed to the Sons of Liberty at a "con-

New York Daily News
Office 19. City Hall Square
New York January 18. 1864

Dear Sir
I have this day connected myself with the Editorial department of the "New-York News." You will remember that the News has, from the first advocated the principles inculcated by Jefferson & his illustrious compeers, and has fearlessly & openly denounced the usurpations of power which have wrested from the citizen his cherished rights, and thrown down the last barrier between him & irresponsible despotism.
The News will be our especial Organ & will be a medium for the interchange of sentiments & opinions of the friends of peace touching the momentous concerns involved in the existing crisis.
I entreat your kind offices & influence in extending the circulation of the News. Throughout the entire field of our labour.

Yours Sincerely,
P. C. Wright

Courtesy, National Archives

Letter written by Phineas Wright, a leader of the Sons of Liberty, offering the services of his newspaper, the New York *Daily News*, as the official organ of the Copperheads. Jacob Thompson sent him $25,000 to trumpet peace.

vention" in New York City. Vallandigham was elected Grand Commander and Wright, secretary.

After the money had been paid to Wright, the editorial pages of the *News* boomed peace, peace, peace.

IX. COUNTERSPY

Too often we fail to realize that history's narrow escapes, daring deeds and great spy dramas were accomplished by men and women of flesh and blood who possessed the fears, hopes, sorrows and dreams we all know; that they hugged the shadows, hearts thundering in their ears, as a patrol passed or hastened to the fatal rendezvous, plagued by doubts as to whether the game was worth the candle. . . .

Such was the case of Felix Stidger, the mild-looking clerk, whose investigation and testimony helped to shatter the Copperheads in the Northwest.

Hines paid him this tribute: "He [Stidger] ruined us all." Stidger left behind him unimpeachable evidence of his counter-espionage for the Union: a package of letters, less than fifty, which he sent to his commander, Colonel Henry B. Carrington, military commander of Indianapolis and bitter foe of the Copperheads.

To read these pages is a thrilling experience. They contain all the conventional props for an Ambler spy drama: a handsome espionage agent, a counter-agent, a beautiful lady agent, secret meetings in candle-lighted back-rooms, midnight raids and a surprise ending.

Stidger's letters were often written hastily, some on bare scraps of paper, on trains, wagons, at brief stops. Although fragile, they are still very legible. Certainly a sense of danger comes through as one reads a scrawl by Stidger after he had attended a secret conference to decide the best means of murdering a man. "They speak of murder . . . I can't trust anyone any more . . . assassination awaits me on the least suspicion. . . ."

Stidger, thirty-one in 1864, was born in Taylorsville, Spencer County, Kentucky. Later his family moved to Mattoon, south Illinois, where he became the owner of a dry goods store. A fervent Union man, he had enlisted immediately after Sumter's surrender, serving first in the Adjutant General's Office, later in the provost marshal's office

97

in Tennessee. It was the latter office which brought Stidger's work to Colonel Carrington's attention.

In April, 1863, Carrington made his first report to the military commander of Ohio on the danger of the Copperhead movement. He demanded a wholesale investigation. Headquarters was not impressed. They took the attitude, as did Washington, that the Copperheads were a petty nuisance and nothing more. However, probably to keep up young Carrington's morale, they gave him the green light. Next he went to Governor Morton, who had a more realistic view of the secret groups infesting the state, and received his pledge of aid. There wasn't much money. Morton's state legislature, dominated by the Copperheads, had cut off his war appropriations. Washington ignored his financial requests.

Finally, Carrington was able to gather a staff of six men. All were amateurs, with no help from the vaunted secret service man-hunters of General Baker, special agent of the War Department.

Carrington now turned to an old friend, Captain Jones, provost marshal of Tennessee. Did he have anyone on his staff who could help break up this "deadly society"? Jones mentioned Stidger, who had been doing good work. Carrington recalled the handsome young man with the mild brown eyes who had been so efficient back in the early days of the war in his Washington office.

Carrington asked Stidger to come up to Indianapolis. There he sold him the idea of worming his way into the society. Stidger accepted the assignment and was indoctrinated into the rituals of the Sons of Liberty.

Go to French Lick, Carrington told the clerk, and see Doctor Bowles. Pose as a Peace Democrat and say you want to help their cause. Can such an approach be called crude today, when we recall the testimony of our counter-agents in the Communist underground?

In May, Stidger was in Indiana, casually working his way along the quiet countryside. At Salem, he met a man in a saloon who talked boldly against "King Lincoln" and his war administration. Stidger began to denounce the President, Grant and the army. Whiskey, and agreement that peace at any cost was the only solution, cemented their friendship. Stidger stayed at the home of his new-found friend. The next day he was asked if he wanted a job with the Order of the American Knights. Was ever a man's luck so good? Stidger said he did. By noon he was on his way to French Lick Springs to see Doctor Bowles. He found the doctor, a black-browed, shifty-eyed scoundrel.

"He cannot look anyone in the face for one moment," Stidger wrote Carrington.

Bowles, for all his bombast, was no fool and questioned Stidger closely about Kentucky. Stidger had learned his subject well. He answered all of Bowles' questions to his satisfaction. The old doctor glowed when Stidger solemnly repeated the first-degree vestibule oath which he said he had taken a week before he had left Kentucky.

Stidger then volunteered the information that he thought Justice Bullitt needed help. There he hit the nail on the head. Bowles slammed his hand down on his desk. Kentucky and his friend Judge Bullitt were Bowles' favorite subjects. He told Stidger he was correct in his assumption that Kentucky "needed more organization" and asked him if he would go down there. Stidger, scarcely believing his luck, said he would.

The next few weeks were busy ones for Stidger. He was introduced to all the Indiana Copperhead leaders by Bowles. In Louisville he took the second-degree oath. Now he was ready to be admitted into the secret councils. For several nights in the back-rooms of farmhouses he listened to the amazing plans of revolution described for him. He read reports from commanders of other states, heard verbal reports from smaller communities of men drilling in schoolhouses, in city parks and of the plan to set up a new Confederacy with Jeff Davis down in Richmond.

On a quiet Sunday morning Stidger attended a secret meeting at which a chemist, hired by the Copperheads, demonstrated the newest type of Greek fire bombs which could be used to destroy transports, military installations and create havoc in crowded Northern cities.

Stidger soon realized that he was now in the inner councils of a band of dangerous men. He began sending his reports to Carrington. From the spidery, minute writing one wonders if his heart was in his throat as each line inked its way across the precious paper.

The first report of May 11 is a long one. It tells of his chance meeting with the Copperhead and the subsequent introduction to Bowles, then of the later meetings with the leaders and the details of their proposed revolution. Ohio, Indiana and Illinois were to fall, guns to be supplied by Captain Hines and Commissioners Clay and Thompson. State heads were to be murdered. Rebel prisoners already had been alerted to begin preparations for mass assaults on their camps. In a few weeks the whole Northwest would be aflame with revolt. He signed his own name and a box number.

Carrington himself knew something of the strength of the movement from his investigations in 1862. But at that time the Copperheads were marching under the banner of the loosely-organized Knights of the Golden Circle. Now they were guided by trained combat veterans financed by seemingly bottomless treasuries. There was discontent in the air. The whole land was grumbling. Carrington, in a direct dispatch to Secretary of War Stanton, told him of the plot.

Stanton mulled over the report, asked Carrington for more details, then, convinced this was no fabrication by a madman, sent Carrington five thousand dollars from a secret fund.

Carrington was jubilant. He sent guarded instructions to Stidger, told him to use the name "Eustis" and to get all the evidence he could. Stidger went to Indianapolis to hear a report read by Dodd of Indiana, who had just returned from a meeting of all Grand Commanders in New York City. Vallandigham had presided. The other state leaders had elected him Supreme Commander. "It was decided to order the uprising at an early date," Dodd told Stidger.

On June 3 Stidger sent Carrington additional details, enclosing endless lists of co-conspirators. His next report is a sinister one. At one meeting he was startled when the name of another Carrington agent came up. Bowles said quietly that he must be murdered "at all hazards." Fittingly, the spy's name was Coffin.

"Coffin is to be murdered. You must send him to another place," Stidger wrote.

The following week Stidger was frantic. Coffin's murder was now a daily topic. Stidger was looked upon as the logical man to commit the crime or to hire the assassin. There was a new note of terror in his reports to Carrington; one of the commanders had questioned his loyalty. Fortunately, Bowles' shrill voice had squelched the suspicious commander.

In June, Bowles surprised Stidger by announcing that he was to be made secretary of the Copperheads in Indiana. It was a fantastic stroke of luck. Orders for the uprising, murders and the distribution of arms were to come through Stidger from Bowles.

Finally, Bowles won out and Stidger was elected as his assistant. But from that day Stidger carried a pistol and a dagger in his boot. Every hour carried a new threat of betrayal and violent death. He implored Carrington "not to speak of me to anyone, nor to tell anyone what work I am doing, for if you do I shall be betrayed and murdered in my sleep."

Stidger met Hines in Louisville. The Confederate master spy had traveled down from Toronto to confer with Bowles on final preparations for the revolution in the Northwest. Hines impressed Stidger, who felt uneasy under the cool gaze of those inscrutable blue eyes. Innocent brown eyes matched his—and won. Hines was completely taken in. In Louisville, Stidger saw him initiated into the Sons of Liberty, probably for purposes of good-will. Stidger says Hines was a night prowler. He seldom moved about during the day, but as darkness crept across the rooftops he would hurry up the Louisville alleys dressed in a somber black suit, his eyes hidden by the brim of a black hat.

Stidger's next dispatch disclosed to Carrington that the uprising had been set for July 4. Bullitt was whispering secrets into his ears to be conveyed to Bowles.

Couriers on fast horses would spread the news across the state from four points. H. H. Dodd, the Indiana Copperhead leader, and Jim Barrett, of Missouri, were in Niagara Falls at the Clifton House waiting to receive their final orders from Hines and Thompson. From there they would travel to New York and to Chicago to spread the word.

While the Blue Grass hummed with intrigue, Morgan, at his headquarters at Saltville, Virginia, was demonstrating that there was still magic in his name. When a dispatch arrived with the news of two columns of Federals moving on Saltville, he gathered his ragged command and rode out with the fours singing, and the standards rippling in the wind. The battle ended with the Union forces fleeing back up the Kanawha valley. The threat had been an important one. Had the Federals been successful they would have cut communications with Lee's army and the Confederacy would have lost all the important salt works.

Two weeks after the battle Morgan suddenly announced that he was ready to launch a raid into Kentucky. General Braxton Bragg was indignant, and called such a move "a most unfortunate withdrawal of forces from an important position at a critical moment." Bragg was right, but what he didn't know was that Hines was conferring with

Bullitt for a revolt in Kentucky. Morgan's raid was to be the signal for the uprising.

As a dispatch from the provost marshal of St. Louis to General Rosecrans reported, "The appearance of Morgan in the state of Kentucky would be the signal for the uprising if the members of the order [Knights of the Golden Circle] in various parts of the state were to aid and assist him in whatever way they could. . . ."

The high command in Richmond could have ordered Morgan to stay in Saltville and defend that important position but did not. Davis, Benjamin and Seddon were more interested in insurrection than in salt.

Unfortunately, the raid was badly timed and mismanaged. Before it would be over the saddles of what had once been the Confederacy's proudest cavalry command would be emptied, and its general would become a lost leader.

It was a tattered bunch that rode out that last time, three brigades, twenty-five hundred men filling the morning with "Cheer, Boys, Cheer, Away with Idle Sorrow." But it would take more than brave songs in the fresh morning to fill the gaps in Morgan's command; St. Leger Grenfel, Basil Duke, George Eastin and most of his captains were gone. There were only Colonel Giltner, commanding the First, composed of his own Fourth Kentucky, and the veteran Colonel Howard Smith, whose beard had been shorn at Columbus. Smith had been the only prisoner to be exchanged by the Union. There was no artillery.

On June 2 they reached Pound Gap, where a sharp skirmish was fought. Colonel Smith led the charge and scattered the Federals. Seven horses were taken and the fours took this to be a good omen.

There was only a short rest before Morgan ordered the advance to continue. Burbridge was in the extreme eastern part of the state. Morgan wanted to reach the supply dumps at Mt. Sterling before Burbridge could hear of his raid.

In seven days Morgan's command made one hundred and fifty miles over mountainous terrain that left men and horses staggering with fatigue. Giltner reported to Morgan he had lost two hundred horses. In central Kentucky their spirits lifted and the fours rode along singing again. At dawn of the 8th, the pickets reached Mt. Sterling. Stores, wagons and a large bag of prisoners were taken. The Mt. Sterling bank was robbed of eighty thousand dollars.

Meanwhile, Burbridge, on his way to assault Morgan's headquarters at Saltville, had turned to counter this attack. In thirty hours his command covered ninety miles to reach the outskirts of Mt. Sterling. In the early hours of the morning, with the campfires low and Morgan's men drugged with weariness, Burbridge rolled in over a dismounted brigade. It was a complete rout. Once again there had been no pickets along the road. There Morgan suffered greatly because St. Leger Grenfel had left him. Morgan fled with those of his men who were not killed or wounded.

Giltner came up to make a gallant but futile counter-attack on Mt. Sterling. But Burbridge's men were entrenched in the houses. The Rebel riders were swept from their saddles by a murderous crossfire as they pounded down the streets. Fifty troopers died in the dust as the rain doves in the trees cooed their warnings of the showers to fall later that day.

After a council on the turnpike, Morgan and his brigades continued on toward Lexington. Corrals were burned and fresh horses taken. After breakfast they made for Georgetown, but then Morgan changed his mind and headed for Cynthiana.

On June 11 they attacked the town. At eight, the houses were burning fiercely and five hundred Federals had surrendered. During the fight in the town more Union cavalry came up. Giltner went out to meet them. They were on their last round of ammunition when Morgan and his brigades charged the bluecoats to save the hour.

This was the moment when the Copperheads were to rise. Morgan waited in vain for the messengers from Louisville. Throughout the state men were being arrested in their homes and charged with treason. Haystacks were torn apart, revealing the stands of rifles; barn floors were ripped up and boxes of Colts confiscated.

It was a desperate moment for Morgan. Across his line of retreat were Federal troops. His men, dirty, exhausted, the fire gone out of their hearts, waited. But Burbridge did not wait. His bugles sounded "Boots and Saddles" and the Federal fours charged, the sun striking fire in the steel of five thousand sabers. Giltner, almost out of ammunition, fought like a madman. The whole command was pushed backward to the Licking River. They crossed in ignominious defeat, to be picked off by Union sharpshooters. Hats, dead horses and gray-clad bodies bobbed up and down in the current.

They reached Sardis, where looting was widespread. Discipline had vanished. The bitter, defeated troopers recognized neither friend nor foe. They wanted food and whiskey and a chance to lie down and sleep away the thunder of the Federal charge, the screams of men and horses crossing the Licking as the Union sharpshooters took their toll.

Flemingsburg and West Liberty were to come, and finally Abington, which Morgan reached on the 20th of June. His star had blinked out. The magic had left his name.

As Justice Bullitt said sadly, "Morgan was too soon; we were not ready for him."

Everything had gone wrong in Kentucky. But there was action on other fronts; besides the military operations there was the peace offensive. Maine and the Northeast Coast were included as prongs of the Conspiracy and Porterfield's agents in New York were still buying up gold despite the Federal agents who were trying to trap the "scoundrels," as General Butler called them.

There was also a dread "pestilence weapon"—a type of nineteenth-century germ warfare. One of the witnesses in the trial of the conspirators in the Lincoln assassination plot (held in the spring of 1865 in Washington) later testified it had been used by the Confederates in an attempt to wipe out President Lincoln and his Cabinet by creating an epidemic of yellow fever. Hundreds of vests, shirts, blankets and overcoats, all "infected" by a Confederate physician with yellow fever, were delivered to the capital by the "informer," who testified he had done so with the approval of Commissioner Jacob Thompson. He quoted the Chief of the Confederate Mission in Canada as saying $200,000 had been appropriated "for the introduction of pestilence" into the North.

In July Hines met with the Copperhead leaders in the Richmond House in Chicago. He discovered that Morgan's defeat in Kentucky had affected all of them. At the meetings in Canada with Vallandigham they had predicted an early uprising in the Northwest but now in the quiet hotel room they had suddenly become cautious.

The date for the uprising had been set for July 4. They asked to postpone the date until July 20. Hines, who was not ready to put on pressure, agreed.

In Kentucky, Justice Bullitt sent out orders to commanders of what he claimed were three hundred thousand members, to attend a "make-believe" barbecue outside Louisville. At a signal they were to start the revolt. Louisville would be taken first. Then they would cross into Indiana to capture Indianapolis, then drive on to take Cincinnati and St. Louis.

While the turnpikes and the backroads were drumming under the galloping hoofs of the horses of the couriers, Colonel Carrington and Stidger were holding one of their last conferences. Carrington told Stidger he wanted to grab the gang in one sweep. Stidger agreed to this plan but advised caution. His life, he said, would be worthless if it were discovered prematurely that he was a Union spy. A pistol shot or the blow of an assassin's dagger would not only kill him but would destroy the government's case. It would be his testimony before a Federal grand jury which would indict the Copperheads; it would be his testimony, corroborated by secret records and membership lists which must be seized, that would convict the indicted leaders.

Carrington saw the wisdom of Stidger's caution. He agreed to hold off until Stidger gave the word. Day and night Carrington's agents watched the secret mail box. At last a single sheet of paper arrived. Stidger had given the green light to Carrington to carry out his raids and arrests.

Justice Bullitt, Stidger said, was returning from Canada where he had collected large sums from the Confederates to buy arms. He had made an appointment to meet him at the Louisville ferry. Bullitt would have in his possession the checks and currency, indisputable evidence of his treasonable dealings.

The arrest was made as Bullitt rode up to the ferry entrance in a carriage. When they saw Carrington's agents closing in, Bullitt knew the game was up. He whispered to Stidger to warn Dodd and Doctor Bowles, the Indiana leaders, at once. To avoid Bullitt's suspicion, Stidger was also taken into custody but released after routine questioning. He rode off for Indiana, keeping Carrington advised of his route.

Bullitt was found to be carrying a valise filled with Federal greenbacks. In an inside pocket were checks drawn on a Toronto bank, signed by Jacob Thompson. Hines and Thompson had both warned Bullitt to cash them as soon as possible. Bullitt had forgotten their warning.

Stidger proved to be a superb counter-espionage agent. He furnished lists of members and secret arsenals. Carrington's official report says his raiders found thirty thousand stands of rifles and revolvers hidden in barns and haystacks. To prove to Colonel Carrington that the Copperheads had that many arms hidden, he produced actual invoices from northern arms factories!

From Indiana, where Dodd had already heard the news of Bullitt's arrest, Stidger went to St. Louis, Missouri, where he saw the beautiful Madam Valesque, the Confederate spy whose black eyes bewitched passes from Union generals. Stidger found the sons of the border strangely quiet. Barrett told him he was not ready. Stidger had all he wanted to know. He hurried back to Louisville.

There he found Carrington pacing the floor of his headquarters. He wanted more evidence, he told Stidger. There was only one way. He would have to arrest his own agent and throw him in with the Copperheads.

Stidger spent some weeks in jail, shifted from prison to prison. From his cell Bullitt sympathized with him. Bowles sent word from Indiana that he was not to worry. Finally, just before the trials began, Stidger was released. But before he appeared in court as a government witness, Bullitt escaped, undoubtedly with the aid of other Copperheads, to join Hines in Toronto.

X. COMMISSIONER HOLCOMB AND THE WILD ROSE

IN EARLY July, a man who might have stepped out of the pages of a tale of high adventure joined Captain Hines. He was Colonel George St. Leger Grenfel, the most colorful as well as the most tragic figure in the Northwest Conspiracy. His life, his adventures, his tragic end rival anything from the pen of Dumas. He lived and fought like D'Artagnan and was imprisoned like Edmond Dantes.

At sixty-two years of age he was still an impressive figure of romance. Slightly under six feet, with light blue eyes and shoulder-length white hair setting off a face darkened by the sandstorms of the Sahara and the winds of the Mediterranean, he had the personal appearance of Brian de Bois-Guilbert, in *Ivanhoe*, as Basil Duke recalled in his memoirs.

Grenfel was the black sheep of an aristocratic English family. At seventeen he ran away to join the Chasseurs d'Afrique. For five years he fought the wild desert tribes. After his enlistment was up, he settled in Tangiers. The Moors liked him and he became a well known figure in the city.

When the French attacked Tangiers, he fought with his former comrades against the Moors. The French, however, suspected his loyalty. He found refuge in the tents of the great chieftain, Abd-el-Kader, under whom he served as a cavalry leader. He next appeared along the Moroccan coast with a commission from the Governor of Gibraltar to clean out Riff pirates. As Hines wrote: "He cleaned them out of this world."

A colonel's commission in Garibaldi's South American legion followed. Tiring of what he told Hines was "irregular service," St. Leger returned to England. In the best romantic tradition he settled down before his hearth with his dogs. Country life soon lost its appeal. St. Leger returned to war in the Crimea and India's Sepoy Rebellion.

When America's Civil War broke out, he hurried to Richmond to become Braxton Bragg's Inspector-General. After Morgan's escape, he again joined his command as Adjutant-General. But the saddles emptied and Grenfel was without a command. He had heard something of the work Hines was doing in the Northwest and decided to join him.

Grenfel ran the blockade to New York, where he casually "paid a call" on General John A. Dix, commanding that area with head-quarters at Fort Lafayette, and told him he had "retired" from the Confederate Army and wanted clearance. Dix sent him on to Washington. There Grenfel saw Secretary of War Stanton, who knew him by reputation. When he asked the condition of the Confederacy's armies, Grenfel told him enormous lies of the strength of Lee's army and their rolling stock. Stanton gave him a pass on his promise he would not "take up arms" against the Union. A week later Grenfel was in Canada.

"I don't think he had the right to ask me such questions," Grenfel indignantly explained to Hines. But Grenfel would pay dearly for those tall tales. Stanton never forgave him.

Grenfel joined Hines at Toronto and offered his services. After Hines had outlined for him "what was going on," Grenfel smiled and replied, "I can see in all this that some lives must be sacrificed. I cannot take part in it"—he winked—"because of my promise to Stanton, but I will go along and witness the executions."

But Grenfel was beginning to feel his years. As he wrote his daughter in London, a few days after he had joined Hines: "Two years and a half of excitement and hard work have told on me. . . . I shall rusticate a month or so—I hope—before I again get into the saddle. . . ."

But only a week after he had arrived, Grenfel was traveling with Hines and Castleman to the Clifton House at Niagara Falls on an important mission.

A few days before Grenfel had arrived, George N. Sanders had demonstrated the enormous influence he now had over the ailing Commissioner Clay. With the Commissioner's blessing and without Jacob Thompson's knowledge Sanders had sent Horace Greeley, editor of the New York *Tribune,* a letter asking for safe conduct for himself and Clay to hold a "peace conference" with President Lincoln.

Greeley replied he understood they were "accredited from Richmond as bearers of propositions looking to the establishment of peace." Therefore he had sent Sanders' note on to the White House with his recommendation that Lincoln grant the safe conduct.

Lincoln, however, was far more astute. Suspecting that Sanders and Clay were acting only on their own, he refused the *Tribune* editor's request but "deputized" Greeley to go to Canada.

Greeley met both Sanders and Clay at the Clifton House, Niagara

Falls. Hines, Castleman and Grenfel tried to warn Clay that Sanders was a scoundrel, but Clay refused to listen to him. The three men met, with Thompson conspicuous by his absence. He had sent word to Hines that his name was not to be mentioned in the meeting, nor was it to appear on any document sent to Richmond.

Sanders took over the whole conference, which soon collapsed over a letter Lincoln had sent to Greeley emphasizing that "the integrity of the whole Union and the abandonment of slavery" were essential before any peace terms could be entered into.

At the Clifton House Sanders archly asked Hines, "Why don't you men go and rob the banks at Niagara Falls and in Buffalo?"

Hines coldly informed him that such an act would imperil the position of the Commissioners in neutral Canada.

"Well, you should try it," Sanders said thoughtfully and went back into the peace meeting with Greeley.

Sanders had a fixed idea that robbing Northern banks would force troops from the Federal armies. Hines ignored his repeated requests. But in the months to come Sanders would finally have his way.

In August Judge Jeremiah S. Black, former Attorney-General, arrived in Toronto with a second "peace move." Hines gives one version of this meeting, Black another, and Stanton still a third. The Confederate version is based on what Black told Thompson, his friend during the days of Buchanan's administration, and Captain Hines. Black later denied it. We are inclined to prefer Stanton's version.

At the first meeting in Toronto, Black told Thompson that he had come north as Stanton's personal emissary. He said the Secretary of War didn't believe that Lincoln could be re-elected and wanted to discuss peace terms.

The only stumbling-block in their discussion was independence. Hines and Castleman, who knew better than Thompson how badly off the Confederate armies were, urged Thompson to send a report of his meeting with Black and the terms proposed to Richmond. Thompson refused. "Independence," he told Hines, "must be in any treaty negotiated between the North and the South."

After several conferences with Justice Black, Hines said, they all traveled to the Clifton House at Niagara Falls to see Commissioner James Holcomb. Hines was dismayed to find that Holcomb, like the ailing Clay, had succumbed to the personality of George Sanders. Holcomb insisted they go to Montreal and see Commissioner Clay.

At Montreal, Clay refused to enter into any discussion of the peace terms unless Sanders were present. Clay and Thompson were barely on speaking terms by this time and it is not hard to picture the scene in the hotel room; Clay, ill and irritable; the bearded Thompson, wiping his feverish eyes; Justice Black, wondering uneasily about the air of hostility in the room; Sanders, debonair, smiling; Holcomb, bored, staring out at the sparkling waters of the St. Lawrence; Hines, Castleman, and Grenfel, impatient men of action, contemptuous of these dreamers and talkers.

Clay at last grudgingly agreed with Thompson's plan to send Holcomb to London to see Mason and Slidell, the Confederate ministers to Paris and London. Thompson thought that Secretary of War Stanton's belief that Lincoln could not be re-elected—as reported by Justice Black—would influence France and England in signing military alliances with the Confederacy.

A copy of Thompson's report to Mason and Slidell of Justice Black's "peace terms" is among the Hines Papers. It ends:

> After these matters are fairly presented to the courts of England and France, I should be pleased to know what we are to expect from them. My advice to the government at Richmond will be modified by your report.

Meanwhile, Black wrote to Stanton, reporting on his meeting with the Confederate Commissioners. He advised the Union's Secretary of War to tell Lincoln "to suspend hostilities for three or six months, and commence negotiations in earnest, unless he had irrevocably made up his mind to fight it out on the Emancipation issue."

Stanton was furious when he received Black's letter. He sent back a biting reply to the former Justice. In it he pointed out that Black had come to Washington as an old friend and "for a friendly visit." Stanton added, "I did not suspect that afterwards you would talk about it as a visit to a 'Cabinet minister.' " Stanton reminded Black that during his visit he had said he would like to go to Canada to see their old friend Jacob Thompson, "who would tell me the real Southern feelings."

At the time, Stanton said, he had thought nothing of the remark, "as it was a matter of trifling importance."

(It was after this Washington visit that Black had traveled to Canada to see Thompson, giving the Confederate Mission the impression he had come at the insistence of Stanton.)

After receiving Stanton's bitter letter, Black sent back a whimpering reply. The Secretary of War never answered it.

The hot summer dragged on. Thompson and Hines waited impatiently for Holcomb to appear with a reply from London. They never received an answer. Holcomb apparently had vanished from the face of the earth. (In November, 1951, while examining captured Confederate documents in the State Department National Archives pertaining to the beautiful Confederate spy, Rose O'Neal Greenhow, this author discovered the reason why Holcomb never returned with an answer from Mason and Slidell.)

Holcomb left Montreal for Halifax on the morning of August 24, 1864. There he boarded the English blockade-runner *Condor*. The London *Evening Mail* described her as "a staunch, three-funneled vessel, superbly adapted for her trade, with a great carrying capacity, drawing only seven foot of water and as swift as a swallow."

The *Condor* was a ship of international mystery. Her skipper was Admiral Hobart Hampden, the eighth Earl of Buckinghamshire. A powerful six-foot man, he had been decorated by Queen Victoria for his service to the Crown in the Crimean War.

He was second in command of H.M.S. *Driver* in the battle of Krönstadt and later led his men aboard a Russian man-of-war. He was a favorite at court and was Queen Victoria's master of her private yacht, the *Victoria and Albert*.

His most famous passenger on board the *Condor* was Mrs. Greenhow, "the Wild Rose," as Washington knew her. Mrs. Rose O'Neal Greenhow was a leader of the female spy ring in Washington which had sent a message to General Beauregard warning him of the Union advance at Bull Run. It had been well hidden in the long tresses of one of its members. Mrs. Greenhow was returning from London in the company of several Confederate and British agents.

The *Condor* was bound for Wilmington, N. C. Why Holcomb, supposedly bound for London, should board her is a mystery.

On September 30 the *Condor* ran the Union blockade in a raging storm off the Carolina capes. Wind shrilling in her rigging, the *Condor* took the bone in her teeth, knifing her way through the heavy seas. Their decks cleared for action, two Federal gunboats took up the chase. At three o'clock in the morning the *Condor* reached the mouth of Cape Fear River, where she went aground on the New Inlet Bar, two hundred yards from the Confederate guns of Fort Fisher.

Mountainous waves jarred the ship. As she wallowed helplessly, Mrs. Greenhow ran up on deck, demanding in the name of the Queen to be put ashore in a boat. Admiral Hampden pointed out such a trip through the breakers would be suicide. But Rose had had one experience in the Union's Old Capitol prison in 1862, and was determined to reach shore.

Finally, Hampden, exhausted by her harangue, ordered a small boat lowered. Holcomb decided to go with her. He stored his mail, including Thompson's report, under the stern seat. He helped Mrs. Greenhow climb in, then took his seat beside her. Four sailors took the oars and the boat was cast free.

The men bent to their oars. Without end the mountainous rollers lifted the tiny boat upward with a rush, only to let it drop sickeningly to the bottom of the deep trough. As the London *Mail* says, "it was near to the beach" when a gigantic wave overturned the boat. Holcomb, Mrs. Greenhow and the crewmen were caught in a terrifying undertow and sucked under.

Holcomb fought his way to the surface where he clung to the keel of the overturned boat. Several times the rollers and the wind almost tore loose his hold but he managed to keep his grip. When he caught his breath he struck out alone, finally reaching the beach, where he lay like a dead man until the crewmen found him.

With torches they searched the beach for Mrs. Greenhow. Her body was found in the morning by a sailor, who stole three thousand dollars in gold she was carrying in a purse (probably the royalties of the best seller she had written in London), then pushed her back into the sea. Holcomb and the others resumed the search the following day. In the afternoon they found the body had washed in again.

Under dripping gray skies she was buried in Wilmington's Oakdale Cemetery, where she rests today. James Holcomb led the mourners from the Seamen's Bethel to the cemetery. Late that same day he left Wilmington for Richmond. What he reported to Davis, Benjamin or Seddon is not known. Neither Hines nor Castleman speak of him. Nor did Thompson in his *Official Journal of the Confederate Mission*. In 1917, shortly before he died, Castleman was still wondering why Holcomb had never returned from London. Mrs. Greenhow's death and Holcomb's rescue were page-one news in London. The story had been sent by the *Mail's* "Richmond correspondent."

Surely it was published in the Confederate newspapers. It is curious that Hines, Castleman or Thompson did not know what had happened to the third man of their Mission, who was carrying such a vital document to the Confederate ministers in London and Paris.

PART IV

THE NORTHWEST CONSPIRACY
The Attacks

———————•◦•———————

XI. THE RAID ON MAINE

H UNDREDS of men pass in and out of the documents and papers relating to the Northwest Conspiracy. They are mostly shadows, men without faces or identity. Nearly all of them used aliases; one had fourteen. Hines himself posed as a doctor, a banker, a teacher and a French-Canadian exporter.

Some were Army officers from Richmond, some wealthy merchants in northern cities acting as Rebel agents in buying arms and gold. One was a doctor gathering medical supplies to be used for Hines' forces. Some were cold-blooded killers, escaped prisoners. But some, like Francis Jones, were men "of high mark," the description given to him by Judge Advocate General Holt in a letter to Secretary Stanton.

Jones was one of the favorites of Richmond society. Slim, handsome, blond and blue-eyed, he typified the cavalier of the times. An elopement, followed by the tragic death of his young wife and child, gave him a brooding, melancholy air which thrilled and touched the hearts of the ladies. Son of the president of St. Louis University, he was well educated and spoke French, Spanish and German fluently.

In 1861, he fought with several guerrilla bands. In 1863 he appeared in Richmond. He charmed Secretary of War Seddon and soon was engaged in espionage work, for what he called "the Confederate Secret Service."

He made thirty-two trips through the Union lines by both land and sea. His favorite route was the blockade-run from Wilmington, North Carolina, to Bermuda, thence by British mail packet to Halifax, then west by train to Montreal, Toronto or Niagara Falls where he would deliver his secret orders and reports to the Commissioners. As a Richmond courier, he was in contact with almost every secret Rebel agent from Maine to New York City.

In July, 1864, while Hines was meeting with the Sons of Liberty in Chicago, Jones participated in one of the most fantastic facets of the Northwest Conspiracy. The plan, which might well have been called the Northeast Conspiracy, was designed to stretch the Union on the rack, torn between sending troops to put down a "scorched earth" campaign from the northern border of Maine to Boston, or to crush the revolution being fostered by Hines in Ohio, Indiana and Illinois.

Curiously enough, Hines, Thompson and Castleman do not mention this operation in their letters or dispatches; there are only vague references to some "activities" in Boston and Maine. Perhaps Richmond had ordered it not to be mentioned to protect their northern agents at all costs. It must be recalled that as late as 1870 men who had acted as spies for either side were being murdered and bushwhacked.

The story can well begin in the spring of 1864 when Hines was planning the Chicago uprising. Then Confederate prospects for a revolution looked good. The Copperheads were promising a great deal. Thompson, believing them, was spending huge sums, and gun-runners were crossing into Indiana with large shipments of rifles and revolvers.

Someone in Toronto (we do not know his name) decided that a major diversionary move was needed to keep the attention of the Federals away from Hines in Chicago at the time he was to set off the revolt in the Northwest. It was decided to organize another expedition, sent against Maine and the Northeast Coast.

Couriers slipped south with messages for President Davis. He gave his approval of an eastern facet of the Northwest Conspiracy. This was the plan, as confessed by Jones to the Assistant Judge Advocate Turner under Holt in Washington.

An army of 5,000 men, with a large number of field artillery, commanded by officers of Morgan's, Mosby's and Stuart's command, who had been summoned to Richmond from the field by Secretary of War Seddon, were to be brought to Canada by eight fast blockade-runners. The troops were to be disembarked on the coast of Maine at night. Detachments were to be sent out first to gather up rolling stock, pack horses, cattle and food. The blockade-runners would then return to Richmond, leaving the small army to subsist on the land. The stock and food were to be brought to a rendezvous in northern Maine. From that point the army was to be split into five columns to fan out, "but within supporting distance of each other" to put Maine to the torch. As Jones said, "The troops were to sack and destroy public and corporative

property of the United States government." Local Sons of Liberty were
to be used as guides or assassins to murder state or municipal officials.
Because the membership of this order in Maine was not too large,
military help from them was not to be relied upon.

The expedition was to be a combined operation. In April, 1864,
Secretary of the Navy Mallory, in Richmond, sent 1,500 seamen and
privateersmen "on special duty" to report to Thompson at Toronto.
They were to man the armed steamers *Tallahassee* and *Florida*, which
were to set sail out of New Brunswick to shell and burn Maine's coastal
cities. Other vessels were scheduled to make a mock attack on Johnson's
Island prison camp, if the U.S.S. *Michigan* guarding Lake Erie could
be scuttled and burned, "to divert the attention of the United States
Government from the real point of attack, the coast of Maine."

Nothing was overlooked to insure the success of the expedition.
On May 14, 1864, fifty engineers and topographers ran the blockade
from Richmond on the *Tallahassee* to New Brunswick. From there they
traveled to Toronto to report to Thompson. The engineers and topographers were briefed on the plan of attack. They were told to make a
plan of the coast, "seeking out unfrequented bays and inlets" where the
Tallahassee and *Florida* could hide and refuel.

During May, June and July, 1864, residents and fishermen along the
Maine coast reported men who said they were "artists" painting and
sketching the coast. By July the finished charts and maps hung on the
walls of a secret hideout "on Barrington Street, Halifax, over a con-
fectionery store, in very good rooms belonging to a colored man."

During the summer of 1864, Confederate headquarters in Toronto
hummed with activity. Jones was traveling about the country, deliver-
ing messages to Rebel agents. In Boston, he met a man who identified
himself as "Major Harris," who was organizing the Sons of Liberty
terrorists for an all-out campaign of destruction. Evidently Jones and
Tom Hines had never met. However, Jones' description of the mysterious major fits Hines, who may have visited Boston to stir up the
Copperheads there to join in the insurrection, which was one of those
planned to divert Federal troops, thereby making it easier for Hines
and his men in Chicago.

Jones returned to Toronto with a troubled heart. He had received
two letters from his mother, whom he described as "a good Union
woman," pleading with him to return to the fold and turn his back on
the Confederacy. There was also a young lady who was writing and
begging him to come home.

While Jones was pondering his decision, a Captain William Collins, formerly attached to General Polk's staff, arrived in Toronto. He was a handsome man with cold eyes and a murderer's heart. The United States consul in St. John's, Quebec, was to describe him as "a man of desperate character, who would not hesitate to shoot his jailer."

Collins, who wore a Colt on his hip in the manner of the later Western outlaws, was to be in command of one of the five raiding columns. He was accompanied by a dim-witted Irishman named Phillips, who had a giant's strength and a child's mentality. Both men reported to Thompson at the Queen's Hotel. Collins was ordered to set up headquarters at St. John's, Quebec, and await further orders. The dapper captain, followed by his lumbering giant, set out at once.

Jones now had come to terms with himself. He decided to return to St. Louis and join his mother and new light o' love. He first sent a letter to Secretary of War Stanton asking to be allowed to take the oath of allegiance and to return home. For some reason Stanton had Assistant Secretary of War Dana answer him personally with a terse refusal. Evidently there were spies in the War Department or Thompson, suspicious of Jones' behavior, had his letters steamed open. His defection was learned. For punishment, as he said, "I was ordered to join Collins and Phillips at St. John's."

Here was a man, found to be a traitor, yet his only punishment is banishment to another troubled area. This is one instance of the curious reluctance of the Confederates to kill informers and traitors discovered in their ranks. Later, Hines himself participated in a more important one when he refused to let the other Chicago raiders kill a young traitor whose loose tongue thereafter would send Castleman to prison and almost to the gallows. Probably the answer is that for cavaliers it was unthinkable to kill in cold blood.

We know from his letters that Jones hated Collins and feared Phillips. On the other hand, Collins, that man of action, detested the scholarly Jones who had been sent to him by the Confederate high command in Toronto. Collins needed a man skilled not in languages, but in the use of a gun.

By the time Jones had arrived, Collins had already killed two men at St. John's, besides gathering together a large force of escaped prisoners. In a meeting with Jones and Phillips, Collins told them they were to make a reconnaissance raid into Washington County, Maine. There do not seem to have been any formal orders from Thompson or

Clay or Holcomb for this raid and undoubtedly it was unauthorized and Collins' own plan.

Too many men knew about it. There was bragging and loud talk in the saloons. United States Consul Howard in St. John's heard the rumors and sent a message in a diplomatic pouch to Secretary of State Seward, who informed Stanton. The War Department communicated with the provost marshal in Portland and the town police and Home Guard were alerted.

The three raiders fanned out in the attack on Washington County. The target was the Calais National Bank. On the morning of July 16, 1864, the three raiders entered the village on horseback. But unlike St. Albans, Vermont, where the Confederates were to rob three banks within fifteen minutes, Calais and its townspeople were ready. Collins had drawn his guns on entering the bank, only to be greeted by a volley from the clerk and bank president. Sheriff Brown had a posse hidden and the bank was surrounded within a few minutes. The three raiders quickly surrendered. Escorted by the Home Guard to prevent a lynching by the townspeople, the trio was taken to the county jail at Machias, Washington County.

Jones' bearing and good breeding impressed Sheriff Brown who, from his letters, was far more intelligent than the usual small-town politician of those days. Jones and the sheriff became friends. They played chess through the bars, discussed crops, the weather and the war. One day Jones said abruptly, "I have been used as a tool by ambitious men and now I think I'm going to pay them back in their own coin."

"What can I do for you, lad?" the sheriff asked.

"Listen to what I have to say," Jones said. "It is important."

Jones talked for hours. The sheriff listened in amazement as the great plan to destroy his state unfolded. When Jones had finished the sheriff sent him back to his cell, convinced that the whole story was a trick on the boy's part to escape trial. But as the days passed Jones filled in so many details that it was obvious there was some truth to his story.

The sheriff then called in the town attorney, who listened "with horrified surprise and indignation." When Jones had finished the attorney told him he wished they had shot them all down. However, he agreed with the sheriff that someone high in Washington should know about it.

Sheriff Brown, in a well-written letter to Secretary of State Seward,

In Jail, Machias, Maine.
July 24, 1864.

Dear Mother,

    Doubtlessly you will be greatly surprised and grieved to hear from me in such a place. We were captured (myself & companions) on the 18th instant. We are accused of attempting the robbery of the Bank at Calais in this State. We were acting under especial orders from President Davis. We were also under the command of a regularly commissioned officer of the Confederate States Army. Had it been otherwise I would have flatly refused to have joined Capt. Wm. Collin's command when ordered to do so by the confederate authorities. We have been committed to this Jail in default of twenty thousand dollars bail, to await our trial before the Supreme Court in November next. Do not come on here and see me for it would be useless besides being very expensive. So do not come unless I should write and expressly request your presence. Enclose a fine to enable me to purchase Tobacco, Needles, thread &c and other little necessaries of prison life.

    As ever your affectionate Son

        Francis.—

Francis Jones' letter to his mother—"a good Union woman"—written in the Machias, Maine, jail after the failure of the bank raid in Calais.

This expedition is to consist of five
columns - can deal at five different
points, but within supporting distances;
and the troops to consist of old experienced raiders from Morgan's, Wheeler's
and Stuart's commands. The various
secret organizations have pledged
themselves, to join in the movement &
become incorporated with it; thereby
to swell this force, as is expected to 12000,
to 15,000 men -

In conjunction with this expedition, there is to be another from Canada
and New Brunswick, comprising 1200 to
1500 men. These men are to embark
in sailing vessels, and convoyed by
two rebel war-steamers - the "Tallahassee"
and "Florida," as is said. At first
it was planned that this raiding force
should be 2000 strong; but finally it
was decided that Gen, Carroll should
take 500 men and make a descent

Courtesy, National Archives

A page from Jones' confession made to Assistant Judge Advocate Turner,
in which he told of the plan to burn and sack the coast and cities of Maine.

gave a résumé of Jones' confession "urging that some person authorized by the government who has a knowledge of these things and could check the truth of Jones' story, be sent at once to obtain his confession."

Seward, who immediately recognized the importance of the letter, sent it over to Stanton the same day he received it. Stanton gave it to Assistant Secretary of War Dana, ordering Assistant Judge Advocate Turner to "go at once to Maine and get the confession from Jones, and to report daily the progress he has made."

Stanton and Seward, daily sifting the reports from their agents in London and in Canada, were well aware of the tremendous luck they had had.

Turner interviewed Jones in the parlor of the sheriff's home. In Turner's papers is the confession, fifteen pages written in a small, cramped hand. Jones told all. He gave names, dates and places. He also disclosed the places where large caches of guns, ammunition, food and medical stores could be found in New York, Cincinnati, Indianapolis, St. Louis and many northern cities. Brooklyn had a warehouse filled with seventeen thousand Henry rifles stolen from the New York Quartermaster Corps, to be used to arm the Sons of Liberty.

Turner, from his boarding-house room in Calais, that night sent Stanton a progress report. He said he was on his way to see the provost marshal at Portland to try to check some of Jones' statements.

"I have no doubt that this man's statement, given in minute detail, is correct," he said.

He described Collins as a cold-blooded killer who "scorns to make any statement," and Phillips as "dull-witted, hard, reckless and obstinate."

Turner, after an interview with the Portland provost marshal, returned to Washington to confer with Stanton, Dana and Judge Advocate General Holt. It was decided to send investigators into Maine to interview fishermen and farm people in an attempt to confirm Jones' statement that Rebel engineers and topographers had been sketching the coast. Other agents and secret service detectives were to trail the men named as Rebel agents in northern cities and to investigate the caches of guns and ammunition.

We will return to Francis Jones, the murderous Captain Collins and the giant Irishman, Phillips.

XII. PASSWORD FOR REVOLUTION

THE Confederate plans had gone awry. Not only was the fighting going badly in the summer of 1864, but the secret Conspiracy was suffering defeats and delays. In June, Morgan's Kentucky raid had fizzled and in July the Maine raid and all the Northeast Coast plans had been uncovered and never materialized. In the Northwest the Copperheads had postponed the uprising from the 4th of July to the 18th. When that day arrived they set the insurrection for the 20th. When they again postponed their actions, saying they were not "prepared," Hines, Thompson and Clay met with Vallandigham and flatly insisted that the day of uprising must be August 29, 1864, the day the Democratic Convention opened in Chicago. There would be large crowds; half the delegates would be Peace Democrats, members of the Sons of Liberty and Knights of the Golden Circle. Chicago would be a powder keg; one spark was all that was needed to touch it off.

"Some sort of violence was needed to make them act," Hines wrote. "We were determined to bring that about." After a conference with Thompson, Hines sent Grenfel on ahead to Chicago to contact Walsh and arm Walsh's "two regiments" with the thousands of rifles and revolvers hidden throughout the city.

Hines now realized that some of the Copperhead leaders were sound and fury, and nothing more. As he wrote: "There was a reluctance on their part to sacrifice life for a cause." With Justice Bullitt in exile he found only four Copperhead leaders he could rely upon for action. They were H. H. Dodd of Indiana, that wild Irishman Charles Walsh of Chicago, who had the strongest organization with two "regiments" under arms; hard-eyed Jim Barrett of Missouri, who knew the bloody Quantrill; and Doctor William A. Bowles of Indiana.

Early in August Hines went to French Lick, Indiana, to confer with Bowles and there had his closest call. Cautious as always, he had Bowles order some of his agents in Indianapolis to warn him if the patrols were sent out after him. Hines was sitting on the porch with Mrs. Bowles when he heard the hoofbeats of an approaching horse.

121

He went inside, and armed himself to wait behind the front door while Doctor Bowles greeted the rider. It was a message from Indianapolis. Hines' presence was known; soldiers and detectives were riding out to capture him. Hines said a quick farewell and vanished in the darkness.

The patrols came up to find Bowles and his wife in bed. While the doctor and his wife taunted the soldiers, the officer in charge grimly went about his task of searching the house. Outside, "Bowles' army" gathered silently, boldly, resting on their rifles and watching the Federals. It needed only the slightest incident to touch off a bloody battle. But the officer in charge was competent and efficient. As soon as he was satisfied Hines had got away, he marched his men back up the road, with the quivering old voice of Bowles screeching insults that echoed in the quiet night.

"Again Hines escaped us," Carrington reported to the assistant chief of staff, Department of Ohio. "This Hines has the full confidence of Morgan and the Rebel command at Richmond. The capture of Hines may elicit no facts from him, but he is one of the most dangerous spies and auxiliaries they [Richmond] have. His headquarters are at Toronto, but he travels in the West under various disguises."

Hines hurried back to Toronto where he was joined by the flower of Morgan's command. Castleman was already there, as were also Lieutenants George B. Eastin, Bennett H. Young, who was to rob the Vermont banks; and Captain George Cantrill, a Scott County, Kentucky, lawyer who was to become one of Hines' most bitter enemies.

There was much to do. Military organization was important. As Hines pointed out, men from all branches of the Confederate services would have to work together, quickly and efficiently. Companies and regiments had to be formed on the spot, the names of officers inside the camps checked and assigned [on paper] to various posts. Regimental headquarters were to be set up in the Invincible Club hall on Randolph and Dearborn Streets, a grimy row of red brick buildings known as "McCormick's row." The password was: "Don't worship the setting sun."

Brigadier-General Charles Walsh of the Sons of Liberty, the political boss of Cook County, was to be the liaison between the marching Copperheads and the Confederate high command.

Hines now had one hundred men in his squadron. He appointed Castleman second in command. Together they selected fifty. Each man received a hundred dollars, a new pistol, ammunition and a round-trip train ticket from Toronto to Chicago. But a new problem presented itself. On the eve of the departure for Chicago, in a farmhouse outside Toronto where he was to give his men final instructions, Hines was dismayed to find not fifty but seventy men on hand.

Castleman, who had just come from Thompson's lodgings, sadly explained the presence of the twenty new recruits. They had been sent by Sanders and Thompson, who had been impressed by their "high connections."

In the flickering candlelight Hines studied each face. There was John C. Maughan, a clerk in a Toronto bank, who had been haunting Thompson's headquarters for permission to accompany the raiders. He was a fawning young man of twenty-one who had been used by the commissioner to deliver dispatches to Cleary in New York. Hines couldn't find anything wrong with him but he knew the boy's love of liquor and inability to stop bragging of his "dangerous missions" made him an undesirable addition. A wagging tongue could send them all to the gallows.

Then there was Colonel Vincent Marmaduke, handsome and dashing. A brother of the Confederate Brigadier-General Marmaduke, he had twice been put under parole by the provost marshal at Boonville, Missouri, "for his treasonable course in conversation." While under parole he was elected to the Constitutional State Convention "posing as a Union man, but he then turned traitor. His influence in the state is really pernicious," the provost marshal's report stated.

Hines always described Marmaduke as "that soldier of great connections." Neither he nor Castleman liked him but Thompson, who admired "high connections," did, and that was enough.

It isn't clear whether Marmaduke obtained his commission by joining the Confederate Army or whether some author in 1866 simply gave him a commission which was repeated down through the years. From his own letters and the records of the Judge Advocate General's Office, Marmaduke was still a civilian in 1863. In June of that year he was sent to City Point for exchange, officially described as "a disloyal citizen of Missouri." There are some later vague references to his buying stores for the Quartermaster Corps in Memphis. He may have been a rear echelon officer or simply an Army contractor.

Hines mentally checked the names. These two would bear watching. He stopped when he came to the next face. He had never seen this tall and lean man with a cadaverous face and unblinking black eyes.

Hines took Castleman aside to ask the name of this stranger. Castleman told him he was a major from a Virginia cavalry outfit who had recently escaped from Camp Douglas. He had reported to Thompson with the request to be "useful." Thompson had been impressed, but Hines and Castleman were suspicious. "Neither Castleman nor myself was taken in by his 'connections,'" Hines said.

In later years Castleman always insisted it had been Hines' shrewd judgment of men that had made them suspicious of the major. Hines by this time had been in communication with the officers inside Camp Douglas who were ready to stage a revolt simultaneously with the Copperhead uprising. Perhaps Hines had information from them. It is more likely that a message warning Hines about him had been slipped north by Mary Morris. Months later Mary would testify that she had sent "verbal" messages north to Hines and Castleman.

The following day they set out for Chicago in pairs and groups of five. Castleman, Hines, Marmaduke, Maughan and the major traveled together.

As Hines recalled, "By seeming to trust and always guarding the treacherous, and by thus unconsciously appealing to a sense of propriety; by quietly demonstrating to the vainglorious the distinction which to him would come when success that he should achieve would be possible only through silence; by cajoling into prudent demeanor the 'highly connected' soldier of the Confederacy; and, yet the most difficult task of all, by warning the idle talker that only by absolute silence could we hope to be successful, and that any careless word might be fatal . . . thus through three days of anxiety concerning our comrades, and through three days of fear . . . we lived in Chicago amidst conditions which our schooled air of confidence and nonchalance made appear agreeable. . . ."

Hines and his men left Toronto in pairs, beginning about August 10. In Chicago, Hines, Castleman and their two charges, Marmaduke and Maughan, joined Colonel Grenfel at the Richmond House. Over their rooms they hung a sign, "Missouri Delegation," and waited to confer with the Copperhead leaders.

As Grenfel wrote to a business associate in London, "We are now on the eve of great events . . . the Northwest is ready for revolt. . . ." Then, always the realist, he gave explicit instructions as to how his estate was to be handled in the event of his death.

One gets a glimpse into the lonely heart of this restless man, as he ends, "I have not heard from all of you for a long time; I was going to say from home, but I forget I have no home. . . ."

Some time before Captain Hines had rounded up his squadron of raiders to strike at Chicago, Colonel Benjamin Jeffrey Sweet, Eighth Regiment, Veterans' Corps, the commandant of Camp Douglas, stood in the doorway of his small wooden house at the entrance of the main gate of Camp Douglas. He shaded his eyes with one hand to look out across the wind-swept enclosure.

Men in worn gray jackets, some without shoes, moved about the seventy acres restlessly, aimlessly, or stood in small groups, huddled against the wind. A black mongrel, its hide corrugated by the rows of ribs, came from around one of the small wooden huts, its tail between its legs.

The only thing they haven't eaten, Sweet mused. The last two dogs had vanished without a trace of a tooth. His clerk told him the Texas Rangers had even made a stew of the bones and hide.

He sighed. There wasn't anything he could do. Food was scarce. Headquarters just wouldn't give him any more. Seventy acres, almost five thousand prisoners, some of them from that damn raider Morgan's command, and those Texans! A tough lot, with only a board fence, made of planks one inch thick and twelve feet high, to hold them back. He shook his head. Hell, there were so many prisoners they had to use them as guards! Even the clerk who issued the rifles and ball and powder for his small garrison of sixteen hundred troops was a prisoner.

A pretty kettle of fish! The prisoners were guarding the jailers! He grunted in disgust and walked inside his hut. He sat down behind his desk to think again about what his mail clerk had told him that morning. For three weeks, the clerk had said, letter writing in camp had suddenly increased. It seemed as if every prisoner was writing to his wife, sweetheart or parents. There was another curious thing about the letters: all were written on long, ruled sheets of paper. But there were only about five lines written on each sheet.

As he thought about it, Sweet clamped his teeth tighter on the cigar. Damn it, something was up! He rose, pacing up and down. At last, as if his mind were made up, he swung open the door, shouting to the mail clerk to bring him some of the Rebels' mail.

When the clerk had left Sweet selected two letters out of the pile of mail. He grunted when he opened them. The clerk had been right; there were only a few lines on each page. He stared at the sheets of paper for a long time, then, struck by a sudden thought, yanked open the door of the stove and held the pages to the heat.

The black words appeared across the paper: "The 4th of July is going up like a rocket and an all-fired sight of powder is going to burn." Another one said: "The 4th of July will be a grand day for us. Old Sweet won't like it."

Colonel Sweet had seen enough. Common sense told him a break was near. He sent a wire immediately to Headquarters asking for more troops but he received only a curt reply; every soldier who was available was in the field. He would have to do with what men he had.

The hot, uneasy days passed. The grapevine brought news to Sweet confirming the 4th of July as the date of the break. Guards slept with their rifles at their sides. Sweet never left his room in the camp. The last part of a confiscated letter read: "A bonfire will be built outside the fence, and we'll salute Old Glory but not with blank cartridges."

When the Democratic Convention was postponed from July to August, the tension eased. Sweet, as he said later, thought the prison break had been called off by its leaders who had got cold feet.

On August 12, just seventeen days before the Convention was to assemble in the Chicago Amphitheatre, Sweet received a letter from a lieutenant colonel, an old friend, commanding in Michigan. The colonel told him he had received a letter from a man in Canada who "represented himself to be a major in Confederate service." The writer of the letter expressed a desire to "reveal a dangerous plot" against Camp Douglas in return for being allowed to take the oath of allegiance and for a reward.

The Michigan colonel wrote he had thrown the letter into the wastepaper basket. A few days later a tall, thin man with a cadaverous face, dressed in torn regimentals and wearing a broad-brimmed hat and enormous jackboots, stamped into his office, "bringing his wares with him." He introduced himself as a major attached to Captain

Thomas H. Hines, in Toronto, Canada. He was willing to sell the plans for an attempted attack on Douglas for blood money.

The colonel refused. He told the major to return with more details. A few days later the major returned with the plans "and his budget." This time he had enough information to make the colonel's hair stand on end.

At the time the Michigan colonel wrote Sweet, he also sent off a dispatch to Headquarters, Northern Department. He enclosed a copy which reads:

> I have the honor to report that I have had another interview with the major—whose disclosures in relation to a Rebel plot for the release of prisoners of Camp Douglas I gave to you in my previous letter.
>
> I have caused inquiries to be made about him in Canada and understand that he does possess the confidence of the Rebel agents and that his statements are entitled to respect.
>
> He now informs me that he proceeded to Toronto, as he stated when he last saw me; that about a hundred picked men of the Rebel refugees in Canada are assembled there armed with revolvers and supplied with funds and tickets to Chicago. That he [the major] and the balance of the men are waiting for final instructions from Captain Hines, commander of the expedition; that Hines left Toronto last Thursday for Chicago and at this time is at Niagara Falls making final arrangements with the chief Rebel agents.
>
> The major says that the general plan [of the Confederates at Toronto] is to accomplish the release at Douglas of the prisoners, and in doing so they will be assisted by an armed organization in Chicago. After being released the prisoners will be armed, and being joined by that organization in Chicago, will be mounted and proceed to Camp Morton [at Indianapolis] and there accomplish a similar object in releasing the prisoners. That for months Rebel emissaries have been traveling through the Northwest; that their arrangements are fully matured; and that they expect to receive large accessions of forces from Ohio, Indiana and Illinois. They expect to destroy the works at Ironton.
>
> The major says further he is in hourly expectation of receiving instructions to proceed from Toronto to Chicago with the balance of the party; that he shall put up at the City Hotel, corner Lake and State Streets, and register his name as

George—that he will place himself in communication with
Colonel Sweet commanding Camp Douglas in Chicago. . . .

The mysterious major never arrived at the City Hotel. His story
ends here. There is no way of knowing what became of him. In 1865,
Sweet told a Chicago *Tribune* reporter in an interview that the major
had been "scared off or murdered by his comrades."

In 1933, the son of Captain Hines, then living in New York, said
in a private interview with Howard Swiggett that his father told him
he had trailed a traitor from Detroit to Niagara Falls and had hurled
him into the Falls. Although Hines, in his letters to friends in Kentucky, labeled as traitors Maughan, the bank clerk, and another Confederate officer, he does not mention the major.

In July, 1865, the *Atlantic Monthly* published an article on the Conspiracy, in which the writer went to great lengths to protect the
identity of the Confederate traitors who had worked for the Union.
In the margins of this article Hines carefully identified each man with
bitter comments on the roles they had played. Curiously, he does not
identify the major, nor does he comment on why he never appeared
again after leaving Toronto.

Castleman recalled a half-century later that several of the raiders
volunteered to murder "the traitors among us" on their way to Chicago, but Hines refused to allow this.

Hines' own accounting to Secretary of State Benjamin shows he
spent $13,600 on the Chicago conspiracy in August. Among the items
were: $3,000 for holsters and ammunition; $2,000 for board for four
hundred men [Copperhead leaders from Ohio and Indiana]; $2,000
for bribes for railroad employees who were to turn their trains over
to the raiders for the prison camp assaults; $3,000 for messengers who
daily delivered reports from Hines to Thompson in Canada; $3,000
for horses to be used for cavalry officers and troopers when they were
released from Douglas; $1,600 for railroad tickets; and $2,000 for
"raising the Irish in Chicago." Certainly this included many bottles
of Monongahela and Old Rifle whiskey.

On the eve of the Democratic Convention the first meeting between the Confederates and the Copperhead leaders took place in

Richmond House. The prospects for revolution were good. "One hundred thousand strangers packed the city from the cellar to the garret" as Ayer, the medicine vender Colonel Sweet used as a spy, reported.

For days men had poured into Chicago, hanging from the sides of trains, on foot, on horseback, in carriages and standing ten deep in the back of farm wagons. Men were sleeping four in a bed in the hotels and boarding-houses. As the night moved across the city, men who could not find lodging "loaded themselves with whiskey and slept in the gutters and alleys of the city." One reporter found ten men huddled together about a lantern under a sidewalk, loading revolvers.

But the stirring portents were wrong. Hines' heart sank as the Copperheads gathered in his suite. They seemed frightened and anxious and not at all like empire-builders who would stop at nothing to gain their ends.

When he asked if they were ready to set the zero hour, Walsh, the Chicago leader, and the others, said that "something has gone wrong." The men who had been ordered to notify the groups in Ohio and Indiana to be ready to strike on the morning of the convention had failed to carry out their instructions. No specific orders had been given.

As Hines realized, there were a hundred thousand Copperheads in the city, enough to take every garrison in the state. But without proper instructions and guidance they were only an aimless, bragging mob who could be dispersed by a company of trained soldiers.

Hines, Castleman and Grenfel were in a rage. But they could do nothing. Another meeting was set for the following morning. It must have been the longest night in his life for Hines, who had promised so much in that June report to Seddon. All his life he was able to conceal his emotions behind those icy blue eyes and sensitive, ascetic face. During that long night, watching the torchlight convention parade wind its way through the city, and waiting for word from Charles Walsh, the Copperhead leader who had promised so much, his gambler's nerves must have been stretched to the breaking point.

Then, as luck would have it, three thousand troops unexpectedly marched into the city, as a result of the pleas of Colonel Sweet, commandant of Camp Douglas. The Confederates were overjoyed. Emphasize to your men, Hines told Walsh and the others, that the troops are here not to arrest us, but to interfere with an orderly Democratic Convention.

"We emphasized that any arrest would mean violent interference with the rights of the people," Castleman wrote. "We knew that an arrest by the troops was our best hope and it mattered little who was arrested. In other words an inflammable mob might thus be led beyond retreat. . . ."

All night blue patrols rode through the streets. But although they could jeer and shout with alcoholic courage the Copperheads never raised a hand against a single trooper. The night passed. As dawn pinked the sagging chimney pots, Hines knew they had failed.

He made another attempt. On the afternoon of the 29th, the day the convention opened, he met with the Copperhead leaders again. When he asked about the attacks on Camp Douglas and Rock Island, which Castleman was to command, they bubbled excuses. "The excuses of our comrades made evident a hesitancy about the sacrifice of life," Hines wrote.

That night he called a last meeting. This time "familiar faces" were missing. The rats were leaving the sinking ship.

"Give me five hundred men and we will attack and capture Rock Island," he said.

Again came excuses.

"Give me two hundred," Hines cried. "Castleman will take a hundred on the nine o'clock train and lead them to the very gates. The garrison has less than a hundred troops. I will take the other hundred and attack the city. . . ."

The Copperheads listened as Hines slammed his fist down on a huge street map of Chicago. He would divide his men into squads of ten, cut the wires leading in and out of the city, destroy the bridges and capture the Federal arsenal. The troops from Rock Island could be equipped with the rifles in their camp. By midnight they would be marching on to Springfield. Hines said he proposed to keep one wire open to flash the word to Indiana, Ohio and Illinois and New York City.

By dawn the Northwest would be in flames. The grandiose plan, in the manner in which Hines presented it, fired the courage of the Copperheads momentarily. They promised to return with the men within a few hours. Surely out of a mob of a hundred thousand they could raise five hundred. Hines paced the floor like a caged animal until at last they appeared. They could raise only twenty-five.

The game was up, certainly for the time being. Hines gathered his squadron together to tell them the Copperheads had failed to rise. He told his men they were free to try to reach home. He would furnish funds for transportation and other expenses. If they wished they could accompany him on a tour through Ohio and Indiana. He would come back to fight another day. Twenty-four took the tickets back home. Grenfel left for Carlyle, Illinois, "to drill the Copperheads." Twenty-three voted to stay with Hines and Castleman. Hines made sure Maughan, the drunkard, stayed with him.

"Our comrades said 'Dead men tell no tales,' and offered to put Maughan in that class, but Captain Hines refused to let the drunkard be harmed. But we wanted him always under our eyes," Castleman recalled.

Before he left Chicago on the second day of the convention the Copperhead leaders told Hines they had prepared the formation of a new "military establishment" within their organizations, to be directed by Jim Barrett and Doctor Bowles.

"Positive action," they said, had been postponed to Election Day in November.

"We doubted this," wrote a sadder but wiser Captain Castleman.

Why did the uprising fail? Jefferson Davis had put his finger on part of the reason two years earlier when he had told Captain Longuemare that the Copperheads had no military leaders. Hines and the Richmond high command also failed to take into account that in the Middle West were men of intense patriotism and deep religious conviction like the father of Hamlin Garland, "son of the border." While an army of Copperheads looked impressive on paper, there were also as many families in the same region who had sons riding with Sheridan or Sherman. They best could understand what Rebecca West was to write more than eighty years later of another treason trial: that treason was the betrayal of that which is near to that which is far.

It has been said Aaron Burr attempted to bring about a revolution because he wanted power and money. The Confederate leaders had not the same singular goals. They did what they thought best for their neighbors. Some leaders of the Copperheads were doing what they believed to be right—Justice Bullitt of Kentucky, Dodd of Indiana, and Vallandigham himself—but there were many others who were consumed by greed.

Stidger, the Union spy, gives a hint of this. In his memoirs, he tells how Doctor Bowles, the Copperhead leader in Indiana, cursed when he heard the revolt had been postponed.

"Those s——o——b——'s," he cried. "It had better be soon, so I can make a dollar on all this!"

Hines was doing what he thought was best for his country. But instead of men fired by intense patriotism, he found most of the men with whom he was dealing to be plotting politicians. He had come to realize this in Chicago and wanted to create a mob incident to force the Copperheads into "a situation from which there could be no retreat."

As a combat officer and a veteran conspirator, Hines should have known the scheme was hopeless. His youth is his only excuse. With Commissioner Clay sick and useless, the major blame rests with the older Thompson, whose political and combat experience and service as a Cabinet member should have served as a counter-balance for Hines' youth, enthusiasm and fiery dreams.

However, because they realized that time was running out for the Confederacy in those bitter, closing months of 1864, Hines and the Confederate Commissioners in Canada were to use the Copperheads again and again in their desperate plots. It seemed better to count them as allies, even though some might be scoundrels, than to fight on alone against overwhelming odds. . . .

While Hines and his men were leaving Chicago, the Copperhead leaders were demonstrating they were stronger with the ballot than with the bullet. The field of four Presidential nominees was led by Major-General McClellan, the little Napoleon whose indecision before Richmond had caused Lincoln to sack him. However, he was still a national figure and a War Democrat. Governor Horatio Seymour of New York, a stronger figure, refused the nomination.

But it was the report of the committee drafting the planks for the party's platform that was eagerly awaited. Vallandigham was its chairman.

The convention opened on August 29, in the Chicago Amphitheatre. After routine business a recess was called until Tuesday noon to hear the decision of the platform committee meeting in the Richmond

House. All day Monday and into Tuesday morning, the committee shouted and argued, while, outside, thousands waited for the news.

Vallandigham was at his oratorical peak; his magnetic personality and bell-like voice dominated the meeting. Men later said he had hypnotized them. Vallandigham's Ohio delegates forced a peace platform down the committee's throat. On Tuesday it was read to the convention. There was no fight. Strangely enough, Sam Tilden of New York, leader of the War Democrats faction, did not stage a protest. After a ringing speech by Vallandigham the platform of "peace at any cost" was adopted.

McClellan was nominated. McClellan, the War Democrat who had said many times that the Union must be preserved at any cost, was now forced to run on a Copperhead peace party platform! Vallandigham's close friend, George H. Pendleton of Ohio, was the party's choice for Vice President.

On September 2, in Georgia, Sherman's pickets moved cautiously through the smoke to enter Atlanta. That afternoon the War Department's telegraph clicked in Washington, with Sherman's message: "Atlanta is ours—and fairly won."

Vallandigham's peace platform cracked. McClellan would fall to defeat. Lincoln had been right. Given enough rope, Vallandigham would ruin his party.

XIII. BALLOTS, IF NOT BULLETS

THE fiasco at Chicago had taught Captain Hines a bitter lesson: that until the secret Copperhead societies, [the Sons of Liberty and the Order of American Knights] had established a military department in their organizations, he could not expect armed assistance from them.

However, since the convention had demonstrated that the Copperheads were more adept at political maneuvering, Hines temporarily switched from violence to politics to further his plans for revolution.

The *Official Journal of the Confederate Mission* shows that after the Chicago failure a committee of Peace Democrats had called upon Commissioner Thompson, bearing a note from Vallandigham, who said it "was of the first importance to secure the election of Mr. Robinson as Governor of Illinois." To attain that goal, however, funds were needed.

In return for Thompson's support, Vallandigham promised that Robinson would turn over to the Confederates and the Sons of Liberty control of the militia and its sixty thousand stands of arms. Thompson, after a conference with Clay, informed the delegation that the money would be paid "whenever proper committees were set up by the State Democratic Central Committee." From Hines' notes it appears that a Chicago lawyer was appointed as chancellor of the exchequer.

Hines and Castleman were directed by Thompson to return to Chicago for an assessment of Robinson's political value. Both Hines and Castleman endorsed Robinson and urged that funds be sent into Illinois to assure his election. But by this time a small fortune had been spent on the Copperheads and Hines told Thompson that some sort of written guarantee should be obtained from Robinson before the gold was turned over to him.

A note among his papers, signed by Hines, reads:

> Robinson was Peace Democratic candidate for the Governor of Illinois. Application had been made to the Confederate Commissioners for funds to carry on the canvass. Desiring,

before giving pecuniary aid, some written evidence as to the course Mr. Robinson would pursue if elected, this letter was written to satisfy the Confederate Commissioners on that point. Verbal assurances from Mr. Robinson, fully committing himself to our movement had already been had. A large amount of money was furnished on these assurances.

In this letter a major political candidate guaranteed, if elected, to turn over his state and its arsenals to a secret movement supported by enemy money and led by enemy officers.

Robinson's letter, dated "Home" and sent just before Election Day, reads:

Gentlemen:

Your letter of inquiry came duly to hand and its contents noted.

In reply I would state that if I am elected governor of the state I will see that its sovereignty is maintained, the laws faithfully enforced and its citizens protected from arbitrary arrest, and if necessary for these purposes will, after exhausting the civil, employ military force of the state.

I will also be happy to avail myself of the counsel and aid of the Executive Committee of the Peace Democracy in the conduct of the organization of the militia of the state, recognizing the fact that a well-equipped militia is necessary for the maintenance of states' rights as well as the rights of the people.

Hoping that the Democracy may be successful in the great contest and that Constitutional liberty may again be reinstated in the full plenitude of her power, I remain,

Yours truly,

James C. Robinson.

The letter addressed to the Ohio and Indiana Copperhead leaders can best be described by Theodore Roosevelt's phrase, "weasel-worded." Robinson wrote this letter with much care. There is nothing incriminating in it, nothing a grand jury could use as "Exhibit A" in an indictment for treason.

But it had been sent to the known Copperhead leaders and Robinson spoke of availing himself of the Peace Democrats in organizing the state militia. For the Confederates that meant the Copperheads would have control of the state's Home Guards and the arsenals. Then again, Robinson had promised a great deal "verbally," though Hines by this time placed little confidence in their glowing promises. Hines and Castleman took Robinson's letter to Thompson, urging him to supply the Central Democratic Committee with unlimited funds.

Fifty thousand dollars in gold, the equivalent of one hundred and forty thousand dollars in the United States currency at the current rate of exchange, was turned over to James Barrett, Vallandigham's Grand Lecturer of the Sons of Liberty, and a Chicago lawyer for distribution throughout the "proper committees" in Illinois during the campaign.

Hines also turned over an additional twenty thousand dollars to Barrett and obtained a receipt. In Chicago, two days later, the Chicago lawyer was given an additional twenty thousand. Again he demanded and received a receipt. Ten thousand more was handed out in smaller amounts. Hines was careful about keeping receipts.

Of all the Peace Committees, the Central Democratic Committee of Illinois was the strongest. Hines, bitterly disgusted at the cowardice of the Sons of Liberty and Order of American Knights at Chicago during the convention, told Thompson it would be far wiser to turn over the Confederate gold to the Peace Democrats than to the fanatical Sons of Liberty or the Knights, some of whom were assuredly lining their own pockets. But Thompson stubbornly refused. He was still convinced the Sons and the Knights could produce a revolt.

"Hines and I were not entirely successful in inducing the Confederate Commissioners to realize that it would be far wiser to supply more funds to the Illinois State Democratic Committee than to the officials of the Sons of Liberty," Castleman later recalled.

XIV. TARGET: TRANSPORTS

IN THE fall of 1864, after the Chicago fiasco, Hines gathered his "squadron" to accomplish what he called "Military Direction." He had had some success with Vallandigham's forcing the convention to adopt the Peace Party platform. Now, Robinson had been bought and the "peace at any cost" campaign was in full flower in Illinois.

There was much to be done to create other troubled areas. Colonel Grenfel was in Carlyle, Illinois, "drilling the Copperheads." Jim Barrett sent word from St. Louis that the Federals had a large number of transports at the city wharf, barely guarded and ready for burning. Other agents sent word that the army warehouses at Mattoon, Illinois, were bulging with supplies.

Hines split his squadron in two; he took ten men, including young whiskey-loving Maughan, to Mattoon. Castleman led the others to Marshall, Illinois. From there Lieutenant George Eastin was sent out to inspect the transports at St. Louis. Twenty-four hours later he returned with the number of ships lying at the city wharf, between which streets, the names of the steamers, their cargo and probable sailings dates.

Castleman ordered his men to leave at once in pairs for St. Louis. They were to meet at the Olive Street Hotel. Upon his arrival he sent a coded message to Hines, who was busy burning Yankee warehouses at Mattoon. Later, with his men he began an inspection of the ships. There were seventy-three steamers at the wharf. Castleman made a list, assigning each man three to five steamers to be burned. For the next two days they walked casually about the ships, swapping plugs of tobacco with the guards or crew members, peering down hatches, and surreptitiously making mounds of wood chips, straw or hay so fires would kindle fast.

The absence of control over military installations by the provost marshals, which Hines and his raiders encountered time and again throughout the war, is amazing. Castleman says no one questioned them

137

as they strolled around the ships. As he said, "Citizens were not denied permission to go at will aboard the boats."

After luncheon they all gathered in Castleman's hotel room. Bottles of Greek fire were distributed. The zero hour was two P.M. One by one, at ten-minute intervals, they departed from the hotel. Castleman and Eastin were last.

Each man selected his ships, found the spot he had picked out and hurled the bottles of Greek fire. Some exploded, some didn't. There was no time to find out what had gone wrong. The explosives which were effective started flames. Wisps of smoke seeped through the seams of the ships. When hatch-ways were opened, crewmen were hurled back by the blasts.

From five to ten transports were destroyed or partially burned. St. Louis was in an uproar and troops were called in. But Castleman was disappointed. As he said, had they used a box "of old-fashioned matches" instead of the highly vaunted Greek fire which the Copperheads assured them they had perfected, "there would have been none of the seventy-three steamboats left on that day at the St. Louis wharf."

Meanwhile, Hines had sent word to Castleman to bring his men to Sullivan, Indiana, to meet the Indiana Copperhead leaders. Castleman ordered his men to leave the city singly. They were to take the train to Terre Haute, then change to the Evansville Road at Sullivan and meet at the railroad depot.

Meanwhile back in Mattoon, Maughan, the young bank clerk, thrilled with the part he had played in the burning of the Federal warehouses with Hines, had bragged too much in a saloon. The inevitable happened. Someone who had heard his story informed the provost marshal. Maughan was arrested and quickly confessed. Hines left Mattoon with the Federals on his heels.

Castleman was not so fortunate. He was the first to arrive at Sullivan, Indiana. Instead of his comrades he was greeted on the platform of the depot by detectives attached to Colonel Carrington, military commander of Indianapolis, who had been notified of the rendezvous by the Mattoon authorities. Carrington had a large dossier on Castleman, Hines and the Copperhead leaders working with them.

Castleman was taken under heavy guard to Indianapolis via Terre Haute. Hines and his crew, upon their arrival in Sullivan, heard of Castleman's arrest from their "friends." They set out in pursuit, determined to free their comrade at any cost.

At Terre Haute, Hines told his men to spread out across the platform. At his signal they were to shoot down the soldiers guarding Castleman, who was slowly pacing up and down, less than a hundred feet away.

Castleman was surrounded by a small crowd of curious onlookers when Hines arrived. One woman asked a guard the identity of the young and handsome prisoner. She almost swooned when he replied, "A dangerous Rebel, ma'am. He burned the steamers at St. Louis."

Castleman suddenly stopped pacing. He had seen the face of Tom Hines in the crowd. The Confederate agent was walking casually toward him. Following him were Eastin and the others. A train chugged in. The last three cars at the end of the platform began to discharge soldiers in blue. Hines and his men, intent on Castleman, didn't see them.

It was clear to Castleman what Hines intended to do. Within a few minutes they would be close enough to shoot down his guards. But what they didn't know was that a hundred Federal soldiers had unexpectedly appeared at the end of the platform, cutting off their retreat. If Hines fired, a hundred rifles would reply. Somehow he must warn them.

Castleman desperately searched the faces of onlookers for someone he could trust with a message for Hines. They stared back at him, blank, curious, laughing or sneering. He tried to whisper to a woman, but she snapped, "Rebel spy," and moved away. Castleman, all hope gone, was waiting "for the ball to open," as they said in those days, when a middle-aged man strolled up. He stopped, stared at Castleman, then said, "It is a terrible thing to see such a young man under arrest."

Castleman recalled that the man's face "instantly inspired confidence." He decided to take the long chance.

"I trust you with the lives of my comrades and beg you to take them a message," he whispered.

The man seemed startled but nodded, "You can trust me, lad."

Castleman nodded to Hines, who was approaching them. "Tell that man that I say go back, and go immediately."

The guard, suspicious of their whispering, had started to walk toward them when the man lifted his hat and walked off. As he reached Hines he took his arm, gave him Castleman's message, then moved off into the crowd. Hines stared for a long moment at Castleman, then turned abruptly to Eastin. They whispered together. In a few minutes they were gone.

In later years Castleman regretted he had not told Hines to follow him. Shortly after they had gone, he was put on another train under a small guard to be taken to Indianapolis. Hines, he said, could have captured the train before it entered the city, run it to the gates of Camp Morton, which had a small garrison, released the prisoners there, "and made at least an effort to accomplish serious results."

The following day Castleman entered the military prison at Indianapolis. But Hines had not given up hope of rescuing his captured comrade.

In Carlyle, Illinois, "a hovel of hogs and Hoosiers," the old soldier, Colonel Grenfel, was thinking of death. The great events he had predicted had fizzled. As he wrote from Carlyle to his daughter in London:

> It does not matter much; we all have got to live a certain time and when the time comes, what difference will it make whether I lived in London or Illinois? And whether I died in a four-post bed with a nurse and phials on the bed table, or whether I died in a ditch? Not that I think it necessary to make myself miserable, *bien au contraire.* . . .

XV. A LETTER FROM LINCOLN

UPON his arrival at the Federal prison in Indianapolis, Castleman was thrown into solitary confinement. His cell was seven foot square and windowless. A twelve-inch grating in the ceiling was the only ventilation. Overhead a guard paced twenty-four hours a day.

Castleman insisted his name was Clay Wilson, of St. Louis, Missouri. The provost marshal's men tore his jacket apart, to find in the shoulder seams maps of northern prison camps, the number of guards and prisoners, letters from Doctor Bowles, the Indiana Copperhead leader and orders from Captain Hines. Castleman still insisted he was Clay Wilson. He told his questioners a former Confederate officer had given him the jacket. He only shook his head when he was asked about Hines and Bowles.

A guard, bribed by Hines, smuggled a small saw in to Castleman, who began work on the three-inch oak floor of his cell. While the "friendly" guard was on watch, Castleman cut a trap-door under his cot. As in the case of the Columbus penitentiary, Castleman found a large air chamber underneath the floor of his cell. He dug a hole through the crumbling mortar of the foundation. He crawled out into the prison yard, only to find sentinels pacing the walls above him.

An alert captain of the guards spotted the saw marks in the floor under the cot. He asked Castleman for the saw, only to receive a shrug. His blankets and mattress were torn to bits. The saw was finally discovered in the lining of Castleman's overcoat.

He was questioned again and finally said, "I brought the saw in with me." Solitary confinement on a bread-and-water diet was his punishment.

On the outside, Hines was working feverishly trying to devise some way to break into the prison. One afternoon was spent in reconnoitering the walls with Eastin. Both men agreed there were too many guards to try to storm the gates.

Hines then decided to work from the inside of the prison. In Indianapolis he bought a Bible. The Copperheads furnished a "loyal" bookbinder and he worked all night—"from midnight to seven in the morning"—carefully taking the binding apart.

Then Hines produced thirteen small saws, made from the mainsprings of a watch. They were glued to one side of the cover along with a note advising Castleman to look on the other side. Three thousand dollars in bills of large denominations were glued to the other side. To call Castleman's attention to the saws and money, Hines un-

Courtesy, National Archives

A true copy of the "expense account" of Captain John Breckinridge Castleman, second in command to Captain Hines in Chicago, which was found sewn in the shoulder seam of his coat when he was captured at Sullivan.

Sept 1st Paid out

    To expense of transportation to Ca $700.00

1st   "   "   Cometees   800 —

10th   "   "Medicine"   150 —

10th Traveling expenses of Shultz, Maughan & Thorp   150.—

11th Additional expenses to Scull in C—a   50 —

11th   "   "   Offutt in J—a   700 —

11th   "   "   Stone Sampson —   400 —

11th To Col. Anderson   .   500 00

   " Shultz traveling expenses & Ca   100 —

13th   " Thomas   Special   do.   100 —

13th   " Ignacio   "   "   100 —

16th   " Shultz   "   "   100 —

    Traveling expenses of self from Ca from Chicago
    & to St Louis   150 —

Thomas alias
     Thomas Snyder
Ignatio
   J. Manael
Shultz
   S. J. Lewis

I certify that the foregoing is a true copy from memorandum book found on E. B. Castleman

              R. S. Burnett
              Judge Advocate D.O.T.M.D.

derlined the following passages in the 14th Chapter of St. John:

1. Let not your heart be troubled; believe in God, believe also in Me.
3. And if I go and prepare a place for you, I will come again and receive you unto Myself; that where I am, there ye may be also.
4. And whither I go, ye know the way.
13. And whatsoever ye shall ask in My name, that will I do, that the Father may be glorified in the Son.
14. And if ye shall ask anything in My name, that will I do.
18. I will not leave you comfortless; I will come to you.
19. Yet a little while and the world beholdeth Me no more; but ye behold Me; because I live, ye shall live also.

Hines sent the Bible to Castleman's mother in Lexington, Kentucky, with a note informing her of her son's arrest and asking her to deliver

If not called for in 5 days, return to
HINES & PORTER,
ATTORNEYS AT LAW
Bowling Green, Ky.

One of the 13 Saws furnished by T. H. Hines to Maj. John Breckenridge Castleman while confined in military prison at Indianapolis Ind. under Sentence of death, Oct 1864.

the Bible. Hines evidently did not mention what the Bible contained, fearful that Mrs. Castleman's nervousness might betray her.

Ten days after Castleman had been arrested, the prison commandant came to his cell.

"If a certain elderly lady has called to see you and says her name is Castleman, and that you are her son, what would you say?" he asked.

"I would say that no matter how extraordinary this statement made by the lady, I would not contradict it," Castleman replied.

A few minutes later Mrs. Castleman was embracing her son. The prison commandant stood in the entrance of the cell holding the Bible in one hand.

"Your mother has asked me to allow you to have this good book," he said. "I recommend its contents."

He placed the Bible containing the money and the saws on a table. "You will be allowed one hour," he said.

After his mother had gone, promising to return the next day, Castleman opened the Bible. As his mother had told him Tom Hines had sent it, he suspected that it contained more than the Great Words. He found the marked messages and recognized them as clues. That night in the light of a carefully shielded candle he took the Bible apart. At last the saws and money fell out on his bunk.

Castleman knew the futility of attempting to escape. The prison was smaller than the one at Columbus, Ohio, where Hines had made his celebrated tunnel, and there were more guards—some of whom refused to take Rebel gold.

The following day he said to his mother, "Mother, tell Hines he must not attempt to rescue me. I must not be the cause of sacrificing others. My love to Tom and tell him and the others I will take care of myself. . . ."

His mother promised she would give Hines his message. After a tearful goodbye, she left. She found Hines at his hideout and gave him the message. Later she saw her daughter, Virginia, and her son-in-law, the famous Judge Samuel Miller Breckinridge. The Breckinridges, like many families of Kentucky, had been split by the war. Sam Breckinridge was a Union man, and his uncle, the Reverend Robert J. Breckinridge, was one of the South's most loyal supporters.

The day after Mrs. Castleman's visit, Judge Breckinridge hired a young lawyer named Porter, later to become the Governor of Indiana, and United States Minister to Italy. After several interviews with Castleman and Colonel Carrington, Porter advised Judge Breckinridge that the young Confederate's case seemed hopeless. Governor Morton was determined to see him hanged to set an example for his Copperhead-infested state.

On November 29, 1864, Judge Breckinridge visited Washington to see his old friend Abe Lincoln. The President, weary and heartsick, welcomed an opportunity to talk of old times.

This was at eight o'clock. At nine forty-five, Lincoln pulled out a watch from his vest, glanced at it, and said, "Well, Sam, I have so much enjoyed your company, and I have been glad for the time to forget grave questions that beset the country."

He squinted at Breckinridge from under his bushy eyebrows. "But we seem to have forgotten the interest that brings you here. We seem to have forgotten young Castleman. Now, I have a Cabinet meeting in fifteen minutes, and I will give you now in the strictest confidence a note only to be used in the case of emergency. Meanwhile, from what I hear, it will be best for that boy's attorney to endeavor to postpone the trial, for those young Confederates have caused the government annoyance and expense."

Then Lincoln sat down and carefully wrote on the stationery of the Executive Mansion:

Washington, Nov. 29, 1864.

Major-General Hovey, or
Whoever may have charge:
at the proper time.
    Whenever John B. Castleman shall be tried, if convicted and sentenced, suspend execution until further order from me, and send me the record.

A. Lincoln

Courtesy of the J. B. Speed Art Museum, Louisville, Kentucky
The original, mentioned on page xx, was located just as this book went to press.

Letter by President Lincoln given to Castleman's uncle, who was pro-Union, to save Captain John Breckinridge Castleman from the gallows.

Thirteen years after the war, Judge Breckinridge gave Castleman Lincoln's letter after he had told him and Captain Hines the story.

Castleman went on trial before the Indiana Judge Advocate. The major-general commanding in Indianapolis forwarded fifteen charges and specific citations against Castleman to Washington, with the comment that the young Confederate officer had been associated with Hines "and is a young man of fine ability, a dangerous enemy and a daring spy."

Evidence found on Castleman when he had been arrested was presented. This included maps of Federal prison camps, lists of disloyal citizens in Ohio, Indiana and Illinois, letters and official orders from Thompson, receipts for money turned over to the Sons of Liberty in Illinois for Robinson's campaign, and papers showing that he and Hines had bargained and bought wheat in the Northwest, which they had hoped to smuggle through the lines to the starving armies of the Confederacy.

These amazing and daring young men could plot revolutions and the capture of whole cities, yet could overlook the obvious fact that documents of this nature, which could send them to the gallows, should be destroyed at once.

Castleman was charged with spying in Ohio, Indiana and Illinois, of attempting to "lay waste" the city of Chicago, of attempting to free the Rebel prisons in Camps Rock Island, Morton and Douglas, and acting in concert with Captain Hines and Jim Barrett, the Missouri Copperhead leader, in the burning of the steamboats at the city wharf in St. Louis. The government's principal witness was his former companion, John Maughan, the drunkard, whom Commissioner Thompson had insisted Hines include as one of his raiders.

There were several adjournments of Castleman's case. Before he went on trial he was exchanged, ordered to leave the country and never to return unless by Presidential pardon. Broken in health, filthy and unshaven from the northern dungeons, Castleman was exchanged at Fortress Monroe. There was almost a last-minute hitch in plans. Governor Morton of Indiana, informed that Castleman had been freed, ordered him returned for trial. However, the Army then sent him to Old Capitol Prison in Washington. A few days later he was returned to Fortress Monroe and ordered out of the country. He was escorted to Detroit, where he took a ferry to Windsor.

Two men waved to him as the ferry pulled in. They were Captain Tom Hines and Colonel Eastin.

XVI. THE INDIANA CONSPIRATORS

IN THE early fall of 1864, the plan of Captain Thomas H. Hines to bring revolution to the Northwest received its most severe blow. Carefully concealing the identity of his counter-spy, Felix Stidger, Colonel Carrington, Union commander at Indianapolis, in one swoop arrested H. H. Dodd, Doctor William A. Bowles, L. Milligan and other Copperhead leaders in the state.

Carrington made sure there were no leaks in his command. He gathered together a picked band of provost marshals and detectives, and at a melodramatic midnight meeting handed out the arrest warrants in sealed envelopes. In isolated farmhouses, secret hideouts and city flats men were taken from their beds. They were forced to listen in sleepy bewilderment as the warrants charging treason were read to them, then were hustled off to the military prison. More than thirty thousand rifles, revolvers and cans of powder were found under floors, in haystacks, and in graveyards.

Earlier, Phineas Wright, the treasonable editor of the New York *Daily News,* had been captured in the Russell House in Detroit, while waiting to cross to Windsor, Canada, to join the Confederates.

Colonel James Hardie, the Inspector General of the Northern Department, ordering his arrest, wrote the Chief of Staff:

> Wright is the New Orleans attorney and owner of a large plantation which has been confiscated by the government. He is connected with the notorious Captain Hines and the leading Confederates in Canada. This information comes from the loyal War Democrats. The order for Wright's arrest is directed to me by the President.

Wright was removed to Fort Lafayette, New York, to await trial there. Jim Barrett, Grand Commander of the Sons of Liberty of Missouri, also had been captured. He was taken to the military prison in St. Louis with some of his command to await a treason trial.

On September 17 the Military Commission met to try Bowles, Dodd

CHARGES AND SPECIFICATIONS

PREFERRED AGAINST

HARRISON H. DODD,

A CITIZEN OF THE STATE OF INDIANA, UNITED STATES OF AMERICA.

CHARGE FIRST.

Conspiracy against the Government of the United States.

SPECIFICATION FIRST.—In this, that the said Harrison H. Dodd, did, with William A. Bowles, of Indiana, Joshua F. Bullitt, of Kentucky, Richard Barrett, of the State of Missouri, and others, conspire against the Government and duly constituted authorities of the United States, and did join himself to, and secretly organize and disseminate, a secret Society or Order, known as the Order of American Knights, or Order of the Sons of Liberty, having a civil and military organization and jurisdiction, for the purpose of overthrowing the Government and duly constituted authorities of the United States. This at or near the City of Indianapolis, Indiana, on or about the 16th day of May, 1864.

SPECIFICATION SECOND.—In this, that the said Harrison H. Dodd, during an existing rebellion against the Government and authorities of the United States, said rebellion claiming to be in the name and on behalf of certain States, being a part of and owing allegiance to the United States, did combine and agree with one William A. Bowles, to adopt and impart to others the creed or ritual of a Secret Society or Order, known as the Order of American Knights, or Order of the Sons of Liberty, denying the authority of the United States to coerce to submission certain citizens of said United States, designing to lessen thereby the power and prevent the increase of the armies of the United States, and thereby did recognize and sustain the right of the citizens and States then in rebellion to disregard and resist the authority of the United States. This at or near the City of Indianapolis, Indiana, on or about the 16th day of May, 1864.

SPECIFICATION THIRD.—In this, that the said Harrison H. Dodd, then a citizen of the State of Indiana, owing true faith and allegiance to the Government of the United States, and while pretending to be a peaceful and loyal citizen of said Government, did secretly and covertly combine, agree, and conspire with one William A. Bowles, of the State of Indiana, Joshua F. Bullitt, of the State of Kentucky, Richard Barrett, of the State of Missouri, and others, to overthrow and render powerless the Government of the United States, and did in pursuance of said combination, agreement, and conspiracy with said parties form and organize a society or Order, and did assist in extending said Secret Order or organization, known as the Order of American Knights, or Order of the Sons of Liberty, whose intent and purpose was to cripple and render powerless the efforts of the Government of the United States in suppressing a then existing formidable rebellion against the Government of the United States. This on or about the 16th day of May, 1864, at or near the City of Indianapolis, Indiana.

SPECIFICATION FOURTH.—In this, that the said Harrison H. Dodd did conspire and agree with William A. Bowles, David T. Yeagle, L. P. Milligan, Andrew Humphreys, John C. Walker, and J. F. Bullitt,—these men at that time holding military positions and rank in a certain Secret Society or organization known as the Order of American Knights, or Order of the Sons of Liberty,—to seize by force, the United States and State Arsenals, at Indianapolis, Indiana, and Columbus, Ohio; to release, by force, the rebel prisoners held by the authorities of the United States, at Camp Douglas, Illinois; Camp Morton, Indiana; and Camp Chase, Ohio; and at the Depot of Prisoners of War, on Johnson's Island; and to arm those prisoners with the arms thus seized; that then said conspirators, with all the forces they were able to raise from the Secret Order above named, were, in conjunction with the rebel prisoners thus released and armed, to march into Kentucky, and co-operate with the rebel forces to be sent to that State by the rebel authorities, against the Government and authorities of the United States. This on or about the 20th day of July, 1864, at or near the City of Chicago, Illinois.

Courtesy, National Archives

First page of the charges and specifications against Harrison H. Dodd.

and the others. A postponement was granted until October. In the meantime Dodd demonstrated that he was still a power in Indiana politics. He objected to remaining in jail and was permitted to occupy a room on the second floor of the Indianapolis post office building.

Mrs. Bowles, after her husband's arrest, proved to be quite a Tartar. The commandant of the military prison at Indianapolis later told how she bustled into his office, demanding to see her husband. He tried to tell her that a pass from Carrington's office was necessary. Mrs. Bowles, after berating him, went out to obtain the pass. She returned with the pass and a package. The commandant asked to search the package. She refused. He managed to twist it out of her hands and untied it. Shiny new bowie knives spilled out on his desk.

"When I had made this discovery, she insulted me in a contemptuous snarling manner, using quite insulting language," the captain wrote to his superiors.

Mrs. Bowles was an endless source of trouble to the captain. When next she returned he was again forced to take a package from her.

"It's only newspapers," she cried.

"We'll see about that," the captain said grimly.

He opened the package to find stacks of Federal dollars, a total of twelve hundred and fifty dollars, which, the captain reported, he was sure was to be used to bribe the guards in an escape plot.

Even in jail Bowles was arming his secret organization and planning revolution. A much-folded scrap of paper smuggled into his cell, signed by an undecipherable name, with several hieroglyphics resembling ancient Egyptian, told him the movement was still working for insurrection despite the arrests. It read:

> The revolvers have all been distributed. Our Society meets tonight here. Great excitement prevails over your arrest. Shall I distribute the balance of the revolvers and rifles to Davis and Granger? Some of our men here are not supplied as yet. I think you should supply them at once. . . .

The Indianapolis trials opened in early October. Bowles, Dodd, Milligan and the others entered the court room with swaggering arrogance. The room was packed with their friends, all hostile to the Commission. Outside, soldiers stood guard, their bayonets keeping at bay the hundreds who milled about, "shouting that Bowles and Dodd and the rest must be freed or they would have their vengeance."

The military tribunal was sworn and took their seats. The first wit-

ABOVE: Clement L. Vallandigham, Grand Commander of the Sons of Liberty, a Copperhead organization.

BELOW: Acting Master John Yates Beall, a Confederate naval hero, who tried to take the U.S.S. *Michigan.*

The U.S.S. *Michigan,* the sole Federal gunboat on Lake Erie guarding the northern lake cities in 1864.

Lieutenant Bennett H. Young, taken after he and his raiders had robbed three St. Albans banks.

A view of the crowded prison yard of Camp Douglas, Chicago, the center of the Northwest revolution mapped out by Captain Hines.

James Shanks, who betrayed Hines' plan for an uprising in Chicago to Colonel Sweet of Camp Douglas.

Rock Island prison camp, one of the primary targets of Captain Hines and his raiders in the revolt which was to take place in August, 1864.

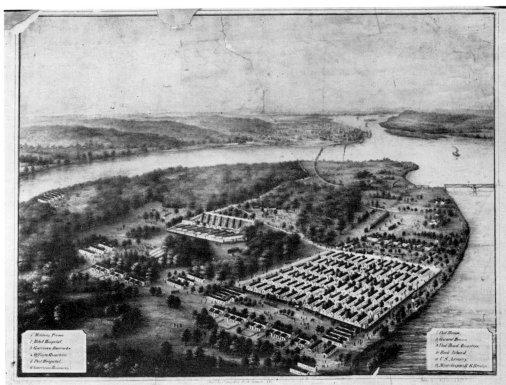

ROCK ISLAND BARRACKS, ILL.

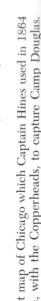

A street map of Chicago which Captain Hines used in 1864 to plan, with the Copperheads, to capture Camp Douglas.

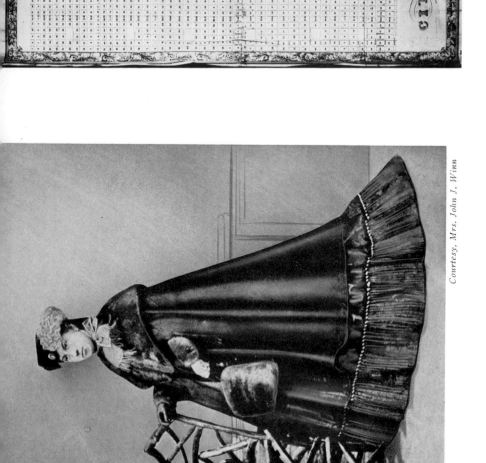

Nancy Sproule Hines, taken in Toronto, where she joined her husband. The dress may have been her bridal grown.

ness shook the courtroom. He was Felix Stidger, former Grand Secretary of the Sons of Liberty, and second in command only to Bowles.

Dodd and Bowles went white to the lips. Stidger testified for two hours. A recess was taken until the next day.

The following morning the Judge Advocate rose to announce to the court that Dodd had escaped at four o'clock by sliding down to the ground from the second floor by means of a rope "furnished by his immediate friends."

By eleven o'clock his description had been sent across the country to all military commanders and provost marshals, with particular attention to Detroit, where it was feared he would try to cross to Canada and join Hines. He was described as "six feet high, weight 180 pounds, eyes blue, and speaks with a fine address."

The official report of the commandant of the post office disclosed that a ball of heavy twine had been smuggled into Dodd's room a few hours after he had returned from hearing Stidger's opening testimony. It was obvious that he and his friends knew the game was up. Dodd had let out the cord to draw up a heavy rope which he attached to his bed.

It is clear that Dodd's escape was arranged with those in high places who feared that Dodd, shocked by Stidger's appearance, might try to turn government witness and name other high Democratic leaders not yet drawn into the net.

There is no doubt bribery played a big part in the escape. Consider the ease with which he got out. First of all, he had been released from confinement in a military prison to be transferred to a room in the post office because it "was understood he would make no attempt to escape, and "had given his word not to" as the commandant's report had it. The street lights, which had been darkened fully an hour before Dodd got away, showed further evidence of outside aid. Yet no one, officers or guards, had had enough curiosity to ascertain the reason. His escape touched off an uproar through the state. The War Democrats charged the Peace Democrats with setting Dodd free; the Peace Democrats charged Colonel Carrington and Governor Morton with a plot to destroy the party before the coming elections.

Meanwhile Dodd made his leisurely way north. Despite the telegraphed alert, no great effort was made to capture him. There is evidence that somewhere along the way he met Hines and together they tried to put together the now leaderless army of the Sons of Liberty.

"Dodd met with Hines, alias Doctor Hunter of the Rebel Army, after he escaped, but they eluded my detectives," Carrington reported to Staff Headquarters.

On October 21, Bowles, Milligan and the others went on trial, with Dodd tried *in absentia*. Fifty-two witnesses, the most important being Stidger, testified against them. The military tribunal found them guilty. They were to be executed by hanging.

Gallows were erected on the parade ground of Camp Chase. The state bubbled with excitement. Riders of the Sons of Liberty galloped along roads and lanes, calling the faithful to arms. Men drilled openly in the yards of schoolhouses, behind churches or on village greens.

As Carrington reported, "The state is ripe for revolution." Carrington and even Governor Morton and Democrats of both factions sent telegrams to Seward and Stanton, predicting that widespread rioting and bloodshed would follow the hangings.

Meanwhile Hines was traveling through the state, slipping with ease out of the traps set for him by the blue patrols and Carrington's detectives. He knew the state was ready for insurrection. If Bowles, Milligan and the others died on the gallows, the flames of revolt in Indiana might set the whole Northwest afire. Hines worked feverishly, talking to leaders of the Castles throughout the state, distributing arms and gold for more arms. It was a dangerous and fateful hour.

But at the eleventh hour, Washington acted. The death sentences were commuted to life imprisonment and order slowly returned to the state.

XVII. THE BATTLE OF LAKE ERIE

A T TIMES it is almost impossible to keep up with Captain Hines. One week he is writing from "somewhere in central Illinois," when we discover a letter written by a man from Toronto casually mentioning that he had just waved to Commissioner Clay, who was walking to the depot with Captain Hines. Hines suddenly appears in Chicago. A week later he is roaming in the backwoods of Kentucky organizing the guerrillas there for a new thrust across the Ohio.

And during this period Hines was also courting Nancy Sproule in Brown's Lock. It is fascinating to consider how one of the most wanted men in America, with a price on his head, was able to court his sweetheart despite the Union patrols, the provost marshal's men, particularly in Kentucky, who had his description, and the traitors, who were always ready to betray him. In one of Nancy's letters there is a hint that Tom had seen her briefly the night before, only to ride off in the darkness after a few moments with his usual farewell—"Goodbye, my darling. . . ."

Hines conferred with many people, moving about the Northwest in strange disguises. But though he could not remain at his headquarters in Toronto, he kept in touch with Thompson about the officers arriving in Canada to serve in the Northwest Conspiracy.

He was in Illinois when Acting Master of the Confederate Navy John Yates Beall, a slender, almost emaciated man of twenty-eight, dressed in black broadcloth and wearing a string tie, arrived at the Queen's Hotel to establish Hines' command on sea as well as on land.

Beall had brought with him to Toronto a plan to capture the U.S.S. *Michigan*, the only gunboat on the lakes, raze the lake cities and storm the Johnson's Island prison. This was not a new plan; it was on Hines' agenda, but the Chicago and Northwest uprising had priority. When Thompson wrote that Beall was begging to put his plan into action, Hines gave his hearty approval. Beall, a University of Virgina student, first served under Stonewall Jackson in the Shenandoah Val-

153

ley campaign of 1862. Badly wounded, he was invalided out of the army. Tuberculosis had already infected one lung.

Beall refused to die in bed. Instead he went to Richmond to lay before Secretary of Navy Mallory the wild scheme which he had spun in his mind during the long days of his convalescence. But the Confederate high command in 1862 was not ready to set into motion the Northwest Conspiracy. Mallory called the scheme "feasible" but ordered it shelved. Capture of the *Michigan,* he told Beall, might embroil the Confederacy with Great Britain.

Beall then asked to be allowed to carry out privateering on Chesapeake Bay. Richmond was still ringing with the exploits of Colonel Zarvona, the famous "French Lady" of the Civil War, who had led several successful attacks on Federal steamers in the Bay while dressed as a woman. The sale of the prizes had netted Richmond several thousand dollars. Mallory told Beall to go ahead with his plan. He commissioned Beall a Master of Privateering and gave him his blessing, but nothing more.

A few weeks later Beall met Bennett G. Burley, a giant Scot, and John Maxwell, a wiry little Highlander. They became his first recruits. By April, 1863, Beall had ten escaped prisoners, young adventurers and seamen without ships. In June, Beall led his motley band in a . guerrilla campaign which warmed the heart of that master guerrilla fighter, Tom Hines.

In July they cut the United States cable to the Eastern Shore of Virginia. In August they blew up the Federal lighthouse on Smith Island. In the first week of September they captured two small sloops. The one painted black was called the *Raven,* the white one the *Swan.*

On September 17, the raiders put out into Chesapeake Bay from Horn Harbor. Beall commanded the *Swan,* Burley the *Raven.* At Raccoon Island they captured two fishing schooners and a sloop. The *Alliance,* a large supply sloop carrying supplies for the Federal garrison at Port Royal, South Carolina, was next taken in a raging storm. A heavy sea was running when the *Raven* and the *Swan* closed in. Grappling hooks flew through the air and Beall and his men swarmed aboard the sloop.

Three more large schooners were taken in the next two days. The captured ships were sent to Richmond with prize crews. Beall and Burley remained aboard the *Alliance,* now their flagship, hidden near the mouth of the Plankatank River, where the French Lady had made his fabulous catches two years before.

In the last week of September Federal gunboats found the *Alliance* and attacked. Beall set her afire after saving ten thousand dollars' worth of Federal stores, which he sent on to Richmond for the Confederate Army.

Beall's escape shook the Navy Department in Washington. On October 1, 1863, Army and Navy forces opened a combined operation to wipe out Beall's tiny command.

On October 5, the Fourth U. S. Colored Regiment, with detachments of four hundred artillery men, and cavalrymen from New York and Pennsylvania regiments, left Yorktown. The infantry and artillery took positions at the mouth of Mathews County, while the cavalry, guided by local "Union men," made a sweeping reconnaissance. Six Navy and five Army gunboats shut off all avenues of escape by water from the Peninsula between Mojack Bay and the Plankatank River. But Beall and his command, like Marion's men, vanished into the deep swamps. Only three officers were captured.

In retaliation, the Army commanders ordered their troops to burn the homes of the natives who had befriended Beall. The colored troops left the countryside in ashes, leaving behind a legacy of hate.

The Burley Papers, National Archives, contain the report to the War Department of that raid. One hundred and fifty small boats and schooners were destroyed. But the *Raven* and the *Swan*, hidden deep in the swamps, had escaped the torch.

For a month Beall and his men were quiet. Then on November 1, the *Raven* and the *Swan* suddenly sailed out of the swamps to skim across Chesapeake Bay again, the Stars and Bars of the Confederacy stiff in the fall wind.

In Tangiet Inlet on the Eastern Shore, they found a large Federal schooner and took her as a prize. Beall remained on board while Burley and Maxwell, on the *Raven* and the *Swan*, searched the Bay for "more bait." One of his officers was captured, and in return for a light sentence, betrayed Beall's hiding place.

The first Eastern Shore Maryland Volunteers in a makeshift armada of pungies, canoes and sloops attacked Beall's port, capturing him and all his followers. General Henry H. Lockwood, in a dispatch to Washington, called it a "highly important arrest."

On November 21, 1863, Beall and his men were indicted as pirates and placed on trial. Richmond immediately took retaliatory measures. Fifteen Federal officers were selected as hostages and put in chains. Washington reversed its ruling and ordered them exchanged.

Beall returned to Richmond, to be given a hero's welcome. As the
lion of the hour, he beseiged Mallory with requests to allow him to
try to capture the *Michigan*, but the Secretary of the Navy put him
off. Restless and in constant pain from the bullet in his side, Beall rejoined the Confederate Army, enlisting in the engineers' corps.

News of Hines' exploits began to filter back into Richmond. Beall
saw an opportunity to put his plan of capturing the *Michigan* into
operation. He resigned from the engineers' corps and made his way
through the Union lines to Detroit. From there he took the ferry to
Windsor, and a train to Toronto, where he found Thompson and outlined his plan.

A few days before Beall's arrival, a Captain Charles Cole, who had
ridden with Morgan and later with Forrest, joined Hines to volunteer
his services. Thompson accepted him, assigning him to Beall. Captain
Cole and Beall met Hines at Sandusky, Ohio. Awaiting their arrival
was another officer, Lieutenant Bennett Young, whom the citizens of
St. Albans, Vermont, would never forget.

Cole, Beall and Young made a two-week reconnaissance of the
U.S.S. *Michigan* and the lake area protected by her fourteen guns.
Cole's report to Thompson, approved by Hines, reads in part:

> Buffalo is poorly protected. There is only one regiment and
> a battalion of invalids. The regiment is at Camp Morgan op-
> posite Fort Huron and between north and south Buffalo and
> the battalion is doing hospital duty and guarding the stores.
> There is a very large amount of government stores there, a
> large quantity of ammunition in U. S. arsenal also some can-
> non, mortar and small arms. The arsenal is situated on Oak St.
> I left for Cleveland and on the passage met a gentleman who
> would be of benefit to our cause at Chicago. He assisted me
> materially in Cleveland and took me around the government
> works and introduced me to the foremen of the cannon shops
> who told me there were about 250 men employed there, and
> that they were shipping large cannons to Sandusky, Mil-
> waukee and Chicago, with 100 rounds of ammunition to each
> gun. I learned the bearings of the lake around Cleveland.
> I met the engineer of the Pacific, who I think money can in-
> fluence. I left for Detroit with him. From Detroit I went to
> Chicago.
>
> I ascertained there the water needed for crossing the bars,
> and the amount of tonnage of the tugs, which would be most
> serviceable in time of need. The new steam tugs are of, say

175 tons, 1 screw engine, and are capable for carrying coal for 36-hour runs; will mount two guns, one large gun at the stern and a small field piece at the bow; are easily managed and will make ten knots an hour even in the severest weather. There is little difficulty in bringing vessels to bear against Camp Douglas. We can run the tugs up the river, and an armed vessel on the lake, bringing guns to bear on the camp. There is an immense amount of shipping and among the first things would be to destroy the different drawbridges, and then the whole city is accessible by water. Milwaukee is an easy place to take possession of. They have no fort and 12 feet of water up to the first drawbridge. The Milwaukee and Detroit steamers are below the first drawbridge; there is a great amount of grain shipment and quantities of coal. Sheboygan supplies all the country from Fond du Lac, sends grain and produce there for shipment. Port Washington is a small settlement with little of advantage, but its people are strong friends, and determined in their resistance to the draft. Mackinaw has natural fortifications, and mounted at the observatory are three guns bearing on the straits. Lake Erie supplies a splendid field for operations. Erie is a difficult place to get at, more so than any city on the lake. I made the acquaintance of Captain Carter, commanding the U.S.S. *Michigan.*

Now a new figure had appeared at Thompson's side in Toronto. He was a quiet, well-dressed man with a nasal twang. He claimed to have escaped from Johnson's Island in 1863. He was less obnoxious than Sanders, but Hines had the uneasy feeling they were brothers under the skin. The stranger's name was Godfrey J. Hyams, of Arkansas.

The Confederate agent warned Thompson to be careful not to confide too much in Hyams, but Thompson waved his warning aside. Hines and the rest of his raiders would always regret they had not disposed of Hyams.

A meeting was held in September, 1864, at Toronto to plot the capture of the *Michigan.* Hyams was present. It was agreed that Cole was to lay the groundwork of the raid by bribery. It seems almost too melodramatic to say that drugged champagne was to be served to the captain and officers at a private dinner party the night of the raid.

Beall and twenty men were to seize the *Philo Parsons,* one of the largest steamboats on the lake. Passengers and crew were to be put ashore. The *Parsons* would then continue along her usual route until she reached Middle Bass Island. With the captain and officers drugged, Cole would shoot off a rocket from the bridge of the gunboat *Michigan* as a signal to the *Parsons* to steam up. The rocket would also announce to the Johnson's Island prisoners that the *Michigan* was in Confederate hands. Armed with rifles and guns smuggled in by bribed guards, they were to storm the prison gates, protected by the *Michigan's* booming guns. The escaped prisoners would march on Sandusky, capture the Federal arsenal there and "form a nucleus of an army, which could be used for greater things," as Thompson put it in his report.

Cole set up his headquarters in the West House in Sandusky. He played the part of a young Philadelphia banker with inexhaustible funds. Through a young woman in town he managed to be formally introduced to Captain Carter of the *Michigan.* Night after night in the barroom of the hotel, Cole listened sympathetically to Carter's denunciation of the Navy Department's brass and its lack of appreciation of his naval talents. Through Carter, Cole also met the *Michigan's* officer. There were rousing parties in the hotel. As Cole said in one of his letters, "sumptuous dinners, dispensed with the choicest wines."

Carter repaid the lavish dinners with repeated invitations for Cole to spend an evening aboard the *Michigan.* Cole at first refused, then seemingly allowed himself to be coaxed. The Confederate was soon a daily visitor aboard the gunboat. He never failed to bring along a box of fine "segars" or a bottle of champagne.

When Cole discovered that Captain Carter knew the commandant of Johnson's Island he hinted he would like to see the prison. Carter was only too glad to introduce his free-spending young friend to his Army friend.

Cole now divided his time between visiting the *Michigan* and Johnson's Island. The prison commandant was soon receiving gifts of cigars and fine wine or champagne. It wasn't long before he took Cole on a personally guided tour of the Rebel camp.

One can only guess the shock Morgan's men received as they saw Cole, once a Morgan captain, strolling casually about the prison yard, arm in arm with the Yankee commandant. Cole cultivated the prison camp commandant until he was allowed freedom of the camp. During the day he lunched with the ship's captain. In the afternoon he would go to the camp. After a few weeks the guards paid little attention to him. Soon the "dangerous Rebel officers" were receiving cigars and lectures on Abolition from the bearded young man who said he was a Philadelphia banker. It is strange the guards never noticed the prisoners failed to smoke their fine cigars immediately. Messages on tiny slips of paper were first removed. In this fashion Cole outlined to the officers the plan of attack.

Cole was also busy in other fields. Evidently he had been put in touch with a new Ohio Copperhead society called "Order of the Star." The secret symbol of the order was a pair of small stars of the kind worn by Confederate generals. The leaders of the society claimed that Stonewall Jackson had begun the movement, but that is nonsense.

Several of the order's leaders were influential people in Sandusky. Soon Captain Carter and his young Philadelphia banker friend were invited to balls and private parties.

Cole had done his part; now Beall did his. Burley, who had followed Beall north, joined his old commander. Thompson commissioned him an acting master and appointed him second in command to Beall.

Twenty-eight seamen, one a gunner, were recruited. Beall furnished each man with a new suit, a Navy Colt, ammunition and twenty-five dollars apiece. On Sunday night, the 18th, Burley took passage on the *Philo Parsons* at Detroit. He asked the captain if the steamboat stopped at Sandwich, a small town on the Canadian side of Lake Erie. The owner said it did not, but that he would make an exception. They arrived there in the evening. Beall and another raider came aboard.

Amherstburg was the next stop at nine o'clock of the 19th. A number of men carrying an old trunk came aboard. At four o'clock the steamer reached Kelly's Island. It was there Beall took over the ship.

He slipped into the wheelhouse, drew a Colt, and, according to the first mate shouted, "This is a prize ship of the Confederacy."

The mate gave him a stunned look. "Are you men Rebels?" he asked.

"We are, sir," was the prompt reply, "and you are our prisoner."

The mate, with a gun pressed in his back, ordered the helmsman to surrender the wheel to one of the raiders.

"Sit there in that chair," Beall told the mate. "And in a while you'll soon see fireworks."

The mate and the helmsman took chairs at one side of the wheelhouse while the *Philo Parsons* continued on her placid journey down the lake. It was a clear, crisp night. A full moon turned the water into molten silver through which the *Philo Parsons* left a bubbling phosphorescent wake.

Beall left Burley at the wheel, and another Confederate with a gun watching the mate and the crewmen. He led the rest of his band down from the bridge to the salon. The passengers were mostly women, who screamed when the Confederates poured into the room with drawn Colts. One man started to raise a chair but was sent sprawling. When quiet was restored, Beall stood on a chair to make a gallant speech for the ladies.

"You need not fear us," he said. "We are Confederate soldiers and gentlemen. We will treat you as our own sisters." But two of his "sisters" apparently didn't trust him and promptly fainted.

The ladies revived, Beall and his men cleared the decks for action by pushing the bales and boxes of freight overboard. The mate later testified Beall robbed the cash box. One account makes the amount eighty thousand dollars but the mate later testified it was only eighty.

The *Philo Parsons* steamed through the night for Middle Bass Island, the Confederates sprawled about the decks, armed with revolvers and rifles and grappling hooks. Soon the *Island Queen*, one of the largest steamboats on the Sandusky-Detroit run, was sighted.

On Beall's orders Burley swung the wheel hard. The *Philo Parsons* cut across the *Queen*'s bow. Signals sounded in the engine room, paddles reversed. The *Parsons* made a wide circle, then came in from the port side. The grappling hooks flew through the air, biting into the wooden decks. The Confederates pulled hard and both steamers slammed together.

Beall, Navy Colt in one hand, led his crew aboard the *Island Queen*. In a matter of moments he had kicked in the door of the wheelhouse.

"This ship is a prize of the Confederate States of America," he cried. "I warn you not to resist."

The *Queen*'s captain, enjoying a last pipe for the night, and the helmsman stared down at the big Colt.

"The ship is yours," the captain said.

The *Queen* had an unexpected cargo. Thirty-five privates and officers of the 130th Ohio Infantry Regiment, all unarmed, on their way home to Toledo, were aboard. Beall and ten men herded them below decks, announcing to the officers that they were now prisoners of war. The odds were in favor of the Federals, but there is no record that any of them attempted to rush the Confederates.

Beall piloted the *Queen* to the United States side of the lake and there he set the soldiers ashore, putting them "on parole." Neither Beall nor the witnesses who testified later gave any details of how this was accomplished, but it is a wonderful picture to visualize: Beall standing on the ladder in the smoky hold, his men perched on bales and boxes holding their rifles, and the captured infantrymen and officers raising their hands and swearing they would never again carry a rifle for the Union.

The *Queen* was then taken to the middle of the lake where she was scuttled and sunk. The cruise continued on the *Philo Parsons*.

At eleven o'clock they reached Middle Bass Island. Half a mile away they could make out the faint lights of the *Michigan* at her anchorage off Johnson's Island.

An hour ticked away. Eyes searched the night. There were no rockets from the *Michigan*. It was evident they had been betrayed. On deck the Confederates began to whisper uneasily among themselves. At last they approached the wheelhouse.

"Get back to your posts," Beall ordered.

"We can't, sir," one of them said. "It's too late."

"What do you mean?" Beall shouted.

"There won't be any rockets. We've been betrayed," a voice said out of the shadows. "To go on means suicide."

"Signal the engine room, John," Beall told Burley. "We'll attack the *Michigan*."

"Then I'm leaving," the ringleader said.

"And me," one added.

"Me, too," another said.

There was a taut silence. The uneasy stirring of the men, the slapping of the water against the sides of the steamer, were loud in the stillness.

"You men refuse to go on?" Beall asked in a voice tight with rage. Voices answered him from the shadows.

"It would be suicide. . . ."

"Turn back, captain. We'll try again. . . ."

The voices died again. "Very well," Beall replied. "We will turn back." He paused. "But I command each one of you to sign a memoir of your treachery and cowardice! Follow me!"

Beall stepped into the ladies' cabin. A lamp was lit. His men whispered uneasily among themselves as they watched their captain, his face pale in the smoking light, scrawl something across the back of a bill of lading. When he was finished, Beall handed the pen to the nearest man.

"Sign your name," he snapped.

The first man stared down at what Beall had written. He read:

> On Board the *Philo Parsons,*
> September 20, 1864.
>
> We, the undersigned crew of the boat aforesaid, take pleasure in expressing our admiration of the gentlemanly bearing, skill, and courage of Captain Beall as a commanding officer and a gentleman, but believing and being well convinced that the enemy is informed of our approach, and is so well prepared that we cannot possibly make it a success, and having already captured two boats, we respectfully decline to prosecute it any further.

Beall later said he never thought his men would sign it. But they did. One by one they bent down under the swinging lantern to sign their names. When it was all over, Beall ordered the steamboat turned back, abandoned and set afire. From the Canadian side in the gray dawn, Beall watched her slowly settle. When the water reached her boilers a dull noise rumbled across the lake. Then with a final upward thrust, in her death agony, she turned over and sank. The fiery glow winked out and the morning mists closed in.

"Bitter, bitter defeat," Beall wrote.

At the turn of the century, Captain Hines loaned Castleman his papers, diaries and memoirs. Among them Castleman found Beall's "cowardice memorial" with the scrawled signatures of his men. Hines, most of all, must have known Beall's bitterness that lonely morning on the Canadian shore as he watched his flagship sink.

Hines tells us what happened to Captain Cole. Just about the time that the *Philo Parsons* was steaming toward Middle Bass Island, servants of the Sandusky Hotel were preparing a sumptuous dinner in the wardroom of the U.S.S. *Michigan* in honor of the captain and his officers. Captain Cole, of course, was footing the bill. At each place there was a slender glass filled with bubbling—and drugged—champagne. There were boxes of cigars and assorted fruits. Brandy was to be served later.

In his hotel room, Cole had just finished dressing. Under his vest was a loaded revolver. A servant had just reported he had delivered the message to "his friend on West Street." "The gentleman said he would see you this evening," the servant had said.

The reply had come from the leader of the Copperheads. When eight thousand Confederate prisoners stormed the walls of Johnson's Island, the men of the Order of the Star would attack it from the outside.

The drugged champagne would take care of the captain and officers

ARREST OF MAJOR COLE
AT THE BANQUET ON BOARD
THE "MICHIGAN"—

Courtesy, Chicago Historical Society

Newspaper sketch of the arrest of Captain Cole, who plotted to capture the U.S.S. *Michigan,* the only Federal gunboat patrolling Lake Erie, by serving drugged champagne to her captain and her officers. Cole was arrested in his hotel room, not on board the *Michigan,* as pictured above.

of the *Michigan*. Beall and his men would take her easily. By dawn, Cole told himself, a Confederate army would be burning the lake cities of the United States.

There was a knock on the door. Before he could call out an invitation to come in, the door was kicked open. A Federal lieutenant and five soldiers, with rifles, and the hotel clerk walked in.

"Are you Captain Cole?" the Federal officer asked.

"Yes, I am," Cole replied with a sinking heart.

"You are under arrest," the Federal officer said. "You must come with me."

"On what charge, sir?" Cole asked, wondering who had betrayed him, what had gone wrong at the moment of victory.

"Treason," was the reply.

Cole was taken to the provost marshal's office in Sandusky. A short time later an outraged Captain Carter of the *Michigan* identified him as the man who had posed as a Philadelphia banker. Cole made "verbal admissions" but refused to sign a written confession. He was charged with twelve specific acts of treason. Receipts in Hines' papers show he and Castleman hired counsel and supplied Cole with funds.

Cole was transferred from Sandusky to Federal prisons in Cincinnati and Columbus, and finally to Fort Lafayette in New York Harbor. He was found guilty by a court-martial headed by General John A. Dix, commanding New York, and sentenced to hang.

In the shadow of the noose he broke down and in his dungeon Cole signed a confession, took the amnesty oath and was released. He was never seen again.

The Lake Erie expedition had not been a complete failure. The engineer bribed by Cole had wrecked the engine room of the gunboat. The news that Confederate privateers were on the lakes made Buffalo and the other large cities shiver with fear. Church bells summoned the Home Guards. General Dix, commanding New York, was forced to divert to the north, to protect the lake cities, troops and cavalry units needed in the field.

In Toronto, Commissioner Thompson acted promptly to take advantage of the North's panic. The two newest recruits for Hines, Lieutenant John W. Headley and Colonel Robert Martin, both of Morgan's old command, along with Beall, were ordered to buy a large lake steamer, the *Georgiana*. Guns were to be mounted on the *Georgiana's* deck to shell Buffalo. Bands of Confederate guerrillas were to slip down out of Toronto and capture the Federal arsenal, when the *Georgiana* appeared offshore. Fires would be set in the holds of schooners and supply ships docked at the Buffalo wharf. With the *Michigan* out of commission until her engines were repaired, the Confederate Stars and Bars would be mistress of the northern lakes.

The *Michigan* was still Beall's favorite target. He told Thompson that after Buffalo had been shelled, he would take the *Georgiana* and ram the Federal gunboat. The plan was approved. Word was sent into Johnson's Island to await the word to begin another riot.

Colonel Martin, Lieutenant Headley and ten men slipped into Colburn on the north shore of Lake Erie, about fifteen miles from Buffalo. Ten more went to Buffalo, to find the city frantic with fear. The Home Guard, they reported, was composed of old men and boys. Colburn was to be the last port of call for the *Georgiana*. There she would pick up Headley, Martin and the raiders for the Buffalo attack.

Headley and Martin waited two days and nights, listening to the church bells tolling, but the *Georgiana* never appeared. On the third day, agents urged them to leave town. General Baker's secret service men had appeared. Troops had arrived from New York City garrisons.

Back in Toronto, Headley learned that the Canadian authorities, under pressure of the United States, had launched a series of raids on the barns and farmhouses where Beall had hidden arms to equip the *Georgiana*. The ship itself had been put under a twenty-four-hour guard. Beall was in hiding. Burley, in trying to escape, had been arrested. Captain Hines, when he heard of his arrest, had tried to help him escape, but Canadian authorities put Burley in irons and under heavy guard to await extradition hearing.

XVIII. THE BANK RAIDS IN VERMONT

THE Northwest Conspiracy was widespread, with varied targets. Let us again review the complex, jig-saw puzzle of troubled areas. The insurrection in Chicago slated for August had fizzled out, the Federal transports at St. Louis had been burned at the cost of Castleman's arrest. H. H. Dodd, Indiana's Copperhead leader and Justice Bullitt of Kentucky, were in exile in Canada. Other Sons of Liberty leaders were convicted and facing death on the gallows. The plan to capture the U.S.S. *Michigan* had misfired, although the vessel had been crippled.

Hines was now in the Northwest preparing another and larger revolution timed for Election Day. Henry rifles, Navy Colts and powder were still being smuggled across the border into Illinois, Ohio, Missouri and even parts of Indiana.

George Sanders, the *ex-officio* member of the Confederate Mission in Canada, now set his favorite plan into action: robbing Northern banks. In August, at the now-famous "peace conference," Hines had scorned such "criminal unlawful acts," but Sanders had just bided his time. With Hines out of the way in the Northwest, Sanders selected Lieutenant Bennett H. Young as the man to fulfill his ambitions. Sanders, of course, sought out Commissioner Clay for official approval. The ailing, fretting old man growled that he thought it was all right. Sanders made it official. He forged Clay's signature. He wanted nothing to spoil this raid.

On the morning of October 11, 1864, two well-dressed, handsome young men arrived at the Lafayette Hotel in Philipsburg, Quebec. After breakfast they asked the clerk if the newspaper from St. Albans, Vermont, had arrived. The clerk said no, but that it would come on the stage later in the day.

166

Several times during the afternoon they sauntered up to the desk to ask the same question. The clerk would remember that. At last the taller of the two "cautiously" asked the distance between Philipsburg and St. Albans, Vermont. The clerk thought it was fifteen miles. The young men thanked him and went up to their rooms.

During the day the hotel had several more guests. Like the first two they were young and well-dressed. The clerk recalled overhearing the name of the Vermont city, St. Albans, several times. But the men were soft-spoken and well-mannered. It wasn't often the clerk got near enough to them to eavesdrop on their conversation.

That evening after dinner, one by one, they gathered in one main room. They sat on the bed, the chairs and on a small table. The tall man, Lieutenant Bennett H. Young, spread out a map on the floor. He motioned to Lieutenant William Hutchinson to kneel beside him. Ringed in ink on the map were the Vermont towns of St. Albans and Sheldon.

"We'll go over it once more," Young said. "The town is about one mile square. There are approximately three hundred homes. The First National Bank, the St. Albans Bank and the Franklin County Bank are located on Main Street in the center of the village, less than a half-block apart. The American House is on the same street with the Fuller Livery stable. . . ."

"Probably all they have are farm plugs," Caleb McDowell Wallace grunted.

"No matter what they are, we'll need all the horses we can get. We can't all ride in. They'll be suspicious," Young said. "Some of you must come by train and carriage."

"What about the Yankee cavalry, Lieutenant?" someone asked.

"There are only a few on leave in the village," Young replied.

"What do you think the banks will have, sir?" another asked.

Lieutenant Young, later described as "a former divinity student but not the type for it," looked up. His face was grim. There were flickers of light in his black eyes.

"The Yankee nerve spot is his pocketbook. If we touch it they'll squeal," he said.

They all nodded. This was what they wanted more than gold: to give the Yankees a taste of what Sherman's and Sheridan's riders were doing in the South.

"Get my carpetbag," Young told one of his men. The bag was opened. Inside were forty small containers of Greek fire.

"I'll call another meeting when we get to the American House," Young said. "We'll divide the bottles of Greek fire between us. After we visit the banks we'll burn the town." He bent over the map. His finger traced the inked line from St. Albans to Sheldon. "After we leave St. Albans, Wallace and Squire Teavis will burn the Sheldon bridge. The rest will follow me into the bank. We'll take that one, too."

"Swanton, too, sir?" Hutchinson asked.

Young nodded. "We'll burn Swanton, too."

"And visit the bank, sir?" another asked with a grin.

"We'll pay their bank a visit," Young replied briskly.

It was now eleven o'clock. Young rolled up the map. He told his men to check out of the hotel between nine and eleven in the morning, leaving the town in pairs. They were to meet in his suite at the American House in St. Albans on the evening of the 17th. On the afternoon of the 18th, the three banks in St. Albans were to be robbed.

"A good start on our frontier campaign," George Sanders would say.

Young and Hutchinson arrived at the American House in St. Albans on the 15th. They were assigned rooms on the second floor. After lunch they strolled about the quiet little town, visiting each of the three banks they planned to rob. The Fuller Livery Stable near the American House had several horses. But Young didn't like the suspicious look Fuller gave him in answer to his questions as to the best roads to Sheldon.

Back at the American House the handsome Young had a romantic interlude. He was coming downstairs to join Hutchinson for dinner when he met her; we don't know her name, but Young said she was pretty, with a sweet smile. Young's cavalier manners captivated her. They had dinner together, under Hutchinson's frowns, then a walk to the village green in the twilight.

What did they talk about as the blue light thickened? Theology. Young, the former divinity student, charmed his young lady with a learned discussion of the Good Book, from which he could quote for hours. The young lady was impressed. She promised Young she would meet him again for another stroll.

Young saw her back to the hotel. He tipped his hat as they passed Fuller, the livery man, who sat outside his stable, the tip of his cigar glowing like a live coal in the gloom.

"Evenin'," Fuller grunted. His eyes followed Young into the hotel. He had taken a dislike to the soft-spoken man in the plum-colored shirt.

Hutchinson didn't approve of Young's striking up an acquaintance with a woman in the village and told his commander, who shrugged off his objections.

"I discovered one thing," Young said. Hutchinson gave him a questioning look.

"We can use the village green to hold our prisoners," Young said thoughtfully. "Two mounted men with revolvers can guard the whole square."

The next day several strangers rode into town and arrived on trains. They stayed at the American House and various boarding-houses. They seemed quiet, well-mannered and well-dressed.

Young, meanwhile, escorted his lady to the village green again that afternoon. It was a wonderful fall day, with the golden and crimson leaves of the big oaks and maples in the park littering the grass. There was another earnest theological discussion. At two o'clock Young brought her back to the hotel. In the evening they met again.

After this brief romantic interlude Young gathered his raiders to discuss the final plans for the bank raid. They all had inspected the banks on some pretext, and knew the roads leading out of the village. Carpetbags filled with gold and Union dollars would be tied to the pommels of their saddles. The bottles of Greek fire were distributed.

Young recalled the cold stare of Mr. Fuller, the livery stable owner. "Be sure that the livery stable is burned," he told his men.

Each man had a Navy six and ammunition. Four men who had arrived on trains were without horses. They would be equipped with mounts from the stable. The time of the robberies was set for three o'clock the following afternoon.

The next day was bright and clear. The morning passed with the usual traffic of farm wagons and riders going in and out of town. Hutchinson and Young had their horses brushed and curried. A stable hand brought them to the hotel, where he tied them to a hitch-up post. Young tipped him twenty-five cents. In the early hours of the afternoon he and Hutchinson took off their long overcoats to show what Young always insisted were Confederate uniforms. This is doubtful in view of the weight of later testimony describing them as dressed "in ordinary street clothes." Hutchinson wore a hunting cap with a narrow rim of black fur.

What they wore may be debatable, but what Young did the next moment is not. All agreed he stood on the steps of the American House, took a Navy Colt from inside his jacket to shout, "This city is now in the possession of the Confederate States of America."

Passersby and farmers dozing on the seats of their wagons coming into town stared unbelievingly at the handsome young man who had just announced that their city was in enemy hands. They laughed. They had never seen a Rebel. For them, Gettysburg, Vicksburg, Perryville, Stone's River had been only terrible names in the St. Albans *Messenger*. The only uniforms they had seen were those worn by Captain George Conger's cavalrymen from Bennington, who had marched behind the village band in the 4th of July parade. But what happened in the next few minutes showed them this young man was the enemy.

Young shouted again that St. Albans was in the hands of Confederate soldiers. At the north end of Main Street four of the raiders danced their horses into a line. Then with a wild Rebel scream they tore down the street, bent low over the necks of their horses, revolvers menacing the sidewalks. Men scattered. Horses tied to hitching posts reared in terror.

The Confederates who were not mounted ran into the street. Young, revolver in hand, walked to the First National Bank. Hutchinson and three of the raiders walked across the street to the Franklin County Bank. Caleb McDowell Wallace led two men into the St. Albans bank.

As Young entered the First National, a man walked out. He stared at the big revolver pointed at his stomach.

"They're robbing the bank!" he shouted.

Young pointed at him. "Take him prisoner," he ordered.

One of the Confederates lunged at the protesting citizen. They struggled furiously for a moment.

"Shoot him down," another raider said, but Young held up his hand.

"He's unarmed. Don't shoot him down in cold blood."

The Confederate was now sitting on his prisoner. "Take him to the village green with the others," Young said.

The Confederate, with his gun in the citizen's back, marched him to the park in the square. Then he waved his pistol at several other men who stared at him, ordering them to join the first man. They did as he said. Several women in the park screamed but the Confederate calmed them with a speech about Southern gallantry. He took off his hat. One of the ladies later recalled he was very handsome, with a brown goatee.

Meanwhile the Confederates were demonstrating the technique Jesse James would use so often a few years later. As Lieutenant Hutchinson walked into the Franklin County Bank, followed by his men, the clerk looked up with a smile. It was a few minutes after three o'clock. Evidently he had not heard the commotion outside.

"Good afternoon, gentlemen," he said.

"What are you paying for gold?" Hutchinson asked.

"We don't deal in such articles," the clerk said. "I must refer you to Mr. Armington."

"Where's Mr. Armington?" Hutchinson asked.

"Just down the street," the clerk said.

"Well, the hell with Mr. Armington," the Confederate said, pointing his Colt at the clerk. "Come out here." Suddenly another man came from the back room. "Who's he?"

"The president," the clerk said.

Hutchinson grinned. "Good." He raised his voice. "Both of you come out here."

The second man hesitated. "Come here, sir," Hutchinson snapped. The bank president hurried to comply with the order. Now the two bank officials stood before him. Hutchinson told them to raise their right hands.

"Repeat after me," he said. "I will solemnly swear to obey and respect the Constitution of the Confederate States of America and its President, Jefferson Davis. . . ."

"For God's sake," the president shouted. "That's a Rebel oath!"

Hutchinson grinned. "We'll make Confederates out of you. In that way we'll only be taking your money on loan to help the Cause. . . ."

"I'll be damned if I'll do it," the clerk said.

Hutchinson cocked his revolver. He wasn't smiling now. "Repeat after me," he said slowly.

There was a dead silence in the bank. Outside shots suddenly rang out. A man screamed. Horses galloped past the bank window.

The two voices rose to repeat in unison: "I hereby. . . ."

As the St. Albans *Messenger* later reported, "Much to the disgust of these two loyal men, they both had to take the oath. . . ."

The president and his clerk were ordered to sit on chairs back of the counter. Then Hutchinson and his raiders cleaned out the vault, throwing securities, gold and Union currency into large carpetbags. Two men were stationed near the door. When they were leaving, Hutchinson pushed the bank president and his clerk into the back room. When the bank officer protested against such "rough treatment," he quoted Hutchinson as telling him, "Well, you people in the North are treating the people in the South in the same manner."

In the St. Albans Bank Wallace and three men cleaned the vault in record time. They pushed the clerk in the vault and locked the door, but they left the key on the outside!

A few minutes later, a depositor, escaping the charging Confederates who were racing up and down the street, ran into the bank. Incredible as it seems, he later said he watched the raiders at work from the bank window. Then, realizing he was alone, he called out, "Hello! Who's there?"

There was a faint, far-off shout.

"Hello! Who's there?" the depositor shouted again.

"Here," the faint voice said.

The depositor finally traced the voice to the vault. He opened it to free the clerk. Together they ran to the window. From these choice seats they continued to watch the raiders.

In another bank, Lieutenant Young repeated the opening Hutchinson had used.

"What are you paying for gold?" he asked the smiling clerk.

"Oh, Mr. Armington does that," the clerk said.

"Well, I can't wait for Mr. Armington," Young said, pulling his Navy Colt from inside his jacket. He pushed the clerk into a chair, then ordered two of his men to fill the carpetbags with the gold and currency in the vault.

The door opened and a smiling man wearing a fur hat walked into the bank. He described for the clerk how four "strangers had stared intently" at him as he had walked in. It is strange he never noticed the tenseness in the room, the frightened look on the bank clerk's face, or the way the four men stared at him.

"What is your name, sir?" Young asked softly.

"Mr. Armington," was the reply.

"Ah, the gentleman who buys gold," Young said quickly.

"The same," the gold buyer said proudly.

"Would you care to buy some, sir?" Young asked.

"Certainly. Have you any to sell?" Mr. Armington said, peering at the Confederate raider over his glasses.

"Yes, sir, right here," Young said, pointing to the carpetbag at his feet.

"Very well, let us get to business," Armington said. He said to the clerk, "Pass me the Boston *Journal*. I wish to see what gold is selling for."

The clerk silently passed Armington the newspaper. He scanned the financial column with interest, cleared his throat and quoted a price. Young said it was "satisfactory" and then proceeded to sell Armington some of the gold the Confederates had just robbed from the bank's vault.

The banker later testified, "It was only afterwards that I learned he [Young] was one of the party."

It was a difficult task to drag the carpetbags filled with gold— Young had ordered the silver left behind—out into the street and loaded on horses. After the first one had been tied to the pommel of a saddle, Young realized he would need more horses. Wallace and two men were dispatched to the outskirts of the village to stop all farm wagons, cut the reins, and bring back the horses.

Meanwhile, Hutchinson, on Young's orders, was dragging out the best horses from Fuller's Livery Stable. Fuller ran after him shouting, "My God, what are you doing?"

"Stealing your horses," replied Hutchinson.

Three banks had been robbed, the town terrorized, its citizens marched up the street at gunpoint, but this remark touched off the first revolt among the peaceful citizens of St. Albans. Mr. Fuller, who loved horses, could not stand a horse-thief, Confederate or Yankee. "Hangin's too good for them," he liked to say. He ran inside to find his Colt.

The town's photographer, Leonard Cross, "hearing the commotion," came out to inquire of Young, sweating and cursing as he struggled with one of the heavy bags of gold, "What are you celebrating here, young man?"

Young turned, stared unbelievingly for a moment, then drew his gun. "This," he snarled as he fired.

The ball sang over the photographer's head. He dived inside his shop, the door slamming behind him.

The bags of gold were finally tied across the saddles of the stolen horses. All the raiders were now mounted. But the villagers were beginning to fight back. A man in an upper window fired at Young but missed. The Confederate whirled. His quick shot hit the man, who dropped his rifle to lie sprawled across the sill, badly wounded.

Another, kneeling on a porch, fired. The ball whizzed overhead. Hutchinson's ball caught him in the chest. The man toppled over. Two other men dragged him inside a house. The wounded man looked down and saw the widening bright red stain. "I think I'm hurt bad," he said. "I had better go to the drug store."

Supported by two men, the dying man calmly stepped into the street, passed the galloping riders who were blazing away at the village's defenders and went into the drug store of Dutcher & Son, located on the short end of Main Street. There, very quietly, he died.

Back in his livery stable, Fuller, now armed, ran out into the street, looking for blood. Through the dust he could see Lieutenant Young, shouting his orders. He was a perfect target. Fuller aimed, then pulled the trigger. There was only a click. He pulled it again. Another click.

The raiders moved up the street. Fuller reloaded, then followed, hugging the sides of buildings or dodging into narrow alleyways. Near "Miss Beattis' Shop" he found another chance. Young twisted in his saddle. His plum-colored shirt was a perfect target.

Fuller aimed carefully. He pulled the trigger. A click. The livery-stable owner jumped into an alley, where he feverishly reloaded. He came out as Young stood up in his stirrup, shouting, "I am an officer of the Confederate service. I have been sent here to take this town. The first one who offers resistance will be shot." It took him a long time to issue his "proclamation." Long enough for Fuller to take aim. He pulled the trigger. Again, there was only a click. The livery man threw down the gun and walked back to his stable. It was not his day.

There was another humorous scene. Hutchinson's hat had been shot off. Evidently he disliked having his long black hair blowing in his face as he rode. He began looking for a hat. He spotted a man cowering near the entrance of the Franklin County Bank.

"Give me your hat," he shouted.

"I'll be damned if I do," said the man.

Hutchinson cocked his revolver and aimed it. "I said give me your hat," he roared.

In reply the man took off his hat, tucked it under his coat and dashed down the street.

"Get him!" shouted Hutchinson.

One of his riders hurtled out of the saddle to give chase. He brought the man down with a flying tackle. He tried to tear open the man's coat to get the hat but its owner fought like a wildcat. Finally he did manage to drag the man to his feet and rip open his coat. Covered with dust, the trooper handed up the hat to Hutchinson, who put it on his head. It was somewhat small and made them all laugh.

"I ought to shoot you for your resistance," Hutchinson told the owner of the hat. "Take him to the green."

The flushed, beaten, but still proud hat-owner walked with slow dignity down the street to the village green. The trooper tried to get him to hurry but received only one reply, "I'll be darned if a Rebel will make me." The trooper who had tasted of real Yankee stubbornness decided to rest on his laurels. They walked at a snail's pace to the green.

It was then that Young decided to sack the town. He ordered his men to form what one villager criticized as "not a very regular line." At his signal they tore down Main Street, shrieking like Comanches, flinging the bottles of Greek fire into doorways, through windows and up against the wooden buildings. The chemical bombs exploded with a whoosh. The Atwood Building was the first to catch. The American House was next. Flames raced up one side, licking at curtains and doors.

The roof of another building began burning briskly. Some of the bottles flared up, then died out. Others failed to explode. But enough caught on to give the shouting raiders the impression they had fired the town.

The man who finally rallied the villagers was nineteen-year-old Captain George Conger of the First Vermont. Ignoring the flying bullets, he found a horse and began riding through the town shouting, "We have a lot of Rebel raiders here. Let's catch them. Get your guns. Fire at the. . . ."

His courage was infectious. The men of St. Albans joined him in twos and threes, sniping at the Confederates from behind trees and from windows of buildings. Their marksmanship was deplorable. Not a Confederate was scratched.

They grew bolder as their numbers increased. Lines were formed across Main Street. But Morgan's raiders were used to these tactics. It was not the first time they had stormed a town. Stirrup to stirrup, reins in their teeth, Colts blazing, they charged. The Yankees broke but under Conger's leadership re-formed. When it was apparent that they were not going to break and that he and his men would only ride into a blazing frontal fire, Young shouted, "That's all, men, the ball is over. Break up."

They wheeled and raced out of St. Albans. But Captain Conger and Fuller managed to find enough horses to mount a posse. In ten minutes fifteen men galloped out of town in a cloud of dust. As Conger testified, "Once out of town it was a running fight. We pressed them hard."

The raiders and the posse tore along the roads, the rifle and revolver shots sounding like splintering wood in the hazy fall afternoon quiet, Neither side scored a hit.

At Sheldon the Confederates had outdistanced the posse, and Lieutenant Young burned a house and two barns, then the bridge—but only after he had allowed an old farmer driving a hay wagon to cross. They passed the First National Bank of Sheldon at a gallop. Young said he "would have liked to stop," but Captain Conger's men were just over the hill.

After Sheldon the raiders broke up into small parties, as had been prearranged, in the best frontier holdup fashion. Conger and his men set off in the direction taken by two of the raiders led by Hutchinson, still wearing his borrowed hat.

Back in St. Albans the *Messenger* put out an extra, charging the Confederates with stealing one hundred and seventy thousand dollars in gold, securities and Union currency.

The headline is a classic of understatement. It reads: "St. Albans Has Been Surprised and Excited Today."

Vermont's Governor Smith declared a state of emergency. The Home Guard was called out to patrol the roads and the borders. In Washington, Stanton described Young and his men as "the Confederate bandits who hide out in Canada."

In New York, General Dix promised a swift court-martial and the gallows for any of the raiders who would be caught. But once again Confederate raiders forced him to divert troops north.

Twice Conger's possemen caught up with small bands of the Confederate raiders. Each time the raiders whirled and charged. Conger was a cavalryman and could stand fast coolly to pick off the charging riders. But not the townspeople; they turned and fled.

Young and Wallace reached the Canadian border at nine o'clock. They abandoned their horses, "donned citizens' clothes" and proceeded on foot to Montreal.

The next afternoon Young heard that seven of his men had been captured near Philipsburg, Quebec, by the posse which had crossed the Canadian border. He decided at once to give himself up. When Hutchinson, who had joined him, protested, Young told him, "I am their leader. Their cause is my cause. I alone had the authority and command of the raid."

With two Navy sixes strapped to his hips, he rode south in the direction of the Canadian-United States border. That evening he stopped at a farmhouse five miles north of Philipsburg. The farmer agreed to give him supper, feed his horse and accommodate him overnight for five dollars. After supper Young stretched out in a chair before a roaring fire, his holster and guns hung over a chair in the bedroom.

Unknown to Young, Captain Conger's possemen had stopped at the house earlier to warn the farmer to keep a lookout for any of the Rebel raiders who might seek shelter. The farmer waited until Young dozed off, then sent one of his hands to find Conger.

Young woke up to find the room crowded with shouting possemen, all pointing pistols at his head. Conger, grinning triumphantly, told him, "You are my prisoner."

Young eyed the unwavering guns. "Had I my revolvers this might be a different story," he replied.

Conger said he thought so, too, but at the moment he wasn't interested in what-might-have-been. He tossed Young his coat. "Mount up, men," he told his riders. "We'll take this Rebel back to the United States."

Young said heatedly, "You are violating British neutrality."

"I'm not interested in any damn laws or in Great Britain either," Conger snapped. "Put on your coat."

The Vermonters were out for blood. Conger testified he had all to do to keep them from hanging Young from the hayloft. The possemen dragged Young into a wagon, put a rope around his neck, "and kept cocking their pistols at him, telling him what they would like to do."

They had started down the farmhouse lane to the main road which led to the United States border, when Conger, who was driving the wagon, turned to shout instructions to the men riding postilion on either side of the wagon.

Young, who later said he thought he was going to be hanged the instant he got back to St. Albans, lunged at Conger. The Federal officer saw him out of the corner of his eye and tried to twist aside. But Young's knee caught him in the pit of his stomach. Conger went down. Young grabbed the reins. The whip cracked. The startled horses leaped forward. Young, the noose still about his neck, cracked the whip again and again. The wagon bounced down the road.

It was a thrilling scene in the moonlight. The shouting possemen started in pursuit. Young laid his whip across the backs of the horses, who squealed in pain. Conger tried to get up, but Young jammed him back with a kick of his heavy boots. Behind him shots rang out. A ball fluttered past his ears. Young cursed his luck at not having his Colts.

But the cumbersome wagon could not outdistance the horses. After a chase of about a half-mile the posse managed to stop the team. Young tried to leap out of the wagon but the possemen swarmed over him, hammering him with the butts of their guns, kicking and punching him.

Young fought back with the ferocity of a man who knows he is headed for the hangman. Suddenly, above the cursing, panting, struggling men, a cool, crisp British voice asked, "Here, here, what is this all about?"

The manhunters stopped pummeling Young to look up. A British major in scarlet had come up the road unnoticed. Conger, who was holding onto Young, acted as spokesman.

"This is the leader of the Rebels who robbed our banks," he said. "He tried to escape."

"Really? Your name, prisoner?" the British officer asked.

"Lieutenant Bennett Young, Confederate States," Young gasped between puffed lips. The officer studied the Confederate. Young was battered and bruised, his shirt and jacket in tatters. Blood streamed down his face from the blows of the gun butts. But he was still full of fight, ready to take on the possemen again.

It was perhaps this display of arrogant courage that made the major lie to the Vermont men. He told them the seven Rebels captured earlier at Philipsburg were to be escorted back across the border and turned over to the St. Albans authorities at ten o'clock the next morn-

ing. He suggested that Young be taken to the British barracks at
Philipsburg, Quebec, along with the others. Conger thought this was a
reasonable suggestion. But some of the others wanted to take Young
back across the border to the United States that night.

The major's voice hardened. As one of them said, "He wasn't
friendly any longer."

"This would be a violation of our neutrality, gentlemen," he
snapped.

"We don't give a damn for your neutrality," one of the Yankees said.

"But you will respect our arms, sir," the major said. "If you leave
with this prisoner I shall send a company of regulars to bring him
back."

There was silence for a moment. British regulars with long steel
bayonets. . . . It was decided to take Young to the barracks at Philipsburg.

At the garrison the Vermont possemen received a cold reception.
A British captain, who took charge of Young, ordered them off his
post. The major had discreetly vanished. The soldiers on guard, obviously pro-Confederate, gleefully "escorted" the manhunters back to
the road. They seemed to delight in dropping the butts of their heavy
rifles on American toes.

Young joined the other seven captured members of his band. The
captain in charge of the garrison post "confined them" in the comfortable barracks, while the soldiers brought them plates of food, beer
and ale. Young, the lion of the hour, told his story of the raid to an
admiring audience of scarlet-jacketed officers.

On the morning of November 5 the raiders were escorted to Montreal to be arraigned on charges of arson, robbery and treason. The
United States, through Secretary of State Seward, demanded their
return to the United States to stand trial.

The preliminary arrangements in the Montreal Police Court at-
tracted huge crowds. At ten o'clock, November 7, 1864, the doors were
closed. Young and his men found themselves defended by one of
Canada's most prominent attorneys. At the request of the defendants
a thirty-day adjournment was granted to permit them to obtain from
Richmond official copies of their commissions and of the Confederate
War Department's orders giving permission to Young to attack St.
Albans.

During the hearing a debonair, smiling man bustled about the
courtroom, whispering to Young, snapping out orders, even telling the

court clerks when to close the doors. The police magistrate seemed awed by his presence. Of course the busy man was George N. Sanders.

The files of the St. Albans *Messenger*, the extradition proceedings, and memoirs written a few years after the raid give a vivid picture of how Sanders planned the raid and, after the capture of Young and his men, took charge of the entertainment, the comfort and defense of the prisoners.

He hired J. G. K. Houghton, "an eminent attorney of Montreal." He issued daily statements to the press—criticizing the local correspondent of the St. Albans *Messenger* as "a coarse fellow"—fought with the United States representatives, informed the magistrate on the more intricate points in the Ashburton Treaty, held court each night in the bar of the local hotel with the pretty Confederate agents and spies, telling them what delicacies and wines to send in to Young and his men. He wasn't above starting a rumor if he thought it would do his cause any good.

On November 10 he issued a statement which the Canadian press carried on page one, stating that General Dix, commanding in New York, had sent an expedition to Canada to remove Young and his men by force. The British garrison was alerted and the cavalry prepared to mount at a moment's notice.

The United States was finally forced to deny the rumor, but the damage had been done. Sanders said casually that Stanton had changed his mind because he knew the British would fight. The city was now more pro-Young than ever before.

Sanders invited the correspondent of the St. Albans *Messenger* to dinner one night. To him he predicted, "The raid on St. Albans is merely the starting point in inaugurating our frontier warfare against the North."

As the correspondent wrote: "He [Sanders] dashed his water freely in connection with oysters on the half-shell, and invited friends to partake of the fun in St. Albans and Burlington when the Rebels strike again."

Beautiful women flocked about Sanders. He began giving the lavish parties he loved so much. There was much champagne, fine food, music and laughter in his suite at the Montreal Hotel. But he didn't forget the prisoners. "He [Sanders] sends in daily to the prisoners chilled wine and cold chicken," the St. Albans correspondent noted.

Sanders appears again during Young's trial, in the web of the Northwest Conspiracy and in the Lincoln Conspiracy trial, still as smiling and as sinister.

XIX. BETRAYAL IN CHICAGO

ELECTION Day, November 8, 1864, was the day of destiny for Captain Tom Hines. At high noon, his private revolution was to break out in the North, from New York to Chicago, from Cincinnati to the small towns of Iowa.

For several feverish weeks, following the burning of the transports in St. Louis, Hines had been traveling through the West, "in various disguises," as Colonel Carrington reported to the Ohio Chief of State, re-forming the scattered bands of the Sons of Liberty into military units to put the country to the torch.

In Chicago, Brigadier-General Charles Walsh, the only remaining high official of the Sons of Liberty not in prison, had convinced Hines that this time there would be no holding back; his men were armed "and ready to shed blood."

Hines was satisfied that this was true. He had spoken to Doctor Edward W. Edwards and Judge Morris and had attended secret sessions of the society in the Invincible Club hall, to instruct the Sons in tactics of cable-cutting, storming prison gates and setting fires to state and municipal buildings. Walsh had a large cache of rifles, revolvers and ammunition hidden under the floor of his kitchen. His house was less than seventy rods from the main gate of Camp Douglas.

He had sent Colonel Ben M. Anderson, formerly of the Second Kentucky, to help arm the guerrilla fighters in Missouri. Anderson had reported three hundred had been given arms and were ready. The largest of the groups was to march through northern Missouri into Iowa and burn as many of the small towns and villages as possible. They were to live off the land and equip themselves with stolen horses.

This time the eastern section of the United States was also to be included in the uprising. New York was to be burned, along with Boston and Cincinnati. It was the most extensive and elaborate of Hines' plots. From all indications it *could* succeed, despite Colonel

181

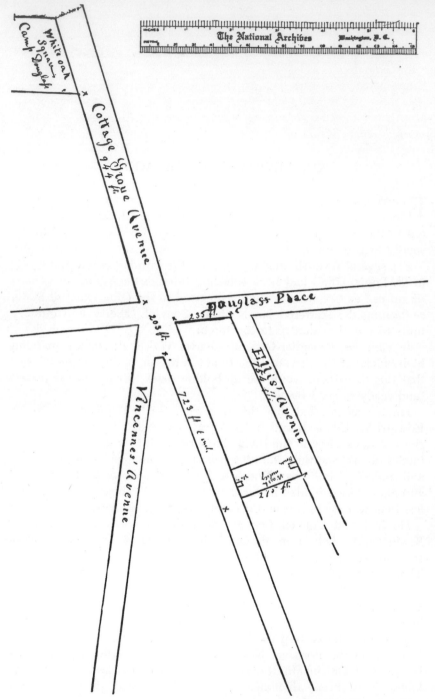

White oak Square Camp Douglas

Cottage Grove Avenue 944 ft.

The National Archives — Washington, D. C.

Douglass Place

Ellis' Avenue

Vincennes' Avenue

205 ft.

235 ft.

723 ft. t ind.

275 ft.

Map used by the government in the prosecution of the Confederate raiders and the Chicago leaders of the Sons of Liberty. Its purpose was to show the military tribunal how near to Camp Douglas was the home of the Copperhead Charles Walsh, whose cellar housed a Confederate arsenal.

Carrington's round-ups during September in Indiana and Bullitt's arrest in Kentucky.

Hines placed the plan before Thompson in Toronto, who immediately approved it. The Confederate Commission was unstinting with gold. Agents took large sums, ranging from two thousand to five thousand dollars to a Captain Churchill in Cincinnati, described by Hines as "a loyal friend but too cautious," a fashionable Boston Back Bay doctor named Blackburn and "Longmire" in New York City.

The last name strikes a familiar note. Headley's Papers in the National Archives and an item in the New York *Herald* further identify him. Another missing piece of the jig-saw puzzle slips into place. Longmire was really Captain Longuemare, the Missouri officer who first presented a skeleton form of the Northwest Conspiracy to Jefferson Davis in 1862.

Longuemare, besides arming and counseling the Copperheads in New York City, was also helping to direct the *Freeman's Journal* editorial policy of "peace at any cost." Editor McMasters was closely associated with the ex-mayor of New York and prominent Copperhead leader, Fernando Wood.

In New York the United States Sub-Treasury on Wall Street was to be seized, City Hall turned into a fortress, Broadway to echo with the tramp of twenty thousand traitors. Policemen who were members of the Sons of Liberty would seize Police Headquarters on Worth Street. The Federal Courthouse and all government buildings were to be taken. Five cans of gunpowder buried under the main gate of Fort Lafayette in the Narrows off Brooklyn would be touched off to pierce the thick stone walls. General John A. Dix was to be held as a hostage in his own dungeon. All Confederate prisoners were to be released and armed. The Stars and Bars of the Confederacy would fly over City Hall in twilight's purple light. By nightfall, as one of them recalled, all New York City would be a "sea of flames."

At the same hour, as the U. S. government was to describe officially, "Chicago was to be sacked, burned, looted and turned into an enemy city." Fifteen thousand howling Rebel prisoners in Camps Douglas and Rock Island, armed with rocks, bayonets and Navy Colts which had been smuggled in to them, would charge the gates. State and municipal officials were to be murdered and replaced with puppets. Brigadier-General Charles Walsh, commanding the Sons of Liberty, would join the released Confederates, twenty thousand strong throughout the state.

Hines sent Colonel Grenfel, who had rejoined him after his siege of "hogs and Hoosiers," out to Chicago to reconnoiter Rock Island Prison. Dressed in hunting tweeds, carrying a fowling piece and followed by a large hunting dog, Grenfel arrived in Chicago. He registered at the Richmond House, using his own name. Every day he went out "for birds." Every evening he returned with his bag filled—and his head buzzing with details of how the camp could be stormed. He wrote Hines a cautious note telling him "the hunting here is good. . . ."

In the first week of November, Hines, Marmaduke, Richard T. Semmes, brother of the Confederate admiral, Lieutenant J. J. Bettersworth and several others left Toronto for Chicago. Eight other officers, commanded by Colonel Martin, with Lieutenant Headley second in command, slipped across the Canadian border at Niagara Falls for New York City, to meet Captain Longuemare and Editor McMasters.

Hines was confident the revolution would come off this time. But a bottle of peach brandy, a traitor and a merry widow would betray him.

From the bitter lines he wrote a year later, from the memoirs of the traitors themselves, and the existing court-martial records, we can reconstruct the story.

It began on a rainy night, November 5, when a former Confederate officer in the pay of the Union as a detective arrived in Chicago from Springfield, trailing a soldier charged with murder. In a saloon an informer whispered to the officer whose name we do not know that "guerrilla Hines is in Chicago to burn it on Election Day."

A few hours later the detective met Doctor Edwards, the Chicago Copperhead leader whom he had known before the war. There was much talk of old times. Then the detective casually asked, "Are any Southern officers in the city, Doctor?"

Edwards smiled knowingly. "Why do you ask?"

"I have heard they are here to burn the city," the detective replied.

The doctor winked. "Marmaduke [Colonel Vincent] is at my house right now with a British passport."

"Oh, I know Marmaduke from St. Louis," the detective said. "Give him my card. Tell him I'm stopping at the Briggs House."

COL VINCENT
MARMADUKE
OF THE CONFEDERATE
ARMY -
HEAD OF THE
CONSPIRACY

Newspaper sketch of Colonel Vincent Marmaduke, who betrayed his comrades in Chicago. The artist was in error. Marmaduke was not the "head of the Conspiracy" in Chicago. He later testified against St. Leger Grenfel.

Courtesy, Chicago Historical Society

Evidently Marmaduke did know the detective. Hines said the next day Marmaduke sent a note to the Briggs House asking the detective to meet him. The messenger took him to a lake-front house where they had a gay reunion. Before the evening was over, Marmaduke, the handsome glory-hunter, had told him they were in contact with Rebel officers inside Camp Douglas and had smuggled in revolvers in preparation for the attack on the camp.

The following morning the detective was in the Camp Douglas office of Colonel Sweet, unfolding the Confederate plot.

"Hines is their leader," Sweet said. "Can you find out where he is hiding?"

The detective sensibly pointed out that Marmaduke had voluntarily told him the plans but might become suspicious under questioning. Sweet thanked the detective, who left. Exit the detective. He never appears again.

After a restless night Sweet began casting about in his mind for prisoners, among the eight thousand in his camp, who might be tempted by gold or freedom to turn on their comrades. He selected two, Lieutenant Maurice Langhorn and Lieutenant James Shanks. Langhorn was a Texan who had served under Forrest and had been captured at Buffington's wharf. Hines bitterly described him as "the former Texas criminal, an infamous traitor who sold his comrades for blood money. . . ."

Sweet had several interviews with Langhorn, each time holding out the opportunity of taking the oath of allegiance and obtaining freedom. Langhorn broke at last. He sat in Sweet's office for five hours, detailing Hines' plan of revolution. His story paralleled what Adjutant-General Holt had outlined in his report to Stanton on October 8; revolution by violence. Langhorn said he had been one of the officers selected by Hines and the Chicago Copperheads to lead the uprising in the prison camp.

"Why have you waited so long to tell us this dastardly plot?" Sweet asked him.

"I intended to, but I was afraid," replied Langhorn. "When I heard of it, I protested against the villainy of such actions. Because of this I am under suspicion."

"We shall see that no harm comes to you," Sweet said.

Langhorn gave him a bleak smile. "If my comrades knew I was talking to you, my life would not be worth a half-dollar."

"What would you suggest we do?" Sweet asked the traitor.

Langhorn replied, "Arrest them as they come into the city." His long finger stabbed at Sweet's jacket. "But, sir, I say to you, more than anything, trap the fox."

"Who is the fox?" Sweet asked.

"Tom Hines," was the reply.

When Sweet suggested that Langhorn return to the prison camp and try to find out where Hines was staying, the Texan gave him a look of horror.

"Please let me go, sir," he pleaded. "I have done my duty. . . ." Langhorn undoubtedly had heard of the traitorous major who had volunteered to trap Hines in August and had mysteriously disappeared. He would play the informer, but not up to the point of no return.

Sweet sent him back to camp, promising to protect him and not to reveal his treason. He himself spent another restless night, after sending off an appeal for more troops to the commandant of Illinois.

The following morning a bearded man wearing spectacles reported to Sweet. He was a United States Secret Service agent named Tom Keefe, who had been ordered by Washington to keep Hines under close watch in Toronto. Keefe had ridden in the train seat behind Hines from Canada to Chicago. But there, he confessed, he had lost the trail. It is curious to note that though Hines was engaged in such high treason and dangerous activities, Keefe did not arrest him when they crossed the border into the United States. We do not know the reason why. However, the explanation may well be that Keefe had been ordered by his superiors to let Hines lead him to the underground leaders of the Sons of Liberty in Chicago and subsequently to their hidden arsenal.

Where was Hines? Sweet shook his head. It was the question he himself wanted so much to be able to answer. Keefe went out, swearing to locate Hines. He never did.

That evening Sweet selected the second of the prisoners who he was sure would turn government informer against Hines. This man was J. T. Shanks. We know Shanks' story from Hines. He was a twenty-two-year-old Texan who had served as a captain under Braxton Bragg, then later in Morgan's command. In 1866 Hines wrote, "He was a Texan by adoption, an ex-convict. A blacker-hearted villain never lived. . . ."

In 1863, on one of Morgan's raids, Shanks had captured a Federal colonel named De Land. The colonel was later exchanged. A year later, in September, 1864, Shanks was captured and sent to Camp Douglas. The camp's commandant was De Land.

De Land and Shanks became friends. The Confederate was appointed camp clerk in the medical department and had the run of the camp. "He was used by De Land to spy on his comrades," Hines recalled and this was probably correct.

A few months after his capture, Shanks met a young Chicago widow who was a member of a ladies' society who brought fruit and cigars to the camp. A romance bloomed within the board fence of the camp. When De Land heard about it, he summoned Shanks to demonstrate that chivalry was possessed not only by Southern cavaliers.

"It is not exactly the right thing to court a lady in a prison, Shanks," he said. "I think you should pay your addresses at the lady's house as a gentleman should do." The happy Shanks was released twice a week to woo his lady. He was accompanied by a guard, who passed the time teasing the maids in the kitchen. When De Land left for the field and was succeeded by Sweet, he explained the situation. True to the romantic times, Sweet allowed the fantastic romance to continue.

As the melancholy November dawn crept across the floor of his bare bedroom, Sweet remembered all this. He summoned Shanks and told him that Langhorn had confessed.

"Are you in this conspiracy, Shanks?" he asked.

Shanks went white to his lips. Under Sweet's hard look, his glance dropped.

"Yes, sir."

"Do you love your friends more than your lady and your country?" he snapped.

Shanks knew what Sweet wanted. "Good God, sir," he cried. "You are asking me to betray my friends! Can I do that in honor?" (In the margin of this passage in the *Atlantic Monthly* article on the Chicago Conspiracy Hines wrote a bitter comment: "How delightfully refreshing!")

Sweet then pictured Shanks as begging for an hour to consider. Of course, in the end, love conquered all. He agreed to act the traitor. "I will do it," Sweet quoted him as saying.

Twice a week a garbage collector visited the camp. To make his plan foolproof, Sweet arranged for Shanks to inform his bunkmates he was going to escape by hiding in the back of the peddler's wagon. His comrades were to engage the peddler while Shanks hid among the debris. The peddler was brought into the plot and promised to play his part.

"What of the guards?" Shanks asked, remembering the jittery Federals at the gate.

"I'll be on hand to see that nothing happens to you," Sweet promised.

Soon Shanks sent a message to Sweet that the escape plan was ready. At six o'clock the scavenger loaded his wagon with the camp's garbage. Shanks was smuggled into the wagon while his friends joked and talked with the driver. The rickety wagon creaked up to the opened gate. The driver whipped his team and started to roll out. Behind in the camp a drum rolled.

"No wagons can pass after the drumbeat," the guard called.

The wagon continued on. Sweet, from the door of his office near the gate, watched.

The sentry raised his rifle. "Halt," he shouted.

"Let him pass, guard," Sweet shouted. The puzzled guard looked back at his colonel and dropped his rifle. The wagon disappeared down the street, the quaking Shanks huddled under the bones, bottles and other garbage.

Lieutenant Bettersworth told what happened next in a pitiful letter to Hines, written a few months after the war had ended. Shanks played his role as an escaped prisoner well. He found Marmaduke, who gave him a pistol. Shanks asked where Hines was hiding out, but Hines had been careful to keep his hideout a secret even from his comrades. Shanks said he would return the following evening "to learn their plans."

In the meantime the sensitive prison camp grapevine quivered with the news that Shanks was not to be trusted. A cryptic note was delivered to Doctor Edwards, who got in touch with Hines. Word was sent to Mary Morris to gather together the raiders at her house. She reached all of them except Lieutenant Bettersworth, who was out of his room at the Richmond House when the messenger arrived.

We do not know how Shanks learned of the meeting but he appeared as Hines was making known his treachery. Mary Morris peeked through the curtains of the front door to tell Hines who was approaching. As Hines said, he warned the others not to say he was present, then hid in an adjacent room with the door half-open. Not knowing he had been uncovered, Shanks entered, "calling out a friendly greeting."

Marmaduke, "who had been alerted to his treachery," gave him a "cool greeting." One wonders why, with so many lives at stake, they did not take him captive or kill him. The explanation may be that Hines, who knew of Shanks' connection with Colonel Sweet, had decided that one wrong move would upset the whole plan and had decided to let the traitor move in the dark.

Shanks undoubtedly felt the chill in the room, for he didn't stay long. "Where is my friend Tom Hines?" he asked.

Hostile faces studied him in silence.

"I must be going," he said, and left.

When he had gone, Hines came out. "Where's Bettersworth?" he asked. "If Shanks gets to him we are lost."

"I left him this afternoon at the Richmond House," Marmaduke said. "He said he was going to stay there until you called on him." Marmaduke must have felt the cold contempt he saw in Hines' eyes.

"Summon a carriage," Hines ordered. "We must get to Bettersworth."

They were too late. Shanks and the pretty widow had found Bettersworth at the hotel. "Ah, Lieutenant Bettersworth!" Shanks said when he came into his room.

"Who are you?" Bettersworth asked suspiciously.

"Lieutenant Shanks of Bragg's staff," the traitor said. "Late of Camp Douglas."

"You escaped?" Bettersworth asked.

Shanks winked. "Under a bag of bones in a peddler's cart."

"Where's Captain Hines?" Bettersworth asked. "I'm waiting for word to join him."

"Captain Hines sent me to pick you up," Shanks explained. "We'll join him later." Then he explained he had a "fair lady" waiting in a carriage and they had to be off. Bettersworth, who had been on edge all day in his lonely room, eagerly went along.

"I wish I had killed him on the spot," he later wrote to Hines. "Had I known what was to happen in those next hours, I would have killed myself before taking one step out of that room."

In the widow's luxurious house, Bettersworth relaxed. Shanks, in his ingratiating way, called for a bottle and the widow brought in peach brandy.

Shanks made sure Bettersworth's glass was never empty. The hours passed. As the brandy bottle emptied, Bettersworth's tongue loosened. By midnight he was lost. He had given the names of the raiders and their whereabouts. It was the night of November 7, the eve of the uprising, and Bettersworth said Hines had planned to spend that night at Doctor Edwards' house.

Shanks, in the widow's carriage, galloped back to camp. When he had finished telling all, Sweet summoned his staff. Names and addresses of the Confederates and the leading officials of the Sons of Liberty were issued. By midnight the patrols were out.

But Sweet was not sure of the strength of the Confederate raiders and their Copperhead allies. His patrols were riding off into the night when he sat down to write a hasty message to Brigadier-General Cook, at Springfield, outlining the plot of "Hines, alias Doctor Hunter of the Rebel Army" to capture the city. He wrote:

> My force is only 800 men to guard 8,000 to 9,000 prisoners. If I arrest prominent people of this city it might lead to riots and great excitement. It seems to me unwise and unsafe to leave a centrally located city open to attack in these doubtful times. . . . I must ask that you again represent [sic] my necessities . . . and use the telegraph at once. . . .

Sweet sent the message to Springfield by a special courier on horse-back. He could not use the telegraph, he informed Cook, "because it might alert those who are interested." He acted wisely. It was learned later that Hines had bribed the army telegrapher inside Camp Doug-las with $1,000 to send him copies of all official telegrams.

St. Leger Grenfel was the first Confederate in the city to be caught. For two weeks he had hunted on the prairies in the vicinity of Rock Island prison camp. He was a familiar figure to the clerk of the Rich-mond House, with his spotted hunting dog trotting behind him, and a bag of birds slung over one shoulder. He had told the clerk he had stopped at the Richmond House "because it was the favorite hotel of my friend, His Royal Highness, the Prince of Wales."

The patrol came in as he sat before a fire sipping a brandy, his dog at his feet, a picture of the traditional English squire taking his ease. A veteran of a hundred such encounters, he surrendered gallantly. "I am your prisoner, gentlemen," he told the lieutenant. They slipped on leg-irons and he hobbled out into the rainy night, captured but unbowed.

The Federals under Colonel Skinner of the Eighth Veterans' Reserve Corps were divided into three parties of a hundred men. Two con-ducted the raids and made the arrests, while the third marched into the city.

The colonel and his men surrounded Walsh's house in the early hours of the morning. After what the *Tribune* called "a great deal of trouble" they broke down the door. Walsh, Captain George Cantrill and several other Confederates, among them Ben M. Anderson, who had armed the Missouri guerrillas, and Richard T. Semmes, were arrested.

The house held a veritable arsenal. There were two hundred and ten double-barreled shotguns loaded with "the largest buckshot"; three hundred and fifty Colt revolvers; a hundred Henry rifles, thirteen thousand rounds of ammunition, three hundred and forty-four boxes of caps; two kegs of powder, cartridge-making molds, pistol printers and assorted boxes of knives, hooks and lances.

Hines and Marmaduke meanwhile had given up their search for Bettersworth. It was ten-thirty when they drove back to Doctor

Edwards' house at 70 Adams Street. For some reason Hines had decided to stay at the Edwards' home for the night. Perhaps, with the uprising scheduled to start on the next day, he wanted to be at the doctor's home, which was to be a sort of command post for the Sons of Liberty when they struck.

It had been a weary, uneasy day. As Hines would recall, he could almost smell danger in the hazy November night. As they blew out the lamps and went to bed, the city was quiet as if holding its breath. Sometime after midnight it began to rain. The drumming of the drops on the roof lulled them all to sleep very quickly. Under Hines' pillow was a Navy Colt and a dagger.

At one-thirty Doctor Edwards, who was attending his wife, feverish from an attack of diphtheria, heard the patrol coming down the street. He pushed aside the curtain. In the light of the street lamp an officer was swinging down from his horse. Rain glistened on the bayonets of his men. The doctor hurried to Hines' bedroom.

"Tom! The patrol is here!" he whispered.

Hines was awake in a moment. "Doctor Edwards," he said, "have you a large box mattress?"

"Yes. Mrs. Edwards is sleeping on it," the bewildered doctor replied.

Hines stuck his pistol and dagger in his belt. "Please show it to me at once."

While the empty house echoed with the banging on the front door, Doctor Edwards, holding a lamp, guided Hines into his room, where his wife moaned in delirium. The mattress she was sleeping on was a huge, cumbersome boxlike affair mounted on cross-ribbed slats, with an air space equal to the depth of the supporting box.

While Edwards held up the lamp, Hines ripped open the side of the mattress with his dagger, passed in his pistol and squirmed inside. The dagger made a ripping sound as Hines made a slit in the bottom of the ticking in order to breathe.

"Let them in, Doctor," he whispered.

The doctor admitted the patrol, who began a room-to-room search. Marmaduke was found in his bed. It is not to Hines' credit that he let Marmaduke be captured. In his later comments on the raids, there is a hint of friction between them. "He [Marmaduke], that man of such high connections. was arrested in another room," Hines wrote as he recalled the night. It is evident that Hines blamed Marmaduke's loose tongue and glory-seeking for leading the Federals to Edwards' house. It was up to him to escape as best he could. But no matter what

faults he had found in Marmaduke, Hines, as an officer and a gentleman, was really duty-bound to aid his comrade in arms to escape.

When Marmaduke went for his revolver, a soldier clubbed him
back into bed with the butt of his rifle. As he dressed under the point
of a bayonet, the Confederate asked Edwards, "Did they get Hines?"

Edwards shook his head. Marmaduke's eyes asked the question:
Where was Hines hiding?

The bluecoats searched every room thoroughly, pulling out the
clothes from closets and looking under the beds. When they came to
the room where Edwards' wife lay ill, the doctor protested, but the
Federal officer pushed him aside. From his hiding place inside the
mattress, Hines could hear the boots crossing the floor, only a few feet
away. Above him tossed the feverish woman.

At last the officer left, after placing Edwards under house arrest.
Two sentries were left on guard. When the front door slammed,
Hines squirmed through the slit in the side of the mattress. He went
to the window and edged aside the curtain. Rain lashed at the pane.
In the light of the street lamp, two sentries paced up and down.

"They have sentries at the door, Doctor," he said.

Edwards, bathing his wife's face, turned to him.

"I don't know what we can do, Tom. . . ."

"I have a plan," Hines said. And he told it to Edwards.

The next day friends of Doctor Edwards received the sad news that
his wife was dying. In twos and threes, they called to pay their re-
spects. Even the sentries—who had been warmed by glasses of whiskey
—told Edwards they were sorry to hear the news.

The persons who arrived at the house had their faces hidden by
umbrellas. The sentries who huddled under the eaves didn't pay much
attention to them. They never bothered to glance under the umbrella
at one young lady and gentleman who hurried out. They would have
found Tom Hines, the fox they were trying to trap, and Mary Walsh,
a daughter of Charles Walsh, Brigadier-General of the Sons of Liberty,
who was now in military prison.

George Scharf, a young resident of Chicago, in his memoirs of the
attempted uprising, now in the Chicago Historical Society, gives a
vivid picture of the panicky city the next day, feverishly preparing

to combat an enemy force determined to burn their homes and sack their community.

As Scharf said, when the news leaked out that Hines and his men were ready to "begin their revolution, the citizens of Chicago formed Home Guard Organizations, the garrison of Camp Douglas was increased, and there was a general rush to arms throughout the city. At midnight the streets were alive with mounted men and infantry."

ATTEMPT OF CONFEDERATE PRISONERS
TO ESCAPE BEFORE THE CONSPIRACY WAS RIPE

Courtesy, Chicago Historical Society

Newspaper sketch showing guards, probably at Camp Douglas, Chicago, firing on Confederates attempting to escape. There is no evidence of this.

The streets, he said, were patrolled all that night and for the next four days.

On November 8 the *Tribune* printed instructions "for all men to appear at Lincoln Hall, corner of Lake and Franklin Streets, at nine o'clock sharp." At three o'clock a proclamation by the mayor was issued and printed in the Chicago *Evening Journal,* "inviting the citizens of Chicago to enlist in the Home Guards for the protection of the city."

That night Scharf, then seventeen, and some friends went to Lincoln

Hall to enlist. It was a lark. They laughed and sang songs and admired the Federal colonel who stamped into the hall, a sword slapping at his side. Within a few hours old men, invalids and young boys were lined up five deep before the enrollment desk. The volunteers were put into one regiment augmented by the Zouave Cadets and the Nineteenth Illinois Infantry, under command of a major.

Enlistment was for three days only. At ten-thirty the order to "fall in" was given. Scharf and his young friends took their places, thrilled at the thought of meeting the Rebels at last in battle.

At State and Lake Streets they commandeered horsecars. The procession of cars, with Zouave Cadets, rifles dangling from their shoulders, and hanging from the front and rear doors, wound its way down State Street, Cottage Grove Avenue to Camp Douglas on the outskirts of the city.

In the camp they lined up before Colonel Sweet's headquarters. The strain of sleepless nights, of dealing with traitors who wanted only blood money, had etched deep lines about his mouth and eyes. He raised a lantern to let its yellow light reflect the eager young faces. He took a deep breath, a weary colonel, his heart weighed down with the indignity of war, talking to children who played at being soldiers.

"Thank you for your prompt response at short notice," he said. "I know you are tired and the hour is late. I order you to go back to your homes. . . ."

It was perhaps the disappointed look on the young faces that made him add, "Your officers will order you to report tomorrow morning at this camp."

The young firebrands gave him three times three and a tiger. They made an awkward turn about the parade, desperately trying to keep in step, then were dismissed by their officers with orders to report the following morning.

At two o'clock that morning, young Scharf arrived home, to describe breathlessly for his mother the thrilling night. The only thing lacking had been the Rebels. They hadn't come out for a fight. We can imagine that his mother, like any mother, thanked God they hadn't.

In his office Colonel Sweet was listing his prisoners for the Commander, Department of Illinois. One finds how carefully he guarded the fate of his informer. Among the prisoners taken that night, he reported, "was one Shanks, a Rebel prisoner."

When Grenfel was questioned, one of Sweet's officers handed him a slip of paper found in his room, on which had been written:

> Colonel—you must leave tonight. Go to Briggs House.
> J. Fielding.

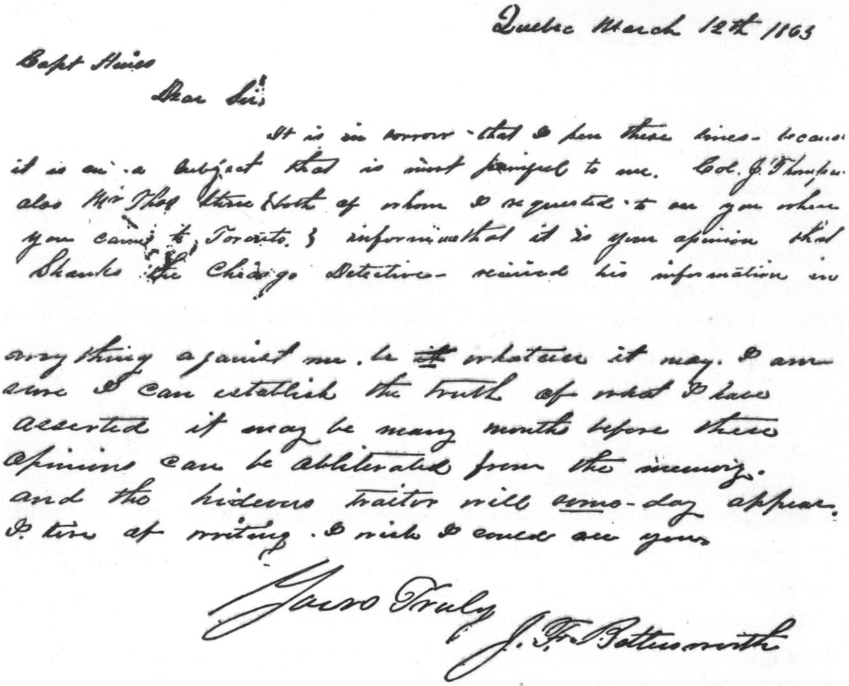

Quebec March 12th 1865

Capt Hines

Dear Sir

It is in sorrow that I pen these lines because it is on a subject that is most painful to me. Col. J. Thompson also Mr Thos Hines both of whom I requested to see you when you came to Toronto. I inform me that it is your opinion that Shanks the Chicago Detective received his information in

anything against me. be it whatever it may. I am sure I can establish the truth of what I have asserted it may be many months before these opinions can be obliterated from the memory. and the hideous traitor will some day appear. I tire at writing. I wish I could see you

Yours Truly

J. F. Bettersworth

Courtesy, Margaret I. King Library, University of Kentucky

Extracts from the letter from Bettersworth to Hines, pleading for a chance to see him and justify his own actions in the betrayal in Chicago.

Who was Fielding? Sweet and Shanks didn't know. In 1866 Hines disclosed his identity. On the back of Bettersworth's letter begging forgiveness, Hines had written to Nancy:

> You will see from this note that Mr. Bettersworth attempts to justify his conduct at Chicago, which in my opinion makes his case worse than has been charged upon him by his friends. I grieves me much to state it, but my conviction firmly establishes that Mr. B. did reveal the whole plan to Shanks while under the influence of liquor. Mr. B., you will remem-

. ber, is from Bowling Green, Ky. Feilding and Bettersworth
are the same. I have had no time to deal with this communication carefully. Please file with the other papers.

Your devoted husband. . . .

It is plain that the unfortunate Bettersworth, in the anguish of re-
morse and the morning after, had tried to warn St. Leger Grenfel,
who had put the letter aside, not knowing Bettersworth had signed a
fictitious name to save his own skin.

Courtesy, Margaret I. King Library, University of Kentucky

Hines' note to his wife written on the back of Bettersworth's letter to him,
commenting bitterly on Bettersworth's part in the betrayal in Chicago.

In August, 1866, after the war was over, Shanks met Sweet again, to recall those exciting nights. It was only then that he learned Sweet had never fully trusted him. As Sweet told Shanks, he had two of his own men in plain-clothes follow him, "constantly at your back, sworn to take your life if you wavered for half a second."

Shanks answered, "I felt it in the air."

XX. THE FOX AND THE HOUNDS

HINES remained in Chicago only long enough to make sure there was no way he could help Grenfel and the others to escape. Mary Walsh told him it was useless. She had seen her father, the "Brigadier-General" of the Sons of Liberty, who was in irons. They were all under heavy guard, she told Hines.

The city was alive with patrols. Additional troops arrived during the morning to augment Colonel Sweet's men. The army of civilian volunteers were armed with rifles and revolvers taken from the Copperhead arsenal. They were trigger-happy, and more than one honest citizen abroad at night found himself in a crossfire from several volunteers who first fired, then shouted a command to halt.

It was one of the darkest hours of Hines' life. The revolution he had been so sure would succeed had fizzled out like all his other great plans; he was now a lost leader alone in an enemy city. Only Mary Walsh could be trusted. And after he had escaped under her umbrella from Edwards' house he had to say goodbye. He told her that if he were captured with her she could expect a long prison term. Ironically, she was arrested the next day.

Somehow Hines got out of the city. It had rained for two days and that might have helped him. He used back alleys, hugging the shadows as the patrols clattered past. Constantly on the move, by horseback, carriage and train, he crossed the Indiana border, traveling south into the lion's mouth at Indianapolis, then swung southeast into Ohio to hide out at the home of his friend Sam Thomas in Cincinnati.

This was probably Hines at his best. Surrounded by traitors, with nowhere to turn, he managed to escape by cunning and improvisation. There were the problems of timing; rendezvous with the few people left whom he could trust; of undependable railroad schedules; of the soldier-detectives and Colonel Carrington's agents through whose territory he rode so calmly. All these had to be surmounted by an enemy agent with a price on his head.

In Cincinnati Hines took a carriage to Sam Thomas' two-story wooden house on Lawrence and Fourth Streets. It was late at night when he knocked at the door. After what must have seemed an eternity, he heard footsteps on the stairs.

"Who is it?" a muffled voice asked.

"Tom Hines."

The door edged open. Thomas held up a candle. "Come in! Quickly!" he said, opening the door.

Inside, he hurried Hines to the kitchen. Mary Thomas came down in her dressing gown.

"Tom! We heard you had been captured in Chicago," she said.

"It was a close call," Hines replied with a grin. "They got Marmaduke and St. Leger. . . ."

"Walsh, too," Thomas said.

Hines asked, "Did you hear from Edwards?"

Thomas nodded. "He said you had left his house but heard the next day Sweet's traitors found you in the old clothes store. Geary was arrested yesterday."

Hines said, "They burned all the papers in a stove before they broke down his door. The others are safe."

The "old clothes store" was one of the Confederate underground stations which sheltered escaped prisoners before sending them to Canada. Located at Madison and Wells Streets in Chicago, its owner, James Geary, was a notorious Copperhead who knew Hines.

Thomas showed him the *Gazette* which told how "the notorious Hines, of Morgan's old command" had been trailed by Federal detectives to Cincinnati. The homes of all suspected Copperheads in the city were going to be searched.

Hines' first thought was to leave at once, rather than endanger his friends. But Sam insisted it would be suicide. All depots and trains were being watched, the *Gazette* said, with patrols on the roads leading in and out of the city.

Somehow Hines must be concealed in the house. Together they feverishly searched the rooms and cellar for a suitable hiding place, while Mary kept guard from a parlor window. In the upstairs bedroom they removed Mary's dresses and Sam's suits to inspect the large clothes closet. It was five feet wide and as many feet deep. The back was faced with wide boards.

"What is behind those boards, Sam?" Hines asked.

"I don't know," Sam replied. "Let's find out."

A crowbar pried loose the boards. They found another old closet, concealed by red bricks and mortar. If enough bricks could be re-moved, it would be a wonderful hiding place if the patrols came. Sam said he knew Dan Weil, formerly of Lexington, Kentucky, "a true friend" who was now a "mechanic" in Cincinnati. He would ask him to come over and advise them how to remove the bricks.

Weil came that night after supper. The three of them, with Mary standing guard at the parlor window, removed enough bricks to make a niche. Then Hines, fortunately a slight man, squeezed into the hole while Sam and Weil put the boards back into place.

"How is it, Tom?" Sam asked.

"Fine, Sam," was the faint reply.

The boards were pulled back and Hines stepped out, dirty and sweating, but grinning.

There was only one hitch. It took too long to put the boards into place. With the Federals banging any minute on the front door the hiding place had to be rigged up with split-second timing.

Hines, Thomas and Weil began experimenting in using the niche. The three of them would sit in the parlor playing cards. Suddenly Mary at the window would hiss, "A patrol!" Hines and Weil would race up the stairs. The boards would be pulled back, Hines would squirm into the hole and the boards would be pushed into position. Then Weil would race back to the parlor. As Hines told Castleman, they "practiced" until the job of concealing him was "easy and effec-tive." Sometimes Thomas took Weil's part in case the mechanic could not be present, or had been arrested.

Suddenly the "dress rehearsal" became reality. "Here's the patrol," Mary said suddenly in a tight voice. Hines and Weil leaped to their feet to race upstairs. The clothes were pushed aside, the boards pulled back. Hines flattened himself into the niche. Weil, sweating, his fingers seemingly all thumbs, pushed the boards back. Weil whispered a last "good luck," then slammed the door. Hines, as he recalled, pressed his mouth and nose to a tiny slit in the boards, sucking in the stagnant air. The warm darkness seemed to throb with the sound of his racing heart.

As Weil reached the parlor, Thomas was at the door waiting. When he saw the mechanic slump in a chair, he yanked open the door and stepped aside. Blue uniforms pushed into the hall.

"We are on government business," the officer said. "You are sus-pected of hiding Rebel spies."

"You are welcome to search our house, sir," Thomas said.

The lieutenant was casually efficient. He had been doing this all day. "Take two men and search the cellar," he told his sergeant. "The rest of you men follow me upstairs."

The soldiers clumped up the stairway. They searched a small spare room, then the bedroom. In his hiding place Hines heard the approaching boots and tried to push himself deeper in the niche. The closet door swung open. A soldier pushed aside the dresses and coats with his bayoneted rifle.

"Nothing here, sir," he said. The door slammed shut. Hines, almost suffocating in the tiny hole, pressed his face against the slit between the boards trying to fill his lungs.

The patrol came out of the cellar. The lieutenant listened to his sergeant's report.

"I'm sorry, sir," he told Thomas. "I am only acting under orders."

"I understand, Lieutenant," Thomas said.

The Federal officer saluted and went out, followed by his men. Through the curtains they watched the bluecoats go up the street. Then Thomas and Weil raced upstairs. The closet door was flung open, the boards pulled back. Hines staggered out into their arms.

"They've gone, Tom," Thomas said.

"Did they leave any sentries?" the practical Hines asked.

Thomas shook his head. Hines gave a sigh of relief and fell into a chair.

"What are you going to do now, Tom?" Sam asked.

When Tom told them, Sam, Mary and Dan Weil gasped. "But how will you do that, Tom?" Sam asked.

"I'll need your help, Sam," Hines said. Then he took out a much folded map, spread it out on a table and showed them how it could be done.

Sam hurried to get the bottle of peach brandy. The glasses were filled and they raised them to toast the future happiness of Tom and his bride.

Tom had told them he had learned Nancy was in an Ohio convent. He was going to spirit her out, bring her to Kentucky and be married there.

XXI. A RAINY WEDDING NIGHT

IT HAD rained all day. When twilight rolled in, mist lay on the ground, heavy as fog in the hollows. It billowed through the orchard outside the convent walls, leaving gray wisps hanging from the naked branches like strings of grimy lace. Night came, wet, windy and filled with expectancy.

Nancy looked out the window of her room on the second floor of the Dunville Institute, a Catholic convent school in Brown County, Ohio. Rain splattered against the pane. She turned up the lamp and sat down to read Tom's letter again, which now she knew by heart.

A man in a carriage was to call that night at eleven o'clock. He would have a message from her father. They would ride to Nancy's cousin's home nearby to tell him she was leaving the convent to join her father. From Brown County the man would take her across the Ohio River into Kentucky. There she and Tom Hines would be married.

Nancy already had her things packed. She hoped the Mother Superior would not notice how quickly she was able to leave. She thought she heard hoofbeats. But it was only the whip of the wind lashing the trees.

During the long wait that night, Nancy, as she later told Tom, reviewed in her heart the last turbulent years. The future, she realized, was stalked by uncertainty. But to be with Tom, to hear his voice, to feel his lips on hers again, was all that mattered.

Before she left Kentucky for the convent school her father had insisted they must wait to marry until the war was over. Nancy told him that if anything happened to Tom she would die. War or no war, she wanted to be his wife more than anything else in the world. Captain Sproule, with a father's caution, pointed out that Hines was engaged in dangerous affairs, that every day brought him nearer to the gallows. The Yankees would have no mercy if they captured the man who had so long been a menace to the security of northern cities.

Nancy could only reply, "I love him, father . . . I will go to him. wherever he is, whenever he asks me. . . ."

The convent was quiet as the thoughts moved through Nancy's head. Above the moaning of the wind, a carriage rattled up the lane almost under her window. But she wasn't listening any more. She was thinking only of "my Tom."

The peal of the doorbell broke the silence. Nancy jumped to her feet. She turned the lamp low and looked out. She could see the horses and the carriage glistening in the rain.

The bell pealed again. She heard the Mother Superior go down-stairs. Nancy opened the door slightly. She heard a man's voice, then the Mother Superior's. She thought she heard her name. When the Mother Superior began climbing the stairs, Nancy put out the lamp and sat in the tense darkness.

The nun knocked. Nancy waited. There was a second knock and her name was called out softly. Nancy answered in what she hoped was a sleepy voice. The Mother Superior told her to come down at once. There was a man at the door with an important message for her.

In a few minutes Nancy faced a strange man whose dripping coat had made a little pool at his feet. She recalled later that he was about Tom's age and had a neat moustache.

"Miss Nancy Sproule?" Sam Thomas asked.

"I am Miss Sproule," she replied.

Sam handed her a telegram from Cincinnati. It read:

Miss Nancy Sproule, Dunville Institute, Brown County, Ohio.
    I am at Burnett House, Cincinnati. Come at once. Call on Cousin John Carter for funds.

(Signed),
Your loving father.

"I hope nothing is wrong, child," the nun said.

Nancy smiled at her. "I'm sure there isn't, Sister."

"You will go to your cousin John Carter's house at once, Nancy," the nun said.

"Yes, Sister," Nancy replied. She said to Sam: "I will be only a minute. . . ."

Nancy came down with a small bag. Sam helped her into the carriage and they drove off, with the Mother Superior watching them from a window.

They stopped first at Cousin John Carter's house. Sam knew the way. He had stopped there before coming on to the convent to show Carter the letter. He had promised he would return with Nancy.

Cousin John seemed puzzled. "Your father sent this young man to escort you to Cincinnati, Nannie," he said. "He said it was most urgent that he see you. . . ."

Nancy gave him her sweetest smile. "Father is probably lonely," she said.

This explanation seemed to satisfy Carter. To warm them for the journey, Nancy was urged to take a cup of steaming tea and Sam, a glass of whiskey. They returned to the carriage, with Cousin John holding a lamp high, protecting the flame with one hand, while his wife called out their farewells. The telegram, the summons for Nancy, didn't sound quite right to Cousin John. He never knew the romantic story until the war was over. "Of course neither Cousin John nor his family knew we were playing off on them," Nancy wrote her father a few days later.

It was a strange journey through the windy night. Once out of sight of Cousin John, Sam lay his whip across the rump of his horses. They rode through the back alleys and lanes to avoid the town watchmen. Once out of town Sam used his whip again. The horses responded. The carriage flew along the countryside. Nancy huddled in a corner of the carriage, a blanket up to her chin, the rain snapping in her face. But Nancy had no thoughts of the weather. Her heart was filled; the waiting would soon be over.

They rode northwest, stopping at Sam's house in Cincinnati to pick up his wife, Mary, who was to be the other witness, then south to the Ohio, crossing over to Covington, Kentucky.

The carriage stopped at a farmhouse on the outskirts of the town. The shutters were drawn and the house looked deserted. Sam leaped down.

"Stay here for a moment," he whispered. The two women watched him walk up to the path. A splinter of light pierced the night when the door opened. Then it closed.

Sam was back in a moment. "The way is clear," he said.

Nancy would always recall how her pulse hammered in her throat as she hurried up the path, holding on to Sam and Mary.

Sam knocked on the door. It swung open. Nancy entered a large room. A lamp, turned low, was on the table. Two men were standing before a fire of flaking coals. One rushed forward.

"Nannie!" Tom said.

As Nancy said, she fell into the arms of her "beloved Tom."

When Nancy at last broke free from Tom's embrace, she saw that the other man, smiling kindly at her, wore a clerical collar.

"We are ready, Father," Sam Thomas told him. Father Butler, pastor of St. Mary's Cathedral, Covington, nodded. He was ready for the marriage ceremony. Sam and Mary Thomas took their places. The solemn words filled the room. Sam gave Tom the wedding ring and he slipped it on Nancy's finger.

This is Nancy's version of her marriage to Tom Hines, as she described it in a letter to her father two days later. However, she knew the Federals were opening her family's mail because she was the sweetheart of Tom Hines, so she carefully obscured some of the details.

The marriage, she said, had taken place "somewhere in Illinois," but the statement Hines asked Father Butler to sign so that there would be no question of Nancy's honor gives Covington as the town. The statement reads:

> On the 10th of Nov., 1864 eighteen hundred & sixty four—Thomas H. Hines & Nancy S. Sproule of Louisville, Ky., were married in the presence of Samuel P. Thomas and Mary A. Thomas.
>
> I hereby testify that the above is a correct extract from the Marriage Register of St. Marys Cathedral Church, Covington, Ky.—that the marriage was performed by me & that I am the usual & proper custodian of the said Register.
> > Signed,
> > T. R. Butler, O. G.
> > Pastor of the Cathedral, Covington, Ky.

The week of their honeymoon, spent somewhere in Kentucky, was the happiest of their lives. They realized every hour was precious and treasured each one. Nancy knew that Tom was to leave her arms in a week to go on a dangerous mission. He had told her something of his work in the Northwest but had carefully avoided details of the narrow escapes, the price on his head and the traitors who were selling them all out. Only after the war would Nancy know the whole story. But she knew enough of it at that time to realize the gallows awaited her husband if he were caught.

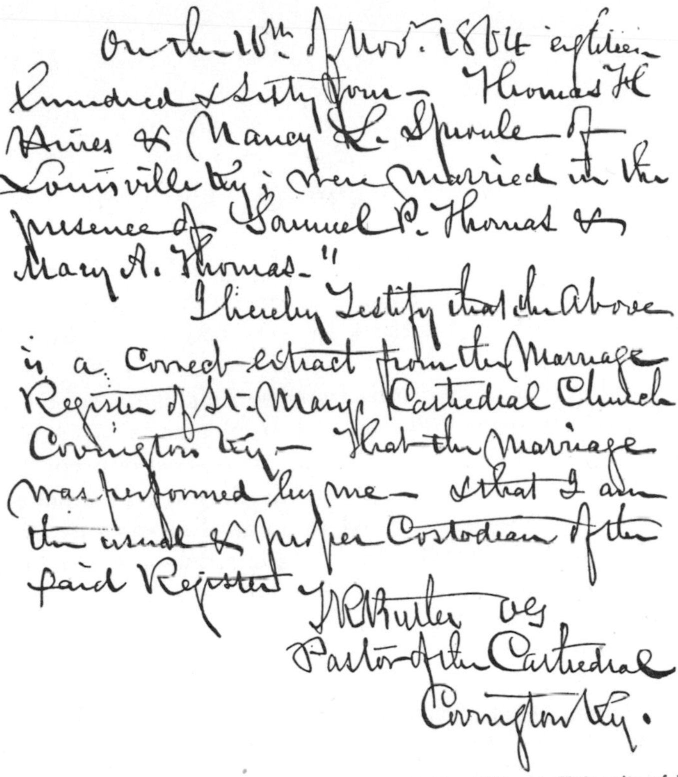

[Handwritten marriage certificate extract:]

On the 16th of Nov. 1864 eighteen hundred & sixty four — Thomas H. Hines & Nancy L. Sproule of Louisville Ky; were married in the presence of Samuel P. Thomas & Mary A. Thomas —

"I hereby Testify that the Above is a Correct Extract from the Marriage Register of St. Mary's Cathedral Church Covington Ky — That the Marriage was performed by me — that I am the true & proper Custodian of the said Register

J. R. Butler
Pastor of the Cathedral
Covington Ky.

Courtesy, Margaret I. King Library, University of Kentucky

A copy of the marriage certificate of Tom Hines and Nancy Sproule. Sam and Mary Thomas hid Hines in a wall of their home in Cincinnati.

Her young heart was full that week. She was gay and never more beautiful to Tom. In the lonely months ahead he would recall this. On the eighth day, their honeymoon ended. Nancy, forcing herself to hold back the tears, kissed Tom goodbye and returned to Bowling Green. Tom slipped through the Federal lines into Ohio, where he hid out at Sam Thomas's house. Then he crossed into Indiana, meeting with Doctor Bowles' Copperheads to encourage and guide them in committing sabotage and stirring up unrest.

Across the country the great plans of Colonel Martin and his raiders to burn New York City had slipped badly.

XXII. THE BURNING OF NEW YORK

FEAR weighed heavily on the heart of Colonel Martin as he read in the New York *Herald* of the mass arrests in Chicago, "which frustrated the dastardly plot to sack the city and turn Chicago into an enemy stronghold."

He turned to the young printer from the *Freeman's Journal* who had just delivered the paper. "Please send my thanks to Mr. McMasters," he said. "Tell him I wish to see him at the earliest opportunity."

The printer nodded and went out. Martin put on his hat and coat to hurry over to the Astor Hotel to show the paper to Lieutenant Headley. Later that night they re-read the article in the small cottage in Central Park which Martin had rented to use as their command post when the uprising was to begin in the city.

They viewed the latest news as another evil omen. Bad luck had dogged their footsteps ever since they had arrived.

At first it had seemed that the city was ripe for revolution. In his office of the *Freeman's Journal* on Union Square, James McMasters, a huge man with a spade beard the color of new rust, told them the Sons of Liberty were ready to march, twenty thousand strong, on City Hall.

The following day they met Captain Longuemare, who introduced them to Katie McDonald, the pretty red-haired daughter of W. Larry McDonald, high in the ranks of the Sons of Liberty. The McDonald piano shop on Washington Square was the secret meeting place for the Copperhead leaders who were planning the insurrection.

Captain Longuemare looked like a firebrand. He was tall and good-looking, with a pointed black goatee. He spoke with a harsh twang and seemed eager to mount the barricades of revolt. He gave Martin and Headley a list of hotels to be burned, beginning with the Hotel Astor, "the most fashionable in the city."

Longuemare sketched for the raiders the military set-up of the Sons of Liberty. With a pencil he drew a rough map of New York City on the tablecloth, showing how important streets would be blocked off

by crowds, thrown into a panic by Copperhead agents, thus preventing the passage of troops or artillery through the city. The attack
would be aided by city and state officials, who would adopt "un-
official neutrality" until the riots were over and the city seized.

On Election Day, the Missouri captain said, a convention of Copperhead societies from New York, New Jersey, Connecticut and several New England states would open in New York. When the first
fires broke out they would appear in the streets with rifles and bombs.
A hundred picked men would turn City Hall into a fortress. Agents
had been assigned to touch off the charges of gunpowder planted
under the gate of Fort Lafayette. Police headquarters on Worth Street
—after its seizure—would become the command headquarters for the
Confederates. Headley and Martin would occupy Superintendent of
Police Kennedy's office.

After lunch Martin and Headley walked down Broadway to the
Battery, their brains awhirl with the great plans. A courier left for
Toronto that night, carrying their coded message to Thompson. Their
dreams, they predicted, would soon be confirmed by success.

The next day they moved to the more luxurious Fifth Avenue Hotel.
That same afternoon Martin and Headley met in secret "the private
secretary" of New York's Governor Seymour. Promises of "official neutrality" were again made. A courier for the Copperheads was sent to
pick up their bags that evening to take them to McDonald's basement
headquarters on Washington Square.

While waiting for Election Day the Copperheads had little to do
but enjoy themselves. There were a lecture by Artemus Ward at
Wood's Broadway Theatre, Henry Ward Beecher's sermons in Brooklyn, riotous meetings of Tammany Hall and a monster torchlight parade up Broadway. They watched former General McClellan review
it on Fifth Avenue. After the parade they joined the thousands that
filled Madison Square. They were amazed at the ferocity of the mob's
feeling against Lincoln. When caricatures of the President were lifted
above the speaker's stand, hisses rose to fill the night with the noise
of a million angry bees.

The crown stayed until the early hours of the morning, alternately
booing the Lincoln administration and cheering McClellan and his
fellow candidates. At that hour, as the Confederates all agreed years
later, the flame of revolt had burned bright. Only an incident would
be necessary to touch off a repetition of the draft riots which had
turned the city into a shambles.

Disaster rose with the sun the following morning. Headley looked out his hotel window to see Federal troops marching up Broadway. They soon discovered what had happened. General Ben Butler— "Beast" Butler as the ladies of New Orleans called him—had entered the city with ten thousand troops to establish martial law.

There seemed no reason why the Army should appear. Copperhead agents tried to find out. They reported back to Martin that there were rumors of a threatened raid on the city by Confederate guerrillas. Had someone betrayed them?

Ironically, Butler and his staff stopped at the Fifth Avenue Hotel, occupying the entire floor below Martin and Headley's room. More than once the Confederates watched the Federal general, his bald head and bulging eyes giving him the look of a disturbed toad, stride through the lobby, followed by his officers.

The *New York Times* applauded Butler's arrival. "The wisdom of the government should be praised in selecting a man who had scattered the howling rabble of New Orleans like chaff and made the Copperheads writhe and squirm in torture."

Headley and his men read uneasily the last paragraph of the editorial, which predicted that Butler would "meet at every point, the Rebel emissaries who would put into execution the villainous threats, made by Richmond papers, of laying New York, Buffalo and northern cities in ashes." It was apparent to all of them that Thompson's airtight secrecy had turned into a sieve. As had often happened, Richmond newspapers and loose tongues had given away much of their plan.

The effect on the Copperheads of Butler's entrance into the city was soon apparent to the Confederates. On the evening of the 7th, the eve of the planned revolt, McMasters, editor of *Freeman's Journal*, informed Martin that the Sons of Liberty officers had cancelled the convention and "postponed all action." Martin and Headley were enraged. But no threats or name-calling could budge McMasters. All he would promise was that the postponement was "temporary." The election passed. Lincoln was returned to the White House.

The Confederates began to trail General Butler, trying to learn when he was going to leave the city. But Butler seemed permanently entrenched in his luxurious quarters at the Fifth Avenue Hotel. Nightly meetings were held with the Copperheads to keep up their dwindling courage. "The more we insisted on the attempt to burn New York City, the weaker Mr. McMasters became," Headley wrote.

Captain Longuemare made violent speeches at these meetings but they did little good. A tentative date for the raid was finally set for Thanksgiving Day, the 25th. But again, at the eleventh hour, the Sons of Liberty sent word that it was off. "We have decided to withdraw from any further connection with the proposed revolution," McMasters wrote Martin.

The Confederate officers voted to go it alone. At another meeting they broke this news to McMasters and Longuemare. The flat statement of action drenched the fire of revolt in Captain Longuemare's heart. He announced, "I am discouraged," and left for a stay in the country. "Until your sensation is over," he told Martin. Before he left, Martin, by threats or money, obtained from him the address of the bomb-maker in the city who was to supply the Copperheads. Longuemare told him he was an old chemist who lived on Washington Square. "All charges have been paid," he said.

Headley found the chemist in a basement on the west side of Washington Square. As he opened the door a bell tinkled in the rear. A gnomelike man with a dirty white beard shuffled out from behind a curtain. He stared at Headley with tiny, button-shiny eyes.

"I have come for the valise," Headley said in the manner of characters of countless modern spy stories.

"Who sent you?" the man asked.

"Captain Longuemare."

The chemist studied Headley for a moment, then walked back through the curtain-door.

Headley never forgot the deadly quiet of the basement room. He could hear the muffled clatter of horses and wagons and the rattling of the horsecars passing the door. A woman shrilled something to a child. In the room a clock ticked loudly. He was alone in a basement in an enemy city. He had exposed himself to a man he had never seen. Suppose. . . .

The curtain was suddenly pushed aside. The chemist was dragging something. He was breathing hard by the time Headley reached his side, to take hold of the valise.

"Thank you," he said, but the man ignored him, vanishing behind the curtain.

The valise, as Headley described it, was four feet long and two or three feet high. It was so heavy he had to stop and rub his hands every ten or fifteen steps. At the corner of Washington Square West he vainly tried to hail a "carriage hack." After several had passed him, he picked up the valise and began to walk.

When he reached the Bowery he boarded a Central Park-bound horsecar. The car was crowded and he had to push his way inside, receiving black looks from passengers over whose feet he had stumbled or whose shins had been barked by the valise. As the car continued north, the passengers thinned out. At last he managed to get a seat directly behind the conductor. With a sigh of relief he sat down, pushing the valise between his legs.

Near Madison Square Headley first noticed the odor—heavy, smelling of rotten eggs. A chill crept up his back. From his knowledge of Greek fire he knew that one of the containers must have spilled. He looked down. There was no tell-tale brownish stain leading from the corners of the valise, but the odor grew stronger. The man next to him moved to another seat. Other passengers gave him hard looks, murmuring suspiciously among themselves.

A woman spoke up. "Something smells dead here," she said loudly. She looked directly at Headley. The Confederate tried to look unconcernedly out of the window.

She sniffed loudly. Headley's nonchalance, hiding a thundering heart, evidently nonplussed her. She held her tongue until Central Park. When Headley rose to leave, she said very loudly, "Conductor, something smells dead in that man's valise."

Headley picked up the valise. He tipped his hat gallantly. "Madam," he said, "I assure you I don't carry dead bodies in my valise. Good day."

He stepped down to the street, deliberately pausing to light a cigar, then went on to the small cottage Martin had rented where they were to meet to be given final instructions. The other Confederates were waiting anxiously. When Headley entered Martin threw his arm about him. "We had thought you lost," he said. With a mixture of laughter and seriousness they listened to his story of the ride on the horsecar.

Headley opened the valise. There were one hundred and forty-four four-ounce bottles of Greek fire. As he had suspected, one had tipped over, spilling its contents. Each man was given ten or more bottles and a list of hotels. They were to register in the hotels under fictitious names. At eight the following evening Headley was to begin with the Astor and give the west side docks a "warm reception." The hour of eight was selected, they said, because of the dinner hour, and "no lives would be lost."

They all shook hands. As Headley recalled, Captain Kennedy said as they walked out into the brisk November night. "Well, we'll make a spoon or spoil a horn tomorrow night."

At six o'clock on the evening of November 25, the Rebels held their last meeting in the Central Park cottage. Two members failed to show up. This was ominous but Martin gave last-minute instructions and information. Once the fires had been started they were to return to the cottage. In the event of capture Martin told them to give their real names, commission and command. They were to say that the raid on the city had been made in retaliation for what Sherman and Sheridan had done in the South.

Headley registered at the Astor, the City Hotel and the United States Hotel. Martin occupied rooms at the Hoffman House, the Fifth Avenue Hotel, and the St. Denis. Lieutenant Ashbrook signed the register at the St. Nicholas, the LaFarge and the St. James. The *Herald's* account has them checking into a total of nineteen hotels.

Headley was given a room on the fourth floor of the Astor directly facing Broadway. As he passed down the corridor he failed to notice that several buckets of water had been placed in a row near the stairway. Inside the room he lit the gas, pulled the curtains together and went to work. Chairs, bureau drawers and a wooden washstand were piled on the bed. Rugs were tossed on top. Newspapers were packed around the base. He unlocked the door and looked out. The corridor was deserted. He closed the door and opened his valise to select a fire bomb. He closed the valise, edged to the door and flung the bottle. There was a whoosh of flame. The bed caught and the newspapers flared up.

Headley went out, locking the door behind him. In the lobby, he turned in his key, telling the clerk he was going to dine with a friend. As he recalled, it took all his will power to walk slowly across the crowded lobby, tipping his hat to the ladies in evening clothes, or standing aside to let one pass. At last he was outside. The doorman wanted to call a hack, but Headley said the night was warm and he would rather walk.

The City Hotel was next. He left with that room in flames. The United States Hotel near the Astor was also on his list. He was given a room on the third floor. As he parted the curtains he could see a "dull glow" in one of the rooms of the Astor.

Frantically he piled chairs, drawers and rugs on the bed. One of the bombs failed to go off. The second exploded with a dull clump. The flames spread so rapidly Headley barely had time to get out. As he started down the stairs he heard the frantic clang of fire engines. For a moment they almost made him betray himself. As he walked across the lobby a voice called, "Sir! Just a moment, sir!"

He wondered if he should run. He gripped the revolver in his pocket and turned around. The clerk, smiling, was beckoning to him.

"Your key, sir—if you are going out!"

"Oh, yes," Headley said. He went back to toss the key on the desk. The clerk was staring at him in a puzzled fashion. Headley felt the sweat bead on his forehead.

"Your bag, sir? Are you leaving so soon?"

Headley smiled weakly. "I'm going to see a friend off," he said. "Goodnight."

He could feel the clerk's eyes stabbing his back until he went out the front door. The United States Hotel was next. When he came out of the last one Headley found Broadway mobbed. Firemen were dragging hoses into the Astor. Flames were shooting out of a fourth-floor window. As he started to turn away another engine company came up Broadway at a gallop, black smoke belching from its funnel.

"Barnum's Museum is afire," someone shouted. The crowd eddied, then went forward with a rush in the direction of the famous museum, sweeping Headley along like a leaf in a mill-race.

A huge crowd had gathered in front of the museum. From where he stood, Headley could see the flames shooting from the upper windows. Two men were sliding down the iron pillars in front of the building. When a woman appeared on the second-floor balcony, the crowd roared, "Don't jump . . . don't jump."

For a moment she stood there, outlined against the glare. Firemen rushed through the crowd, bowling people aside like ninepins. A ladder went up. The crowd roared its approval as a fireman raced nimbly up the ladder to rescue the swooning lady.

Now above the crowd's roar came the sound of frenzied animals: the trumpeting of a bull elephant, the roar of a tiger. A manager kept running through the crowd, shouting, "Save the animals . . . save Mr. Barnum's animals. . . ."

A terrifying figure suddenly appeared in the front doorway. She

Lieutenant John W. Headley, one of the Confederate raiders who attempted to kidnap Andrew Johnson.

Colonel Robert M. Martin, who was in command of the raiders who attempted to burn New York in 1864.

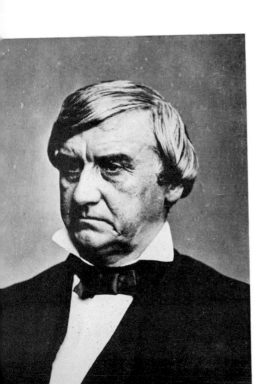

Judge Advocate General Joseph Holt, who vigorously investigated and prosecuted Copperhead leaders.

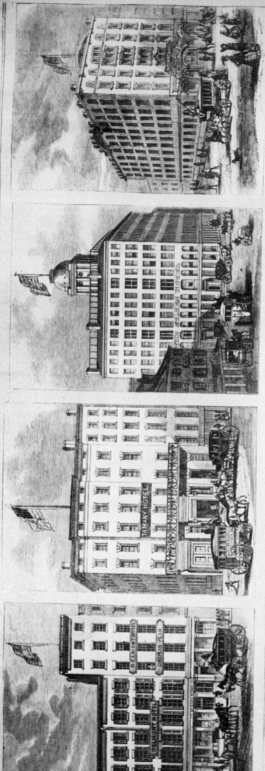

New York hotels which were targets of the Confederates: from
left to right and from top to bottom: the Belmont, Tammany,
United States, International, Metropolitan, Fifth Avenue, Astor,
St. Nicholas, La Farge, Barnum's, Howard, St. James', Lovejoy's.

ABOVE: Fort Jefferson in the Dry Tortugas, where Colonel George St. Leger Grenfel was imprisoned for his part in the Northwest Conspracy.

BELOW: A view of the moat a shark, the "Provost Marshal," patrolled.

was easily seven feet tall, with a shock of thick black hair. She had enormous shoulders and arms like fence posts. Her voice sounded like the frightened bellowing of a bull moose. Mr. Barnum's giantess— "the most spectacular female on earth," as his posters claimed—had gone berserk. She flailed about wildly, screaming in terror. Two men tried to hold her, but she tossed them aside with ease. A fire captain and the museum's manager ran up, only to go down under a hammer blow of those big arms.

She plunged through the crowd. A human aisle quickly opened for her. On the opposite side of Broadway she ran into the lobby of the Powers Hotel. Five firemen and several spectators followed her. The clanging fire bells, the pall of smoke, the crackling of flames, the roar of crowds and the wild-eyed men moving in on her turned the museum's giantess into a raging Amazon. She fought fiercely, shouting that she did not want to get burned, that the flames were all around her. Finally, by sheer weight of numbers, she was overpowered. After a doctor administered a sedative she was put into a room of the Powers Hotel with two of Barnum's employees standing guard. The firemen went back to battling the blaze, which was soon brought under control.

Headley, according to plan, hurried down Broadway. At Bayard Street he turned west to the North River piers. Against the star-shot night, barges and schooners were hulking clots of bows, cross-bars and rigging. The street was pitch-black. Headley opened his valise, selected a bottle and hurled the fire-bomb. It broke on the deck of a barge. Flames began spreading.

Headley started down the street on the run, hurling his bottles of Greek fire at the shadowy ships. His last throw was the best. The bottle broke on the hay barge *Marie* and exploded with a gushing flame. He turned east, coming back on Broadway just above the burning Barnum's Museum. Firemen were still clambering up and down the ladders. Others were leading animals out into the street which was still packed with spectators. Fire bells were echoing up and down Broadway. Headley pushed through the crowd, crossing the square to the Bowery where he caught a horsecar.

"Those damn Rebels have started the city on fire," a conductor shouted. At the Bowery, opposite the Metropolitan Hotel, the car was halted by a crowd. The hotel was afire. Headley jumped off "to see how Ashbrook was doing."

He had gone only a block when he saw Captain Kennedy pushing his way through the crowd. Headley hurried up to him. He touched him on the shoulder. The Confederate whirled about.

Headley caught the glimpse of a gun in his hand; in that instant, as Headley said, his life hung in the balance. Kennedy almost slumped down in relief when he saw his comrade's face.

"Damn you for giving me such a scare!" he said. "I should shoot you down."

"What about Ashbrook?" Headley demanded.

"I just left him. There he goes," Kennedy said, pointing to a man crossing the street.

Without saying another word they linked arms, continuing on up Broadway. On their way, Kennedy told Headley how he had started fires in the Tammany, LaFarge and Lovejoy Hotels. After starting a fire in the Lovejoy, he had gone into the museum, intending to get lost in the crowd.

He was in the basement looking at the animals when the first fire bell had sounded. He was rushing upstairs when an idea came to him. He still had two bottles of Greek fire. He waited until the crowd had gone out, then hurled his bottles against a step and a basement wall, "as you would crack an egg."

When they arrived at the Astor, the fire had been extinguished. Lynch law was in the air. The crowd was shouting to the soldiers now patrolling the city that the Rebels must be hanged.

"They know we are here," Kennedy said. "If Butler catches us, he'll hang us."

Two more of the raiders joined them outside the Astor, whispering as they came up that "they had done their jobs."

"The Rebels have started a fire in Niblo's Garden Theatre," someone shouted. The crowd pushed forward. The Confederates flattened themselves against the wall of a building. Another engine clanged up Broadway.

"Hang the Rebels," a man shouted. The crowd chanted it like a battle cry as they followed the mounted patrol up Broadway.

By eleven o'clock Martin had gathered together his raiders. It was obvious that if they traveled in a group they would be caught. Martin told them to split up into pairs and join him at Carter's Restaurant in Union Square. They were to take separate tables.

The restaurant was crowded. Kennedy, Martin and Headley selected a table in the rear. The others came in, glanced over at them, and ordered coffee. The morning papers arrived to create a stir in

THE NEW YORK HERALD

WHOLE NO. 10,318. NEW YORK, SUNDAY, NOVEMBER 27, 1864. PRICE FIVE CENTS.

ATTEMPT TO BURN THE CITY.

Discovery of a Vast Rebel Conspiracy.

Twelve Hotels Fired by Turpentine and Phosphorus.

SIMILAR ATTEMPTS ON THE SHIPPING.

Prompt Frustration of the Scheme.

GREAT PANIC AT BARNUM'S MUSEUM

Excitement at Niblo's and the Winter Garden.

Full Development of the Plot.

ARREST OF FOUR OF THE PRINCIPALS.

One of Morgan's Guerillas Implicated.

HIS ARREST AND IMPRISONMENT.

Vigorous Orders of Major General Dix.

The Perpetrators to be Tried by Court Martial and Hanged Immediately.

Rewards Offered for the Arrest of the Guilty.

OPERATIONS OF THE DETECTIVES.

THE LATEST PARTICULARS,

&c., &c., &c.

The details published in yesterday's HERALD respecting what turns out to be a vast and fiendish plot to burn down our grand Empire City gave rise to the most profound excitement among all classes of our citizens. There was no panic, no evidence of ridiculous fright or the wild apprehension that might naturally be expected to result from the discovery of a conspiracy, which, if successful, would have been accompanied by such unspeakable horrors. Our people took the affair very collectedly, taking all things into consideration; but they did not the less on that account realize the fact that they had escaped,
by a miracle, from a dreadful calamity, wh...
have left half the city in ashes and cons...
of innocent persons—men, women ...
... capable of dealing. Vi...

States authorities were not moved by a slight cause when, just preceding the election, they warned the Mayors of all our principal cities to be on the alert against an extensive plot of incendiarism. The result would seem to fully justify the alarm then created, and even the apparently harsh measures recommended and adopted. The attempt to burn down this city by one common means, and at about the same hour, and on the same night, is evidently a part of the conspiracy then partially discovered.

OUR SOUTHERN RESIDENTS.

It will be remembered that Major General Dix issued an order in the latter part of October requiring all the Southern residents in the Department of the East to register their names at General Peck's headquarters before the third day of November. This order has been obeyed only in a very few instances. It is believed that there are not less than twelve or fourteen thousand Southern refugees resident in this city; but of that large number only a part have thought proper to obey General Dix's order by registering their names, and the disregard of the rest is looked upon as a very suspicious circumstance. All that was required of them was to come forward and show their loyalty; and having refused to do so, they can hardly consider themselves deeply wronged when they learn that the authorities view them as suspicious characters, unfriendly to the government and likely to join in any wild scheme for its overthrow. It may be that many of them are honest and harmless, only desiring to live in quiet and peace, but the fact that they have not complied with Gen. Dix's order leaves no room to discriminate.

PROMPT ACTION OF GENERAL DIX.

In view of the developements yesterday, Major General Dix has issued the following remarkable orders, indicating what sort of punishment the perpetrators will receive, and calling again upon Southern residents to come forward and register themselves:—

GENERAL ORDERS—NO. 92.

HEADQUARTERS, DEPARTMENT OF THE EAST, }
NEW YORK, Nov. 26, 1864. }

A nefarious attempt was made last night to set fire to the principal hotels and other places of public resort in this city. If this attempt had succeeded, it would have resulted in a frightful sacrifice of property and life. The evidences of extensive combination, and other facts disclosed to-day, show it to have been the work of rebel emissaries and agents. All such persons engaged in secret acts of hostility here can only be regarded as spies, subject to martial law, and to the penalty of death. If they are detected, they will be immediately brought before a court martial or military commission, and, if convicted, *they will be executed without the delay of a single day*. By command of Major General DIX.

D. T. VAN BUREN, Colonel and Assistant Adjutant General.

GENERAL ORDERS—NO. 93.

HEADQUARTERS, DEPARTMENT OF THE EAST, }
NEW YORK CITY, Nov. 26, 1864. }

The Major General commanding renews the notice given by General Orders No. 80 to all persons from the insurgent States to register their names at the headquarters of Major General John J. Peck, second in command in the Department, at No. 37 Bleecker street, within twenty-four hours after their arrival in this city. If any such person fails to comply with this requirement he will be regarded as a spy and treated accordingly.

Keepers of hotels and boarding houses are requested to send to the same headquarters the names of all persons from the insurgent States taking lodgings with them immediately on the arrival of such persons. It is not doubted that the danger which the city has just escaped will insure a compliance with this request. If any one fails to comply with it *he will be held responsible for any evil consequences which may result from the omission.*

By command of Major General ...
D. T. VAN BUREN, Colonel and Assista...
General.

THE MODUS ...

The plan of firing the hote...
some person well versed ...
engaged in it. In ...
rials used seem ...
phosphorus. The ...
glass vials of six ...
were sealed with ...
coming in contact ...
to explain that, ...
phosphorus unde...
found in the room...
floors, unsealed, ...
pentine, which ...
ran in solution ...
attention be...
readily ...
of the ...
complet...
truly ...

boarders were naturally very nervous, and it is to be presumed did not sleep quite as soundly as last week.

THE CHIEF CONSPIRATOR

is believed to be a member of Morgan's old command, and one of the prisoners, it is said, who escaped with others of Morgan's men from the penitentiary at Columbus, Ohio. He was captured on the blockade runner Roses, while trying to make his way into the confederacy to join his command, and was sent to Fort Lafayette. While there he made oath to being a British subject, and a long correspondence ensued between Secretary Seward and Lord Lyons in relation to him, which resulted in his release from Fort Lafayette, about two weeks since. A portion of that time he has been staying at the Lafarge House, and was there, occupying room No. 283 at the time of his arrest. He was examined yesterday afternoon.

OPERATIONS OF THE POLICE.

From the moment it was ascertained that the fires were the work of incendiaries, President Acton directed that the whole machinery of the police should be brought into requisition to ferret out the perpetrators. Mr. Superintendent Kennedy seconded his efforts so ably that in a brief space of time two parties were under arrest and the officers were upon the scent of others concerned in the plot, and who were making what subsequently proved to be vain endeavors to escape. Orders were sent out to the police of New York, Brooklyn and Williamsburg to notify all the hotel keepers within their respective precincts of the *modus operandi* of the incendiaries, and caution them to be on their guard.

THE DETECTIVE FORCE,

under Chief John Young, went to work with the most commendable energy, and have thus far succeeded in discovering the entire plan of organization, the names of the parties concerned, how they obtained the means to carry on the enterprise, and who were the principal instigators and directors of the whole affair.

THE PLAN.

The original plan of the marauders was to have simultaneously fired the hotels at the lower and upper parts of the city, and while the Fire Department and the police had their attention distracted to these remote portions of the city, to fire the hotels and other public building...
in the more central points. The next step would ...
been to have fired the shipping, beginning w...
barges, which they had the idea could ...
pushed up alongside the shi...
and thus destroy a vast amo...
... of these scen...
the gang were to ha...
the iron-clads now ...
provided them...
which was a ...
possible, the...
least so clo...
the police ...

In ca...
to trust ...
been lo...
Importa...
burg an...
ful work...
of men ...
but co...
as t...
afo...

day in and out the hotel ...
time he kept a fire in his ...
three to four persons ...
times they would remain ...
times to a late hour in the ...
that he was a chemist, fro...
and that he is the same p...
years ago, confined in Fort L...
called a telegraph tapper. ...
of his own, he would apply t...
intercept messages from one ...

The damage done to the ...
furniture, will not fall sho...
covered by insurance. ...
low, was mostly damaged by...
to the porters and engineer ...
manner in which the fire w...

The Bel...

Notwithstanding the ...
is issued on Friday ...
was promptly notified ...
fire, he, like others ...
daring plot. About ...
covered ...
floor, and ...
various employes ...
the room was ...
tents discovered ...
strong odor of p...
not having gaine...
tinguished. Up...
were found satu...
of the furnitur...
bag containin...
it appears...
gistered ...
Army. ...
to th...
nigh...

Courtesy, New York Public Library

First page of the New York *Herald* the morning after the fire raid on New York City. The *Herald* devoted twenty-eight columns to the story.

the restaurant. Headley bought one from a newsboy who was shouting the headline story.

The *New York Times* and the *Herald* devoted most of their extras
to the fire raid. Headley felt a cold hand clutch his heart as he
read the story of an interview with the clerk of the United States
Hotel. He had been described down to the color of his eyes, hat and
overcoat. As he looked up he thought every man in the room was
staring at him.

He passed the paper to Martin, who glanced down the columns
swiftly. "Good God," Martin whispered, "they know all about us."

They drank their cups of coffee as casually as they could, with
hearts pounding against their ribs and the shadow of a noose dangling before their eyes. When they left, Martin told each man to
register for the night at side-street boarding-houses or inns. They were
to gather at the Central Park cottage in the morning.

From the *Herald's* account the raiders had done considerable damage. There is no doubt that had the Copperheads risen, the city would
have been given an incredible blood bath.

All leaves of police and firemen were cancelled. The firemen worked
from nine that night until six the next morning. The blaze in the
Astor had been discovered by a night watchman. Damage was slight.
"Had the window been open to create a draught," the reporter
quoted the manager, "the whole building would have been in flames
in a short time." The buckets of water at the stairway, which Headley
had overlooked, helped considerably in extinguishing the fire. The desk
clerk described Headley as a nervous man "who had made many visits
to the barroom and his room."

When the fire had broken out in the Belmont Hotel adjacent to the
Herald office, reporters, editors and firemen dragged the hoses
through the city room to fight the blaze. Two floors were burned out
before the fire was brought under control. Barnum's Museum—with
the giantess now sleeping peacefully—reported a thousand dollars'
damage. The fire at Lovejoy's Hotel had been put out with small
damage. The Metropolitan had two whole floors destroyed. The St.
Nicholas was completely gutted, with damage estimated at ten thousand.

At Niblo's Garden Theatre tragedy had been narrowly averted. The house was packed for the opening of *The Corsican* when the fires broke out. As fire bells clanged outside the audience stirred uneasily. Suddenly someone cried, "Fire." Men and women leaped from their seats. However, a quick-witted stage manager named Wheatley ran up on the stage, "shouting a speech." In a moment boys were running up and down the aisles holding placards aloft on which had been scrawled "No Fire." Mr. Wheatley's "speechifying" made the audience laugh, then relax. A fire in the basement was put out and the Corsican strode back on the stage.

At the Winter Garden, next to the LaFarge Hotel, Julius Caesar was saying his lines when a coil of smoke seeped from under the stage. The dreadful cry of "fire" rose in the darkened theatre. Happily, Superintendent of Firemen Leonard was in the dress circle. He rose to shout, "That's only a drunken man. Go on with the play." Caesar stared up at him, then quickly recovered himself to accuse Brutus. The audience hesitated, but as Shakespeare's words rolled out, they relaxed. Leonard ran down to the basement and with the help of stage hands put out the blaze.

The St. James, Albemarle and Fifth Avenue Hotels reported large damage. The United States Hotel at Broadway and Maiden Lane and the Bancroft at Broadway and 12th Street were wiped out. The New England House at Bayard Street and Broadway had its first and second floors destroyed.

Headley's sabotage along the west side wharfs had done some damage. The hay barge *Marie* had been sunk. A merchant ship was pronounced a loss. Two other barges had been damaged. A sailing vessel's deck was charred. Other ships reported trifling damages.

By midnight two arrests had been made. "There will be many more, before long," announced Superintendent of Police Kennedy, whose office the Rebels had hoped to occupy.

The following morning, the 26th, the Confederate raiders met at Central Park. It was an unseasonable day, and the raiders loafed, smoked and waited for the newspapers. Late in the afternoon Martin told them to break up for dinner.

Headley, Ashbrook and Kennedy met at a 12th Street restaurant.

After a leisurely dinner, for some unexplained reason they decided to visit McMasters at his office in the *Freeman's Journal* in Union Square.

As they neared the *Journal's* office, Headley said, "I think it will be dangerous if we all go in. I'll see McMasters and join you later at the cottage." Martin and Kennedy agreed. They said goodbye and walked to the corner, where they hailed an approaching horsecar.

As he started down the two steps to the *Journal's* basement office, Headley saw Katie McDonald staring at him through the glass door. Behind her were several men talking to Editor McMasters. When she saw Headley, Katie's eyes widened in terror. Then she closed them, raised her hand to her mouth and shook her head.

It was enough for Headley. He skipped back up the steps. The horsecar which Martin and Kennedy had taken was starting up the street. Headley ran after it. He kept pace with it for a few minutes, until Martin, staring idly out of the window, looked down and saw him. He yanked the bell cord and the car ground to a stop. Headley climbed aboard, with the conductor growling at him to get on at the regular stops.

Martin and Kennedy knew something had gone wrong and kept silent. When the car turned into Madison Square, they all got out. The nearest saloon was their first stop. Headley took one whiskey neat before the color returned to his face. Then he told them what had happened.

"The game is up," Martin said. "We can't help McMasters."

"What about Katie?" Kennedy said.

Martin shrugged his hopelessness. They drank a silent toast to the pretty redhead with the gay laugh and so much courage.

Before they left, a newsboy came into the saloon, shouting the headlines. Martin bought a paper. He glanced down, then looked up, frightened rage in his face. He pushed the paper over to Headley and Kennedy.

"My God! It can't be true!" Headley said.

"It is. We must leave at once," Martin said.

Now they knew who had betrayed them. The traitor was Godfrey Hyams, the mysterious stranger who had appeared at Toronto at the time John Yates Beall was about to launch his raid on the U.S.S. *Michigan*. The story also disclosed that Hyams had betrayed Beall and Captain Cole to the Federals. The Union had paid him seventy thousand dollars in gold.

As the story revealed, he had first approached Union agents in To-

ronto, offering details of the New York City raid for a price. Skeptical
Washington headquarters told Hyams he would first have to prove
it. The informer had then turned over a list of names of the raiders
going to New York and Chicago, including those of Hines and
Headley.

The Federal authorities entered into a deal with the Confederate
Judas. Unknown to Headley or the others, they had been shadowed
for twenty-four hours a day from the moment they had entered the
city. Strangely enough, their mild behavior and gentlemanly manner
had fooled the detectives. Two days after they had registered at the
hotels the investigation had been abandoned.

Hyams had been furious. He added a list of New York City Copperhead leaders who were involved in the plot. Federal detectives
who knew of the treasonable activities of the Copperheads named
urged Washington to take some precaution. Stanton sent in Butler and
his troops. The "disgraceful plot" was still believed to be the figment
of a bargaining traitor. Only after the first fire bells had clanged in
the night did the Federals know how reliable the "information" had
been.

McMasters and twenty-five Copperhead leaders were arrested on
the 26th. It had been Federal detectives Headley had seen talking to
McMasters in his office.

At noon of the 26th, Major General Dix issued General Order No.
92, which said in part:

> A nefarious attempt was made last night to sack and burn
> the principal hotels and public resorts in this city. Had it
> succeeded, it would have resulted in a frightful sacrifice of
> human lives and property. The evidence of extensive combi-
> nations and other facts disclosed today show it to have been
> the work of Rebel emissaries and agents. All such persons
> engaged in secret acts of hostility can only be regarded as
> spies subject to martial law and penalty of death. If they are
> detected they will be immediately brought to trial before a
> military commission, and if convicted, executed without the
> delay of a single day.

Two hours later Dix's office issued orders for "all persons of insurgent states" to register at the Office of the Adjutant General, 37
Bleecker Street. Hotel owners were told to report any suspicious persons who registered.

That night the alarm of fire again terrified the city. The firm of Halsted and Haines at White Street and Broadway, one of the largest dry goods houses in the East, was completely destroyed. Firemen fought the blaze all night. Dawn found the house a smoldering ruin. Damage was estimated at $200,000. Bottles of turpentine and phosphorus, sealed with plaster of Paris, were found by the fire marshal's men, who described the blaze as having been set by "Rebel incendiaries." It is more likely the fire had been set by one of the more courageous Copperheads. None of the Confederates mentioned this fire, reported by both the *Herald* and *Times*.

This blaze resulted in a general round-up of all enemy residents. Day and night the raids went on. Sixty blockade-runners, Confederate agents and former officers under Morgan were arrested and thrown into dungeons at Fort Lafayette. Among them was Captain J. D. Allison, whom we will meet again.

Damage from the raids, based on the *Herald's* estimate, was placed at $422,000. The largest loss was Halsted and Haines; the smallest, the Astor with only $100. The fire marshal's office reported that bottles of unexploded Greek fire had been found in some of the hotels, along with boxes of cartridges soaked in turpentine. A note found in a wastebasket had been pasted together, revealing the postponement of the raid from Election Day to Thanksgiving Day.

"The chief conspirators were members of Morgan's old command, led by the guerrilla Hines," the marshal announced. A study of the fictitious names used by the Confederates in registering at the hotels gives a hint why the marshal named Hines. Headley, when he had registered at the Astor, signed himself as "Haines."

On the 27th, with the city still dreading the approach of night while enemy arsonists ranged free, the Hotel Keepers' Association of New York posted a $2,000 reward for information leading to the hiding place of the Confederates.

The raids also changed the usually cooperative hotel clerks, always ready to wink at a gentleman bringing in a lady for a rendezvous, into paragons of virtue. The *Herald* told of a gentleman and a lady who tried to register at the Albemarle. The clerk took one look at the gentleman's small black valise and "indignantly" refused him a room, threatening to call the police. The red-faced man and his fair lady retreated in confusion. The *Herald* gallantly informed its readers that "the pair probably had nothing to do with the Rebel incendiaries."

On the evening of the 27th, Colonel Martin and his men slipped out of New York, the Federal detectives nipping at their heels. They found a train leaving the city for Albany at eleven o'clock, with sleepers open for passengers at nine. Again breaking up in pairs, they went to the New York Central Depot, where one of them not possibly known to the detectives bought the tickets. At nine they slipped into the sleeping cars, retiring at once to their berths. They drew the curtains but did not undress. Martin found a rear door to the car and unlocked it. He passed word to the others that if detectives came aboard to search the berths, they were to "open the ball" and escape in the crowd at the station. It was to be every man for himself.

When the cars backed into the depot, they watched the platform through slits in the window-shades. Several men, obviously detectives, "carefully scrutinized" every passenger as he came aboard. Curiously enough, they never bothered to examine the car before the gates were opened. Gold possibly had passed from Confederate hands to the conductor's.

The train pulled out at eleven. At six the next morning they arrived at Albany. It was Sunday and no trains were running across the border. Martin told his men to seek lodging at small boarding-houses or hotels. At four on Monday afternoon, they crossed the Suspension Bridge, each man holding a revolver in his overcoat pocket.

Tuesday morning they arrived at the Queen's Hotel in Toronto. That night they gave Thompson a full report. Despite the treachery of Hyams, they would have left the "queen city" of the nation in ashes, they said, had they not been given an inferior grade of Greek fire. They agreed that the fire in "Captain Longmire's" heart had winked out. Under the pressure of the New York Copperheads he probably had told the old chemist to water down his bottles of Greek fire. Compared to the fires set by Sherman's torches, they had struck only a match.

XXIII. THE MAINE COAST EXPEDITION

WHILE Hines was dodging Federal patrols in Indiana, Judge Advocate Turner's agents had completed their investigation of the confession of Francis Jones, still languishing in the county jail at Calais, Maine. Collins, the leader of the raid on the Calais bank, was openly threatening to kill Jones, and the sheriff had him removed to another part of the jail.

There had been rumors that the Confederates in Montreal were openly boasting of their plans to storm the jail. Portland had sent troops who, with the Washington County Home Guard, surrounded the jail day and night with a ring of bayonets. Companies of horsemen constantly patrolled the roads leading in and out of the county.

War Department,
Bureau of Military Justice,
Washington, D.C., Nov. 2ᵈ 1864.

Hon. E. M. Stanton,
Secretary of War:
Sir—
Upon the sworn statements of Francis H. Jones — a rebel prisoner now confined at Calais, Maine — referred

Courtesy, National Archives

Extracts from a report of Judge Advocate General Holt to Stanton, in which Holt evaluated for him the confession made by Francis Jones.

Portland, Me. – Major Dudley Harris – alias "Spencer", alias "Barbour"

Boston – Col. J. D. Martin.

New York – Col. Geo. & Maj. A. Hawthorne.

Brooklyn, N.Y. – J. Taylor, tavern-keeper.

Philadelphia – Maj. Chur Rice.

Baltimore – Col. Wm. Hamilton.

Chicago – Maj. Morris or Maurice, – alias "Sam Ober"

Springfield, Ills. – Capt. Thos. Terier, alias "Oliver Ditson".

St. Louis – Wm. Kendall and Capt. Lewis Kennerly.

St. Joseph, Mo. – John or Wm. Ritchie.

New Madrid – James Hunter.

Cape Girardeau – Col. Wm. Harper.

Memphis – Capt. Pope.

Nashville – Col. Thos. T. Tunstall.

Cincinnati – Maj. Heikirmere.

Louisville – Capt. M. J. Garrett.

It is also added by Jones

that Wm. O. Massie of Water Street, New York City, and three other individuals whom he speci-

the highest considerations connected with the public safety.

J. Holt.

Judge Advocate General.

R 12./45.

Holt's signature on the report to Stanton.

Farmers had been ordered to warn the county officials of the presence of any strangers.

War Department detectives and Turner's personal agents correlating their findings in Washington found that Jones' report, as Turner had suspected, "checked in minute detail."

On November 23, 1864, Stanton asked Judge Advocate General Holt for a summary of Jones' confession and his own findings. Holt made a lengthy reply, basing his conclusions on Major Turner's report of his investigation of Jones' confession. Describing Jones as "possessed of unusual intelligence and well educated," Holt wrote in part:

> The most important feature of his [Jones'] disclosures is the statement that while employed in the secret service of the enemy he became acquainted with many of their principal Agents within our lines, with some of whom he personally communicated as bearer of dispatches to them from "Southern generals," and who, as he describes, are stationed at various points in the North for purposes of facilitating correspondence and communicating with the South—aiding the transportation of contraband goods, the running of the blockade, collecting deserters from the Rebel Army, etc., etc. He [Jones] reports their names and stations as follows:
>
> Portland, Me. . . . . Major Dudley Harris—*alias* "Spencer," *alias* "Barbour"
> Boston . . . . Col. J. D. Martin
> New York . . . . Col. Geo. & Maj. A. Hawthorne
> Brooklyn, N. Y. . . . . J. Taylor, tavern-keeper
> Philadelphia . . . . Maj. Ohue Rice
> Baltimore . . . . Col. Wm. Hamilton

Chicago ....Maj. Morris or Maurice,—
                                        alias "Sam Ober"
Springfield, Ill. ....Capt. Thos. Sevier,
                                        alias "Oliver Ditson"
St. Louis ....Wm. Kendall and Capt.
                                        Lewis Kennerly
St. Joseph, Mo. ....John or Wm. Ritchie
New Madrid ....James Hunter
Cape Girardeau ....Col. Wm. Harper
Memphis ....Capt. Pope
Nashville ....Col. Thos. J. Tunstall
Cincinnati ....Maj. Heikermere
Louisville ....Capt. M. J. Garrett

It is also added by Jones that W. O. Massie of Water Street, New York City, and three other individuals whom he specifies as Hoffman, Donovan and Woods (and whom he believes to be Custom House officers) have been actively engaged in that city in shipping munitions of war to the Rebels. Furthermore, the names of the Rebel Agents, at sundry points outside the United States, as Quebec, Montreal, Halifax and Bermuda, are also designated.

Holt then went on to say that his own and Major Turner's investigations had convinced them that Jones was telling the truth and that the confession and disclosures could be described as "affirmative." Then Holt broke down Jones' confession into points which he said had been proven to be correct by the investigation of Turner's agents.

Details of the plan to raid the state had been confirmed by U. S. Consul Howard at his listening post in St. John's, New Brunswick. Turner's counter-espionage agents working in Toronto had wormed some of the secrets out of the Confederate Commissioners. Fishermen and farmers had given affidavits stating they had seen men posing as "artists" who had sketched the coastal bays and inlets. They said the men "seemed unfriendly and not eager to discuss their work."

As for the names of the secret Rebel agents in the North, Holt said some of them, he had learned, were already under investigation by agents of Colonel Carrington in Indiana and General Dix in New York. Evidence of their "treasonable activities" had been gathered, "and I would urge most vigorously that they all be arrested at once, to be confined in Fort Lafayette, New York, under the closest guard."

Holt also had a startling disclosure to make. In late September, he said, a strange, low-slung steamer with a sharp bow, painted a deep gray, the color of all blockade-runners, had been sighted off the Maine coast. It was a ghostlike ship, slipping in and out of the ocean mists. Several fishermen had come close enough to her to read her name: *Tallahassee*.

As Holt wrote:

> Major Turner in his report calls attention to the fact that Jones specifies the *Tallahassee* as one of the vessels to be employed in convoying the transports of the secret piratical expedition to the coast of Maine; and in connection therewith, to the further fact that this very vessel had been lately cruising in the same neighborhood. Jones was placed in confinement in July last, and did not know then and does not know now, that this steamer was near the coast. From these considerations he derives a further corroboration of the statement of the prisoners. Other points have been verified, such as the Rebel engineers and topographers who have been seen on the coast of Maine posing as artists, making his confession accurate and truthful.

Stanton wrote back a terse reply: "Arrest them all."

Turner arranged for the warrants and arrests. On November 24, with the New York raiders ready to act, Turner's investigators along with Secret Service operators, closed in on every important Rebel agent in New York, Cincinnati, St. Louis, Baltimore, Indianapolis, Portland and Boston. Numerous arrests were made. Caches of arms, ammunition and medical supplies were found and confiscated. Plans of Federal buildings, prison camps, bridges, Federal storehouses, shipping centers, and arsenals throughout the country, all "subject to attack," were uncovered. The arrests were made swiftly and in secret; neither Hines nor the New York raiders under Colonel Martin knew about them immediately. The agents were charged with treason. A cross-check of the *Official Records* under individual names shows that some were sent to Fort Lafayette or the Dry Tortugas for long prison terms at hard labor. Curiously, despite overwhelming evidence of treason, none was hanged. But the "piratical expedition" against Maine, as the Federals called it, never materialized.

What of Jones, the killer Collins and his dim-witted follower, Phillips? In late November Jones wrote a sad letter to his mother telling her he was now in jail, a criminal charged with robbery. The sheriff, who evidently liked him, sent a copy of the letter to Stanton and Turner. His mother, that "good Union woman," wrote back that she would stand by him.

Meanwhile, Collins raged and fumed in his cell. Evidently they were all tried by a military tribunal, with Collins and Phillips receiving the death sentence. Collins wrote a bitter letter to his sister the night before he was to be executed accusing the "traitor I thought was a loyal soldier of the Confederacy" of betraying him. He reviewed his war record as a staff officer under Polk, and ended by saying he was not eager for "death" but would "swing off like a man."

There the story ends. There are no formal documents of execution, or commutations, as can be found in all other cases of the captured and condemned men of Hines' command, or of the leaders of the Sons of Liberty.

Turner's last report in the case to Judge Advocate Holt does not tell us what happened to the three men. Did Collins die like a man as the trap sprung, and did the moronic Phillips have to be tied before they could hang him? And what of Jones? Did he finally return to his mother, that "good Union woman" in Missouri, that dark and bloody ground, where for years assassins' bullets would cut down the informers who had sold out to the Union?

XXIV. SHOOT THEM DOWN

IN DECEMBER, 1864, Hines was in the Northwest, and in Canada Thompson was planning the most infantile scheme to be executed by the Confederate raiders. It was a plan to capture a train transferring several Confederate generals, colonels and lieutenant colonels, from Johnson's Island to Fort Lafayette in New York harbor. The information came from the secret "Order of the Star" in Sandusky, Ohio, through which Hines may have been sending intelligence to Toronto.

On December 10, Martin, Lieutenants Headley and Ashbrook, and Acting Master John Yates Beall met on the windy platform of the Dunkirk, New York, depot. The plan was for Martin to ride the train from Erie, Pennsylvania, to Dunkirk and there signal the others on the platform. They would come aboard, and, four miles outside Buffalo, take over the train, kill the guards and free the Confederate officers. The passengers were to be made to undress and give their clothes to the prisoners. "If they resist, shoot them down," Thompson had told them.

Beall had been sent out ahead and the others had followed. While in Buffalo, Beall had "recruited" a young boy named Anderson who was familiar with the countryside. Anderson's fondest dream was to wear a sword and join Jeb Stuart's raiders.

After a "practice" run on the Dunkirk depot platform they returned to Buffalo, and registered at the Genessee House. They slept that night with pistols under their pillows. The Buffalo papers had prominently displayed stories about General Ben Butler's latest order: "Rebel guerrillas are to be shot on sight, if possible while in the commission of their crimes."

The next day they boarded a train for Dunkirk. Headley, Beall, Ashbrook and young Anderson got off at Dunkirk. Martin continued on to Erie, Pennsylvania, where he was supposed to board the train bringing the Rebel prisoners east.

The three Confederates and their latest recruit, Anderson, waited for hours on the windy Dunkirk depot platform. Finally at three

230

o'clock the train from Erie chugged into the station. Colonel Martin stepped down, his face gloomy. The officers, he said, had not yet been removed from the prison camp. The transfer was supposed to take place the following night, when they would be brought to Buffalo on the Buffalo Express of the Lake Shore Railroad.

They returned to their rooms in the Genessee House in Buffalo. The following day they checked the railroad and found the express was scheduled to arrive at six o'clock that evening. It was decided to derail it four miles from the city, at a point where the Buffalo Road crossed the tracks, return in sleighs to Buffalo with the Confederate officers and take a late train across the Suspension Bridge into Canada.

The planning was infantile, the timing off. Apparently it never occurred to them that their generals might be killed in the derailment or that they could linger four hours in an aroused city while waiting for a train to Canada.

Their methods were blundering. They hired two sleds and drove out to the point where the road crossed the tracks. Anderson had not produced a crowbar. A small iron rail was placed across the tracks. The express came roaring out of the winter twilight, headlights piercing the snow which had begun to fall, tossing the rail aside like a matchstick.

The train ground to a stop two hundred yards from the spot, perhaps as an afterthought by the engineer, who feared he had hit a sleigh at the crossing. When they saw the conductor approaching with a lantern they all ran to their sleighs and dashed back to the city. The whole plan had been foolhardy and they knew it.

That night Martin and Headley walked across the bridge through the snow in to Canada. Ashbrook took a train to Detroit and ferried across to Windsor. Beall and Anderson said they would follow on the night train. Martin, Headley and Ashbrook reported in to Toronto the next day. That afternoon Thompson received word from New York that Beall had been arrested with young Anderson in the Niagara Falls depot. Beall and his recruit were captured by a policeman in the depot restaurant. The two were sleeping on a bench when he had idly tapped Beall's feet with his nightstick. But in a moment the frightened Anderson was babbling out their plans.

They badly needed Hines that night. The master spy would never have permitted such blundering.

XXV. THE KIDNAPPING OF THE VICE PRESIDENT-ELECT

I N EARLY December, 1864, Hines joined Nancy at her father's house, then continued on through Kentucky to report to Richmond. It was a journey filled with stirring adventures and close calls. The Blue Grass was swarming with detectives. Somewhere along the line word had gone out that Hines had slipped across the Indiana border and was heading south. One night he hid out at the home of one of his friends but was forced to leap out a back window with Federal rifles flashing in the night, the balls smacking the tree trunks near him or fluttering past his ears. But, as always, he got away. In a nearby village he stole a horse from a livery stable and left a goldpiece to pay for the mount.

About December 10, he was in Richmond. He saw Seddon and Benjamin Davis and gave them full reports on the fiascos in New York and Chicago. It was a negative report, but evidently the high command thought enough Federal troops had been diverted for him to continue his harassing tactics. Benjamin told Hines that Thompson had sent in a long report, asking to come home. They had placed an ad in the New York *News* ordering him to remain at Toronto and continue his guerrilla war. Davis and Benjamin may also have been influenced in their decision to send Hines back to create more troubled areas in the North by the report made public that fall by Judge Advocate General Holt in which he described the scope and revolutionary goals of the Copperhead Sons of Liberty. Admitting the total might be "exaggerated," Holt estimated the membership of the society as from 500,000 to 800,000. The members, he asserted, were fully armed and led by veteran Confederate officers.

On December 16, 1864, Benjamin gave Hines orders to report back to Toronto. The order read:

> Capt. Hines will report with Private Thomas for duty, to Hon. Jacob Thompson, Toronto, C. W. In case of his absence, to Gen. E. G. Lee at Hamilton, C. W. If Gen. Lee is absent ask his address of Captain F. Lee Esq. at Hamilton. . . .

Capt Hines will report with private Thomas for duty, to Hon Jacob Thompson, Toronto, C.W. — In case of his absence to Genl S. G. Lee at Hamilton C.W. — If Genl Lee is absent ask his address of Capers F Lee Esq Hamilton

J P Benjamin
Sec of State

19th Dec '64

Dec 19

Courtesy, Margaret I. King Library, University of Kentucky

Secretary of State Judah Benjamin's order to Hines sending him back to Toronto in 1864 the Northwest and Northeast Conspiracies had failed.

A three weeks' pass was issued to Hines about this time. Presumably he went back to Nancy for a last goodbye before starting on the hazardous journey to Canada.

In Toronto, Christmas was celebrated in the Queen's Hotel with a large tree, a great deal of whiskey, brandy and tears. Men in exile thought of past Christmases at home and tried to hide their feeling by roaring out Morgan's old song, "Song of the Raiders," or "Here's to Morgan and Duke, Drink Them Down." But the women wept and when the songs were all ended and the braggadocio forgotten, the men did, too. They were in exile. When they would return home they didn't know.

But Thompson shed no tears. For him the war had not been lost. Poring over the maps, trying to read between the lines of cautiously written letters and dispatches from friends and agents in the south, he and his raiders tried desperately to breathe life and hope into dying dreams. In the end, like other lost leaders, Thompson was moving and rearranging regiments which no longer existed.

His last scheme was his most fantastic. Dabbing at his feverish, watering eyes, he outlined the following plan to Lieutenant Headley and Colonel Martin:

The Confederate forces north of Sherman's positions and the new force being organized by Beauregard in North Carolina would be combined with Lee's army, to evacuate Richmond and Petersburg. The total was estimated at about 100,000 troops.

Both armies would be concentrated between Richmond and Lynchburg, marching to Staunton and on to Pennsylvania, leaving the South abandoned. They would threaten Washington and Philadelphia. Meanwhile, the cavalry would gather up all the horses in the country and mount the infantry, until eventually the whole command was mounted and mobile. After threatening Washington, this new mounted army would fall back and capture Pittsburgh, locating "the seat of government at Wheeling, some forty miles west." The army would then face east and guard the line from the Ohio to Lake Erie, some one hundred miles.

With the railroads and bridges destroyed, Grant and Sherman "would require some time to meet the new conditions of affairs." For the Confederates their new position, the mountains of western Virginia, the Ohio in the South and Lake Erie in the North were natural bastions. Included in this mad plan was a cavalry movement of ten thousand troopers against New York. Thompson based this move on the ease with which Sherman was marching to the sea. If the Yankees could do it, why couldn't A. P. Hill?

Fantastic as it may seem, Thompson still included in his plan an uprising by the Sons of Liberty, who would attack Camps Douglas and Chase. Chicago and Indianapolis were the points of "rendezvous." Many of the Copperheads had been arrested in November, their arsenals taken by the Federals, their plans betrayed, the leaders not arrested were in hiding, yet this naïve man could make such plans! It is surprising that Colonel Martin and Lieutenant Headley took it all seriously.

The second part of the plan envisioned Grant's actions. His command would join with Sherman and come up the Atlantic Coast on transports to Washington, Philadelphia and New York. Such a long operation would, of course, "enable Lee and Johnson to establish the new base." Then, when the Federals did come up to establish a new front in the northern cities, the Confederate army was to retreat westward, "gathering strength on the march and creating consternation all over the North." E. Kirby Smith, Forrest and Taylor were not neglected. They would all join commands to march west of the Mississippi River and, with sixty thousand men, move into Iowa, gather up all the horses and swing east in support of Lee and Beauregard.

As Headley wrote in his memoirs, "None of us could see the propriety of making a last stand in the South when the gates of the North and then to the West stood wide open. We felt certain that the South could afford to have the seat of war transferred to the North where we could win or lose at the expense of the enemy."

Of course, the lack of rolling stock, the starving armies, with men falling to the side of the road from sheer exhaustion and lack of food, the spread of disease and the weary hearts, once filled with fire and now laden with the bitter ashes of defeat, were not taken into account. Nor was Grant with his mighty Federal armies.

Headley and Colonel Martin were selected by Thompson to take this plan to Secretary of War Breckinridge, who had replaced Seddon. Martin had been chief of scouts for Breckinridge at Shiloh and knew him well. It was hoped the Secretary would approve the plan and take them in to see President Davis.

They crossed the frozen Detroit River at night to Detroit. To avoid the detectives they hired a carriage and drove to the home of a Frenchman six miles down the river. Hines had used the Frenchman's farm as a hideout on his trips across the border, and Martin and Headley knew it.

The Frenchman was not at home and they drove back to the depot in the early hours of the morning. To make sure the detectives didn't see them they climbed to the top of a pile of firewood, shoveled out a hole in the snow and sat there, hugging each other and flapping their arms to keep warm. A bottle of brandy helped. By the time the Detroit train whistled off in the distance they were almost frozen. Headley had to help Martin down from the pile of ties. They were both numb to the marrow of their bones.

From Toledo they went on to Cincinnati, to find the streets filled with Federal troops moving to the steamboats and railroads. At first they planned to steal two cavalry horses but decided it would be impossible to get out of the city. They left Cincinnati by steamer for Louisville, arriving the following morning. They knew the city intimately, which was both an advantage and a disadvantage. Old friends could hide them, but loyal Union men could betray them to the provost marshal.

For two days they stayed in their hotel room, eating and sleeping. On the third day they found a boarding-house keeper on a side street who offered to rent them a sitting-room and a large bedroom—on the condition they share the bedroom with another man. Anxious to get out of the hotel with its suspicious hotel clerks, they agreed.

They met their roommate at dinner that night. Headley gulped. He was a Union major recovering from wounds "received in vigorous action against the guerrillas of Kentucky and Missouri," as he told them proudly.

After the landlord introduced them, the major began describing a recent battle with the guerrillas. As Headley wrote, "He went into a frenzy" as he told how the Rebel guerrillas operated.

"Those infernal villains," he said, "come up on the outskirts of the city and shoot the guards. They hide in the woods and caves all around the state and we have to have cavalry in all the county seats and infantry and stockades at all the railroad bridges and tunnels or the scoundrels would ruin everything. They dodge about, shoot our men from ambush, murder Union men, steal horses and everything else they want, they pay for nothing. . . ."

The major was bellowing now and pounding his fist on the table. Headley felt the sweat trickle from under his arms.

"What do they look like, Major?" he asked.

The major growled. "They are a great deal like the average Rebels in appearance and wear all sorts of clothes and are regular daredevils."

Colonel Martin changed the subject to horse racing.

They stayed in the city for two days. During that time Headley, through old friends, managed to reach one of the members of Hines' underground. Through him they got the name of a physician who was a secret Confederate agent. That night, in the home of the physician, they studied a map of the area with the Federal garrisons carefully marked off.

"The commandant of the section has ordered all captured spies and guerrillas shot down on sight," the physician told them. Headley gave the doctor money to buy two saddles and blankets. He was to hide them in his barn and wait for instructions.

Back at the boarding-house they played a game of euchre with the major, who insisted on interrupting the game to describe his battles with the Rebel guerrillas.

"I will personally hang the first one I capture," he roared.

"Your deal, Major," Martin said quickly.

Headley never forgot the next evening, when he and Martin planned and almost succeeded in kidnapping the Vice President-Elect of the United States, soon to become President.

They had sat down to supper when the major called their attention to an article in the paper announcing the arrival of Johnson on his way to Washington. He was to stay at the Louisville Hotel. Headley toyed with his food. Suddenly he said he felt sick, and went up to his room. Martin, who knew something must be up, followed him.

He found Headley pacing the floor. When the door closed he told Martin he had a plan to kidnap Johnson and bring him to Richmond and hold him as a hostage. Headley quickly outlined his plan. Martin caught some of his enthusiasm. In the morning he said he would go over to the hotel "and make observations," while Headley contacted the physician to see if there were any escaped Confederates hiding out in the city. Later in the morning Headley told Martin the physician was in touch with three young Confederate officers who had recently escaped from Johnson's Island.

Martin reported he had watched Johnson's movements from nine to eleven o'clock. He had learned he usually retired at seven with only a colored servant in the sitting room.

Headley told Martin he had met Johnson before the war at a political convention and the Vice President-Elect "would recognize him." His plan was to first "disarm Johnson by chatting with him," reminding him of their meeting when Johnson had been military Governor of Tennessee. After which he was to begin an earnest conversation about a Federal appointment. While he was thus engaged, Martin was to enter with drawn pistol.

Martin was to say, "This doesn't mean any harm, Mr. Johnson. Just keep quiet a minute and I will tell you what it does mean, otherwise you will be killed in seconds."

Their fantastic naïveté is best understood by Headley's own words, "We took it for granted that Johnson would have enough curiosity to listen rather than be killed."

Then Martin, "with earnest eye and voice," was to explain to Johnson that actually they were secret agents ready to kidnap him and take him to the enemy capital where he was to be held as a hostage!

A closed carriage would be engaged and brought to a short distance from the hotel's front door. Headley and Martin would walk up to the second floor, enter Johnson's suite and at pistol-point tie him up and bring him down a back stairway, called the Ladies' Entrance, a coat thrown over his shoulders. If anyone questioned them they were to say they were taking a friend to the nearby hospital.

The next night the three escaped Confederates met Headley and Martin at the doctor's home. They turned out to be two of Forrest's staff officers and a young lieutenant of the Second Kentucky who had been captured on the Ohio raid. They pledged their support and said they would meet outside the hotel at six o'clock.

One of them was to stand by the Ladies' Entrance of the hotel. When he saw Headley and Martin bringing down the Vice President, he was to call out, "Oh, George." This was the signal for the officer driving the carriage to pull up to the door.

The next day Headley hired a carriage. Martin reported that Johnson was moving about the hotel according to schedule. The other Confederate officers sent word they were ready. Headley and Martin had dinner that night with the fierce major, rumbling on about what they were going to do to some guerrillas a patrol had captured that afternoon.

At six o'clock Headley and Martin watched the carriage pull up to the Ladies' Entrance in the rear of the hotel, at the corner of 6th and Main Streets. While Martin waited outside, clutching a revolver in his coat pocket, Headley walked around the block and into the hotel's main entrance. He crossed the crowded lobby and climbed the stairs to the second floor. The door to Johnson's suite was half-open. The Confederate could see Johnson bidding several people good-night.

Headley hurried down the back stairway to the Ladies' Entrance. There was no one in sight. It was a splendid opportunity. But as always in all their plans, something went wrong. Headley went out to alert Martin. He found his fellow officer pacing up and down under the trees. He looked troubled. Headley soon found the reason why. Only one officer, the driver of the carriage, had appeared. The other two had failed to show up. The Federals had learned of their hiding place, forcing them to move to another farmhouse. It was decided to put off the kidnapping until the following evening.

The next night at six, the carriage was outside. In it this time were the other Confederate officers, all armed. Headley and Martin quickly rehearsed the plot with them. Headley was to go into the hotel, wait at the top of the stairs for Martin, who would join him in a few minutes. Headley, as he had done the night before, walked around the block to enter the hotel's front door. The lobby was not as crowded as it had been the previous night. The clerk looked up as Headley started up the stairs. The Confederate gripped the butt of the revolver in his coat pocket and smiled. The clerk smiled back, returning to his newspaper.

Headley waited at the top of the stairs. In a few minutes he was joined by Martin. They walked down the hall to Johnson's room. The door was open a few inches. Headley glanced up and down the corridor. It was deserted. He took a deep breath, pulled out his revolver and rushed into the room. Martin remained on guard outside.

He found himself in a large living room. There were some cigar butts and glasses on a table. The door to the bedroom was closed. Headley was about to enter when he heard voices outside in the corridor. He opened the door and looked out into the hall. Several Federal officers and their ladies were standing outside the door of another suite, talking and laughing. Martin greeted him as though he had just come up the stairs.

One of the Union officers glanced at them curiously, then turned away. Headley launched into talk of a fictitious cotton deal. Martin kept nodding, quoting prices. It seemed a lifetime before the Federals left. Once again the corridor was deserted. This time they both entered the suite with drawn guns. Headley tried the bedroom door. The knob turned. He flung it open suddenly. The room was deserted, the bed unmade.

For a moment they felt a great surge of combined relief and disappointment. Sure that Johnson had gone out for a short stroll after dinner, they returned to the lobby.

The clerk again looked up as they passed. On an impulse Headley asked, "Clerk, do you know if Governor Johnson is in?"

"Oh, no, sir," the clerk said. "He's not."

"Has he gone to dinner?" Headley asked.

The clerk shook his head. "He left on the five o'clock boat for Cincinnati."

Headley stared at Martin. "I guess we missed him," Headley said.

Later they learned that Johnson, for some unknown reason, had suddenly decided to go by boat to Cincinnati instead of by train later that night. Ironically, had they known of his intention to travel by boat, their task, as Headley said, "might have been much easier." On board an unarmed steamer, late at night, it would have been comparatively easy to take a man prisoner in his stateroom and capture the ship, rather than to try to kidnap a man from his hotel room. In this Headley was correct. There are innumerable instances in the Civil War of small bands of armed men capturing large steamers.

It was a night of bitter disappointment. Headley and Martin joined the other three Confederates waiting outside, bought them a drink and wished them godspeed.

One wonders what might have happened had Johnson been in his bedroom when the two armed Confederate officers walked in and how history would have been affected had they succeeded in their wild plan. . . .

Only a few months later John Wilkes Booth was to fire his fatal shot, and Andrew Johnson became President of the United States.

PART V

THE AFTERMATH
Dispersion and Reunion

———————•◦•———————

XXVI. A STRANGER IN A STRANGE LAND

"THE president of the court-martial described me as the white-haired leader of the conspirators, riding a white charger into Chicago. Nothing can be further from the truth. . . ."

This was Colonel George St. Leger Grenfel, writing from his cell in McLean Barracks, Cincinnati, to the editor of *Harper's Monthly,* begging for an opportunity to present his case to the public. But the editor, who certainly missed getting the inside story of one of the most glamorous figures of the Civil War, wrote back a stuffy note saying he would never consider "communicating with a Rebel."

The editor, of course, was doing his duty as a citizen in refusing to communicate with the enemy, but one feels he went too far in enclosing Grenfel's letter along with his own suggestion to the prison commandant that the matter be investigated. Grenfel had bribed a guard to mail the letter. The commandant of the barracks threw the old soldier into solitary confinement, when he refused to name the guard.

For a time it seemed as if the government could not make up its mind when and where to hold the trial of Grenfel, Colonel Marmaduke, Charles Walsh, Judge Norris, Richard T. Semmes and the other Confederate agents and Copperhead leaders arrested by Sweet's patrols in Chicago on Election Night. It was more than a month after the raids before the government acted.

On December 14, 1864, Judge Advocate Burnett of the Department of Ohio reported to Judge Advocate General Holt that he had gone to Chicago "with my photographic recorder, Mr. Pitman," for "a full investigation of the Rebel attempt to sack, burn and destroy the city of Chicago and set up a Northwest Confederate States."

Burnett stayed in Chicago five days, questioning and cross-examining witnesses. At the end of that time he ordered the release of the son of Brigadier-General Charles Walsh and Mary Morris, wife of Judge Morris.

Grenfel, Marmaduke, R. T. Semmes and the others were ordered

241

confined to the McLean Army Barracks, Cincinnati, for trial, which Burnett strongly urged should be held in Cincinnati, hinting that an attempt might be made to release the prisoners by mob rule. Burnett knew Hines. The Confederate agent was still on the loose and would stop at nothing if he thought he could release Grenfel, whom he had admired and respected since the early days of Morgan's command.

On December 21, 1864, the prisoners were taken under heavy guard on a special train to Cincinnati.

On the 23rd, John Maughan, whose loose tongue had betrayed Castleman, was brought to Cincinnati to be questioned by Colonel Burnett. He babbled all night, pouring out secrets he had overheard and learned from the others. Christmas Eve he signed a confession to become a government witness. Burnett showed his appreciation. In the tradition of all grateful prosecutors who are forced to deal with turncoats, he had young Maughan transferred out of McLean Barracks to a comfortable suite at the Skinner House.

Barley soup, a thin slice of beef and bread and unsugared tea was the Christmas dinner for the Confederates and Copperheads at the barracks. For Maughan it was a chicken dinner. But the soft white meat stuck in his throat and the coffee they poured for him tasted like mud.

"The prisoner said he felt sick," the captain of his guards wrote Burnett. It was a sickness of the soul and not of the body, as Judas could have told them.

That Christmas week was a momentous one for the conspirators. On the 23rd, Vincent Marmaduke wrote a long and imploring letter to Major-General Hooker from his cell in the McLean Barracks, Cincinnati. "Writing with a ball and chain on my leg," he outlined the details of his arrest, his denial of having participated in the Conspiracy, which he had made in a sworn statement to Colonel Sweet at Camp Douglas, or having any "links" to Tom Hines. His defense was a weak one.

"I had come to Chicago and as a total stranger in the city, had sought refuge at the home of Doctor Edwards," he wrote. "I know nothing about the Conspiracy of which I am charged." Marmaduke then went on to boast of his connections in Missouri as brother of

General Marmaduke, who would certainly have been shocked at his sniffling letter. Curiously enough, the Federals believed him. A week later Hooker ordered his release. He was allowed to take the oath of allegiance at McLean Barracks. He does not appear again.

The new year turned. The trial of the Chicago conspirators took place in Cincinnati. The chief witnesses were Shanks, Langhorn, John Maughan, and a surprise witness, Sergeant George Hull, Company E, Second Kentucky. St. Leger Grenfel had ordered Hull arrested for stealing his horses during the 1863 raid on Gallatin, Tennessee. A horse-thief, a forger, and two traitors who played both ends against the middle for money. It was not a proud hour for the Union.

An examination of the ninety-year-old evidence shows that justice slipped badly in Grenfel's case. His attorney was Roger Hervey of Chicago, hired by Hines. Hervey was a young and fiery lawyer who fought vigorously to release his client long after the war was over.

The first witness was Shanks. He told a long and rambling story of how he had spied for Sweet, his voice echoing in the long room in the barracks above the bubbling and rumbling of the pot of water on the pot-bellied stove.

Hervey rose to ask in a contemptuous voice, "Were you ever convicted five times for forgery while you were employed in the land office at Austin, Texas, Mr. Shanks?"

Shanks cried, "I was never arrested."

Hervey gave him a cold glance. "I would like the court to examine this document," he said. It was a statement of the head of the land office. Shanks, he said, had been indicted and convicted five times for forgery. Hervey also introduced evidence that Shanks had forged an endorsement of a thirty-dollar draft belonging to another prisoner while at Camp Douglas, all unknown to Colonel Sweet, "who had hired him, not knowing his true nature."

Colonel Burnett, the Judge Advocate presenting the evidence for the government, examined the documents, then told the board, "I wish to announce to the president of this board, that I must abandon the witness. He is not worthy of credit." It was a brave statement for this young and ambitious colonel to make. The favorite of Judge Advocate General Holt, he had sent a long and imposing list of traitors and spies to the gallows.

Maurice Langhorn, who had betrayed his comrades in Chicago, next took the stand. Hervey bombarded him with a furious cross-examination. He was forced to admit the provost marshal of Detroit had

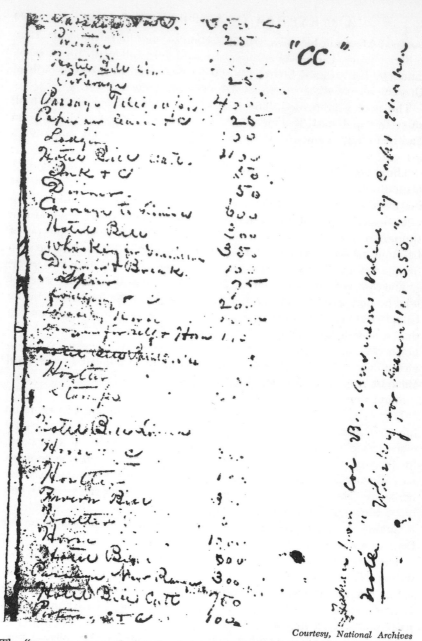

The "expense account" of Colonel Ben M. Anderson, who was sent by Hines to arm the guerrillas of Missouri. "C C" indicates that it was a government exhibit. "Note: whiskey for guerrillas, 3.50," was noted on the margin.

booted him out of his office when he tried to sell him false information.

Sergeant Hull, "scarcely more than a moron," followed him. Hervey damaged his testimony when he quickly brought out that Hull "hated" Grenfel for ordering his arrest for stealing horses on a battlefield.

The traitor John Maughan was next. Aware that soldiers on both sides detested traitors, Hervey shrewdly made Maughan tell how he had been befriended by Hines in Toronto, only to sell him out to save his own skin.

There were two other surprise witnesses presented on the last day: Captain Cantrill and Colonel Ben M. Anderson who had armed the Missouri guerrillas. In return for testifying, Cantrill was allowed to take the oath of allegiance. His testimony sketched out the details of the attempt to sack Chicago and the Northwest. But under Hervey's hammering cross-examination he failed to link Grenfel with Hines.

In Toronto, Hines was following the trial closely. Maughan as he had suspected, had turned traitor. But it was Cantrill's treachery which enraged him. He sent a note by courier to one of his friends in Chicago, telling him to get word into the barracks "to inform Cantrill that if he testifies against Grenfel and the others, he will wish he had never been born." But the warning came too late. Cantrill told all. Eventually, he must have received the warning from Hines, however, because extra guards were put "in and out of his cell."

Anderson's testimony, although false, connected Grenfel with Hines. When he left the stand Anderson was a trembling, frightened man, far from the swaggering, blustering leader of the terrible Missouri guerrillas.

His lies came back to haunt him that night. With a small stiletto he had hidden in a seam of his coat he slashed his wrists and lay back on his cot to die. The guard found him in the morning, near death.

"Get Hervey," he whispered. When Hervey arrived they conferred in whispers. Hervey wrote out a statement and Anderson scratched his name to it and died, the pen in his hand.

The last witness was Colonel Sweet. He was on the stand all day telling how he had frustrated the August and November Chicago conspiracies. Hervey could not shake him. Sweet admitted he had given Langhorn a thousand dollars in gold for betraying his comrades but had only "used a Rebel to catch a Rebel."

Although he pinpointed Hines as the leader of the insurrection, Sweet failed to link Grenfel to the plot. Looking back over the old evidence, we know that Grenfel was to aid Hines in storming the gates of Camp Douglas and Rock Island. But the government had failed to prove it.

Grenfel was found guilty and sentenced to hang. Richard T. Semmes, "brother of the Rebel pirate," was given three years at hard labor in the Ohio penitentiary at Columbus; Walsh was given five years, Mary Morris two years, Judge Morris, five years; Cantrill was released. Some of the lesser lights of the Sons of Liberty were acquitted or given short terms.

While awaiting sentence Grenfel was put into a small, damp prison cell. It was a rainy, snowy winter. The walls of his cell continually dripped moisture and the floor was sometimes inches deep in water. In February he was in constant pain from inflammatory rheumatism. On February 15, the commandant of the McLean Barracks wrote a strong letter to headquarters recommending that a doctor be sent in to examine Grenfel. On the 30th, an army physician ordered him to remain in his cell.

"His health is too good to recommend hospitalization," was his report.

The same day a headquarters staff colonel sent by courier a message to the prison commandant, rebuking him for his naïveté in believing that Grenfel could be really ill.

"Look out that Grenfel is not playing some sharp game to escape," he wrote. "I have no confidence in him and warn you not to give him a chance."

Hervey, Grenfel's attorney, never gave up the fight to save his client. He constantly hammered away at Stanton, Lincoln, Seward and the British minister. In the spring of 1865, he filed a long brief, summing up the testimony, and cross-examination of the government's witnesses. It was twenty pages long and proved beyond a doubt that the government witnesses were perjurers and thieves, but, more importantly, proved the government had failed to prove a case based on corroborative testimony.

Hervey ridiculed the charge that "a man of such brilliant military background in many countries about the world could undertake such a hazardous enterprise with this man, Doctor Hunter [the alias used by Hines] whose object it was to pillage and destroy a city of 200,000 inhabitants, without knowing or being known to one single subordinate, or having any knowledge of the men he was expected to lead."

Hervey was particularly scornful of Shanks and Langhorn. He quoted Colonel Burnett's own "abandonment" of Shanks and went on to show how they had lied under oath about their backgrounds. Hervey also introduced new evidence when he produced a signed statement, written by the guerrilla chief Ben M. Anderson on his deathbed, that his testimony had been false.

He summed up the case against his client by pointing out that the orderly book of Captain John Breckinridge Castleman and Captain Hines' letters and orders, found when Castleman had been arrested in Illinois, had not shown Grenfel's name; that the Britisher's luggage had not contained "one scrap" of incriminating evidence; that he had signed his own name on the hotel register while the other conspirators had used aliases.

As Hervey described him, "He is a stranger in a strange land; a man without a friend within thousands of miles. . . ."

Grenfel's case became an international one. The London *Times* ran a daily story on the court-martial proceedings. Parliament resounded with demands that England intercede.

Under the international pressure, President Johnson commuted Grenfel's sentence to life on the Dry Tortugas. In a letter to Hervey, who had informed him of the Presidential commutation, Grenfel wrote: "I am a soldier, I can bear my fate."

We shall return to Grenfel on a windy night as he and three men, as desperate as himself, tried for the freedom they loved so much.

XXVII. THE TRIALS AND OTHER TRIBULATIONS

THE four hundred and twenty pages of the official transcript of the extradition proceedings against "Lieutenant Bennett H. Young and Command" are fascinating reading. It contains the whole story of the St. Albans raid, with its hilarious scenes and its grim moments. It also shows the slippery George N. Sanders at his best. The proceedings leave no doubt that the raid was Sanders' idea. Confederate Commissioner Clay had tentatively approved it, but had signed no formal order. Sanders had forged the order after Hines had scorned such criminal acts.

The president of the bank told how he and his clerk had been forced to take the Confederate oath. Mr. Armington, the St. Albans gold buyer, testified how he had bought gold which only a few minutes before had been stolen from the bank vault; Mr. Fuller, owner of the livery stable, was still bitter about his stolen horses and said so. More than fifteen witnesses from St. Albans testified.

The testimony of Young and his twelve men did not vary. They described themselves as officers who had served under John Hunt Morgan. Cleary, the secretary of the Confederate Mission in Canada, and Sanders also testified. The surprise government witness was the traitor Godfrey J. Hyams.

Sanders insisted that Commissioner Clay had approved the raid. He produced a letter from Clay to Bennett H. Young which read:

> Your suggestion for a raid on accessible towns in Vermont commencing with St. Albans is approved. You are authorized and required to act in conformity with that suggestion.

But Sanders had shrewdly put the blame on a missing witness. Clay had started south on December 18. Sanders said he had spoken to the ailing Commissioner who "irritably informed me several times he had approved the raid."

However, Sanders let slip that in his last talk with Clay no formal orders had been written out and signed. Sanders admitted that the letter "had not been written up to that time."

"Mr. Clay gave him [Bennett Young] four hundred dollars to burn the town and sack the banks," he said. The checks, Sanders said, had been drawn on Clay's personal account, and signed at his private residence at St. Catharine's, Canada.

The case now hung in the balance. Was it an officially approved military raid, or only a criminal felony, extraditional under the Ashburton Treaty between Great Britain and the United States?

Obviously, nobody believed Sanders. Official sanction of the raid had to be obtained from Richmond. The case was postponed for several weeks until couriers were sent south. Thompson requested permission from Washington to send a messenger under a flag to Richmond. The request was refused.

There was more bad news. The trial of B. G. Burley, the giant Scot who had served under John Yates Beall in the attempt to capture the U. S. S. *Michigan* on Lake Erie, had begun. He sent a note to Toronto asking for money for his legal counsel, and requesting that someone be sent to Richmond for copies of his official orders.

A young Kentucky widow whose name we do not know, Lieutenant Sam B. Davis, of Madison, Kentucky, and Reverend Stephen Cameron, a Virginia army chaplain, all volunteered to try to reach Richmond to obtain copies of the official orders in both cases.

Lieutenant Davis never arrived at Richmond. Hines sent word back to Toronto from somewhere in the Northwest that Copperhead friends had told him Lieutenant Davis had been captured by Federal detectives in Ohio.

Davis was tried and sentenced to death. He was sent to a military prison in Albany, New York, where the execution was to take place. However, Lincoln commuted his death sentence to imprisonment in Fort Lafayette for the duration of the war.

Down through the years young Davis has been confused with the famous Confederate hero of the same name who was executed November 28, 1863, at Pulaski, Tennessee, for spying. Some historians have accepted the fact that the Davis who had left Toronto to help the St. Albans raiders was the same Davis who died on the gallows in Pulaski. The trial records and personal papers of the Sam Davis whose life was saved by Lincoln disprove this.

The days dragged on in Canada without word from the Kentucky widow or the army chaplain. Finally, the United States government attorneys forced the Montreal magistrate to reopen extradition proceedings. With no evidence at hand of their military status, it seemed clear they would be found guilty of committing a felony and returned to the United States to stand trial.

The hearing opened in a crowded, tense courtroom. The attorneys for the raiders were sitting with Young and his men at the defendants' table when the door of the courtroom opened. There was a slight disturbance. Heads turned. Suddenly a guard pushed his way through the crowd, leading a young woman. Once again circumstances had turned the tables for them. The young woman was the Kentucky widow who had safely made the journey from Richmond. The package she handed to the counsel for the Confederates contained copies of their commissions and official sanction for the raid.

"Madam, you must be rewarded for this," Young said.

"I am only doing my duty as a woman of Kentucky," she replied.

Two days later Reverend Cameron arrived in Toronto with a duplicate set of copies of their orders given to him by Jefferson Davis, Judah Benjamin and Secretary Seddon.

These "official" orders are most curious. Sanders in his testimony had said the orders came from Clay, not Richmond. Evidently the orders had been sent by Richmond to Toronto in an effort to save the lives of Young and his raiders.

An examination of the papers brought from Richmond, later marked into evidence, shows that Secretary of War Seddon signed three official orders for Young in one day, not one of which mentions the St. Albans raid. In the first he was to "collect twenty escaped Confederate prisoners and execute such enterprises as may be indicated to you." The twenty men were entitled to pay, rations, clothing, and transportation. The second order had him "reporting to Messrs. Clay and Thompson." The last did not mention the Commissioners, but said simply his "organization was under the direction of the Confederate War Department and as such could be disbanded at its pleasure. . . ." However, the orders signed by Davis and Benjamin approved the raid.

Reverend Cameron had also brought copies of Bennett G. Burley's commission as an Acting Master and official orders. Hines sent these on to the attorney whom he had hired for Burley's defense. But Burley was found guilty of committing a felony and ordered extradited back to the United States to stand trial for piracy. Hines sent word to

Burley's attorney to appeal the decision "of this police judge." "A dastardly decision," he wrote.

On January 21, Thompson sent off a bitter note to Mason, Confederate minister in London, denouncing the Burley verdict as an "outrage and an insult to the Confederate States." He urged Mason to intercede at court. Nothing was heard until February. The police recorder, who had been advised by Burley's attorney, through Hines, of the letter sent to London, had held off signing the extradition document. Meanwhile, three detectives from Washington waited impatiently.

On February 10 London sent word to Toronto to set Burley free. The big Scot was released from jail the next day. He later sailed for England where he would become a member of Parliament.

The band was breaking up fast. Lieutenant Ashbrook and Captain Robert Cobb Kennedy, who had been on the fire raid in New York, told Hines and Thompson they were going to try to get through the Union lines to Richmond and then home. Kennedy said he hadn't seen his mother and father for three years.

They were supplied with funds and after a farewell drink in the bar at the Queen's Hotel they set out. They left on the Grand Trunk Railroad, traveling west to Lake St. Clair, crossing over to the St. Clair depot in Michigan. There they boarded an express going south and west of Detroit.

It was a bitterly cold night and snowing hard when they crossed into Michigan. The coach was crowded and the Confederates took separate seats, Kennedy in the front of the car, Ashbrook in the rear. A few minutes later two men bundled in overcoats and mufflers entered the door at the front of the car. They stared at the sleeping passengers swaying on the hard wooden seats. One pointed to Kennedy, who was dozing, his head on his chest. The other nodded. They went down the aisle, drawing revolvers. As they came up to Kennedy, he lifted his head. One of the men put a revolver against his head.

"You are a Rebel spy and our prisoner," he said loudly. "I call upon you to surrender."

It was enough for Ashbrook. He was already yanking open the rear car door before the man had finished talking. He hung to the door rail for a moment, then pushed himself off into the darkness. He never forgot that moment of slipping through space, then having the wind knocked out of him as he hit the edge of a slope and sliding down into a small frozen lake.

His head spinning, he stood up to watch the coach lights of the trains wink out through the snow. He walked all that night. In the morning, half-frozen, he came on a farmhouse. The farmer believed his story of a runaway team and gave him food and lodging for the day and one night.

But the detectives had discovered where he had jumped the train and the telegraph crackled with his description. He worked his way slowly to Cincinnati where Sam Thomas hid him. A week later he arrived in Lexington, Kentucky. The spring thaw was breaking up the ice in the rivers when he walked up the lane to the porch of his home, to fall into the arms of his mother.

In 1866 he wrote Hines that he had learned detectives had followed them from the Queen's Hotel the night they had left, and had wired their descriptions to the provost marshal's office in Detroit.

Captain Kennedy was sent to New York City, where he was tried by a court-martial at Fort Lafayette. On March 20, 1865, he was found guilty of spying, and of taking part in the raid on New York, described by the court-martial as "the greatest atrocity of the age . . . nothing in the annals of barbarism evinces greater vindictiveness. . . ."

On the 25th, six hours before he was to die, Kennedy, in the presence of a *New York Times* reporter and the commander of Fort Lafayette, signed a confession that he was one of the New York raiders. After describing the burning of the hotels, he added that neither he nor any of the Confederates intended to harm women or children. He admitted taking part in the burning of Barnum's Museum but gave the excuse it was for "only a joke." "I had been drinking and went there with a friend—to scare people."

As he said, "We only wanted to let the people of the North understand that there are two sides to war; and that they can't be rolling in wealth and comfort, while we in the South are bearing all the hardships and privations. . . ."

At noon, while the church bells tolled across the Bay, Captain Robert Cobb Kennedy, age 26, blond and handsome, walked to the gallows. His last words, in a loud, clear voice, were, "I die like a Southern officer and a gentleman. I do not regret the road I have followed."

Then the sword of the officer commanding the execution party flashed downward in the sun. The trap sprang for the second spy to die on the gallows in New York. Nathan Hale had been the first.

Below the gallows of Fort Lafayette, Kennedy had found war to be grim and deadly. But in the front parlor of Montreal police chief Guillaume Lamothe, which had been turned into a "cell," Lieutenant Bennett Young found war amusing and gay. After a day's court session, he wrote a long letter to the St. Albans *Messenger*. It read in part:

> Please send me two copies of your daily journal. I am extremely sorry I cannot visit your town to subscribe to your valuable journal in person. My present business in Montreal prevents my coming. Please address me care of the Montreal jail.

The letter enclosed a three-dollar bill. As the *Messenger's* editorial writer commented, "We fear that the three-dollar bill did not come into Young's possession honestly."

It was an understatement, or written with tongue-in-cheek. The three-dollar bill had been one stolen from the Franklin County Bank. The *Messenger*, however, did send Young two papers daily, until the three dollars had been used up, "so that it may help them open their eyes to the enormity of their crimes."

Young also wrote a letter to the manager of the hotel where they had stayed.

> You will probably remember I was a guest at your house. I regret I neglected to settle my hotel bill. Nevertheless, I am enclosing five dollars drawn on the Bank of St. Albans. Please tender my regards to Mr. Bishop [Cyrus Newton Bishop, the teller in the St. Albans Bank who had been forced to take the Confederate oath], in hopes he still bears faith and allegiance to the Confederate States of America, which he so solemnly swore to do.
>
> We have heard nothing of the old gent, president of the institution at the time we suspended him and began running his bank, I presume he is still faithful to the pledge and is fixed to that old armchair. If so, tell the old "boozer" his term of sentence has now expired.

Young in his letter also asked about a "ruffled shirt" which he had left behind and "a flask of Old Rifle Whiskey, which we had intended to use in case our ammunition was all used up. It is warranted to hold uphill [sic] at 150 yards."

In his final paragraph in this arrogant letter, he inquired about the mysterious lady he had met in the hotel.

"Please remember me to the lady next door," he ended, "whose good opinion I had the fortune to win, on account of our theological proclivities. Make to her your best bow. . . ."

In a long and momentous decision, Judge Charles J. Coursol of Montreal ruled that the St. Albans raid was "a hostile expedition by the Confederate States against the United States," and that no act had been committed which could be conceived of as a felony and therefore extraditional under the existing treaty. The raiders were re-arrested for violating Canada's neutrality, but this was only a formality. In three weeks they were found not guilty and were finally freed.

XXVIII. THE HANGING OF A HERO

THE second member of Hines' command to die was John Yates Beall. His trial and execution enraged the Confederates in Canada even more than had young Kennedy's death in New York. The courage, audacity and unquenchable fighting spirit stored up in his frail body had moved them all.

"He was a brave, wonderful man, who showed the Yankees how to live, to fight and to die. I salute him," Hines wrote. Castleman echoed these sentiments.

The account of Beall's trial and execution is contained in the original transcript of the hearing held by the court-martial board on February 1, 1865, at Fort Lafayette. Beall was charged with violation of the laws of war, and acting as a Confederate spy. The first charge had six specifications outlining the capture of the *Philo Parsons* and the attempt made on the U. S. S. *Michigan*. The second charged him with spying in Ohio and in New York.

Young Anderson became a government witness, describing for the court the attempt to capture the Buffalo Express. The clerk and part-owner of the *Philo Parsons* identified Beall in the courtroom and testified how Beall had captured his vessel, then seized and burned the *Island Queen*.

The trial records show that James T. Brady, one of the great lawyers of his day and a strong Peace Democrat, volunteered to defend Beall without cost. His cross-examination of Anderson, the owner of the *Philo Parsons* and the crew of the *Island Queen* was long and vigorous, but the witnesses never wavered from their original stories.

He thundered that Anderson was "a weakling and himself a spy," but the frightened boy, reduced to tears, did not change his testimony. After the second day he was excused, to be taken home by his mother, his dreams of wearing a sword and riding out of the West like Lochinvar cruelly shattered. Beall sent him his forgiveness through a minister, telling him to live "a brave and true life as a man." "It was my fault," he wrote. "I thought I had recruited a man but he was a child

255

in a man's clothing." Affidavits from Thompson in Toronto were introduced, but the court refused to mark them as evidence.

Finally, on February 8, Beall was sentenced to death. On the 14th, he wrote a long, brave letter to his brother William, serving before Richmond in Jackson's old foot cavalry. He said simply that he was sentenced to die on the gallows and that it was an unjust verdict. "Vengeance is mine, saith the Lord, and I will repay; therefore, dear William, do not show unkindness to the prisoners, they are helpless. . . ."

He wrote another letter to his brother which said in part: "I die for my country . . . should you be spared through this strife stay with Mother and be a comfort to her in her old age. Endure the hardships of the campaign like a man. Give my love to Mother and the girls. May God bless you all, now and forevermore, is my prayer and fervent wish for you. . . ."

Before his execution Beall had been confined in irons in a dungeon at Fort Lafayette. The diary manuscript of Captain J. D. Allison, who was among those arrested following the fire raid on New York City, gives a wonderful, little known picture of the prison life of the old fort.

He tells of "Captain Bell's [Beall] arrival," then goes on to describe that Christmas Eve. Dinner had been a small piece of boiled soup beef, a cup of rice and a thin slice of bread. He had sat up all night "washing out my under and over shirt, drawers, socks and hdkf. to be clean for the holidays."

On Christmas Day a St. Louis, Missouri, judge, who was drunk most of the time on what they called "blockaded" whiskey, read the Christmas services. Beall attended under heavy guard.

On the 31st a heavy snow fell. The prison monotony had grated their nerves raw. Allison found himself unable to read "with any degree of satisfaction."

On January 5 the guards, who had heard rumors of an attempt to free Beall, conducted a surprise raid on all their cells. Beds, books and drawers were pulled apart by the guards "looking for saws." A few days later to the cry of "fresh fish" a new batch of prisoners were brought in. A young lieutenant produced a bottle of whiskey.

"Lock that damn door!" he cried. The door was locked. He held up the bottle. "Let's make a night of it," he cried. At midnight they became "so boisterous" that the officer on guard came in and removed the owner of the bottle. There were two more intense searches for saws during the next week. Food grew scarce. A pet cat disappeared, probably finding its way into a pot.

Allison was granted permission to buy a game of darts. It helped to pass the weary days. The newspapers were devoting long columns to Beall's trial and to the fact that Lincoln had granted his mother permission to pass under a flag of truce to New York.

Beall saw his mother for a half-hour. In their cells the men who saw the white-haired old lady pass wept and cursed the court-martial board which had doomed Beall.

Darts and games of euchre passed the time for Allison and his fellow prisoners. He wrote in his diary, "I won the bed linen, shirt, cravat and a mince pie he is expecting" from a cellmate.

News spread through the prison grapevine that Beall had again appealed his execution. The news touched off a fight between the prisoners. As Allison said, shovels, pokers and knives "flourished in a way truly alarming." Some of the prisoners were wounded before the guards broke up the riot. One of the wounded men "tried to be peacemaker but was hooted down." Peace was restored when the prisoners began to tease Allison about "burning New York." What the "feud" was about we do not know, but it may have begun when someone said Beall was ready to accept clemency in return for making a full confession, naming his co-conspirators, and making a case for extradition against the Confederates in Canada.

On the 13th of February, the prison commandant summoned Beall.

"I have bad news for you, Captain," he said. "But I know you are a brave man and can stand it." Allison remembered that the frail Navy man stood straight as a poker and told the Federal colonel to read on.

Beall was told he was to hang at two o'clock on the 24th. Allison wrote, "God! What a lamentable death for one so far from friends and home, a prisoner in the hands of bitter, bitter enemies."

On the 14th Allison heard that Beall had sent a note to the prison commandant. "He seems prepared to go."

On the 16th, a tug landed at Fort Lafayette to take Beall to Governor's Island. Allison wrote, "I was not allowed to go down and see him. When he walked from his cell into the yard he saluted me and several others. He spoke pleasantly to me and walked with a steady step to the tug that was to bear him to his place of execution. . . ."

On the 19th, a Sunday, there was no service. The Missouri judge was drunk "and had fallen from grace."

On the 23rd Allison read in the *Herald* that Beall would be executed the next day.

Brady, Beall's attorney, tried desperately to save his client. He got up a petition signed by the country's leading clergymen, statesmen and numerous congressmen. He personally handed it to Lincoln. But the most compassionate of men would not be influenced.

"The case of Captain Beall is closed," he said. "General Dix can do as he pleases. I will not interfere."

Brady and his staff hurried back to New York to plead with Dix in a last-hour interview. But Dix, who had a bitter hatred of Rebel guerrillas, refused to commute the sentence.

"The President must decide," he said. The White House was silent.

On the afternoon of February 24, 1865, Beall stepped out of the sallyport of Fort Columbus on Governor's Island. For a moment he was out of step with his guards but quickly skipped a step to pick up the pace. Behind him a drum rolled out the death march.

At the foot of the gallows was a pine coffin. He stared at it impassively, then walked up the five steps. The news of the execution had drawn a crowd of five hundred. The Confederate ignored them. He looked out across the Bay and asked the hangman, "Is that Lafayette?"

"It is," the hangman replied in a low voice.

"I have a great many friends there, hangman," he said with a smile.

For nine minutes the lieutenant in charge of the execution party read the specifications of the court-martial and its verdict. Beall stood up when the young lieutenant began, but when he heard himself described as a "citizen of the insurgent state of Virginia," he reached around with his foot in a contemptuous gesture to pull a chair forward and sat down. At one point he laughed out loud.

Someone in the crowd called out, "The captain wants to be swung off quickly." Others took up the shout. Beall nonchalantly stretched out his legs, folded his arms and stared down for the first time at the chanting crowd.

The scowling lieutenant, determined to do his duty, raised his voice and continued reading. For a few minutes there was a grim contest between the officer and the howling mob. At last it was finished. In the sudden silence Beall rose. The noose was placed about his neck. A sudden gust of wind blew off his hat. When the hangman offered to retrieve it, Beall said, "Never mind, hangman, I won't need it where I'm going."

A Brooklyn Presbyterian minister began reading the prayer for the dead. In the sudden hush his voice sounded unnaturally loud. When it had ended, he stepped back.

Beall turned to him with a smile. "As some author has said, Reverend, we may be as near God on the scaffold as elsewhere."

The drums rolled. The young lieutenant dropped his sword. The trap sprang. The third spy died on the gallows in New York.

XXIX. THE EXPATRIATES

THERE was no darker or bloodier ground than the gentle Blue Grass of Kentucky in the spring of 1865, where murder bred murder and justice was distributed on the barrelhead. Confederate guerrillas bushwhacked, burned and looted; Federals made their prisoners draw straws and shot those who held the short ones.

In March, Richmond sent a colonel and a major on secret orders into Kentucky to create unrest. They were captured and put into irons. Richmond retaliated by selecting two officers of the One Hundred and Ninetieth Pennsylvania Regiment, both prisoners in Libby Prison, in Richmond, and put them into the dungeon of Richmond's penitentiary. Washington ordered the major and colonel released. Richmond sent the two Pennsylvanians back home.

This was the last exchange. Four more officers on secret service in Kentucky were caught. This time they were hanged as spies. Richmond threw more officers from Libby into the dungeons. In Lexington three staff officers were hanged in the cold dawn after pleading for a firing squad. Ten prisoners marched into the provost marshal's office in Lexington and in a dramatic scene selected straws from a can. Five were returned to their cells; five were hanged.

When General Breckinridge's brother Robert, a colonel, was captured, he was sent to the penitentiary at Columbus and put in the same block of cells which had once held Morgan and Hines. Ever since the escape, the officers who had remained behind were kept under the most strict discipline. Twenty out of twenty-four hours they were confined to their small cells.

It was a bloody, cruel business on both sides, but it was a troubled area suitable for Hines' talents. In the winter of 1865, after conferring with Thompson, he left Toronto for the Blue Grass, as he put it, "to form a new command."

In their reports, Colonel Sweet in Chicago and Colonel Carrington in Indiana, linked Hines with Captain Jessee, leader of one of the largest band of guerrillas in Kentucky. Like Quantrill in Missouri, Jessee's men were a fierce-looking lot of bearded mountain men, escaped prisoners, Copperheads with prices on their heads, farmers who had seen their homes go up in smoke, deserters and former cavalry troopers whose commands had vanished in the cannon smoke of Gettysburg, Perryville and Stone's River. They rode fine racehorses, slept with their rifles and Colts, struck with savage swiftness to burn, kill and vanish. While he was in Kentucky, Hines hid out in their strongholds, deep in the woods.

In April, Richmond fell in flames. Lee surrendered. The news came to the backwoods of Kentucky with stunning swiftness. In his hideout Hines gathered his men about him. As he wrote his father:

> I shall not attempt—language is inadequate—to express my feelings when the awful calamity burst upon us. It is a grief almost too sacred for words. I was at the time—fall of B [Breckinridge] and surrender of Lee—in Kentucky forming a new command. I addressed my men, telling them our cause was hopeless, that I was no longer in authority. I advised them to seek shelter for themselves, for to remain with me would be dangerous. After many adventures I succeeded in getting to Canada. . . .

Captain Hines' son [in 1933] described his father's "adventures." Two days after Lincoln's assassination Hines arrived in Detroit. Unshaven, and bone-tired from the hazardous journey north, he walked into a saloon near the Windsor Ferry for a drink and some supper. As he sat down at a table a man at the bar studied him intently. Suddenly the man shouted, pointing at Hines, "That's John Wilkes Booth, I saw him many times in Baltimore and New York!"

In a moment the place was in an uproar. Hines kicked the chair back. In a moment his revolver was in his hand. He clubbed the first man who tried to grab him. Another got Hines' boot in the stomach. He menaced the others with his Colt. As they hesitated, he backed out of the saloon.

With the city clanging with alarm, Hines scaled back fences and made his way to the wharf. A ferry had just come in. Hines waited until the passengers and wagons had disembarked. Then he casually went aboard and made his way to the captain's bridge.

The skipper of the ferryboat was sipping a cup of coffee when Hines walked in. The cold steel of the Colt barrel touched the back of his head.

"Take me across at once," Hines ordered.

The captain signaled the surprised engine room and the ferry pulled out. On the Canadian side Hines gave the captain five dollars, apologized for "the inconvenience" and then disappeared into the darkness.

Back at Detroit, the ferryboat captain was questioned by police. He told them a man who looked like Booth had commandeered his boat at pistol point and made him cross to Canada. Until Booth was shot some days later, it was believed he had indeed made his way across the border.

In Toronto Hines joined Thompson, Castleman, Bennett H. Young and his St. Albans raiders who had been freed by the Montreal court. It was a colony of lost men, asking themselves the same question: What shall we do now?

For them there was no Appomattox. Secretary Stanton had made it clear he regarded them as bandits. Warrants had already been issued for their arrest. Hines had a thousand-dollar reward on his head. Stanton had sworn to hang Thompson. Young and his raiders were bank-robbers in the eyes of the Union. Stanton had invited them to return home "to stand trial for their infamous conduct." Young, who still regarded the whole raid with a whimsical eye, had refused.

Clay, who had left Toronto in December for Kentucky, had told Thompson, "I'm sure they won't harm a sick old man." He was soon to learn how the Union felt about him.

Of the other members of Hines' command, Beall and Kennedy were dead, Burley had gone back to England, Captain Cole had vanished. Lieutenant Ashbrook was dodging the provost marshal's men in Kentucky. Lieutenant Headley and Colonel Martin were with Jefferson Davis and his cabinet. Lieutenant Bettersworth was writing Hines letters imploring forgiveness for his loose tongue in Chicago. Grenfel was in prison waiting to be transferred to the Dry Tortugas for life. Marmaduke, the glory-hunter, was on his way home to Missouri with his tarnished honor; John Maughan, the traitorous clerk, had vanished after the Chicago trials. Of the Copperheads, Justice Bullitt and H. H. Dodd were in exile in Canada. The others, in New York, Indiana, Illinois and Missouri, were under sentence of death or serving long terms in military prison.

Hines, the realist, knew he might never be able to return to the United States. So instead of sitting about the Queen's bar listening to Thompson's wild ideas, he wrote Nancy to join him as soon as possible, sent off a note to his father not to expect him for some time, then

Bill of sale of the *Canadian Eagle,* on which the Confederate agents hoped to escape.

Courtesy, Melville Nichols, Summit, N.J.

rented a small flat and entered Toronto University to study French and literature. He began reading law at night with Justice Bullitt. Castleman joined him at the University to study medicine.

Meanwhile Thompson had formulated his plans. There was enough gold left in the treasury to buy a schooner, equip it and sail to the Rio Grande. Thompson asked Hines and Castleman to go along, but they refused. The schooner *Canadian Eagle* was purchased through agents of the Sons of Liberty in Portland. A captain was hired and the ship was brought to St. John's, New Brunswick. But the alert Portland provost marshal's men heard of the deal and contacted the Canadian authorities who arrested the agents. Drafts drawn on a Montreal bank were found on them. They confessed that the schooner was to be used "to help the Rebels in Canada to escape."

On April 20, Assistant Secretary of War Charles A. Dana alerted all border commands and provost marshals along the East Coast to watch out for the schooner "and to arrest all Rebels aboard." He enclosed Thompson's description, pointing up his swollen eyes, "which make it almost impossible for him to see at times."

Agents on the St. Croix River, a center of Copperhead activity, warned Toronto that Federal gunboats were searching the waters off the Maine coast for the *Canadian Eagle*. The escape never came off. The ship lay in the harbor for five months. In the summer of 1866 "the ship the Rebels intended to escape on" was sold to a Canadian merchant.

On the night of April 26, John Wilkes Booth was shot and captured by Lieutenant Colonel Everton J. Conger's pursuit party. (Colonel Conger was not related to the Captain George Conger who roused the townspeople of St. Albans, Vermont, against the Confederate raiders.) By this time Greeley's *Tribune* and other leading newspapers in the North were openly charging that the Confederates in Toronto had plotted Lincoln's murder. Letters from informers offering "evidence" to link the Confederate Mission in Canada with the assassination poured into the offices of Secretary Stanton, Judge Advocate General Holt and General Baker, Chief of the National Detective Force in Washington.

One "G.S.C." of New York wrote that while in Toronto on business he had read a letter from John Yates Beall to Thompson, written before his execution, demanding that his hanging "be speedily and terribly avenged." In the Queen's bar he had listened to Bennett Young promise his raiders, "We'll make the Yankees soon howl," and

"We'll soon have news from Washington that will make the people stare."

The informer said this was on Friday morning, April 17. The next day he received word of Lincoln's death. In the Queen's bar the Confederates called it "good news this morning," and "damn well done."

Judge Advocate Burnett, who had tried Grenfel and the other conspirators in Chicago, sent Baker a letter from an Englishman working with the Confederates "but who found the murder too much for him."

The Englishman had written that he had heard that one of the figures in the plot, he wasn't sure if it had been Booth, had wired Thompson shortly after the shooting at Ford's Theatre advising the Confederate Commissioner to expect him "shortly." Whoever the conspirator was, he never showed up. The best clue came from St. Albans, Vermont. The sheriff reported that three men had arrived just after the assassination. One had dropped a handkerchief in a railroad depot with the name J. H. Surratt [John Harrison Surratt, son of Mary Surratt, later to be hanged for her part in conspiring with John Wilkes Booth to assassinate Lincoln] embroidered in one corner.

The letter produced a great deal of excitement at Baker's headquarters in Washington. A detective was dispatched to St. Albans to bring back the handkerchief. Meanwhile the provost marshal at Portland had sent an agent into Canada to trace the three men. He found them hiding out in a small town. He had Surratt's picture and none of them compared with it. After a drinking bout, he learned they were deserters, "as desperate a trio of characters as I ever came across," but not implicated in the murder plot. How they obtained Surratt's handkerchief is still a mystery.

Baker received numerous letters accusing Thompson and the Confederate command in Toronto of plotting the murder of Lincoln. Of course they were the most likely suspects. Thompson's best man even looked like Booth. Baker would have been delighted to be able to link Thompson, Hines, and the others to the murder. But he realized that despite the sometimes eerie twists of coincidence, there was not one shred of evidence to place the murder at the door of the Confederate Commission in Toronto.

At times, the bitter hate they felt toward Hines' raiders obscured the thinking of some of the Union leaders. Judge Advocate General Holt was one. He tried desperately to link Clay, Thompson and Hines to the Lincoln assassination plot but, like Baker, failed. In his attempts to do so, he was used by swindlers and confidence men who in the end made him a ludicrous public figure.

The principal swindler was a penniless newspaperman who had been fired from his job for drunkenness. He sent Holt a telegram informing him that he had news "of the greatest importance" involving the Confederate Commissioners in the Lincoln murder.

Holt eagerly sent word for him to come to Washington. The newspaperman, an intense young man with a spade beard, impressed Holt, who told him to go ahead and find his "witnesses."

The newspaperman disappeared. Soon Holt was being bombarded with telegrams from all over the Northwest: "Have witness who confesses he heard Clay admit his part in the Lincoln Conspiracy. . . ."

Of course, with every telegram was a request for money. Holt was generous. Weeks went by. Finally the newspaperman, several hundred dollars richer, appeared with a batch of "confessions." Holt was jubilant. He immediately conferred with Congressional leaders who were then trying to decide what to do with Clay and Davis. It was decided to call the witnesses and hear their stories. The inevitable happened. One of the wild stories told by a witness fell apart after a Congressional prober pointed out that Clay could not have been in Toronto when the witness said he was, because he had been in jail. The witness, under the threat of perjury, confessed that he had been paid by the newspaperman to lie.

The other witnesses also testified they had been bribed. Congress was rocked by the revelations and Holt shocked. He had the provost marshal's men bring in the newspaperman. He said he also was "shocked" and, with a great deal of bluster, promised Holt he would go at once to New York with the Congressional probers and locate a witness who would "prove" that Clay and Davis had ordered Lincoln murdered.

Holt swallowed his story. The newspaperman and the Congressional attorneys left for New York City. There the reporter gave the party the slip by going out the rear door of a saloon. He was never seen again. Later it developed that Holt, incredibly gullible, had given him an extra $100 for "expenses."

The chagrined Holt was forced to admit in a letter to the Congressional committee that he had been hoodwinked by a smart swindler. It was the last attempt by the government to prove that the Confederate Mission in Canada had any part in the Lincoln murder.

The mists of history have hidden two important links between the

Confederate Mission in Canada and the assassination of Lincoln. John Harrison Surratt was a known Confederate spy and mail courier who had traveled the overland route from Richmond to Canada many times. Had he dropped his handkerchief in the St. Albans depot while he was reporting to Thompson?

There is evidence that John Wilkes Booth had been in Montreal during the winter of 1864–65. What he did there—and his draft on a Montreal bank used by the Confederates—has never been fully explained.

In all the Hines Papers, the Baker-Turner Papers and the Lincoln Conspiracy Papers this author did not find anything which could be remotely classified as *evidence* that the Confederates in Canada had helped to pull the trigger that sent the bullet into Lincoln's brain.

In Toronto, Hines, very lonely without Nancy, was writing in his diary: "Weary, weary day . . . no word from Nannie. . . ."

Finally a note arrived from Nancy. She was on her way to join him in exile. The long days dragged on. For Hines they seemed never-ending. War, conspiracy, exile were no longer important. In the morning and afternoon he and his friend "Breck" Castleman stood on the Windsor wharf watching the passengers come ashore from the Detroit Ferry. Every boat without Nancy was a bitter disappointment for Hines. As they walked back to their lodgings on May Street, Castleman did his best to cheer up his friend.

The waiting became almost unbearable. Hines wrote in his diary: "No dispatch yet from my darling. When will she arrive?"

And the next day, after the weary vigil at the ferry: "My darling not yet arrived . . . Weary, weary days! . . ."

And the next: "Still no news of my wife."

Then the glorious day: "Nannie arrived in the evening from Ky."

It was a wonderful meeting. Tom saw Nancy hesitantly step off the ferry. With a shout he elbowed his way through the crowd, Castleman close behind. Nancy dropped her bag and ran toward him. Hines grabbed his wife in his arms and swung her about. Castleman took off his hat and waited to kiss the bride, while the other passengers stood around grinning at the happiness shining in their faces.

The gambler's impassiveness, the cold, steady eye, the carefully

December,   Monday, 18.   1865.

Tuesday, 19.

Wednesday, 20.

December,   Thursday, 21.   1865.

Friday, 22.

Saturday, 23.

Two pages from Tom Hines' diary. "Nannie" is Nancy, his wife.

controlled voice had vanished. Tom Hines at that moment was only a young man of twenty-six, deliriously happy and deeply in love.

A few days after Nancy arrived, Tom found a larger flat with "a nice Kentucky family." Life was not all grimness. None of them had any money left—Hines wrote he hadn't been paid by the Army in fourteen months—but from entries in his diary, there were visits and tea parties, and they rode, fished and danced. Hines continued studying law under Justice Bullitt and French at Toronto University. Breck Castleman was their first Sunday visitor and made Nancy blush with his compliments about her cooking.

On May 29, 1865, President Johnson signed the Amnesty Act which granted pardons to ex-Confederates—except certain officers—on the condition that they take the oath of allegiance. Hines did not rush to sign the oath, as many of the former officers in Toronto did. For two months he nosed about, writing cautiously worded letters to friends in Kentucky. Finally, he bowed to the inevitable. He decided

Letter written by Hines to a friend in Kentucky giving the date he took the oath of allegiance to the United States, July 20, 1865, in Detroit.

to take the oath, but to remain in Canada until the situation at home was clear. On July 20, with Nancy, he crossed on the ferry to Detroit and took the oath in the provost marshal's office.

Evidently there was no special reason to refuse Hines clearance, although the provost marshals in Lexington and Bowling Green had patrols watching the roads for his return. Hines was one of those "certain officers," at least to the Federals in Kentucky, and to Colonel Carrington in Indianapolis, who told the Chief of Staff, Department of Ohio, that Hines should be arrested as soon as he crossed back into the

United States, and returned to Indianapolis for trial. In Columbus, Ohio, the provost marshal said the authorities would like to question Hines about Sergeant Moon's part in the Ohio penitentiary escape. He forgot to say whether or not the thousand-dollar reward was still in effect.

That summer Hines received the first of letters from home warning him that the Federals were out to get him. In an obviously disguised handwriting, "your friend" wrote, "Watch out, there is a guard at the bank [sic] to catch you. . . ."

The forced gaiety soon wore thin. Home was in all their hearts. Some of them tried to sneak back into the States and were caught. In Kentucky, the provost marshal reported the arrest of Lieutenant John W. Headley, "a slick fellow who can't be trusted."

Commissioner Clay, who thought the Federals wouldn't harm a "sick old man," had been arrested in Kentucky. He had been put into jail without ceremony, a guard in and out his cell twenty-four hours a day. Clay's illness took a turn for the worse. The constant guards, he said, "make me fret." The provost marshal of Lexington wrote headquarters, recommending that the old man be sent to the hospital. Headquarters deliberated for a month, then at last sent orders to remove the guards from inside the cell but to keep one outside "at all times." A doctor was permitted to examine Clay. He added his recommendation to the provost marshal's that the former Confederate Commissioner be removed to a hospital. Again headquarters pondered. A few weeks passed. Then came the order sending Clay into the hospital at Lexington. A short time later he was paroled and finally freed.

In Toronto, Thompson, who knew what fate awaited him if he returned to the United States, left for London to see Judah Benjamin. Castleman, who found the Canadian winter aggravated the illness he had contracted in prison, decided to join Thompson for a grand tour of England, Scotland and Ireland. The evening before he left was a sad one. While Nancy played the piano they sang the old songs. Breck told stories of old Isaac Byrd, one of the slaves on the Castleman plantation, and Tom, who had a wonderful gift of mimicry, showed how Scotty, the old trusty in the penitentiary at Columbus, used to shuffle down the prison corridors in soft slippers to try to catch them with a candle lit after curfew. Perhaps at no other time during the exile did they feel such terrible loneliness and longing for home. At last the evening was over. Nancy kissed Breck goodbye and Tom showed him to the door. The night was bitterly cold. Overhead the Canadian sky quivered with star-fire. They shook hands, then Breck was gone.

It was a hard winter for them in Canada. Nancy, who, as she admits in her letters, had never thought twice about the value of a dollar, now found value in pennies. But despite the lack of money and sometimes food, Tom and Nancy would recall those days as happy ones. After all the uncertainty, danger and separation, they were at last together. That was all that mattered.

The next year turned. Hines began to hear from friends of his father's; the simmering hate had commenced to cool. Clay, Lieutenant Headley and Colonel Martin had been freed. Even Bennett Young was back home in Scott County, although Vermont's governor was talking about reopening the case and having him stand trial. But nothing had come of it. Basil Duke wrote he had gone into the produce business in Cincinnati and was prospering. He added one significant line: "Our friends at last have control of the state, and we will have things decently conducted at last. . . ."

Across the world in London, Charles Francis Adams, writing from the American Legation, forwarded to Secretary of State Seward a petition several feet long, signed by the residents of hundreds of towns and villages in England, asking President Johnson to pardon Colonel Grenfel and allow him to return home.

As Adams wrote, "This man already owes to the intervention of influential men his rescue from the fate [from hanging] which [you] informed me at the time he richly deserved. The proposed move is to release him altogether. . . ."

Hervey, the attorney Hines had hired in Chicago to defend Grenfel, personally delivered another appeal to the White House. Johnson sent out word his mind was made up: Grenfel would spend the rest of his life in the Dry Tortugas. Hervey rode over to the State Department and Seward told him the case was closed.

On January 4, 1866, Hines received a letter from Hervey which for a time dampened their spirits: Judge Advocate General Holt had formally advised Hervey his appeal had again been denied. Grenfel was to be held at McLean Barracks in Cincinnati to await transfer to Key West Naval Depot—the last mile before the Dry Tortugas.

Hines sent some money to Grenfel—and perhaps a message that he was already planning his escape.

Before spring arrived, Hines had completed his study of law under

Justice Bullitt, who was talking of going home. The other Copperhead leader, H. H. Dodd, said he would wait—the death sentence passed by the Indianapolis Military Tribunal was still valid.

Under heavy pressure from his party, President Johnson paroled Jim Barrett, the Missouri Copperhead leader, from prison on April 8, 1866. There is a wonderful series of communications between Barrett and the captain of the prison in charge of political prisoners. The Judge Advocate General's office had demanded a bond of five hundred dollars from Barrett. But the Missourian wrote back to the captain, "I shall pay only half that; take it or leave it." The government took it.

A week later the United States Supreme Court, in what it called one of its "most momentous decisions" (*Ex-parte Milligan*), ruled that the military tribunal which had tried the Indiana Copperheads had no jurisdiction. A few days later all of them were released. In Canada, Bullitt and Dodd hastily packed their bags, said goodbye to Tom and Nancy and set out for home.

Ironically, among the government attorneys who had argued the case was General Ben Butler, who had felt the Copperhead fangs when New York City was almost burned about his ears. Arguing for the conspirators was the same Justice Black who had tried to bring about a spurious peace at the Niagara Falls meeting in the summer of 1864.

In May, Hines and Nancy packed for home, to join the exodus of former Confederate officers and their families who were leaving Montreal, Toronto and Amherstburg. No longer would the bar at the Queen's Hotel resound with the crash of broken glasses and the voices roaring out the words of "Morgan and Duke Ride Tonight. . . ."

Tom and Nancy had a particular joy in leaving; their first child, expected in June, would be born in their beloved Blue Grass. . . .

XXX. THE ORDEAL OF THE GALLANT TEMPLAR

THE setting for the last scene had changed. Gone were the Queen's bar in Toronto, the hideout in Halifax, the windy train platforms, hotel rooms in Chicago, jails and prisons in the Northwest. Instead it was the dark hold of a freighter, reeking of hemp and coral on a June day in 1866. The *Alice Carter*, its beams still holding the smell of death from her blackbird days, had left Key West Naval Depot bound for Fort Jefferson, the United States Military Prison on Garden Key, largest of the Dry Tortugas.

They had been in the hold less than an hour but the prisoners lay in a sea of their own sweat. When they moved, their heavy chains rattled. The ten "common prisoners" who had joined the five political prisoners at Key West made the trip miserable with tales of the sun-scorched, barren island to which they had been sentenced for life.

But Colonel George St. Leger Grenfel, who had felt the glare of the desert sun, shook his long mane of white hair and countered with tales of Abd el-Kader, who had ordered the eyes of unbelievers burned out with hot sticks and mounds of coals shoveled into their open bellies. Even the convicted criminals grew silent as the clear voice with the crisp British accent filled the suffocating darkness.

Suddenly a rifle butt banged on the hatch cover. A voice shouted for them to get ready. Then the hatchway swung back and the men in chains rose to their knees to sniff at the sweetness of the ocean air. One by one they climbed the few steps, managing their chains with the skill of men whose bodies had lived with them for months.

The young New Hampshire private, the more friendly of their five guards, grinned as he herded them on deck. Grenfel saw they were pulling into a rickety wooden wharf jutting out from a small sandy island. Three other islands of various sizes were scattered about the sea. One, with a lighthouse, he judged to be about three miles distant.

The young soldier pointed with his bayonet to the island which they were approaching.

"There's your prison, Rebs."

"What's it called, Yankee?" called out a man who had been convicted of murder.

"Garden Key," the guard replied. He pointed to another island in the distance. "That's East Key."

"What's the little one?" the prisoner asked, pointing to an island scarcely more than a strip of sand, less than a half-mile from Garden Key.

"Bird Key." The guard chuckled. "There's a lot of good Rebs over there!"

The prisoner squinted in the sun. "Don't look like anybody's on it," he murmured.

The guard chuckled again. "That's the cemetery."

Grenfel studied Garden Key as the freighter was being tied up. It was less than fifteen acres in width, dominated by an enormous fort. Swarms of squeaking seagulls wheeled about the wharf. Numerous pelicans strutted about the beach. The island was perfectly flat, less than three feet above sea level. Its surface was covered with brushwood, clumps of sea grass and shrubs with inch-long spikes which he later learned were called prickly pear.

But what interested Grenfel most was Fort Jefferson itself. There, in the words of his commutation, he had been sentenced to spend the rest of his "natural life."

It was a huge, six-sided fort, three tiers high and bristling with guns, which his practiced eye told him were 11-inch Columbians. Built of bright yellow brick, the fort was dazzling in the glaring sunlight. The reflection was so strong the prisoners shielded their eyes as they stared at the massive mountain of masonry. The guard told them they would soon get used to it, that everybody, prisoner and soldier alike, found the reflection of the sun off the sides of the fort almost maddening, and for the first few hours found it almost impossible to keep his eyes open.

The prisoners were lined up on deck and marched down the gangway. On the wharf they were counted and checked. The skipper of the freighter was given a slip signed by the captain in charge of the guards. Back at the naval depot he would turn it in for fifty dollars.

Fifty Negroes, ironically, leased by their owners in Key West to the Abolitionist government, appeared to unload the cargo. The prisoners passed them on their way to the fort.

Grenfel's first impression of Fort Jefferson was a wide moat. As they crossed the drawbridge one of the prisoners shouted and pointed down. Grenfel followed his finger. A shark's fin cut the clear water. He could see the ugly, blunt snout.

"We call him 'Provost Marshal,' " the guard said. "He's there just to make sure you boys don't get any notions."

They crossed the drawbridge to enter an enormous sally port. Inside the walls Grenfel had the impression he was once again in the courtyards of Morocco. Exotic flowers, exuding a heavy perfume, bordered the five-foot cement walk. In the center a fountain tinkled, the water sparkling in the sunshine. They walked across a thick carpet of Spanish grass. On one side was a square patch of flowers, red as newly spilled blood. In contrast were the men in chains, listlessly chipping and polishing mounds of yellow bricks. Other men under guard, carrying their chains and large iron balls, shuffled across the yard.

A guard pointed to one of the prisoners, a short man with sun-bleached hair. He was wearing tattered gray pants and no shirt. His chest and arms were tanned the color of old leather. This was Johnny Adare. A grudging note of admiration crept into the guard's voice as he told them how Johnny had made two attempts to escape. The first time he had broken out with a Negro slave, and, using a plank to support his ball and chain, had swum the three miles to Logger Key. At the lighthouse there they stole a boat and made the ninety-mile trip to Cuba. In Cuba Adare broke off his chains. But to get money to escape to Europe he tried to sell his Negro comrade back into slavery. The slave complained to the Cuban police, who arrested Johnny. A month later he was back at the Dry Tortugas. The second attempt—this time, in addition to the iron ball, he had chains around his neck and waist—ended on Logger Key when he was caught by a corporal of the guard who heard him stealing a lifeboat.

"What about the Provost Marshal?" one of the prisoners asked. "How did he get by that shark?"

"Johnny swam across the moat," the guard said. "When the shark went for him, Johnny punched him in the nose. The Provost Marshal wanted no more of Johnny."

Grenfel met the provost marshal of Fort Jefferson, a sadistic young lieutenant named Robinson, "who warned him he was aware of his reputation as one of Morgan's bandits." Grenfel contemptuously informed him he was an officer of the Confederate States and a gentleman. The commandant's reply was that he would be treated like any other prisoner. "Work or don't eat," was the order.

After the interview Grenfel went to the blacksmith's shop and had a 30-pound ball and chain welded around his leg. Then he was assigned to his bunk in the huge, domelike gun room. Johnny Adare, that "hard case," had the next bunk.

On June 30, 1867, Grenfel was permitted for the first time to write a letter to his daughter in England. It is moving and stark. In it Grenfel described the brutal treatment inflicted on him by the sadistic Lieutenant Robinson during his first year at Fort Jefferson. From the first day of his arrival, Grenfel wrote, he had worked in the "chain gang" from 6 A.M. to 5:30 P.M. under a blazing sun, unloading coal and bricks from the holds of freighters. After a frugal evening meal he had scarcely enough strength left to fall onto his straw pallet. But Grenfel had lived most of his life in the field and his body was hard as whipcord. The laborious work had not impaired his health, he wrote, and the only malady he suffered were occasional attacks "from my old enemy, rheumatism," and weak spells, brought on by "old age" and poor food. He was then sixty-six years old.

Evidently Grenfel's family was powerful enough to bring heavy pressure on Downing Street to obtain Grenfel's release, because his daughter had written that a Brigadier-General Hill, answering protests sent to the State Department by the British Minister to the United States that Grenfel was imprisoned under "barbaric conditions," had personally written the Grenfel family to say that Grenfel "was completely satisfied with his life in the Dry Tortugas, and had been assigned duties which are very light."

As Grenfel wrote, "The lying old sinner knew perfectly well that by his own order I was being treated worse than any other prisoner on the island. The very day that he dates his letter I was working with niggers unloading 450 tons of coal from a vessel under a sun hotter than your hottest July weather, and kept at work 'till I could barely stand." Grenfel revealed that in April, when he was so stiff with rheumatism he could not bend, he was ordered by Lieutenant Robinson to pick up bricks in the prison yard. Grenfel said he refused but told Robinson he would do anything "that would not make me bend."

As Grenfel reconstructed the scene this is what happened:

"Pick up those bricks," Robinson ordered.

"I am sorry but I cannot bend."

"This is your last chance—pick up those bricks!" Grenfel shook his head. Robinson then ordered the old soldier tied to a grate outside the prison walls. He was left there from 7 A.M. until 4 P.M. when he was cut down, more dead than alive.

"Will you pick up those bricks?" Robinson asked.

"I cannot," Grenfel whispered.

Robinson then returned with two other officers and three soldiers. They dragged Grenfel down to the wharf. His hands were tied behind him, "so as to cut all the skin from the wrists," and he was pushed off the dock into twenty-five feet of water. A strong swimmer, Grenfel managed to reach the surface. "Haul him up," Lieutenant Robinson shouted. The soldiers hauled Grenfel back to the wharf. Robinson ordered his legs tied this time. Again the old colonel was flung off the dock.

As he wrote, "Still, by great exertion, I managed to float and I was once more hauled in." This time Robinson attached weights to Grenfel's feet before he ordered the troopers to push him into the sea. He sank like a stone. When they pulled him back up on the wharf, he was strangling. Robinson kicked him back to consciousness. "Are you going to carry those bricks, Grenfel?" he asked.

The old soldier weakly shook his head. "Throw him over again, boys," Robinson ordered.

Three times they threw him into the sea, pulling him up each time as he was about to drown. Robinson kicked him unmercifully, "my ribs, elbows and hands were stripped of skin" until after the last time, when he remained unconscious for a long time. They left him on the wharf as the twilight deepened into night. Later a kindly guard brought Grenfel a blanket. In the morning, bruised and sick, retching constantly, he stumbled back into the prison yard.

Robinson was there to greet him. "Going to pick up those bricks, Grenfel?" he asked.

Grenfel looked him in the eye and shook his head. For a long moment both men were locked in silent battle. It was Robinson who broke. He grunted and walked away, leaving the gallant old Templar undefeated on the field.

Lieutenant Robinson practiced his cruelty not only on the prisoners but on the soldiers in the garrison as well. As Grenfel wrote his daughter, three young recruits, whose bayonets did not gleam as brightly as Robinson thought they should, were sentenced to the "ring." This punishment consisted of walking about a large circle in the courtyard carrying a 250-pound shell. One boy, "with tears streaming down his face," suffered sunstroke, another fainted and was kicked back on his feet, while the third lasted until 2 P.M. before he collapsed. Grenfel was near him when he fell and helped to carry him to the infirmary. But the next day he was back in the ring. This time his punishment was slightly relaxed; he was allowed to roll the heavy shell about the circle from sunrise to sunset, never once allowed to get off his knees. The other two soldiers were delirious for days.

Grenfel warned his daughter not to let any of the stories he had told her leak out, "because it will subject me to worse treatment than I have received." He also warned her not to pay "notice" of the stories in her return letter. The rest of the letter is a moving account of a gallant man waiting, even praying for death . . . "I am dying by inches . . . the sooner the better. . . ."

The few brief moments of "sunshine," as he put it, were reading and rereading his daughter's letters and remembering the home which, ironically, he had spurned all his life. Another consolation, he said, were the letters he received from his friends in the South. The Confederacy's leaders never forgot Grenfel. Jefferson Davis, from his own cell in Fort Monroe, sent him a "cheery note," a package of tobacco and $20; General Braxton Bragg wrote "a kindly" note; and the Florida legislature had passed a resolution, which was sent on to Stanton, pleading for Grenfel's release.

As Grenfel said, he knew all attempts to secure his release would be useless while Stanton was in office. Sir Frederick Bruce, the British Minister, had made a personal call on Johnson, but the President had referred him to Stanton. Grenfel was bitter over Bruce's attempts, which he thought were very feeble. "The British lion puts his tail between his legs when Jonathan gets mad. Seward rules in Downing Street as much as in Washington. . . ." He ends with, "Adieu, with love to all who once loved me. . . ."

While Grenfel was confined in the dungeon, a new batch of prisoners arrived. Among them were Doctor Samuel Mudd, who had set John Wilkes Booth's broken leg; Edward Spangler; Michael O'Laughlin and Samuel Arnold, all convicted in the plot to murder Lincoln. Mudd was given a straw pallet in the gun room. The other prisoners at first refused to talk to him, but gradually the gentle, soft-spoken man broke down their resistance. They accepted him, tough Johnny Adare dubbing him "Yankee Sawbones."

Grenfel emerged from the dungeon, broken in health but not in spirit. If anything, he was more rebellious. As one guard recalled, he never let an occasion pass to remind them "with spice of satisfaction" how he had seen Secretary of War Stanton and had deceived him about the Confederates' strength.

"Stanton has never forgiven me for that," he would say.

As the guard wrote, "We would be surprised if he did."

During the terrible days and nights in the dungeon, Grenfel had made up his mind to escape from the Dry Tortugas. "I must have freedom or perish," the New Hampshire guard quoted him as saying.

The night after he was released from the dungeon, Grenfel sought out the escape artist, Johnny Adare. They were seen that night in the gun room talking in low tones with Joseph Holroyd and James Orr, "two prisoners of notoriously desperate character."

Grenfel had not yet met Doctor Mudd. The physician took his place in the dungeon "for insulting a guard."

Fate, in the form of Major J. Stone, the new commandant of the fort, who arrived the morning after Grenfel's release from the dungeon, delayed the escape. With Stone was his five-year-old son. When he heard of the treatment of Grenfel and the others by Lieutenant Robinson, the new commandant sent the provost marshal back to Key West under charges and relaxed the inhuman rules.

The major's young son soon captivated the love-starved garrison, soldiers and prisoners alike. Johnny Adare made a plate for the child from the shell of a turtle and Grenfel told him stories of fighting and adventure that seemed to have come out of the pages of the Arabian Nights.

It lasted only a few days. The major had brought the germs of yellow fever from Cuba. In the night the dread "black vomit" had appeared. Stone's son died as the blood-red dawn crept out of the sea. By noon Major Stone had joined his son in death. Grenfel was heartbroken. To him fell the task of writing the major's brother and telling him of the double tragedy. The fever spread with the speed of a prairie fire. In a week the prison surgeon was dead, and a company of soldiers had died.

Now Grenfel played his greatest role. Robert Hervey, his attorney, painted the opening scene in his moving appeal to President Johnson for Grenfel's release.

A week after the epidemic struck, Grenfel walked into the office of the prison commandant. He was clad in a dirty, ragged shirt and torn pants. Through his shirt his skin, like old leather, was stretched tightly over his chest, the ribs showing clearly. His white hair was shoulder-length. He was barefoot. There was no speech, no dramatics. He had simply come to volunteer to nurse the sick and the dying.

"Why do you do this, Grenfel?" the commandant asked.

"Can you tell me a better way of dying, sir?" Grenfel replied.

A blacksmith struck off the chains. Grenfel was escorted to the gun room, which was used as the pesthouse, by a guard who carefully held a handkerchief over his face. Grenfel was pushed inside and the door slammed behind him.

The stench was almost overpowering. Hanging on the wall was an oil lamp. In the feeble light Grenfel could see the staring eyes brilliant with the raging fever, the open mouths of the dead men, others with the horrible black vomit bubbling on their lips.

He bent down to pick up a basin of water. He looked up as someone came toward him. Grenfel's bad eyesight and the dimness of the room prevented him from making out the white blur of the man's face.

"Who are you?" he asked. "A nurse?"

The man held up a candle to his face. "I'm surprised, sir, I thought everyone in America knew Doctor Mudd."

The man who set the broken leg of John Wilkes Booth and the old soldier of fortune stared at each other in the candlelight.

"I've come to help, Doctor," Grenfel said. "What can I do?"

"Thank God you've come," Mudd replied. "I have made a dispensary at the back of the room. If you will follow me. . . ."

The "murderous physician" and the man of "reckless and impetuous temperament—a born revolutionist," walked together down the aisle of dying men. It was to be, as Grenfel would write: "Doctor Mudd, Chief Physician; Colonel Grenfel, Chief Nurse."

The memoirs of the young New Hampshire private, Hervey's letters to Johnson, Grenfel's personal notes, and his letters tell us what happened in the pesthouse.

For three months Grenfel and Doctor Mudd worked together in the stinking gun room. Grenfel, as the surgeon general of Key West officially declared, scarcely slept or rested during that time. He administered the medicine made by Doctor Mudd, washed men burning with fever, fed them, wrote their letters, their wills and wiped the black vomit from their cracked lips. Death had always carefully avoided Grenfel on the battlefield; in the pesthouse he also kept his distance.

In three months not a boat or a schooner touched the fortress. Once a small boat made the journey from Key West to deliver medicine and some supplies. At night soldiers who had recovered from the fever, or who had successfully avoided getting it, made up parties to hunt the giant tortoises. They would hide in the grass at twilight. As night fell with tropical rapidity, the lumbering sea giants would emerge to crawl up on the beach, to lay their eggs or engage in weird dances in the moonlight. Soldiers with bayonets or swords would rush out of their hiding places, and working in pairs, overturn the tortoises, and gather their eggs. Soup was made from the flesh and the eggs were served to the sick.

The death rate increased. According to the prison records, there were three hundred cases of yellow fever and forty deaths. The surgeon general attributed the fact that most of the sick men were kept alive to the care of Mudd and Grenfel. In the first month the most deaths occurred. Burial parties were leaving almost every hour to row across to the tiny cemetery on Bird Key. As Doctor Mudd himself described it: "The burial parties arrive to take a drink of whiskey to infuse a little more life in them. They move quickly. In a half-hour after a man dies he is put in a pine coffin, nailed down, rowed to the adjacent island, the grave dug, covered up and the parties return."

Before the epidemic finally died out Mudd himself was stricken. He was cared for by Spangler, Arnold and Grenfel. Grenfel emerged from the pesthole, bearded and gaunt, stinking of vomit and death, his eyes sunken in his head, so completely exhausted he could barely lift a glass of whiskey given to him by the grateful commander of the garrison. There were to be no more chains for Doctor Mudd or for Grenfel. "I will immediately communicate with the Secretary of War and with the President to inform him of your heroic conduct," he told them.

Grenfel went back to his bunk next to Johnny Adare, who had been in charge of the burial parties. Grenfel surely told Adare that all escape plans must be forgotten. There was a chance his sentence might be commuted and he would be returned to England.

Surgeon Whitehurst, of the U. S. Surgeon General's Office, wrote from Key West directly to President Johnson of Grenfel's heroism. He wrote, "By his services to those dreadfully afflicted with yellow fever in the hospital, where night and day he was zealous, careful, I have no doubt [he] contributed by unwearied and continued service, to the restoration of the health of the troops."

Major Andrews, commandant of Fort Jefferson, also forwarded a copy of his congratulations to Grenfel to President Johnson. "I can only give him the highest recommendation for his services during the epidemic," he wrote.

Grenfel followed with a letter of his own to Johnson. It was dignified, not begging for mercy, but asking "only for a fair inquiry to be made as to facts, one in which I may be heard." Grenfel then attacked the government witnesses, citing Colonel Burnett's own admission that Shanks "as a witness was not worthy of credit."

Grenfel was sure he would be released. Varina Davis, formerly the "first lady" of the Confederacy, sent him two shirts and $20. There was also a note from Basil Duke and some other officers of the Ninth Kentucky. But as the days dragged by and there was no word from Washington, his hopes dwindled.

On December 26, after a melancholy Christmas, Grenfel wrote his daughter, answering her letter of May 16. He apologized for his failure to write sooner but explained that only that day had he received the few cents to pay the postage. He outlined his prison life: "as to the food . . . 'Halte là ma voisine' it is a dangerous topic. . . ."

Sir Frederick Bruce had recently died, Grenfel noted without any regret, and he hoped his successor would continue the battle to free him. It was a short note, with Grenfel telling his daughter how he was picturing her and his grandchildren in the gardens of their home near the Thames, "with its flowers and fruits, [and] your young barbarians at play. . . ."

In January, 1868, he wrote to a business acquaintance in London that Basil Duke and Carleton Morgan were fighting for his release "with all the influence they can command." William Pendleton, the Copperhead friend of Vallandigham and the Vice-Presidential nominee on McClellan's ticket, also had written Grenfel he was in Washington trying to get Johnson to free him. The President had again been approached, Pendleton wrote, and although Johnson had promised to review his case, he had said "there are several hard points in his case."

A new commandant had given Grenfel some privileges, perhaps in gratitude for his courageous service with Mudd in the pesthouse. Grenfel wrote his daughter that he was no longer unloading ships but now had started a large garden. He boasted of his "radishes, tomatoes, and peppers in bloom, and peas and beans at maturity." As he wrote, "They have turned my sword into a shovel and rake and I am at the head of my profession."

There were also changes brought about by the new commandant, Grenfel wrote. Now they had minstrels and dramas, with Doctor Mudd "playing the violin for drunken soldiers to dance to or to form part of a very miserable orchestration. . . ."

Then at last the letter came from Washington. When he read it, Grenfel's weary old heart faltered. It said simply: "Your application for clemency has been denied. Signed, Holt, Judge Advocate General, on order of the President."

The storm which struck Fort Jefferson the morning of March 7, 1868, was the most violent that any of the guards remembered during their thirty months of service. "It was a wild night and stormy beyond precedent," the New Hampshire private wrote.

In his casement cell on the second tier of the fort, Grenfel listened to the howling wind. It was midnight when he heard the guard changed. He leaned over and nudged Johnny Adare. They waited, in silence, listening to the measured steps of the guard coming down the corridor. They came nearer, then at last stopped at the cell door. In the dim lantern light they could see the pale blur of the face of Private Noreil, Company I, Fifth Artillery, the midnight to eight o'clock guard.

"Quickly," Noreil whispered, "we haven't much time."

The key ground in the lock of the cell door. Grenfel and Adare jumped to their feet.

"Have you got the rope?" Grenfel asked.

Noreil held up a length of rope. "It's long enough," he said.

The three men hurried to the end of the corridor, and pushed open the window. The wind, like a living thing, swept into the corridor. Grenfel tied the rope to a bar and threw it out the window. One by one, they slid down the rope to the beach.

The wind tore at them, forcing them to bend over to walk. They made their way, "apparently with great difficulty," as the official report of the escape said, to where the fishing boat of Company I, Fifth Artillery, was anchored.

They were approaching the boat when they saw two men coming toward them. One seemed to be dragging something along as he walked. As they came near, they saw it was "those two desperate characters," Joseph Holroyd and James Orr. Holroyd was walking alongside Orr, carrying Orr's 30-pound iron ball attached by a chain to his right leg. The five men walked to where the fishing boat was tied to a stake. The knot was untied and they pushed the awkward boat through the boiling surf.

It was a tremendous struggle. It seemed as if they would never pull it out beyond the high waves. Finally they made it. Orr, who had been put into the boat because of the iron ball attached to his leg, leaned over and helped his comrades get in. Oars were slipped into the locks, the blades swung into a rough rhythm. They were soon hidden by the curtain of rain, never to be seen again. Grenfel had at last found the peace for which he had searched so long.

This is the story of the escape of Grenfel and the four others as it was reconstructed by Brevet-Captain George Crabb, First Lieutenant, Fifth Artillery, officer of the day, in the early hours of the 8th. The Coast Survey steamer *Bibb* searched the area for seven hours but failed to find any survivors or the wreckage of the fishing boat.

Bribery had won over Private Noreil, but Captain Crabb reported there was evidence that someone on the outside had helped to engineer the break. Private Noreil had received several mysterious letters and had seemed rather prosperous.

We can only guess the "outside help" might have been Captain Hines. . . .

XXXI. A NEW ROLE: RECONSTRUCTION
AND RECONCILIATION

Now the story of the Grand Conspiracy ends. True to the traditional role of hero and heroine in their tale of love and high adventure, Tom and Nancy in real life lived happily ever after. Tom's first job after he returned to the States was as editor of the Memphis *Daily Appeal*. On June 1, his first child, a daughter, was born. Nancy, in Kentucky, wrote him:

> . . . Oh, how I wish you could see the little darling in bed with me. I wish she could send you some word or kiss. Of course she is a precious little piece of humanity, and by the time you see her she will be all white and pretty. Of course, pretty to us. You don't know how thankful I was when the doctor said she was wonderfully and perfectly formed and all right. Then I wished for you, my darling. But you must not let this desire trouble you. I know I must not think of it until I am well enough to come to you. . . . I have made up my mind I must do without you for a time, and have gone through all the worst. . . .

Nancy told Tom his father had come to see the baby, and described the old gentleman cooing over the infant, like any proud grandfather. Nancy ended with, "I think of you walking the floor all night with her . . . now isn't that a pleasant prospect?"

Nancy, whose letters show she possessed a fine sense of humor, may have had the contrasting picture in mind: the Confederate agent, master spy, revolutionist, conspirator, hard-riding cavalry officer in nightshirt and slippers, hushing his squalling newborn, as he shuffled up and down the room, hoping for the dawn to steal through the window, just as fathers in every age have done and will continue to do.

On June 12, Hines passed the bar examination with high honors. On the same day, Basil Duke wrote him a note from Cincinnati, where he was still in the produce and commission merchant business, congratulating him on the birth of his daughter, "for whom I wish only the brightest and happiest future, and although not given to salutatory performance, hope to dance at her wedding."

It is the first of many notes destroying the legend that Hines and Duke bitterly disliked each other, during and after the war. Duke, always in the dark about the plans between Hines and Morgan, had excellent reasons as senior officer to be irritated with the devil-may-care captain of Company E. But Duke, a man of excellent character, also recognized Hines' qualities as a splendid officer. No matter what personal feelings he may have felt, he kept them carefully hidden on the field. After the war Hines and Duke were the closest of friends. Duke, in the letters Hines kept among his papers, told how he never failed to stop off at the Hines' home on his travels through the South.

Hines returned to Kentucky after his admission to the bar, and formed his own law office in Bowling Green. The fame of his Civil War days stayed with him. To the ex-Confederate officers and soldiers he was always "Captain Hines, who rode with Morgan."

But Hines was not the back-slapping, professional veteran who liked to gather at the neighboring club or saloon to swap lies about the war. In civilian life he still remained the soft-spoken, aloof, almost cold man who had traveled through the Northwest. He carefully kept up his studies, reading the classics in French whenever he could. Nancy and his children were his whole life.

In 1882 Hines first thought about writing the full story of the Northwest Conspiracy for the *Southern Bivouac*, published by Basil Duke and R. W. Knott. He wrote to Castleman offering "all my private papers bearing on the matter, including original orders, etc. What say you?"

Castleman wrote back that he thought they should first confer with Jefferson Davis, then enjoying the peace of Beauvoir Plantation facing the blue waters of the Gulf of Mexico. Hines wrote to Davis asking for a private interview. He never received an answer. Hines respected the unspoken wish of his former commander-in-chief. But in 1885 Duke again asked Hines for his memoirs. Hines, busy with his law practice, gathered his papers and sent them on to Castleman, urging him to write the whole story.

In 1886 Castleman prepared the article. The *Bivouac* informed its readers that in subsequent issues the full story would be told. It was then that Davis moved with all his still powerful prestige to stop the series. He wrote a strong letter to Duke, who replied:

> As you are doubtless aware, I had no connection with the transactions which this narrative will record, and no personal knowledge of them. I have only the general knowledge which may be gathered from conversations with the principal actors and inspection of documents as are shown to me . . . much of this intelligence would be intelligible to me both as regards persons and events. . . .

Hines, Castleman and Duke must have conferred together and decided to respect once again the wishes of Davis, who wanted to protect the names of the Northern traitors. Twenty years was too short a time.

Two articles were finally published in 1887. As we now know, they were abridged. The part played by Morgan, Bowles, Dodd and the rest of the leaders of the Sons of Liberty were conspicuous by their absence. But the abridgment was not lost on the former Confederate officers and editors of Southern newspapers who had heard rumors of the roles Hines, Castleman and the others had played. In an editorial Emmett G. Logan, of the Louisville *Times*, and one of the South's great editors, took Hines and Castleman to task for failing to tell the whole story. As his editorial said in part:

> That a movement was planned, organized and partially executed which in scope was of gigantic and far-reaching dimensions, has been a matter of common knowledge ever since its miscarriage, but the men through whose sympathy and aid only could it have been consummated, succeeding in withdrawing themselves behind a veil of obscurity which the most curious have failed to penetrate . . . from a disinterested point of view no tenable reason exists why the names of the Northern associates should be withheld . . . therefore Messrs. Hines and Castleman should have told their whole tale. For instance the February paper [in the *Bivouac*] stated that a candidate for governor in 1864 made his canvass on money furnished by Jacob Thompson and his followers. What a colorless, insipid passage this is. . . .

The editorial went on at length urging Hines and Castleman to tell all, but they remained silent. Davis had asked them to keep faith with the men in the North, some now dead, with whom they had intrigued, and they were obeying his wishes. Hines never again attempted to publish the story of his adventures. On October 10, 1890, Castleman addressed the Confederate Veterans' Association of Kentucky on the subject of Hines and the Northwest Conspiracy. On the 12th a delegation of the association sent Castleman a letter urging him to publish a full account of the inside story of what happened in those stirring days of 1864-65. Heading the list of thirty members who signed the letter was Basil Duke.

Castleman conferred with Hines, who enthusiastically endorsed the idea. Once again he gave Castleman all his papers, which Nancy had kept carefully hidden. Although he had all the Hines Papers, Castleman again failed to tell the whole story. He was writing in the twilight of his life, remembering the brave days, and like the gentleman he was, he refused at that late date to name the men who had betrayed them, even though Hines had identified them. Details of the Chicago fiasco were omitted, along with many other stories.

The Papers were returned to Hines. This may have been the transfer in which some of the important documents were lost.

In 1875 Hines entered public life. He was elected Chief Justice of Kentucky's Court of Appeals, defeating the well known jurist of that state, Caswell Bennett. Hines served two terms.

Now there was a second child, a boy named William. Nancy, still loving and adoring, was content to stay in the background. In 1890-1 Hines represented Frankfort, the state capital, in the Constitutional Convention.

Hines was the distinguished Chief Justice of the Court of Appeals, but he was still the gamecock. The story is told today in the Blue Grass country of the lawyer who insulted him in a courtroom. Hines, white to the lips, faced the man who had made the remark. What it was we do not know.

Hines picked up his cane. He rapped it sharply on the floor. A slender sword slid out of its sheath. Hines flexed the blade.

"Now, sir," he thundered, "repeat that!"

Court attendants hustled the frightened lawyer out of the courtroom. When the room emptied, Hines slid back the sword into the cane, picking up his valise of papers, then walked out, tipping his hat to the ladies as he strode up the street.

Hines was Chief Justice the year Horace Greeley, with the joint support of the Liberal Republican and the Democratic Parties, ran against Grant for the Presidency. Greeley immediately became the center of a violent political controversy. His old Republican Party associates regarded him as a renegade; the Democrats gave him only half-hearted support, while the shadow of George N. Sanders, the mysterious figure of the Northwest Conspiracy, stalked him during the entire campaign.

Grant's supporters released copies of the Jacob Thompson report on Hines' activities which he had sent to Judah Benjamin in 1864. The documents were described as part of the "captured correspondence of the leaders of the Rebel Government."

Among the Hines Papers are three long newspaper accounts, many columns long, on the Thompson report. The headline reads, "The Terrible Thompson," and the story goes to great lengths to connect Greeley, Thompson and Clay in the abortive peace meeting at Niagara in the summer of 1864. George Sanders, the stories charged, was an intimate of Greeley "and enjoyed his confidence." The inference, of course, was that Greeley had dealt with traitors and had their support. Greeley gave a dignified reply outlining his meeting with the Confederate Commissioners at Niagara, adding, "I did nothing then that I am ashamed of now."

Sanders was pictured in the stories as a mysterious but little known figure in Washington who had the ear of those in high places. Debonair and poised as always, Sanders met the press and waved aside the charges. "The charge that I have any influence with Mr. Greeley is without foundation," he said. "The meeting with Mr. Clay, Mr. Thompson, myself and Mr. Greeley was a proper attempt to bring about a peaceful end to a horrible war."

And on this last pious note, Sanders slipped back into the shadows. During the campaign there were veiled references to his "powerful connections" in Washington, but Sanders kept a discreet silence. It was his last known participation in public affairs.

Now what of the other raiders of his "old squadron," as Hines liked to call his northern command?

Lieutenant Bennett Young, the leader of the St. Albans raid, became president of the Monon Route, a railroad running between Louisville and Chicago. He later became president of the Louisville Southern Railroad, and of the Kentucky and Indiana Bridge Company. He was a member of the Louisville delegation at the Constitutional Convention in 1890–91, where he met Tom Hines again. Like Hines, Young had studied law in Canada under Justice Bullitt, and in the late nineties he opened his own law office in Louisville. He became a celebrated orator and the author of several surprisingly good books on the war, all very rare. One, entitled *Confederate Wizards of the Saddle,* is a collection of fine cavalry stories. Curiously enough, he never wrote anything about the most thrilling chapter in his own life—the Vermont raid.

Colonel Martin settled in Evansville, Indiana, where he engaged in the tobacco warehouse business. In 1874 he moved to New York—the very city he had tried to burn—to become manager of tobacco inspections for the David Dowes Company. In 1887 he returned to Louisville, still in the tobacco business. In the winter of 1900 an old wound in his lung reopened and he almost died. He returned to New York for special treatment. That March there was a last and sad farewell with Lieutenant Headley at the Louisville station. They were both old men now and knew they would never meet again.

On April 18, 1900, Martin died in Brooklyn, and was buried in Green-Wood Cemetery, Brooklyn.

Lieutenant Headley, who was also in the tobacco business, moved frequently about Kentucky. In 1891 he entered public office and was elected Secretary of State of Kentucky, serving until January, 1896. He later left the state. The date of his death is not known.

Castleman, like Hines, had a particularly distinguished career. When the Spanish-American War broke out he interrupted the writing of his memoirs to enlist in the Army. He served in Puerto Rico as a colonel under General Nelson Miles, who highly praised his bravery. Shortly after his return to the states, he was commissioned a Brigadier-General by President McKinley. He returned to Kentucky to serve as the state's Adjutant-General. In 1900, when Governor Goebel was assassinated and Kentucky was in a state of insurrection, it was Castleman's cool-headedness and decision which prevented mobs from storming arsenals and state buildings. Castleman later served as chairman of the Louisville Board of Parks. It was due to his imagination and unceasing efforts that the city's Cherokee Park became a model of municipal splendor.

Nearly all of the former raiders rose to superior positions in business and statesmanship. Lieutenant Ashbrook became head of the Underwriters' Association of Kentucky and Tennessee; Cleary, the secretary of the Confederate Mission, became a leading Kentucky corporation lawyer; Clay, a sick man when released from prison, returned to his native Huntsville, Alabama, to die; Thompson, who had lost more than a hundred slaves and a great deal of property but was still a wealthy man, went home to Oxford, Mississippi. He remained one of Jefferson Davis' closest friends and visited him often.

Life flowed on for all of them. Felix Stidger, the Federal spy, in 1902 was writing the Pension Bureau, War Department, asking for a copy of his war record. He was then sixty-five years old, and owner of the Stidger Progressive American Twentieth Century Shortland School in Chicago. Stidger revealed that he had been a hunted man after the war. He was constantly threatened and once was almost assassinated on a Louisville street. Finally, "weary of being afraid of going out on the street after hours," he left the South "forever." There is no date of his death.

In January, 1898, life stopped for Tom Hines. Nancy died unexpectedly. His friends and old comrades rallied to his side but he could not be consoled.

Among his papers is a touching letter from Colonel, later General, William C. P. Breckinridge, who had commanded the Ninth Kentucky of Morgan's Cavalry:

> If I were with you, I would not say a word but only hold your hand in love and sorrow. What can I write? It has been so long since we first met, so long since she now dead in your house, met me in Canada. So much has happened, so much to sadden, to bend, to break our hearts, that really it doesn't matter much if the end came and we found what was on the other side of the river. My heart is with you tonight, as it always has been with you and her. You have faced death with equal pulse and calm face so often, what was death to you? But we cannot face the death of our beloved with calmness and courage. And yet, dear comrade, death is but for a moment, and then . . . and then, what? We are not afraid of that "What," for whatever is best in Heaven is hers, won by her life here on earth. . . .

There is a moving last line:

> Old friend, old comrade, here is my hand and my heart.

Hines carefully folded the letter and put it among his papers. He wrote on the envelope: "From Col. Wm. C. P. Breckinridge, C. S. A., commanding Ninth Kentucky" . . . "Oh, Nannie . . . Nannie. . . ."

His heart was breaking. Three weeks later, at eight o'clock on a quiet Sunday morning, he joined her.

State houses flew their flags at half-mast and the long obituaries recalled the escape from the Ohio Penitentiary, Morgan's great raids, and Hines' "service to the Confederates in Canada." But even in death he held on to his secrets; none of the stories about his life told of his attempts to bring about a revolution in the Northwest.

Perhaps it would be fitting to end the story of Tom Hines and his raiders on a note both of solemnity and high frivolity. It concerns the last years of Bennett H. Young, who led the St. Albans raid. In May, 1904, Vermont decided to include the re-enactment of the St. Albans raid, during a state centennial celebration. When they learned that Young was still living they invited him to lead the "raid" personally.

Young sent back a note of acceptance, but the Grand Army of the Republic adopted a resolution asking Vermont's governor to cancel Young's appearance on the ground that the pageant "had aspects of a commercial proposition." The controversy raged in the nation's newspapers until Young gallantly sent a note to the pageant committee saying he would be detained elsewhere and would be forced to cancel his appearance.

Young was elected head of the Confederate Veterans' Association. On a frosty day in 1914, with guns of a more deadly war than the one he had fought in ready to rumble across the sea, he dedicated the Confederate Monument in Arlington Cemetery. The reporters at the ceremony were impressed by the old man in Confederate gray who stood straight as an arrow shaft, his white beard blowing in the wind, speaking of battles and men now in the history books.

Young died in 1917. Hundreds followed his coffin and the traditional boots stuck backward in the stirrups, while the muffled drum beats rolled out in the dull winter morning.

The last of the old squadron had crossed the river to rest under the heavenly trees.

A FINANCIAL ACCOUNTING
OF THE NORTHWEST CONSPIRACY

Shortly after the war was over and he was in exile, Hines made an accounting, probably for Secretary of State Judah Benjamin, then in London, of the money he had spent. The total came to seventy-four thousand dollars in gold. However, there are many receipts made out to him, Castleman, or unknown members of his band, for sums of from twenty to fifteen hundred dollars, "for returning funds to the government." What those funds were or what they totaled is not known. (See Hines' financial accounting, and miscellaneous vouchers, receipts, etc., **H. P.**)

By their own letters and memoirs Hines, Castleman and others in the Conspiracy spent untold thousands in buying arms for the Copperheads. Castleman says Hines, on one trip north to Canada, delivered three hundred thousand dollars aboard a ship in New York to be smuggled to the Confederate ministers Mason and Slidell, who were in communication with Thompson and the Confederate Commissioners in Canada. There is no documentary evidence of this. (See *Active Service,* also *Southern Bivouac.*)

Fifty thousand dollars was spent by Hines and Castleman to buy the gubernatorial candidate of Illinois, James Robinson. Another twenty-five thousand was given to the editor of the New York *Daily News* and his editorial pages for their "peace move." (See **H. P.**, also *Active Service;* also **Phineas Wright Papers, W. R., N. A.**)

Lieutenant George Eastin, one of Morgan's officers who joined Hines in the fall of 1864, robbed a train in the spring of '64 of a Federal payroll said to be seventy-five thousand dollars which he delivered to the Confederate Mission. (See undated newspaper clipping, **H. P.**; also *Active Service.*)

In a raid in June of that year by Morgan on Mt. Sterling, Kentucky, the town's bank was robbed of eighty thousand dollars in gold, silver and Federal currency. Twenty-four hours later, Captain Castleman left Morgan to join Hines in Toronto. There is no direct evidence that Castleman took the money with him. However, a colonel later testified that he saw Castleman's brother Humphrey with some of the money.

Morgan would never permit an inquiry by his officers into the Mt. Sterling robbery and the disposal of the money. The reason is obvious when one learns that the Kentucky raid was made with the secret approval of the government in Richmond, following reports made to Seddon by Hines and Commissioner Thompson that the Copperheads were ready to move immediately but wanted, as evidence of good faith, a raid by General Morgan to take place simultaneously with their uprising. (See Giltner-Alston and Smith testimony, **O. R.**, Series I, Vol. 39, also Swiggett's *The Rebel Raider; also* **Bowles Papers, W. R., N. A.**)

There is evidence that a small band of Copperheads on a rainy spring night in 1864 robbed a Federal payroll train. Several horses were used to carry off the gold and currency. The loot was two million dollars!

Official notice of the robbery can be found in a letter written in 1865 by Colonel Burnett, Judge Advocate in Ohio, to Judge Advocate General Holt in Washington. The letter was a résumé of the role played by James Barrett, the Missouri Copperhead leader, in the uprising in Chicago and his connection with the "notorious Hines."

> Barrett had a meeting of the leaders of the Order [Sons of Liberty] in Chicago on July 29, when the uprising was agreed upon. At this meeting Barrett said that he had at his disposal, furnished by the Confederate government to be used for the purchase of arms and furthering an insurrection in the North, two million dollars which had been captured from the U. S. paymaster on Red River. That one hundred thousand dollars had been sent to H. H. Dodd to be used in Indiana and the same sum to each of the grand commanders of the state.

Burnett, one of the ablest Judge Advocates in the North, possessed a precise legal mind. He never repeated exaggerations or wild reports. His information undoubtedly came from Felix Stidger, the Union spy, whose integrity and reliability cannot be doubted.

Stidger, who survived fantastic adventures to break the back of the Copperhead movement, presents this story as fact. He said the gold was used to arm the "Castles" of the Knights of the Golden Circle in Illinois, Ohio and Indiana.

In 1865 Ayer, a patent medicine peddler who also played a minor role as a spy in Chicago during the uprising there, quoted Doctor Bowles, the military leader of the Indiana Copperheads, as saying that the robbery had taken place on the Red River. The payroll, he said, "was used to arm the Sons of Liberty in Ohio and Indiana." (See Burnett's letter to Holt, **Barrett Papers, W. R., N. A.**, also Stidger's *Treason History of the Sons of Liberty*, also Winslow Ayer's *The Great Northwest Conspiracy*.)

In the fall of 1864, some of Hines' raiders, without official orders, cleaned the three banks of St. Albans, Vermont, of one hundred and seventy-five thousand dollars in gold. A large part of this money went for bribes and for the defense of the men who were captured after the Lake Erie raid, the fire raid on New York City, the St. Albans raid, the Chicago uprising and the attempted derailing of the Buffalo Express. (See John Branch's *The St. Albans Raid;* also the St. Albans *Messenger,* also, *The Investigation into the Acts at St. Albans of Lieutenant Bennett H. Young and Command.*)

Commissioner Thompson stated in his report to Richmond in 1864, that he had spent fifty thousand dollars buying up gold in New York to create a financial panic. (See Thompson's report to Benjamin, **O. R.**, Series I, Vol. 43.)

Approximate Accounting
of Income and Expenditures

Let us attempt to add the incomes used to finance the conspiracy which we know to be factual:

Money taken in the St. Albans bank raid and probably turned over to Commissioner Thompson	$ 175,000
The military payroll taken by Lt. Eastin and brought to Canada	75,000
The Mt. Sterling bank robbery	80,000
The approximate total of funds brought to Canada from Richmond by Thompson	200,000
The Federal payroll robbed on the banks of the Red River, Arkansas, which the Federal spy, Stidger, and Judge Advocate Burnett, said was used to arm the Copperheads in the Northwest	2,000,000
Total	$2,530,000

Now, let us try to deduct the outgo:

The Hines itemized accounts of monies spent, 1864–65 (Computed from the Hines Papers)	$ 74,000
Miscellaneous vouchers for various amounts paid out to the members of the Hines command	3,000
Money turned over to Phineas Wright, editor of the New York *Daily News*, for editorial support of the Confederate peace movement	25,000

Toronto, Canada West, Feb. 7th 1865

Account of Monies received from the Confederate Government for the release of Prisoners of War in the North West
& for the purpose of aiding in freeing the North West
in effecting a Revolution—

Received of the Government at Richmond, March 19th 1864,
five thousand dollars in Confederate five dollar notes= $5000.
Received of Government at Richmond, March 20th 1864, one
thousand dollars in gold= $1000.
Received of Col Jacob Thompson—Toronto, about 1st June
1864, two thousand four hundred & ninety dollars in gold=$2.490.
Received of Col J. Thompson—Toronto. about the 24th Aug '64,
two thousand five hundred in Green Back= $2500.
Received of Col J. Thompson—Chicago Ill (through James A. Barrett),
about the last of Aug. 1864, seven thousand four hundred
dollars in Green Back= $7400
Received of Col J. Thompson (through James A. Barrett) Chicago
Ill about the last of Aug. 1864, five hundred dollars
in gold, making one thousand & fifty dollars in G.B. $1050
Received of Col J. Thompson (through J. Maughan) Chicago Ill.
about the 28th Aug 1864, ten thousand dollars in
Green Backs= $10000
Received of C. C. Cley at St. Catharines C.W., about the
20th October 1864, four thousand one hundred dollars
in gold—sold at 2-10 giving eight thousand six hundred
& ten dollars in U.S. Currency= $8610
Received of C. C. Clay (through Charly Lesley) at Chicago Ill,
about the 30th October '64, thirty thousand dollars in
United States Currency= $30.000

Paid to Mrs Lendry (of Chicago) by request of Mrs Morris, for satisfaction
of expenses & trouble in caring for my men—four hundred
dollars U.S.C. $400

June 21st 1865. Amherstburg C.W. 11

On the 11th January 1865 I had remaining in my hands government funds to the amount of three thousand nine hundred & ninety nine dollars United States currency— which I immediately converted into gold at two twenty-five ($2.25) giving one thousand seven hundred & seventy six dollars gold $1776—

Also eight hundred & ninety dollars in gold—

Making the sum total unaccounted for = ($&ct)

April 4th 1865. Out of this amount I gave to Miss Mary Walsh for the benefit of her father, then on trial for conspiracy at Cincinnati, twelve hundred dollars in gold=

Same date I employed three hundred in gold for the equipment of men there organizing in Ky. Making in all used upon that day fifteen hundred dollars—; Leaving unaccounted for one thousand one hundred & sixty-six dollars ($1166) gold.;

My expenses for travel &c from the 1st of April '64 to the first of April '65 have been something over two thousand dollars in gold—Leaving the Government in debt to me about eight hundred & thirty four dollars in gold =($834).

After depositing three thousand dollars in Confederate notes to the credit of the government at Grenada Miss. I had remaining two thousand dollars in Confederate notes; fifteen hundred of this was expended for a horse & equipment; two hundred for my expenses of myself from Richmond to Ky. The remaining three hundred I left at my home as I passed in April '64. It is of course of no value at present=

T. Henry Hines
Formerly Capt. P.A.C.S.

Hines' accounting of money spent in the attempt to bring about an insurrection in the Northwest—virtually an "expense account for revolution."

Money spent by Thompson to buy up gold in New York City	50,000
Money turned over to the Illinois Central Democratic Committee for support of the gubernatorial candidate, James Robinson	50,000
Money turned over to a "Reverend Johnson" of Mississippi, not further identified, who told Thompson he was "organizing" the Sons of Liberty in Indiana............	3,000
Approximate sums turned over to couriers, supposedly from Richmond, who later turned out to be "scoundrels" as Hines called them, who were lining their own pockets..	10,000
Total	$ 215,000

After deducting the outgo, there remains unaccounted for, $2,315,-000. What happened to this fortune? Hines was almost penniless when the war was over. He had used most of his family's funds for the Confederacy in the Northwest and had to depend on the generosity of friends to help him start his law practice in 1866. Castleman had scarcely any funds left after he was released from prison and had to call on his family. Thompson, who had been a wealthy man before the war, had his slaves and property confiscated and lived only modestly in later years. As their meticulous accountings show, they were all scrupulously honest.

Thompson's naïveté and his poor judgment of men may be part of the answer, along with the fact that most of the money, like the Federal payroll taken on the banks of the Red River, never reached Toronto but was sidetracked to the Copperhead leaders in the Northwest "for arms," although the Confederate Commission was spending large sums in New York City buying rifles and smuggling them across the Canadian border into Indiana, Ohio and Illinois.

In the winter of 1864, when he returned to Toronto, Hines was horrified to learn how easy it was to get gold out of Thompson. Every "scoundrel" who dreamed up a wild tale of how he was preparing to spread havoc among the Federals by burning army transports or military installations, would come to Thompson and demand anywhere from $10,000 to $50,000, "to equip my organization," as one said. Thompson usually turned over the money. Thompson himself tells how one man who had come from Richmond supposedly on the orders of Secretary Benjamin demanded $10,000 for arms but couldn't produce his official orders. He promised to return to Richmond to get another copy—if Thompson gave him $3,000. Thompson did. The supposed raider, of course, never again appeared.

SOURCES

NOTE: I have listed here the sources on which I have based this history. Nothing in this book is fiction, not even the conversations, which may seem to some to be "fictionized." All are based on documents: trial transcripts, newspaper and other reports, magazine articles, interviews, letters, memoirs and other writings of the principals, all of which—excepting only minor letters and other such items—I have listed.

J. D. H.

Chapter I

THE MOST DANGEROUS MAN IN THE CONFEDERACY

The description of Buckner's Guides, who joined General Albert Sidney Johnston's command in April, 1861, is taken from the long, unpublished story of Hines' life by Doctor James Blanton, Cumberland County, Virginia, in 1864, hereafter known as the **Blanton Mss.** Much of the material was contributed by Hines, General John Hunt Morgan and a Captain Cunningham. Blanton was probably trying to sell the story to the *Atlantic Monthly*.

See also letter from Hines to his father, August 23, 1864, in the **Hines Papers,** Margaret I. King Library, University of Kentucky, Lexington, hereafter to be known as **H. P.** See also "History of the Hines Family," a series by Mrs. Frank P. Moore, Kentucky Library staff, published in the Lexington, Kentucky, *Daily News*. This series is among Hines' personal papers owned by Mrs. John J. Winn, Mt. Sterling, Kentucky.

Hines traced his family antecedents in a letter to a Mrs. Watts Parker of Denver, Colorado, August 27, 1895, **H. P.,** in which he wrote that his father's great-grandfather, Thomas Hines, was a Scotch physician and army surgeon who came to America in 1745 with the British Army. He settled near Hobb's Hole, Virginia, and there married a Miss Jones. His sons, Henry and James, served in Washington's army. James was killed. Henry Hines, his father's grandfather, married and had six sons and three daughters. All moved to Kentucky about 1800. Hines' father, Warren Walker Hines, was still living in 1895. His mother died in 1893. Hines' grandmother on the paternal side was a daughter of a Captain William Walker, Cumberland County, of French descent, who served under Washington. His maternal grandmother was a Dinwiddie of Virginia. See also the *Biographical Encyclopedia of Kentucky,* J. M. Armstrong and Co., Cincinnati, 1878, and *Lawyers and Lawmakers of Kentucky,* H. G. Levin, editor, Lewis Publishing Co., Cincinnati, 1897.

Chapter II
MORGAN'S RAIDERS

For Colonel George St. Leger Grenfel's background see appeal of Robert Hervey, attorney for Grenfel, hired by Hines; personal papers of Grenfel, **War Records, National Archives,** hereafter to be known as **W. R., N. A.** See Grenfel's own letters to his daughter, 1864, owned by J. Packe, Burnham, Bucks, England. See also "The Northwest Conspiracy," *Southern Bivouac,* 1887. Grenfel's name is usually spelled with two l's. But he signed his name with one l. His name is also spelled this way in the military indictments and warrants of 1864–65.

For background of Lieutenant Bennett H. Young, see memoirs of Bennett H. Young, The Filson Club.

An account of Hines' first raid into Kentucky when he was bushwhacked by Federal guerrillas can be found in the **Blanton Mss.** See also *History of Morgan's Cavalry* by Basil Duke, Cincinnati, 1866, and **Official Records of the Union and Confederate Armies,** Series I, Vol. 23, hereafter to be known as **O. R.;** Moore's "History of the Hines Family."

The romance of Tom and Nancy is reconstructed from their loveletters which are among Hines' personal papers owned by Mrs. John J. Winn. The letters are fragile, but fortunately Nancy wrote a clear and legible hand.

For Hines' raid into Kentucky in February, 1863, see the **Blanton Mss.,** which quotes some of his troopers, and **O. R.,** Series I, Vol. 23; also Hines' letter to his father, undated, 1863, **H. P.,** and Duke's *Morgan's Cavalry.*

Chapter III
FIRES OF THE COPPERHEADS

For Captain Longuemare's own account of his interview with Jefferson Davis, see the **Maule Papers,** Western Reserve Historical Society; for Carrington's report to Lincoln on early activities of the Knights of the Golden Circle, see **O. R.,** Series II, Vol. 5. An excellent source on early Copperhead movements is provided by the **Yates Papers,** Chicago Historical Society, also **Samuel Henry Eells Mss.,** Library of Congress. See also Chicago *Times,* December 27, 1862, and March 6, 1863; the Chicago *Tribune,* February 18, 1863; the Davenport (Iowa) *Daily Gazette* of February 3, 6, 7, 1863; the Detroit *Free Press,* January 1, 13, 1863. See also *The Hidden Civil War* by Wood Gray, The Viking Press, 1942, New York.

See Felix Stidger's reports to Colonel Carrington, Bureau of Military Justice, **W. R., N. A.,** and his *Treason History of the Order of the Sons of Liberty, Succeeded by Knights of the Golden Circle, Afterward, Order of American Knights,* Chicago, 1903; reports of Edward Hoffman, agent for Colonel Sanderson, provost marshal, St. Louis, Missouri, **O. R.,** Series II, Vol. 7.

For a history of the Knights of the Golden Circle, see Bibliography.

For background and activities of "Doctor" George Bickley, see the **Bickley Papers,** Adjutant General's Office records, **W. R., N. A.;** copy of the *Rites and Oath of the Knights of the Golden Circle,* government exhibits, Indiana Conspiracy treason trials, **W. R., N. A.,** also **O. R.,** Series III, Vol. 2.

For report of the Federal grand jury investigations into the treasonable activities of the Knights of the Golden Circle, see Cincinnati *Gazette,* February 20, 1863. See **Phineas Wright Papers,** Indiana conspiracy trials, **W. R., N. A.**

For Vallandigham's trial, conviction, exile, see **O. R.,** Series II, Vol. 6 and **O. R.,** Series II, Vol. 5.

Chapter IV

ON THE OHIO

See Hines' letter to his father, April 2, 1863, "leaving for a dangerous mission," **H. P.;** Duke's *Morgan's Cavalry:* Howard Swiggett's *The Rebel Raider,* Bobbs-Merrill Company, New York, 1934.

For Duke-Davis correspondence, see chapter sources for "A New Role: Reconstruction and Reconciliation."

For Colonel Carrington's report to the assistant chief of staff, Department of Ohio, definitely putting Hines in Indiana with Bowles, paving the way for Morgan's raid, see **Bowles Papers, W. R., N. A.;** see also "Raid of Captain Hines into Ohio and Indiana," **Blanton Mss., H. P.**

For Burnside's offer of reward for Hines' capture, see **O. R.,** Series I, Vol. 23.

An excellent account of Hines' Indiana raid can be found in the Louisville *Journal,* June 15, 1863, which charged him with breaking open the Adams Express Company safe at Elizabethtown, Kentucky, and stealing an undetermined amount of Federal greenbacks; also see the New Albany *Daily Ledger,* June 14, 19, 22, July 9, 1863; also the Indianapolis *Daily Journal,* June 22, 1863; also the Madison *Courier,* June 24, 1863; also the Indianapolis *Sentinel,* July 13, 1863; also the Indianapolis *Daily Journal,* June 23, 1863. These newspapers carefully followed Hines on his journey north, publishing news of his train robberies, his inquiries for Doctor Bowles, his raids on Federal cavalry horse depots, and his battles with the Union cavalry, only hours after the incidents had taken place. These newspapers are also excellent source material on Morgan's raid.

For Duke's meeting with Hines on Brandenburg wharf and Morgan's raid into Indiana, see Duke's *Morgan's Cavalry,* also memoirs of Captain Hockersmith, **H. P.**

Chapter V

PRISON

For telegrams of Generals Burnside and Judah singling out Hines among the captured Morgan captains, see **O. R.**, Series I, Vol. 39.

For account of their imprisonment at Johnson's Island, see Hockersmith memoirs, **H. P.**, also Castleman Letters to Hines, **H. P.**, also letters of James Hines, Tom's brother, Kentucky Collection, Western Kentucky State College, Bowling Green.

Chapter VI

THE ESCAPE

The story of the escape is based on the **Blanton Mss., H. P.,** Hockersmith's memoirs, and Hines' version, **H. P.** Also see Secretary of War Seddon's communication to General Leonidas Polk, Seddon's Letter Book, **W. R., N. A.,** Dessellem's report to Governor Tod of Ohio, **W. R., N. A.,** reprinted in **O. R.**, Series II, Vol. 6. See also report of investigation of General Wright to Tod, **O. R.**, Series II, Vol. 6. See also Hines' version, *Southern Bivouac*, 1887, and the abridged version in G. W. Cable's *Famous Adventures and Prison Escapes of the Civil War*, London, 1894; also Swiggett's *The Rebel Raider*. The Cincinnati *Gazette* gave extensive coverage to the escape in issues during the weeks of November 25, 1863, and December 1, 1863. See also Castleman's *Active Service, Courier-Journal* Job Printing, Louisville, Kentucky, 1917.

Chapter VII

THE MISSION IN CANADA

For Hines' own version of the origin of the Conspiracy, written on the first page of an article in the July, 1865, *Atlantic Monthly* about the Chicago Conspiracy, see **H. P.** Hines carefully annotated the article, correcting errors and unmasking the traitors by name, though they were carefully disguised by the author. He even gave the name of the anonymous author—Edmund Kirk—and the price he received for the article—$100.

For Hines' first interview with Davis, Benjamin and Seddon, see Hines' notebook, **H. P.**

For comments on the Northwest Conspiracy, see Hines' notebook, **H. P.** For Hines' engagement party and his summons to Richmond, see interview with William Hines by Howard Swiggett on April 7, 1933, in New York City, also questionnaire interview by the author with Mrs. John J. Winn, January, 1954.

For Seddon's order to Hines, see Seddon's Letter Book, Series IX, Vol. 17, **W. R., N. A.** See also Castleman's *Active Service*.

For order to find Hines a suitable "cipher key," see order to Signal Officer, March 16, 1864, **H. P.**

For amendment of Hines' authority, see *Southern Bivouac,* 1887. See Seddon's order to Colonel T. L. Bayne, Ordnance Officer, Richmond, March 18, 1864, **H. P.**; Hines' letter to his father, Columbia, S. C., **H. P.**

For Hines' recruiting de l'Isle brothers on his own authority, see captured correspondence of Captain Hines, **W. R., N. A.**

For Hines' meeting with President Lincoln and wager, see Swiggett's interview with William Hines, 1933.

For memorandum marked "for the President alone," see J. B. Jones' *Rebel War Clerk's Diary,* Philadelphia, 1866. See also Hines' letter to his father, April, 1864, **H. P.**, and letters of Colonel Grenfel to his daughter, owned by Mr. A. H. Packe, Bucks, England. Copies are in The Filson Club, Louisville, Kentucky. For Davis's letter to Senator Hunter of Virginia, see Hines' captured correspondence, **W. R., N. A.**

For Davis's letter to Thompson, see *Active Service.* For Cleary's description of the Commission running the blockade, see *Southern Bivouac,* 1887.

Chapter VIII

THE FOX AND THE COPPERHEADS

Colonel Benjamin Jeffrey Sweet, commandant of Camp Douglas, first described Hines as "the fox" in his *Atlantic Monthly* article, 1866, **H. P.** See Hines' letter to Castleman, May 16, 1864, **H. P.**

For Hines' evaluation of the three Confederate Commissioners, see *Southern Bivouac,* 1885.

For order of Jefferson Davis giving Thompson absolute authority over Conspiracy, see Thompson Papers, **W. R., N. A.**

For Sanders' background, see undated newspaper clipping, **H. P.** See also **George N. Sanders Mss.,** Library of Congress. These contain twenty-seven letters written to Sanders by prominent Peace Democrats and Confederate leaders.

For Porterfield's financial manipulations in New York City, see Thompson's letter to Benjamin, December 3, 1864, **O. R.,** Series I, Vol. 43.

For Hines' comments on Vallandigham and the Copperheads, see Hines' notebook, **H. P.** See Hines' report to Seddon, giving details of the plans for the release of prisoners in the Northwest, June, 1864, **H. P.** See Thompson's letter re Davis, quoted in *Active Service.*

For buying of arms, see Hines' accounting of funds spent, also receipts, **H. P.** See also Carrington's report to the Assistant Chief of Staff, Department of the Ohio, **W. R., N. A.**; also **Bowles, Wright** and **Barrett Papers, W. R., N. A.** For the letter from Duke to Hines identifying "faithful Schultz," the courier, as Lieutenant G. E. Severn, see **H. P.**

Chapter IX

COUNTERSPY

See Stidger's reports to Colonel Carrington, Bureau of Military Justice, W. R., N. A., also his memoirs and government exhibits, Indiana Conspiracy trial, W. R., N. A.

For Thompson's report to Judah Benjamin, see O. R., Series I, Vol. 43.

For Morgan's raid, see Duke's *Morgan's Cavalry*.

For Giltner-Alston and Smith testimony in Mt. Sterling bank robbery, see O. R., Series I, Vol. 39.

Chapter X

COMMISSIONER HOLCOMB AND THE WILD ROSE

See **Greenhow Papers,** captured Confederate correspondence, Records of the War Department and of the State Department, **N. A.** See accounts from "our Richmond correspondent," London *Evening Mail*. See letter from the Earl of Buckinghamshire to the author, November, 1951, also letters of Mrs. Greenhow, owned by Mr. Foreman M. Lebold of Chicago and Thomas L. Taylor's *Blockade Running*, Charles Scribner's Sons, New York, 1896.

For references to the peace meeting at the Clifton House, see the **Greeley Papers,** Manuscript Division, New York Public Library, also Greeley's *The American Conflict*, O. D. Case and Company, two volumes, 1867.

Chapter XI

THE RAID ON MAINE

Sources for the Northeast facet of the Northwest Conspiracy not mentioned by Hines can be found in the **Baker-Turner Papers,** which were ordered opened to the public September 29, 1953, Box 3317, **W. R., N. A.,** which give an account of the raid on the bank in Calais, Maine. The papers contain the confession of Francis Jones of St. Louis, Missouri, Jones' letters to his mother; Turner's report to Holt and Stanton; Holt's observations to Stanton on the proposed raid on Maine; Collins' letters to his mother and sister; letters from the sheriff to Holt and Stanton and Seward; Turner's final report to Holt; list of Rebel agents in the United States, Canada and Bermuda and his "minute" investigations; also report of U. S. Consul Howard, St. John's, New Brunswick, to Seward; also letters from Major Young, 1863–66, pertaining to the Copperhead activities of the St. Croix River area, owned by Mr. Henry A. Tompkins, of Milltown, New Brunswick.

It is curious to note that news of the raid and the subsequent investigation never appeared in the Maine newspapers of the time. When Turner arrived in Portland on his investigation, he may have pledged the provost marshal to secrecy. The Maine Historical Society reports nothing can be found on the Calais raid.

Chapter XII

PASSWORD FOR REVOLUTION

For Hines' conference with Bowles, see the **Bowles Papers, W. R., N. A.** See Hines' comments on the Chicago fiasco, Hines' notebook, **H. P.** See Lieutenant Bennett H. Young's memoirs, The Filson Club; Grenfel's letters to his daughter, The Filson Club; the Chicago *Tribune*, November 17, 1864, and February 19, 1864. See Stidger's reports and memoirs. See letter to Hines from J. J. Bettersworth, **H. P.; Marmaduke Papers, W. R., N. A.;** interview with William Hines, 1933; Castleman's *Active Service; Southern Bivouac*, 1887; Sweet's memoirs; Langhorn's confession and memoirs, "a new version," Chicago *Tribune*, July 31, 1898. "Republican Opinions about Lincoln, 1864" Democratic National Committee document No. 18, **O. R.;** Series II, Vol. 7; the Columbus (Ohio) *Crisis*, August 18, 1864, quoted in the Chicago *Times*; **O. R.**, Series III, Vol. 4; and **O. R.**, Series I, Vol. 45; **Richard Yates Mss.**, Chicago Historical Society.

For an accounting of the money Hines spent, see his budget for revolution, **H. P.;** see William Bass, "Biographical Sketch of the Late General J. B. Sweet," *History of Camp Douglas*, Chicago, 1878; also *Atlantic Monthly*, July, 1865.

Chapter XIII

BALLOTS, IF NOT BULLETS

See Hines' memorandum on James C. Robinson, **H. P.** See also *Active Service*. See "McClellan's Changing Views on the Peace Platform of 1864," *American Historical Review*, Vol. VIII, April, 1933; also the Richmond (Virginia) *Examiner*, August 31, 1864.

Chapter XIV

TARGET: TRANSPORTS

Captured correspondence of Captain Castleman, **W. R., N. A.** Appeals of Hervey, attorney hired by Hines through Mary Walsh for Grenfel; **Grenfel Papers, W. R., N. A.**

For Castleman's expense account, see **Castleman Papers, W. R., N. A.** See recollections of William Hines, 1933. See also *Active Service* and letters from Hines to Castleman, **H. P.**

Chapter XV

A LETTER FROM LINCOLN

One of the thirteen saws Hines smuggled into Castleman in prison, made from the mainspring of a Swiss watch, can be found among the **Hines Papers** in the Margaret I. King Library, University of Kentucky, Lexington. It is believed Castleman gave it to Hines as a memento after he was released from prison. He had kept the saws concealed in the Bible while in prison. The Bible was lost and cannot be found. A picture of it was reproduced in *Active Service*. There are guarded references to the attempted prison break in the letters from Castleman to Hines, 1864, **H. P.**; see also Castleman's *Active Service*. The Lincoln letter was first reproduced in Castleman's memoirs, *Active Service*, published in 1917.

Chapter XVI

THE INDIANA CONSPIRATORS

For the arrests, trial and convictions, see **Bowles Papers; Wright Papers; Dodd Papers;** Stidger's reports, government exhibits, Indiana Conspiracy trials; **Bullitt Papers, W. R., N. A.**

For testimony in the trial, see the original Pitman Transcript, **W. R., N. A.**

Chapter XVII

THE BATTLE OF LAKE ERIE

See Hines' letter to Doctor Stuart Robinson, undated, 1864, **H. P.** See **Bennett G. Burley Papers,** captured correspondence of Burley, Maxwell and Beall, **W. R., N. A.**

For Captain Cole's champagne dinner plot, see Chicago *Tribune*, July 31, 1898.

For trial and testimony of John Yates Beall on charges of unlawful acts of war, see Beall trial records, **W. R., N. A.**; also *The Trial and Conviction of John Yates Beall*, author unknown, New York, 1866; also *John Yates Beall, Forgotten Hero*, author unknown, Toronto, 1865; also U. S. Navy Department of History, Washington, D. C.

Chapter XVIII

THE BANK RAIDS IN VERMONT

An on-the-spot account of the bank raids can be found in the St. Albans *Messenger* for October 11, 12 and 13, 1864. See Lieutenant Bennett H. Young's letter to the editor of the *Messenger*, also *The St. Albans Raid*, John Branch, St. Albans, 1935. See also the extradition proceedings against "Lieutenant Bennett H. Young and Command," Toronto, 1864; Thompson's report to Secretary Benjamin, December 3, 1864, **O. R.**, Series I, Vol. 43; *Les Raiders de Saint Albans Episode de la Guerre Americaine*, David Tetu, Amerikai Veszonyak, Quebec, 1891; Headley's *Confederate Operations in Canada and New York*, Neale, New York, 1906; undated clippings, **H. P.**; Hines' comments on Sanders, **H. P.**

Chapter XIX

BETRAYAL IN CHICAGO

For Hines' comments on the Chicago Conspiracy, 1864, see **H. P.** See **Ben M. Anderson Papers, W. R., N. A.;** Grenfel's letters to his daughter, July and August, 1864; Grenfel's letter to Hunter (Hines' alias), July, 1864, The Filson Club; report of Thompson to Secretary Seddon, December 3, 1864, **O. R.,** Series I, Vol. 45.

For Colonel Sweet's appeal for more troops, see **O. R.,** Series II, Vol. 1. For trial of the Chicago conspirators, with Hines named as leader of the plot to sack the city, see Chicago conspiracy trial transcript, also the verdict of the military tribunal, **W. R., N. A;** also Headley's *Confederate Operations in Canada and New York.* See also letter of Bettersworth to Hines, **H. P.;** also Langhorn's confession and a new version, Chicago Sunday *Tribune,* April 21, 1895. See also Attorney Hervey's appeals for Grenfel, which contain his views on the government's witnesses.

For Shanks' own story, see Chicago *Tribune* of April 21, 1895; January 15, 1875; February 20, 1887; September 23, 1876; September 22, 1890; February 15, 1891.

For Hines' identification of Bettersworth as one of the Chicago traitors, see his comments to Nancy, on the back of Bettersworth's letter, **H. P.** See also **O. R.,** Series III, Vol. 4; also Chicago *Tribune* of November 17, 1865, and February 19, 1882 and January 27, 1865, and *New York Times* and New York *Tribune* of November 26, 27, 28 and 29, 1864.

For money spent by Hines for arms and horses in Chicago, see Hines' accounting, **H. P.** See also Scharf and Strong memoirs, Chicago Historical Society.

Chapter XX

THE FOX AND THE HOUNDS

For Hines' comments on his escape, see margin of the July, 1865, *Atlantic Monthly* article, **H. P.;** interview with William Hines; *Active Service;* interview with Mrs. Winn.

Chapter XXI

A RAINY WEDDING NIGHT

The story of the wedding and the way in which Nancy was spirited out of the convent is taken from Nancy's own account in a letter to her father, November 27, 1864, Hines' personal papers owned by Mrs. Winn.

For Tom and Nancy's marriage certificate, see **H. P.**

Chapter XXII

THE BURNING OF NEW YORK

See *New York Times,* New York *Tribune,* November 25, 26, 27, 28, 1864; Headley's *Confederate Operations in Canada and New York;* **Headley Papers, W. R., N. A.**

For Turner's report to Holt, on rebel agents in New York City, see **Baker-Turner Papers,** Calais bank raid, **W. R., N. A.**

For Hines' hiring attorney for McDonald, see Hines' accounting, **H. P.**

For Eastin's letter to Hines, see **H. P.**; also **O. R.,** Series I, Vol. 45.

Chapter XXIII

THE MAINE COAST EXPEDITION

For report of Turner to Holt; report of Holt to Secretary Stanton; confession of Francis Jones; warrant for arrest of Rebel agents; the Calais bank robbery attempt; the Rebel attempt to burn coastal cities, see **Baker-Turner Papers, W. R., N. A.**

Chapter XXIV

SHOOT THEM DOWN

See Thompson's report to Secretary Benjamin, December, 1864, **O. R.,** Series I, Vol. 43. See *The Trial and Conviction of John Yates Beall,* New York, 1865; *New York Times,* December 14, 1864; **Thompson Papers, W. R., N. A.**

Chapter XXV

THE KIDNAPPING OF THE VICE PRESIDENT-ELECT

This chapter is based solely on Headley's account in his *Confederate Operations in Canada and New York.* Headley seems to have confused the dates. He placed the attempt as February, 1864, a month before Hines left for Canada for the first time. Headley did not join Hines in Canada until late September of that same year. The events he cited in which he took part show he meant the year to be early in 1865, in which he and Eastin tried to kidnap Vice President-Elect Johnson. Headley seems to have confused dates on other occasions. He places the death of his close friend Colonel Martin as 1901. I checked the funeral and cemetery records in Brooklyn, which show that Martin died a year earlier.

Chapter XXVI

A STRANGER IN A STRANGE LAND

For Grenfel's trial, conviction, and appeals, letters of editor of *Harper's* to the commandant, McLean Barracks, Cincinnati; the doctor's recommendation after Grenfel's examination; appeals of Grenfel; communication of Charles Francis Adams, London Consulate; petitions from residents of English counties; letters from Hervey, Grenfel's attorney, to Holt; Holt's letter to Stanton; Indiana Conspiracy trials; **Grenfel Papers, W. R., N. A.;** *see also* **Marmaduke Papers** and **Ben M. Anderson Papers, W. R., N. A.**

Chapter XXVII

THE TRIALS AND OTHER TRIBULATIONS

See extradition proceedings against "Lieutenant Bennett H. Young and Command," Toronto, 1864. See **Lieutenant Sam Davis Papers, W. R. N. A.; Kennedy Papers,** also **Ashbrook Papers, W. R., N. A.**

Chapter XXVIII

THE HANGING OF A HERO

For Hines' letter to Doctor Robinson, Toronto, 1865, see **H. P.** *The Trial of John Y. Beall as a Spy and Guerrilla by Military Commission,* D. Appleton Company, New York, 1865; account of the execution of John Yates Beall, *New York Times,* February 26, 1865; memoirs and diary of Captain Allison, The Filson Club. Headley, in his *Confederate Operations in Canada and New York,* said Beall was buried in Green-Wood Cemetery, Brooklyn, New York. A check of the cemetery records shows Beall was buried on February 26 ("the corpse died of strangulation on Governor's Island," the report reads) but on March 22, his mother, Mrs. Jeanette M. Beall, had the body exhumed. There is no record of the reburial. Presumably it was in his native Virginia.

Chapter XXIX

THE EXPATRIATES

See Headley's *Confederate Operations in Canada and New York;* Hines' letter to his father, Toronto, April, 1865, **H. P.;** Hines' letter to a Mr. Prentice, Kentucky, 1865, **H. P.**

For Hines' near-capture as John Wilkes Booth, see interview with William Hines, 1933.

For Rebel attempt to escape by ship, see papers of Clement C. Clay, **W. R., N. A.**

The manifest of the schooner *Canadian Eagle,* in which they attempted to escape to Rio Grande, is owned by Mr. Melvin Nichols of Summit, New Jersey.

For Assistant Secretary of War Dana's order for Thompson's arrest and confiscation of the schooner, see **Thompson Papers, W. R., N. A.**

For Dana's order to the Portland provost marshal, see **W. R., N. A.** See also General L. C. Baker's *History of the United States Secret Service*, Philadelphia, 1867; Hines' diary, 1853, **H. P.**; for Hines' taking oath, see letter to Mr. Prentice, Kentucky, 1865, **H. P.**

Chapter XXX

THE ORDEAL OF THE GALLANT TEMPLAR

For Hervey's appeal to Stanton, see **Grenfel Papers, W. R., N. A.** See also *Galaxy* Magazine, 1866; "Thirty Months on the Dry Tortugas": "Gibraltar of the Gulf of Mexico," Florida Historical Society *Bulletin* XXI, No. 4, April, 1943; *Life of Doctor Mudd*, N. Mudd, editor, New York, 1906; *Harper's Weekly*, February 23, 1861; letter of Richard Wood, **W. R., N. A.**, to the author November, 1953, outlining method of Grenfel's escape; letters of Grenfel to his daughter from the Dry Tortugas, The Filson Club.

Evidently Grenfel did die after all, despite what the New Hampshire private had learned from the dispatches in "the Southern papers." According to Grenfel's grandson, Mr. Packe, Grenfel disappeared at sea and was never seen again. See Packe's letter to The Filson Club, 1950. See also the Dry Tortugas *Prison Book* and box of miscellaneous clippings on the yellow fever epidemic which struck Fort Jefferson, 1868, in **W. R., N. A.**

Chapter XXXI

A NEW ROLE: RECONSTRUCTION AND RECONCILIATION

See Nancy's letter to Tom, June, 1866; **H. P.**; Duke's letter to Hines, 1866, **H. P.**; Hines' letter to Castleman, 1885, **H. P.**; Davis's letter to Manly Tello, editor of the *Catholic Universe*, published in Cleveland; Swiggett's *The Rebel Raider*. See also the *Rise and Fall of the Confederacy* by Jefferson Davis, New York, 1881. See also *Active Service* and Headley's *Confederate Operations in Canada and New York*.

According to the records of the Green-Wood Cemetery, Colonel Martin died April 18, 1900, and was buried on April 22, Lot 24209, Section 200. Each Memorial Day veterans' organizations decorate the graves of the dead of all wars who are buried in Green-Wood, one of the largest and oldest of New York cemeteries, and a sprig of spring flowers is always left on Martin's grave, along with a small American flag. For Hines' obituary, see **H. P.** See Stidger's pension appeals, U. S. Army pension records, **W. R., N. A.**; also **Stidger Papers, W. R., N. A.**

For Young's invitation to lead the St. Albans "raid" of 1904, see *The St. Albans Raid*, John Branch, St. Albans, 1935.

BIBLIOGRAPHY

The main sources for "Confederate Agent" are the Baker-Turner Papers, War Records, National Archives, and Hines' own papers, ten volumes, one hundred and twenty-two pieces, in the Margaret I. King Library, University of Kentucky, on perpetual loan from Mrs. John J. Winn, of Mt. Sterling, Kentucky, the granddaughter of Captain Hines. However, many other unpublished sources were consulted, both in the United States and Great Britain, in an effort to find and fit in the missing pieces in this strange Conspiracy. Parts of the puzzle, still missing, may turn up as the years pass. But there is no doubt that much of it went up in smoke the night Richmond fell, when Secretary of State Judah Benjamin burned his correspondence with the Copperheads.

I. UNPUBLISHED SOURCES

Allison, Captain J. D., diary of, The Filson Club, Louisville, Ky.

Baker-Turner Papers (General Lafayette Baker and Assistant Judge Advocate Levi Turner), War Records, National Archives.

Beall, John Yates, Papers of, War Records, National Archives.

Bickley, George W. L., Papers of, War Records, National Archives.

Bowles, William, Papers of, War Records, National Archives.

Bullitt, Joshua, Papers of, War Records, National Archives.

Burley, Bennett, G., Papers of, War Records, National Archives.

Clay, C. C., Papers of, War Records, National Archives.

Captured Confederate correspondence, Greenhow Papers, State Department, National Archives.

Dodd, H. H., Papers of, War Records, National Archives.

Douglas, Camp, miscellaneous military papers, Chicago Historical Society.

Eells, Samuel Henry, Mss., Library of Congress.

Grenfel, Colonel George St. Leger, letters to his daughter, 1863–68, owned by Mr. Packe, Bucks, England, copies in The Filson Club.

Grenfel, Colonel George St. Leger, Papers of, War Records, National Archives.

Hines, Thomas Henry, Papers of, Margaret I. King Library, University of Kentucky, Lexington.

Hines, Thomas Henry, Personal Papers, owned by Mrs. John J. Winn, Mt. Sterling, Kentucky.

Headley, John W., Papers of, War Records, National Archives.

Holt, Joseph, Mss., Library of Congress.

Indianapolis Conspiracy Trial Records and Government Exhibits and Benn Pitman Transcript, War Records, National Archives.

Martin, Colonel George, Papers of, War Records, National Archives.

Marmaduke, Colonel Vincent, Papers of, War Records, National Archives.

Milligan, L., Papers of, War Records, National Archives.

Newspaper clippings, miscellaneous reports in connection with the yellow fever epidemic, 1868, Fort Jefferson, the Dry Tortugas.

Prison Book, Fort Jefferson, the Dry Tortugas.

Sanders, George N., Mss., Library of Congress.

Scharf, Albert Frederick, Memorandum regarding the Camp Douglas Conspiracy, Chicago Historical Society.

Seddon, Secretary of War, Letter Book of, War Records, National Archives.

Seward, William H., Secretary of State, Letter Book of (Secret Service Activities, 1861–62), War Records, National Archives.

Stanton, Edwin M., Secretary of War, Letter Book of, War Records, National Archives.

Stidger, Felix, reports of, Bureau of Military Justice, War Records, National Archives.

Strong, Henry C., *Civil War Reminiscences of Life as a Member of Company H, 93rd Illinois Infantry, Including Incidents Regarding Camp Douglas Conspiracy*, Chicago Historical Society.

Thompson, Jacob, Letter Book of, War Records, National Archives.

United States Congress. House of Representatives. Executive Document No. 50. 39th Congress, 2nd Session. Message from the President of the United States, in answer to a Resolution of the House of the 19th of December, transmitting papers relative to the case of George St. Leger Grenfell, January 21, 1867.

United States War Department. Provost Marshal General's Office, Historical Report of the Acting Assistant Provost Marshal General for Illinois from Organization to May 31, 1865. National Archives.

Wright, Phineas, Papers of, War Records, National Archives.

Young, Bennett H., Memoirs of, The Filson Club.

SECONDARY SOURCES

Adams, Henry, *The Education of Henry Adams*, Houghton Mifflin Company, New York, 1918.

Adams, Henry, "The Great Secession Winter of 1860–61, *Proceedings*, 1909–1910, Massachusetts Historical Society, Vol. 43, 1910.

Allen, T. F., "John Morgan Raid in Ohio," *Ohio Archaeological and Historical Publications*, Vol. XVII, 1908, pp. 49-59.

Annual Report, American Historical Association, Washington, D. C., Government Printing Office, Vol. II, 1889; Vol. II, 1904; Vol. I, 1905; Vol. I, 1908.

Appleton's Annual Cyclopaedia and Register of Important Events, 1876–1903.

Arnold, Samuel B., "The Lincoln Plot," New York *Sun*, 1902.

Ayer, I. Winslow, *The Great Northwest Conspiracy*, U. S. Publishing Co., Chicago, 1865.

Ayer, I. Winslow, *The Great Treason Plot in the North during the War:* Most Dangerous, Perfidious, Extensive and Startling Plot Ever Devised: Imminent Hidden Perils of the Republic: Astounding Developments Never Before Published, U. S. Publishing Co., Chicago, 1895.

Baker, L. C., *History of the United States Secret Service*, published by L. C. Baker, King & Baird, printers, Philadelphia, 1867.

Baker, William Washington, *Memoirs of Service with John Yates Beall*, C. S. N., Richmond Press, Richmond, 1910.

Bartsch, P., "Bird Rookeries of the Dry Tortugas," *Annual Report*, Smithsonian Institution, 1917, Washington, D. C.

Basset, George W., "A Discourse on the Wickedness and Folly of the Present War." Delivered in the Courthouse at Ottawa, Ill., on the Sabbath, August 11, 1861.

Bassett, George W., "A Northern Plea for the Right of Secession," Office of the *Free Trader*, Ottawa, Ill., 1861.

Battles and Leaders of the Civil War, 4 volumes, The Century Co., New York, 1884–87.

Beehler, William H., *The American Gibraltar*, Governor's Island, N. Y. H., 1910.

Belmont, August, *Letters, Speeches and Addresses*, New York, 1890.

Benjamin, L. N., *The St. Albans Raid: or Investigations into the Charges against Lieutenant Bennett H. Young and Command for Their Acts at St. Albans, Vermont*, Montreal, 1865.

Berry, Thomas F., *Four Years with Morgan and Forrest*, Oklahoma City, 1924.

Billings, John S., A report on barracks and hospitals, with descriptions of military posts, Government Printing Office, Washington, 1870. From the Surgeon General's office, Fort Jefferson, Florida.

Bingham, John A., Speech of Hon. John A. Bingham, of Ohio, in the House of Representatives, January 22, 1861, Office of the *Congressional Globe*, Washington, 1861.

Biographical Encyclopedia of Kentucky, J. M. Armstrong and Co., Cincinnati, 1878.

Birdsall, D. C., "McClellan and the Peace Party," *The Century Illustrated Monthly Magazine*, XXIX, New Series XVII, February, 1890.

Black, Jeremiah S., "The Doctrine of the Democratic and Abolition Parties Contrasted—Negro Equality—The Conflict between Higher Law and the Law of the Land," Speech of Hon. Jeremiah S. Black, at Philadelphia, *The Age* office, 1864.

Bovey, Wilfrid, "Confederate Agents in Canada during the American Civil War,"*The Canadian Historical Review*, Vol. II, March, 1921.

Bowers, Claude, *The Tragic Era*, The Literary Guild of America, New York, 1929.

Boyer, Margrette, "Morgan's Raid in Indiana," *Indiana Magazine of History*, Vol. VIII, December, 1912.

Brevard, Caroline M., *A History of Florida from the Treaty of 1763 to Our Own Times*, Edited by James A. Robertson, The Florida State Historical Society, Deland, Fla.

Bridges, C. A., "The Knights of the Golden Circle: A Filibustering Fantasy," *The Southwestern Historical Quarterly*, Vol. XLIV, January, 1941.

Bross, William, "A Biographical Sketch of the Late General B. J. Sweet," *History of Camp Douglas*, Jansen, McClurg & Co., Chicago, 1878.

Browne, Jefferson B., *Key West: The Old and the New*, The Record Company, St. Augustine, Fla., 1912.

Burnett, H. L., *Reply of the Judge Advocate, H. L. Burnett, to the Pleas of the Counsel for the Accused, to the Jurisdiction of the Military Commission, Convened by Major-General Hooker, Commanding Northern Department, in Case of United States vs. Charles Walsh, Buckner S. Morris, Vincent Marmaduke, R. T. Semmes, Charles Travis Daniel, George E. Cantrill, G. St. Leger Grenfell, Benjamin M. Anderson, Charged with Conspiring to Release the Rebel Prisoners at Camp Douglas, Chicago, Illinois, and to Lay Waste and Destroy That City*, Moore, Wilstach & Baldwin, Cincinnati, 1865.

Cable, G. W., *Famous Adventures and Prison Escapes of the Civil War*, The Century Co., New York, 1898.

Callahan, J. M., "The Northern Lake Frontier during the Civil War" (with remarks of Gen. H. B. Carrington), *Annual Report*, The American Historical Association, Washington, D. C., 1896.

Callahan, James Morton, *Diplomatic History of the Southern Confederacy*, privately printed, Baltimore, 1901.

Carpenter, Francis B., *Six Months at the White House*, New York, 1866.

Castleman, John B., *Active Service*, Courier-Journal Job Printing Co., Louisville, Ky., 1917.

Chesnut, Mary Boykin, *Diary From Dixie*, D. Appleton Company, New York, 1909.

"Chicago Conspiracy, The," *Atlantic Monthly*, Vol. XVI, July, 1865.

Chicago Copperhead Convention, The: The Treasonable and Revolutionary Utterances of the Men Who Composed It: Extracts from All the Notable Speeches Delivered in and out of the National "Democratic" Convention —a Surrender to the Rebels Advocated—a Disgraceful and Pusillanimous Peace Demanded—the Federal Government Shamefully Vilified and Not a Word Said against the Crime of Treason and Rebellion, Congressional Union Committee, Washington, 1864.

Cochran, William C., "The Dream of a Northwest Confederacy," The State Historical Society of Wisconsin *Proceedings* of 1916, Madison, 1917.

Cist, Henry M., *The Army of the Cumberland*, Charles Scribner's Sons, New York, 1882.

Clay-Clopton, Virginia, *A Belle of the Fifties*, G. P. Putnam's Sons, New York, 1904.

Coleman, Charles H., "The Use of the Term 'Copperhead' during the Civil War," *The Mississippi Valley Historical Review*, Vol. XXV, September, 1938.

Connelley, William Elsey, *Quantrill and the Border Wars: The Story of the Border*, The Torch Press, Cedar Rapids, Iowa, 1910.

Cook, Frederick Francis, *Bygone Days in Chicago & Recollections of the "Garden City" of the Sixties*, A. C. McClurg & Co., Chicago, 1910.

Cooley, Verna, "Illinois and the Underground Railroad to Canada," *Transactions*, Illinois State Historical Society, 1917.

Copperhead Catechism for the Instruction of Such Politicians as Are of Tender Years, The: Carefully Compiled by Learned and Designing Men: Authorized and with Admonitions by Fernando the Gothamite, High Priest of the Order of Copperheads, Sinclair Tousey, New York, 1864.

Copperhead Conspiracy in the North-West, The: An Exposé of the Treasonable Order of the Sons of Liberty—Vallandigham, Supreme Commander, Union Congressional Committee, New York, 1864.

Crenshaw, Ollinger, "The Knights of the Golden Circle," *The American Historical Review*, Vol. XLVII, October, 1941.

Dahlgren, J. V., *Memoirs of Colonel Dahlgren*, J. B. Lippincott Company, Philadelphia, 1872.

Dana, Charles A., *Recollections of the Civil War*, D. Appleton & Company, New York, 1899.

Davis, Jefferson, *The Rise and Fall of the Confederate Government*, 2 volumes, D. Appleton & Co., New York, 1881.

Davis, Jefferson, *Jefferson Davis, Constitutionalist: His Letters, Papers and Speeches*, 10 volumes, edited by Dunbar Rowland, Jackson, Miss., 1923.

Davis, Varina, *Jefferson Davis*, 2 volumes, Belford Company, New York, 1890.

Davis, William W., *The Civil War and the Reconstruction in Florida*. New York, 1913. (Published also as *Studies in History, Economics and Public Law*, Vol. LIII.)

Denison, G. T. A., *History of Cavalry*, T. Bosnorth Co., London, 1913.

Dewitt, David Miller, *The Assassination of Abraham Lincoln and Its Expiation*, Macmillan Co., 1909.

Dictionary of American Biography, 20 volumes, edited by Allen Johnson and Dumas Malone, Charles Scribner's Sons, New York, 1932.

Dix, John Adams, Letter from John A. Dix to the War Democracy of Wisconsin, New York, Sept. 10, 1863.

Doster, William E., *Lincoln and Episodes of the Civil War*, G. P. Putnam's Sons, New York, 1915.

Duke, Basil W., *History of Morgan's Cavalry*, Miami Printing Co., Cincinnati, 1866.

——, *Reminiscences of General Basil W. Duke, C. S. A.*, Doubleday, Page & Co., Garden City, N. Y., 1911.

Dyer, Frederick H., *A Compendium of the War of the Rebellion*, Dyer Publishing Co., Des Moines, Iowa, 1908.

Early, Gen. Jubal A., "The Story of the Attempted Formation of a N. W. Confederacy," *Papers*, Southern Historical Society, Vol. X, April, 1882.

Early, Jubal A., *A Memoir of the Last Year of the War*, 1866.

Echo From the Army, The: What Our Soldiers Say about the Copperheads (Loyal Reprints, No. 1), Wm. C. Bryant & Co., printers, New York, 1863.

Ellis, Mrs. L. E., "The Chicago Times during the Civil War," *Transactions*, Illinois State Historical Society, 1932.

England, George A., "Tortugas Tales," *Saturday Evening Post*, October 2, 1926.

Ewbank, Louis B., "Morgan's Raid in Indiana," Indiana State Historical Society *Publications*, Vol. VII, No. 2, C. E. Pauley & Company, Indianapolis, 1923.

Fahrney, Ralph Ray, *Horace Greeley and the Tribune in the Civil War*, Torch Press, Cedar Rapids, Iowa, 1936.

Fesley, Mayo, "Secret Political Societies in the North during the Civil War," *Indiana Magazine of History*, Vol. XIV, September, 1918, Bloomington, Ind.

Foulke, William Dudley, *Life of Oliver P. Morton:* Including His Important Speeches, 2 volumes, Bowen-Merrill Co., Indianapolis and Kansas City, 1899.

"Gibraltar of the Gulf of Mexico, The," *Florida Historical Quarterly,* April, 1943.

Gorham, George C., *Life and Public Service of Edwin M. Stanton,* 2 volumes, Boston, 1899.

Gray, Wood, *The Hidden Civil War,* Viking Press, New York, 1942.

Great Northern Conspiracy of the "S. O. L., The; "Resistance to Tyrants is Obedience to God"; The Votes of the Copperhead in the Congress of the United States, Union Congressional Committee, Washington, D. C., 1864.

Greeley, Horace, *The American Conflict,* O. D. Case Co., N. Y., 1867.

Green, Edwin L., *School History of Florida,* Williams & Wilkins Co., Baltimore, 1898.

Greene, Thomas W., *Historic Families of Kentucky,* privately printed, Cincinnati, 1889.

Greenhow, Rose O'Neal, *My Imprisonment and the First Year of Abolition Rule at Washington.* R. Bentley, London, 1863.

Halliburton, Richard, *Seven-League Boots,* The Bobbs-Merrill Co., Indianapolis, 1935.

Harrington, Fred Harvey, editor, "A Peace Mission of 1863," *The American Historical Review,* Vol. XLVI, October, 1940.

Headley, John W., *Confederate Operations in Canada and New York,* Neale Publishing Company, New York, 1906.

Heitmann, Francis B., *Historical Register and Dictionary of the U. S. Army, 1789–1903.* Government Printing Office, Washington, D. C., 1903.

Henry, Robert S., *The Story of the Confederacy,* The Bobbs-Merrill Company, Indianapolis, 1931.

Hines, Thomas H., "The Northwest Conspiracy," *The Southern Bivouac:* (written by John B. Castleman) conducted by Basil W. Duke and R. W. Knott, New Series, II, June, 1886–May, 1887.

History of Lexington, Ky., Cincinnati, 1872.

History of the Late War in the Western Country, Bowling Green, Ky., 1919.

Holder, C. F., "The Key of the Gulf—the Tortugas Islands," *Scientific American,* April 16, 1898.

Holder, J. B., "The Dry Tortugas," *Harper's Magazine,* July, 1868.

Holt, Joseph, *Report of the Judge Advocate General on "The Order of American Knights," alias "The Sons of Liberty":* A Western Conspiracy in Aid of the Southern Rebellion, Union Congressional Committee, Washington, D. C., 1864.

Johnson, Adam R., *The Partisan Rangers of the Confederate States Army,* G. G. Fetter Co., Louisville, Ky., 1904.

Jones, J. B., *A Rebel War Clerk's Diary,* 2 volumes, Philadelphia, 1866.

K. G. C., *A Full Exposure of the Southern Traitors;* The Knights of the Golden Circle; Their Startling Schemes Frustrated; From Original Documents Never Before Published, E. H. Bullard & Co., Boston, 1860–1.

Keefe, Colonel Thomas H., "How the Northwest was Saved," from "The Secret Service Records of the Civil War," *Everybody's Magazine,* Vol. II, January, 1900.

Keefe, Thomas H., *The Great Chicago Conspiracy of 1864:* Thomas H. Keefe's Narrative of the Discovery of the Plot to Release the Confederate Prisoners of War in Camp Douglas, Chicago, Ill., The Desplaines Press, Chicago, 1898.

Kelley, William D., *Lincoln and Stanton,* G. P. Putnam's Sons, New York, 1885.

Keyes, E. D., *Fifty Years' Observation of Men and Events,* Charles Scribner's Sons, New York, 1884.

Kimball, E. L., "Richard Yates: His Record as Civil War Governor of Illinois," *Journal,* Illinois State Historical Society, Vol. XXIII, April, 1930.

Kirkland, Edward Chase, *The Peacemakers of 1864,* Macmillan Co., New York, 1927.

"Knights of the Golden Circle," *American Historical Review,* Vol. XLVII, October, 1941.

Lawyers and Lawmakers of Kentucky, H. G. Levin, editor, Lewis Publishing Co., Cincinnati, 1897.

Leland, Charles G., "The Knights of the Golden Circle," *The Continental Monthly,* Vol. I, May, 1862.

Leovell, John, *Memoirs of John Yates Beall:* His Life, Trial, Correspondence, and Diary, J. Leovell, Montreal, 1865.

Leslie's Illustrated Weekly, 1861–65.

Lossing, Benjamin J., *Pictorial History of the Civil War,* 3 volumes, T. Belknap, Hartford, Conn., 1868.

Matthews, Albert, "Origin of 'Butternut' and 'Copperhead'," The Colonial Society of Massachusetts *Publications,* Vol. XX, April, 1918.

McClure, H. H., *Old Capitol and the Dry Tortugas,* Lancaster, Pa., 1865.

McCrellis, J. B., *Military Reservations, National Military Parks and National Cemeteries,* Washington, D. C., 1898.

McFarland, R. W., "The Morgan Raid in Ohio," Ohio Archaeological and Historical *Publications,* Vol. XVII, 1908.

Meade, George, editor, *The Life and Letters of George Meade,* G. G. Meade, Amber, Pa., 1924.

Miller, F. T., *Photographic History of the Civil War,* 10 volumes, The Review of the Reviews Company, New York, 1912.

Milton, George Fort, *Conflict:* The American Civil War, Viking Press, New York, 1941.

——, *Abraham Lincoln and the Fifth Column,* Viking Press, New York, 1942.

Minahan, Mary Canisius. "James A. McMasters: A Pioneer Catholic Journalist," The American Catholic Historical Society, *Records,* Vol. XLVII, June, 1936.

Moore, Frank, editor, *The Rebellion Record,* 12 volumes, D. Van Nostrand Company, New York, 1861–65.

Mudd, N., editor, *Life of Dr. Samuel A. Mudd,* Neale Publishing Co., New York, 1906.

Paris, Comte de, *History of the Civil War in America,* 4 volumes, Porter and Coates, New York, 1875–88.

Pendleton, George H., Speech of Hon. George H. Pendleton of Ohio, on the State of the Union, delivered in the House of Representatives, January 18, 1861, Lemuel Towers, printer, Washington, D. C., 1861.

Pendleton, George H., Speech of Hon. George H. Pendleton, of Ohio, in the House of Representatives, December 10, 1861.

Pendleton, George H., "The Resolution to Expel Mr. Long, of Ohio," Speech of Hon. George H. Pendleton, of Ohio, delivered in the House of Represenatives, April 11, 1864.

George H. Pendleton, The Copperhead Candidate for Vice President: His Hostility to the American Republic Illustrated by His Record as a Representative in the Congress of the United States from the State of Ohio, Union Congressional Committee, Washington, D. C., 1864.

Perrine, C. O., An Authentic Exposition of the K. G. C., Indianapolis, 1861.

Pitman, Benn, editor, The Trial for Treason at Indianapolis, Disclosing the Plans for Establishing a North-Western Conspiracy: Being the Official Record of the Trial Before the Military Commission Convened by Special Order No. 129, Headquarters, District of Indiana, Moore, Wilstach & Baldwin, Cincinnati, 1865.

Pollard, Edward A., Secret History of the Southern Confederacy, National Publishing Co., Philadelphia, 1869.

Pomfrey, J. W., A True Disclosure and Exposition of the Knights of the Golden Circle Including the Secret Signs, Grips and Charges, of the Three Degrees, as Practiced by the Order, printed for the author, Cincinnati, 1861.

Pomeroy, Samuel C., Speech of Hon. S. C. Pomeroy, on the Platform and Party of the Future, and National Freedom Secured by an Amended Constitution, delivered in the Senate of the United States, March 10, 1864, McGill & Witherow, Washington, D. C., 1864.

Poore, B. P., Life and Public Services of Ambrose E. Burnside, Providence, R. I., 1882.

Proceedings of the Democratic State Convention, Held at Columbus, Ohio, Friday, July 4, 1862: Containing the Speeches of Hon. Samuel Medary, Hon. C. L. Vallandigham, Hon. Rufus P. Ranney, and Hon. Allen G. Thurman. The Address and Platform, Balloting for Candidates, and Names of Delegates in Attendance, Dayton Empire Press, Dayton, 1862.

Proceedings of the Great Peace Convention, Held in the City of New York, June 3, 1863, Speeches, Addresses, Resolutions, and Letters from Leading Men, Abridged from the Elaborate Report Published in the New York Daily News, June 4, 1863.

Quartermaster's Department, Outline descriptions of the U. S. military posts and stations in the year 1871, Government Printing Office, Washington, D. C., 1872.

Rarick, Rowland H., "Memories of Florida," The Southern Historical Association, Vol. I, Atlanta, 1902.

Report on the House Committee on Military Affairs, Congress 1, Session V, 11, Report 407.

Russ, William A., Jr., "Franklin Weirick: 'Copperhead' of Central Pennsylvania," Pennsylvania History, Vol. V, October, 1938.

Sanger, Donald Bridgman, "The Chicago Times and the Civil War," Mississippi Valley Historical Review, Vol. XVII, March, 1931.

Seitz, Don C., Braxton Bragg, The State Co., Columbia, S. C., 1924.

Senour, Fauntleroy, Morgan and His Captors, C. F. Vent and Co., Cincinnati, 1864.

Sherman, John, "Vallandigham's Record Reviewed; a Political Traitor Unmasked," Speech by Hon. John Sherman, U. S. Senator from Ohio, delivered at Delaware, Ohio, July 28, 1863, *Daily Journal,* Dayton, 1863.

Shinn, Josiah H., compiler, *Fort Jefferson and Its Commander, 1861–1862.* Governor's Island, N. Y. H., 1910.

Sigaud, Louis A., "Mrs. Greenhow and the Rebel Spy Ring," *Maryland Historical Magazine,* September, 1946.

Simms, J. H., *Last Night and Last Day of John Morgan's Raid,* East Liverpool, Ohio, *Morning Tribune,* 1913.

Simpson, Elizabeth M., *Bluegrass Houses and Their Traditions,* Transylvania Press, Lexington, 1932.

Smith, Bethania Meredith, "Civil War Subversives," *Journal,* Illinois Historical Society, Vol. 45, autumn, 1952.

Smith, Edward C., *The Borderland in the Civil War,* Macmillan Company, New York, 1927.

Stidger, F. A., *Treason History of the Order of Sons of Liberty, Succeeded by Knights of the Golden Circle, Afterward, Order of American Knights,* privately printed, Chicago, 1903.

Swiggett, Howard, *The Rebel Raider,* Bobbs-Merrill Company, Indianapolis, 1934.

——, editor, *A Rebel War Clerk's Diary* by J. B. Jones, Barnes and Noble, Inc., New York, 1935.

Taylor, Thomas L., *Blockade Running,* Charles Scribner's Sons, New York, 1896.

"Thirty Months on the Dry Tortugas," *Galaxy Magazine,* February, 1869.

Thompson, Taylor, "The Northwestern Confederacy," *Confederate Veteran,* Vol. XXIV.

Trial of Hon. Clement L. Vallandigham, The, by a Military Commission: and the Proceedings under His Application for a Writ of Habeas Corpus in the Circuit Court of the United States for the Southern District of Ohio, Rickey & Carroll, Cincinnati, 1863.

Trial of John Y. Beall as a Spy and Guerrilla by Military Commission. D. Appleton Company, New York, 1865.

Tuttle, E. B., *The History of Camp Douglas:* Including Official Report of General B. J. Sweet, with Anecdotes of the Rebel Prisoners, J. R. Walsh & Co., Chicago, 1865.

U. S. Inspector General's Office. Outline descriptions of the posts and stations of troops in the geographical divisions and departments of the United States. Government Printing Office, Washington, D. C., 1872.

United States, War Department, *The War of the Rebellion:* a Compilation of the Official Records of the Union and Confederate Armies, 70 volumes, Government Printing Office, Washington, D. C., 1880–1901.

Vallandigham, Clement L., *Speeches, Arguments, Addresses and Letters of Clement L. Vallandigham.* J. Walter & Co., New York, 1864.

Vallandigham, Clement Laird, Speech of Hon. C. L. Vallandigham, of Ohio, delivered in the House of Representatives, February 20, 1861, Henry Polkinhorn, printer, Washington, 1861.

Vallandigham, Clement Laird, "After Some Time Be Past," Speech of Hon. C. L. Vallandigham, of Ohio, on Executive Usurpation, in the House of Representatives, July 10, 1861.

Vallandigham, Clement Laird, "The Great Civil War in America," Speech of Hon. Clement Laird Vallandigham of Ohio, in the House of Representatives, January 14, 1863.

Vallandigham, Edward N., "Clement L. Vallandigham, Copperhead," *Putnam's Monthly*, August, 1907.

Vallandigham, James L., *Biographical Memoir of Clement L. Vallandigham*, J. Walker and Company, New York, 1864.

Wall, Alexander J., *A Sketch of the Life of Horatio Seymour, 1810–1866*, New York, 1929.

Wallace, Lew, *An Autobiography*, 2 volumes, Harper & Brothers, New York, 1906.

War Department Official Records of the Union and Confederate Armies, Government Printing Office, Washington, D. C., 1880–1901.

Waterloo, Stanley, "The Great Chicago Conspiracy," *Nickell Magazine*, March, 1897.

Wharton, A. F., *Trial of the Crew and Officers of the Privateer Savannah on Charges of Piracy*. Baker & Goodwin, New York, 1862.

Williams, T. Henry, *Lincoln and the Radicals*, University of Wisconsin Press, Madison, Wis., 1941.

Williamson, James J., *Prison Life in Old Capitol*, privately printed, West Orange, N. J., 1911.

Wilson, Charles R., "McClellan's Changing Views on the Peace Plank of 1864," *The American Historical Review*, Vol. XXXVIII, April, 1933.

Wood, Benjamin, Speech of Benjamin Wood, of New York, on the State of the Union, in the House of Representatives, May 16, 1862. McGill, Witherow & Co., printers, Washington, D. C., 1862.

Wood, Benjamin, "Peace," Speech of Benjamin Wood, of New York, in the House of Representatives, February 27, 1863.

Woodburn, James A., "Party Politics in Indiana during the Civil War," *Annual Report*, American Historical Association, Washington, D. C., 1903.

Woods, F. L., "Fort Jefferson, Bastille of the Gulf," *Travel*, February, 1936.

Yates, Richard, *Message of His Excellency, Richard Yates, Governor of Illinois, to the General Assembly, January 5, 1863*, Baker & Phillips, printers, Springfield, Ill., 1863.

NEWSPAPERS

Chicago Daily Post
Chicago Daily Tribune
Chicago Evening Journal
Chicago Morning Post
Chicago Times
Cincinnati Daily Enquirer
Cincinnati Daily Gazette
Cincinnati Weekly Gazette
Cleveland Plain Dealer
Daily (Columbus) Ohio State Journal
Daily (Columbus) Ohio Statesman
Daily (Madison) Wisconsin Patriot
Daily (St. Louis) Missouri Democrat
Daily (St. Louis) Missouri Republican
Davenport (Iowa) Daily Gazette
Indianapolis Daily Journal
Louisville Journal
Madison Courier
New Albany Daily Ledger
New York Daily News
New York Times
New York Tribune
New York World
Saint Paul Press

INDEX

Abington, Ky., 104
Adams, Charles Francis, 271
Adare, Johnny, 275, 279, 281, 283
Albany, N. Y., 223, 249
Alexandria, Va., 23
Alliance, 154, 155
Allison, Capt. J. D., 222, 256-59
American House, 168, 169, 175
Amherstburg, Mich., 75, 159, 272
Amnesty Act, 269
Anderson, Col. Ben M., 181, 191, 244, 245, 247
Anderson, George S., 230, 231, 255
Andrews, Maj., 282
Appomattox, 262
Armington, Mr., 171-73
Arnold, Samuel, 278, 281
Ashbrook, Lieut. Philip, 216, 219, 230, 231, 251, 252, 262, 290
Astor Hotel, 213, 214, 222
Athens, Tenn., 57
Atlanta, Ga., 133
Atlantic Monthly, 65, 78, 128, 188
Augusta, Ga., 78
Austin, Tex., 243
Ayer, J. Winslow, 59

Baker, Conrad, 30
Baker, Gen. L. C., 98, 165, 264, 265
Baltimore, Md., 226, 228, 261
Bardstown, Ky., 27
Barnum's Museum, 214, 215, 218, 252
Barrett, James J., 90, 101, 106, 121, 131, 136, 137, 147, 148, 272
Bayne, Col. T. L., 76, 78
Beall, Acting Master John Yates, 3, 153, 154, 155, 156, 160, 161, 164, 165, 220, 230, 231, 249, 255-59, 262, 264
Beauregard, Gen. G. T., 111, 234, 235
Beauvoir Plantation, 286
Belgique, Corps de, 15, 94
Benjamin, Secr. of State Judah, 16, 22, 42, 67, 93, 232, 233, 250, 270, 289
Bennett, Capt. J. C., 43, 44, 47-50, 53, 55
Bennington, Vt., 170
Bermuda, 79, 80, 113, 227
Bettersworth, Lieut. J. J., 184, 188, 189, 190, 191, 196, 197, 262
Bibb, 284

Bickley, "Doctor" George W. L., 16, 33, 63
Black, Jeremiah S., 109, 110, 272
Blanton, Dr. James, 7, 60, 78
Boonville, Mo., 123
Booth, John Wilkes, 5, 79, 240, 261, 264, 265, 267, 278
Borah's Ferry, Ky., 6
Boston, Mass., 22, 181, 226, 228
Boston *Journal*, 173
Bowles, Dr. William, 25, 26, 27, 98, 99, 100, 121, 122, 131, 132, 141, 148, 150, 151, 152
Bowling Green, Ky., 6, 10, 12, 13, 197, 207, 269
Brady, James T., 255
Bragg, Gen. Braxton, 9, 12, 19, 22, 23, 41, 101, 107, 187, 190, 278
Brandenburg, Ky., 28, 33
Breckinridge, Col. William C., 292
Breckinridge, Gen. John Cabell, 7, 41
Breckinridge, Judge Samuel Miller, 145, 146
Briggs House, 184, 185, 196
Bristown Station, Ky., 10
Brooklyn, N. Y., 120, 183, 209, 226, 290
Brown, Sheriff, 117
Brown's Lock, Ky., 12, 69, 153
Brownsville, Tenn., 25
Bruce, Sir Frederick, 278, 282
Buchanan, Pres. James, 80, 87
Buckner's Guides, 4, 5, 7, 13
Buell, Gen. Don Carlos, 12
Buffalo, N. Y., 32, 109, 156, 164, 165, 210, 230, 231
Buffalo Express, 231, 255
Buffington, Ohio, 33, 34, 35
Bull Run, Va., 111
Bullitt, Chief Justice Joshua, 10, 34, 90, 102, 104, 105, 106, 131, 166, 183, 262, 264, 269, 271, 272, 290
Burbridge, Brig.-Gen. S. G., 102, 103
Burley, Bennett G., 154, 155, 159, 160, 161, 165, 249-51, 262
Burlington, Vt., 180
Burnett, Judge Advocate H. L., 241, 242, 243, 247, 265, 282
Burnside, Gen. A. E., 20, 21, 28, 33, 35, 39, 41, 90
Butler, Gen. Ben, 89, 104, 210, 221, 230, 272

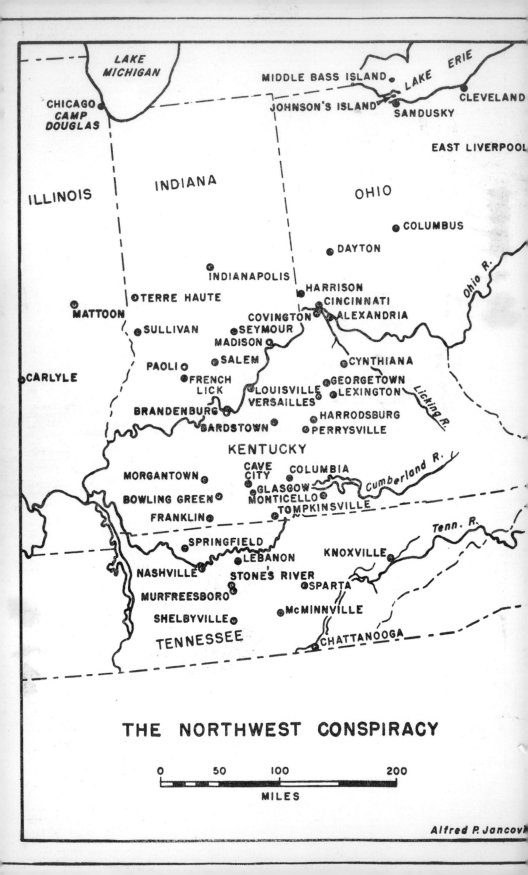

THE NORTHWEST CONSPIRACY

```
0        50       100              200
MILES
```

Alfred P. Jancovic